FROM THE AUTHORS

The "Elkins' Comprehensive Tax Guide, 2014 Edition" was written as an easy to use, understandable reference for anyone, including tax professionals. The Guide follows the flow of a tax return, from filing status and requirements through tax credits. It is primarily for use in preparing individual and small business tax returns, with chapters that include detailed discussions on employee travel and entertainment expenses, depreciation, and carrying on a trade or business as a sole proprietor, partnership, farmer, and S-Corporation. Within the chapter on carrying on a trade or business are informative discussions on classifying workers as employees vs. independent contractors, and reasonable salaries for S-Corporation shareholders. The Guide also includes chapters on the alternative minimum tax, estate and trust income, and estate and gift taxes.

A unique feature in this Guide compared to others is a chapter devoted to dealing with the IRS, including applicable penalties for underpayment of taxes, failure to file, failure to pay, and how to avoid paying penalties and interest. The chapter includes a detailed section on IRS audits that discusses IRS notices and the Agency's latest concentration on an audit-by-mail program. The chapter discusses surviving an IRS audit, how to handle a dispute over a tax liability, how to prepare a request for appeals, closing agreements, and offers in compromise. We believe this chapter alone is worth getting this Guide as a reference.

Perhaps the most important chapter in the Guide is a detailed discussion of the "Patient Protection and Affordable Care Act," also known as Obamacare. This chapter discusses in detail all of the compliance and tax provisions of the law, including the additional 0.9% Medicare surtax on high-income earners, the 3.8% surtax on "net investment income" of high-income earners, and the 2.3% excise tax on medical devices. The individual and employer mandates are also discussed in detail, including penalties, exemptions, and the IRS role in implementing the mandates.

While some IRS regulations and court cases are referred to in the Guide, our aim was to keep such references to a minimum. We believe that the vast majority of the content meets our "understandable" goal for all readers. This Guide was compiled over several years based on our experiences in preparing tax returns, as well as from various interpretations of tax laws and IRS regulations. It is also worth mentioning that we have extensive experience in working for the IRS, the U.S. Tax Court, and the Tax Division of the U.S. Department of Justice. While we believe in the accuracy of the content of this Guide, it is intended to be used as general tax information only and not tax advice, which should be provided on a case by case basis. As always, please consult your tax advisor for more detailed information on tax issues and for advice on your specific situation.

If you have questions or comments about anything in this guide or wish to schedule a consultation, please feel free to contact Chad Elkins, CPA, MBA at (703) 217-6646 or Tim Elkins CPA, MBA, at (806) 463-3128.

HOW TO USE THIS TAX GUIDE

To find a specific topic in this Guide, you must first refer to the Contents page and then to the Detailed Table of Contents. The Contents page shows the page where each chapter in the Guide starts. For example, the chapter on "Taxable Income" starts on page 17 and goes to page 56.

To find out the sections included in the chapter "Taxable Income," refer to the Detailed Table of Contents. For example, one of the sections included in Taxable Income is "Distributive Share of Partnership and S-Corporation Income," which as shown in the Detailed Table of Contents is located on page 19 of the Guide. When you go to page 19 and read what is says about Distributive Share of Partnership and S-Corporation income, you will see a reference in bold that says **(SEE "Carrying on a Trade or Business," Partnerships, and S-Corporations)**.

Again, go to the Contents page to find that the chapter on "Carrying on a Trade or Business" starts of page 144 and goes to page 186, and according to the Detailed Table of Contents the section on "Partnerships" is located on page 172, and the section on "S-Corporations" is located on page 178. You will need to read those pages to find out more about Distributive Share of Partnership and S-Corporation income.

You'll also notice when looking at the Detailed Table of Contents that there are subsections under sections. For example, under Partnerships is the subsection "Limited Partnerships" located on page 177. When you go to that page to read about Limited Partnerships, you will see a reference in bold that says **(SEE "Taxable Income," Passive Activity Income; and "Carrying on a Trade or Business," Passive vs. Nonpassive Income)**.

The Detailed Table of Contents shows that the "Passive Activity Income" section is located on page 24 of the Taxable Income chapter, and the "Passive vs. Nonpassive Income" section is located on page 147 of the Carrying on a Trade or Business chapter. Finally, when you read about Passive vs. Nonpassive Income, you will see a reference in bold that says **(SEE "Taxable Income," Passive Activity Income)**, which is a cross-reference back to the Passive Activity Income section in the Taxable Income chapter.

You will see references and cross-references throughout this Tax Guide that should be followed in order to get further information and clarifications about a particular topic.

CONTENTS

PERSONAL EXEMPTION AND STANDARD DEDUCTION 1

2013 TAX BRACKETS 2

FILING REQUIREMENTS 4

FICA – OASDI (SOCIAL SECURITY) AND MEDICARE TAX 15

TAXABLE INCOME 17

INCOME EXCLUSIONS 57

DEDUCTIONS FOR COMPUTING ADJUSTED GROSS INCOME (AGI) 77

ITEMIZED DEDUCTIONS 85

TAX CREDITS 103

EMPLOYEE TRAVEL AND ENTERTAINMENT EXPENSES 122

DEPRECIATION 130

CARRYING ON A TRADE OR BUSINESS 144

ALTERNATIVE MINIMUM TAX (AMT) 187

TAX RETURN OF DECEASED 194

ESTATE INCOME AND TAX RETURN 196

TRUST INCOME 199

ESTATE AND GIFT TAX 203

PATIENT PROTECTION AND AFFORDABLE CARE ACT (ACA) 209

OTHER IMPORTANT TAX PROVISIONS 228

DEALING WITH THE IRS 235

TAX PLANNING 272

DETAILED TABLE OF CONTENTS

PERSONAL EXEMPTION AND STANDARD DEDUCTION 1

2013 TAX BRACKETS 2

FILING REQUIREMENTS 4
    DEPENDENCY EXEMPTION 4
    ELECTION TO INCLUDE A QUALIFYING CHILD'S INCOME 6
    MARITAL STATUS AND DIVORCE 8
    HEAD OF HOUSEHOLD 11
    SURVIVING SPOUSE 12
    SAME SEX COUPLES 12
    U.S. CITIZENS LIVING ABROAD 12
    ALIENS 13
    INTERIM TAX IDENTIFICATION NUMBER PROCEDURES 13
    FILING YOUR RETURN AND RECEIVING YOUR REFUND 14

FICA – OASDI (SOCIAL SECURITY) AND MEDICARE TAX 15

TAXABLE INCOME 17
    TIPS 17
    NONCASH COMPENSATION 18
    UNEMPLOYMENT COMPENSATION 18
    SEVERANCE PAY 18
    INTEREST 18
    DIVIDENDS 19
    ROYALTY INCOME 19
    DISTRIBUTIVE SHARE OF PARTNERSHIP AND S-CORPORATION INCOME 19
    DISTRIBUTIVE NET INCOME FROM ESTATES AND TRUSTS 19
    CAPITAL GAINS AND LOSSES (FORM 8949) 20
    PASSIVE ACTIVITY INCOME 24
    RENTAL INCOME 27
    QUALIFIED RETIREMENT PLANS AND TRADITIONAL IRAS 30

REQUIRED MINIMUM DISTRIBUTIONS 32
RETIREMENT PLANS INHERITED BY BENEFICIARIES 34
ROLLOVERS FROM TRADITIONAL IRAS TO ROTH IRAS 35
DISTRIBUTIONS FROM "NONQUALIFIED" TAX DEFERRED ANNUITIES 38
NET UNREALIZED APPRECIATION 39
SOCIAL SECURITY BENEFITS 40
ALIMONY/SEPARATE MAINTENANCE 41
PRIZES 42
GAMBLING WINNINGS 42
SOCIAL SECURITY DISABILITY INCOME 44
CANCELLATION OF DEBT 44
ABANDONMENT OF PROPERTY 48
CASH SURRENDER VALUE OF A LIFE INSURANCE POLICY 48
PERSONAL INJURY AWARDS ASSOCIATED WITH NON-PHYSICAL INJURIES 49
SALE OF DEMUTUALIZED STOCK 50
INCENTIVE STOCK OPTIONS 50
EARNINGS ON UNIFORM TRANSFER TO MINORS CUSTODIAL ACCOUNTS 50
REIMBURSEMENTS OF MEDICAL EXPENSES 50
STATE AND LOCAL INCOME TAX REFUNDS 51
PROPERTY TRANSFERRED TO A TAXPAYER IN EXCHANGE FOR SERVICES 51
EMPLOYER PROVIDED VEHICLE 51
CONSTRUCTIVE DIVIDENDS 52
SERVICES RENDERED FOR THE BENEFIT OF A CHARITABLE ORGANIZATION .. 52
BARTERING 52
NET OPERATING LOSS 52
INSTALLMENT SALE 54
JURY DUTY PAY 54
DAMAGES RECEIVED FOR DISCRIMINATION 54
BEQUESTS MADE IN EXCHANGE FOR SERVICES 55
REQUISITION OF PROPERTY BY THE GOVERNMENT 55
NET INVESTMENT INCOME (FORM 8960) 55
ALTERNATIVE MINIMUM TAX 56

INCOME EXCLUSIONS 57

INTEREST ON MUNICIPAL BONDS 57
CONTRIBUTIONS TO QUALIFIED EMPLOYEE RETIREMENT PLANS 57
ROLLOVERS FROM QUALIFIED EMPLOYEE RETIREMENT PLANS 59
DISTRIBUTIONS FROM COVERDELL EDUCATION SAVINGS ACCOUNTS 59
DISTRIBUTIONS FROM QUALIFIED TUITION PROGRAMS 60

U.S. SAVINGS BOND REDEMPTIONS 63
QUALIFIED SCHOLARSHIP AND FELLOWSHIP GRANTS 63
DISTRIBUTIONS FROM HEALTH SAVINGS ACCOUNTS 63
CONTRIBUTIONS TO FLEXIBLE SPENDING ACCOUNTS 64
FORGIVENESS OF STUDENT LOANS FOR MEDICAL PROFESSIONALS 64
FOREIGN EARNED INCOME EXCLUSION 64
FOSTER CARE INCOME 65
CHILD SUPPORT PAYMENTS 65
GIFTS AND INHERITANCES 66
QUALIFIED DISTRIBUTIONS FROM ROTH IRAS 66
VA PENSIONS OR ALLOWANCES 66
LONG-TERM DISABILITY INSURANCE BENEFITS 67
STATE PAID VETERANS BONUSES 67
EMPLOYER PAID ASSISTANCE PROGRAMS 67
CLERGY FURNISHED HOUSING 69
STOCK DIVIDENDS 69
PERSONAL INJURY AWARDS 69
PROPERTY DAMAGES 69
WORKERS' COMPENSATION 70
GAIN ON THE SALE OF A PRINCIPAL RESIDENCE 70
MORTGAGE DEBT 72
GAIN ON THE SALE OF SECTION 1202 SMALL BUSINESS STOCK 73
LIKE-KIND EXCHANGES (SECTION 1031) 74
LIFE INSURANCE PROCEEDS 75
MILITARY PERSONNEL COMBAT PAY 75
STATE PAYMENTS FOR COMBAT SERVICE 75
INTEREST EARNED ON TAX-EXEMPT HOUSING BONDS 75
PAYMENTS TO VOLUNTEER FIRE FIGHTERS AND MEDICAL RESPONDERS 76
REBATES RECEIVED FROM TANGIBLE ASSETS 76
AIRLINE MILES 76
NATIONAL HEALTH SERVICE CORPS AND ARMED FORCES SCHOLARSHIPS 76

DEDUCTIONS FOR COMPUTING ADJUSTED GROSS INCOME 77

EDUCATOR EXPENSES 77
STUDENT LOAN INTEREST 77
TUITION AND FEES FOR HIGHER EDUCATION (FORM 8917) 77
CONTRIBUTIONS TO HEALTH SAVINGS ACCOUNTS (FORM 8889) 78
MOVING EXPENSES (FORM 3903) 79
TRADITIONAL IRA CONTRIBUTIONS 80

ALIMONY/SEPARATE MAINTENANCE (FORM 3559) 82
SELF-EMPLOYMENT TAX 82
SELF-EMPLOYED HEALTH INSURANCE PREMIUMS 82
SELF-EMPLOYED RETIREMENT CONTRIBUTIONS 82
PENALTY FOR EARLY WITHDRAWAL OF SAVINGS 83
BUSINESS EXPENSES OF STATUTORY EMPLOYEES 83
BUSINESS EXPENSES OF STATE AND LOCAL OFFICIALS 83
OVERNIGHT TRAVEL COSTS OF RESERVISTS & NATIONAL GUARD MEMBERS 83
BUSINESS EXPENSES OF PERFORMING ARTISTS 83
ATTORNEY FEES PAID IN CONNECTION WITH UNLAWFUL DISCRIMINATION .. 83
DOMESTIC PRODUCTION 84

ITEMIZED DEDUCTIONS 85

MEDICAL EXPENSES 85
TAXES 89
MORTGAGE INTEREST 90
INVESTMENT INTEREST 92
CHARITABLE CONTRIBUTIONS 92
CASUALTY, DISASTER, AND THEFT LOSSES 98
MISCELLANEOUS ITEMIZED DEDUCTIONS SUBJECT TO 2% AGI FLOOR 100
MISCELLANEOUS ITEMIZED DEDUCTIONS NOT SUBJECT TO 2% AGI FLOOR. 101

TAX CREDITS 103

REFUNDABLE TAX CREDITS 103
    RECAPTURE OF FIRST-TIME HOMEBUYER CREDIT (FORM 5405) 103
    EARNED INCOME CREDIT (EIC) 104
    ADDITIONAL CHILD TAX CREDIT (FORM 8812) 105
    40% OF THE AMERICAN OPPORTUNITY EDUCATION CREDIT 105
    CREDIT FOR FEDERAL TAX PAID ON FUELS (FORM 4136) 105
    HEALTH COVERAGE TAX CREDIT (HCTC) 105
    AMT CREDIT (FORM 8801 105
NON-REFUNDABLE TAX CREDITS 106
    FOREIGN TAX CREDIT (FORM 1116) 106
    CHILD AND DEPENDENT CARE CREDIT (FORM 2441) 107
    ELDERLY AND DISABLED CREDIT (SCHEDULE R) 108
    ADOPTION CREDIT (FORM 8839) 108
    EDUCATION CREDITS (FORM 8863) 109
    SAVERS CREDIT (FORM 8880) 110

- CHILD TAX CREDIT 111
  - MORTGAGE INTEREST CREDIT (FORM 8396) 111
  - RESIDENTIAL HOME IMPROVEMENT CREDIT (FORM 5695) 112
  - RESIDENTIAL ENERGY EFFICIENT PROPERTY CREDIT (FORM 5695) 112
  - PLUG-IN ELECTRIC DRIVE VEHICLE CREDIT (FORM 8936) 113
  - LOW SPEED 2 & 3 WHEEL PLUG-IN ELECTRIC VEHICLES CREDIT 113
  - CREDIT FOR PRIOR YEAR MINIMUM TAX (FORM 8801) 113
- NON-REFUNDABLE BUSINESS TAX CREDITS 114
- THE GENERAL BUSINESS TAX CREDITS (FORM 3800) 114
- INVESTMENT CREDIT (FORM 3468) 114
- REHABILITATION TAX CREDIT (FORM 3468) 114
- BUSINESS ENERGY CREDITS (FORM 3468) 114
- QUALIFYING ADVANCED COAL PROJECT CREDIT (FORM 3468) 115
- QUALIFYING GASIFICATION PROJECT CREDIT (FORM 3468) 115
- WORK OPPORTUNITY TAX CREDIT (WOTC) (FORM 5884) 115
- HEROES AND WOUNDED WARRIORS WOTC (FORM 5884) 117
- R&D TAX CREDIT (FORM 6765) 117
- DISABLED ACCESS CREDIT (FORM 8826) 118
- FEDERAL HUD ZONE TAX CREDIT (FORM 8844) 118
- NEW MARKETS TAX CREDIT (NMTC) (FORM 8874) 119
- CREDIT FOR SMALL EMPLOYER PENSION PLAN STARTUP (FORM 8881) 119
- EMPLOYER PROVIDED CHILD CARE TAX CREDIT (FORM 8882) 119
- ENERGY EFFICIENT HOMEBUILDER TAX CREDIT (FORM 8908) 119
- ENERGY EFFICIENT APPLIANCE CREDIT (FORM 8909) 119
- ALTERNATIVE FUEL VEHICLE REFUELING PROPERTY CREDIT (FORM 8911) 119
- CREDIT FOR EMPLOYER DIFFERENTIAL WAGE PAYMENTS (FORM 8932) 120
- SMALL BUSINESS HEALTHCARE TAX CREDIT (FORM 8941) 120
- OTHER GENERAL BUSINESS CREDITS 120

EMPLOYEE TRAVEL AND ENTERTAINMENT EXPENSES 122

- CLAIMING TRAVEL AND ENTERTAINMENT EXPENSES 122
- VEHICLE AND OTHER TRANSPORTATION EXPENSES 127

DEPRECIATION (FORM 4562) 130

- BONUS DEPRECIATION 130
- SECTION 179 FIRST-YEAR EXPENSING 131
- DEPRECIATION METHODS 132
- RESIDENTIAL RENTAL PROPERTY 134

LISTED PROPERTY 135
LISTED PROPERTY OTHER THAN VEHICLES 136
NOT LISTED PROPERTY 137
NOT LISTED PROPERTY OTHER THAN VEHICLES 137
OTHER METHODS OF DEPRECIATIONS 138
ENERGY-EFFICIENT COMMERCIAL BUILDING DEDUCTION (FORM 3115) 138
COST SEGREGATION STUDY 139
DECONSTRUCTION 139
REPAIRS VS. CAPITAL IMPROVEMENTS 139
DEPLETION 142
AMORTIZATION OF INTANGIBLE ASSETS 142

CARRYING ON A TRADE OR BUSINESS 144

BUSINESS EXPENSES ARE "USE OR LOSE" 144
FEDERAL UNEMPLOYMENT TAX ACT (FUTA) 144
ACCRUAL METHOD OF ACCOUNTING 145
BUSINESS OR HOBBY 145
AT-RISK RULES 146
PASSIVE VS. NON-PASSIVE INCOME 147
START-UP AND ORGANIZATIONAL COSTS 148
REQUIREMENT TO FILE INFORMATION RETURNS (FORM 1099-MISC, ETC) .. 149
BUSINESS BAD DEBT 150
BUSINESS CASUALTY AND THEFT LOSSES 150
SALE OF BUSINESS PROPERTY (FORM 4797) 151
PAYMENTS TO NON-EMPLOYEES 153
INDEPENDENT CONTRACTORS 153
STATUTORY EMPLOYEES 156
HIRING YOUR TEENAGE CHILDREN TO WORK FOR YOUR BUSINESS 157
EMPLOYEES' MILITARY SERVICE/RETIREMENT PLAN 158
MARK-TO-MARKET ELECTION 158
CASH TRANSACTIONS OVER $10,000 159
SMALL BUSINESS ADMINISTRATION (SBA) LOAN LIMITS 159
CHANGING A TAX YEAR (FORM 1128) 159
INTEREST ON CREDIT CARDS 159
BUSINESS OUTSIDE OF USA 159
BEST SMALL BUSINESS TAX PRACTICES 159
SOLE PROPRIETORS/SELF-EMPLOYED (SCHEDULES C & SE) 161
    SELF-EMPLOYMENT TAX (SE) 164
        HOME OFFICE EXPENSES (FORM 8829) 165

PROFIT OR LOSS FROM FARMING (SCHEDULE F) 167
    FARMING EXPENSES 170
    FARM OPTIONAL METHOD 170
    FARM INCOME AVERAGING... 171
    NET OPERATING LOSSES 171
    SALE OF FARMLAND 171
    FARM ACT OF 2008 (4-H ACT) 171
PARTNERSHIPS (FORM 1065) 172
    LIMITED PARTNERSHIP 177
    FAMILY PARTNERSHIP 177
S-CORPORATIONS (FORM 1120S) – ELECTION MADE ON FORM 2553 178
    REQUIREMENTS TO BECOME AN S-CORPORATION 181
    SHAREHOLDER'S STOCK BASIS 182
    S-CORPORATION INCOME VS. DISTRIBUTIONS 183
TAX EXEMPT ORGANIZATIONS (FORM 990) 184
E-COMMERCE TAXATION 186

ALTERNATIVE MINIMUM TAX (AMT) (FORM 6251) 187

    TAX PREFERENCES 188
    ADJUSTMENTS 190
    DEPRECIATION 190
    RENTAL PROPERTIES 191
    AMT CREDIT.. 192

TAX RETURN OF DECEASED 194

ESTATE INCOME TAX RETURN (FORM 1041) 196

TRUST INCOME (FORM 1041) 199

    GRANTOR/REVOCABLE TRUST... 199
    NON-GRANTOR/IRREVOCABLE TRUST 201

ESTATE AND GIFT TAX... 203

    ESTATE TAX RETURN (FORM 706) 203
    PORTABILITY OF THE ESTATE TAX EXEMPTION 205
    BASIS OF PROPERTY ACQUIRED BY BENEFICIARIES....................... 205

GIFT TAX RETURN (FORM 709) 206
GENERATION-SKIPPING TRANSFER TAX (FORM 706, FORM 709) 207

PATIENT PROTECTION AND AFFORDABLE CARE ACT (ACA) 209

PROVISIONS EFFECTIVE BEGINNING IN 2010 210
    COMPLIANCE PROVISIONS 210
    TAX PROVISIONS 211
PROVISIONS EFFECTIVE BEGINNING IN 2011 214
    COMPLIANCE PROVISIONS 214
    TAX PROVISIONS 214
PROVISIONS EFFECTIVE BEGINNING IN 2012 214
    COMPLIANCE PROVISIONS 214
PROVISIONS EFFECTIVE BEGINNING IN 2013 215
    COMPLIANCE PROVISIONS 215
    TAX PROVISIONS 216
PROVISIONS EFFECTIVE BEGINNING IN 2014 220
    COMPLIANCE PROVISIONS 220
    TAX PROVISIONS 220
PROVISIONS EFFECTIVE BEGINNING IN 2015 225
    TAX PROVISIONS 225
PROVISIONS EFFECTIVE BEGINNING IN 2018 227
    TAX PROVISIONS 227

OTHER IMPORTANT TAX PROVISIONS 228

MANDATORY E-FILING 228
REQUIREMENT TO REPORT FOREIGN BANK AND FINANCIAL ACCOUNTS 228
FOREIGN ACCOUNT TAX COMPLIANCE ACT (FATCA) 229
DEDUCTIBLE LEGAL FEES 231
TAX BENEFITS FOR PERSONS WITH DISABILITIES 232
MILITARY SERVICE CONNECTED BENEFITS 233

DEALING WITH THE IRS 235

RECORD KEEPING 235
POWER OF ATTORNEY AND DECLARATION OF REP. (FORM 2848) 236
FILING AN AMENDED RETURN 236
IDENTITY THEFT PROGRAM 236
INTEREST RATES 237

AVOIDING TAX PENALTY FOR UNDERPAYMENT OR FAILURE TO PAY 237
AVOIDING A LATE FILING PENALTY 239
INSTALLMENT AGREEMENTS 240
FIRST-TIME PENALTY ABATEMENT 241
WHAT HAPPENS TO NON-FILERS 241
TAX PENALTIES AND INTEREST 243
INNOCENT SPOUSE RELIEF 246
DISCLOSURE STATEMENT (FORM 8275) 246
REPORTABLE AND LISTED TRANSACTION DISCLOSURE (FORM 8886) 247
UNCERTAIN TAX POSITIONS (SCHEDULE UTP) 248
ECONOMIC SUBSTANCE DOCTRINE 249
TAX REFUND OFFSETS 249
TAX PREPARER RESPONSIBILITIES AND PENALTIES 249
IRS AUDITS 254
DISPUTE OVER A TAX LIABILITY 263
U.S. TAX COURT 270
TAXPAYER ADVOCATE SERVICE 270

TAX PLANNING 272

GENERAL PLANNING 272
PLANNING FOR THE AFFORDABLE CARE ACT (ACA) 273
PLANNING TO AVOID THE ALTERNATIVE MINIMUM TAX LIABILITY 275
PLANNING FOR EDUCATION EXPENSES 277
ESTATE TAX PLANNING 278
AVOIDING AN AUDIT 278

Filing 2013 Tax Returns

Personal Exemption and Standard Deduction

Personal Exemption
$3,900 ($3,800 in 2012). Both the personal exemption and the itemized deduction phase-outs are reinstated in 2013. The personal exemption phase-out is reinstated at adjusted gross income (AGI) thresholds of: $250,000 single (**S**); $300,000 married filing jointly (**MJ**) and surviving spouse (**SS**); $275,000 head-of-household (**HH**); and $150,000 married filing separately (**MS**). Personal exemptions are reduced by 2% for each $2,500, or portion thereof (2% for each $1,250 for married filing separately) by which the taxpayer's adjusted gross income (AGI) exceeds the applicable thresholds. Exemptions are fully phased-out when AGI is: $372,501 (**S**); $422,501 (**MJ**) and (**SS**); $397,501 (**HH**); and $211,251 (**MS**). The threshold amounts will be adjusted for inflation after 2013.

Standard Deduction
- **S** under 65—$6,100; **S** over 65 - $7,600
- **MJ** under 65—$12,200; **MJ** one over 65 - $13,400; **MJ** both over 65 - $14,600
- **SS** under 65—$12,200; **SS** over 65 - $13,400
- **HH** under 65—$8,950; **HH** over 65 - $10,450
- **MS**—$6,100
    - Added amount for each person aged 65 or blind—$1,500 (**S**, **HH**)
    - Added amount for each person aged 65 or blind—$1,200 (**MJ**, **SS**, and **MS**)
- Single dependent's standard deduction is the greater of (1) $1,000, or (2) $350 + earned income up to a maximum of $6,100.

SS - A qualifying widow(er) with a dependent child
Blind - You can't see better than 20/200 in your better eye with corrective lenses, or your field of vision is 20 degrees or less.
If your 65th birthday is on Jan. 1, 2014, you are considered 65 on the last day of 2013.

2013 Tax Brackets

Married Filing Jointly

If Taxable Income Is	The Tax Is
$0–$17,850	10% of taxable income
$17,851–$72,500	$1,785 + 15% of the excess over $17,850
$72,501–$146,400	$9,982.50 + 25% of the excess over $72,500
$146,401–$223,050	$28,457.50 + 28% of the excess over $146,400
$223,051–$398,350	$49,919.50 + 33% of the excess over $223,050
$398,351–$450,000	$107,768.50 + 35% of the excess over $398,350
$450,001 +	$125,846 + 39.6% of the excess over $450,000

Head of Household

If Taxable Income Is	The Tax Is
$0–$12,750	10% of taxable income
$12,751–$48,600	$1,275 + 15% of the excess over $12,750
$48,601–$125,450	$6,652.50 + 25% of the excess over $48,600
$125,451–$203,150	$25,865 + 28% of the excess over $125,450
$203,051–$398,350	$47,621 + 33% of the excess over $203,150
$398,351–$425,000	$112,037 + 35% of the excess over $398,350
$425,001 +	$121,364.50 + 39.6% of the excess over $425,000

Single Taxpayers

If Taxable Income Is	The Tax Is:
$0–$8,925	10% of taxable income
$8,926–$36,250	$892.50 + 15% of the excess over $8,925
$36,251–$87,850	$4,991.25 + 25% of the excess over $36,250
$87,851–$183,250	$17,891.25 + 28% of the excess over $87,850
$183,251–$398,350	$44,603.25 + 33% of the excess over $183,250
$398,351–$400,000	$115,586.25 + 35% of the excess over $398,350
$400,001 +	$116,163.75 + 39.6% of the excess over $400,000

Married Filing Separately

If Taxable Income Is	The Tax Is
$0–$8,925	10% of taxable income
$8,926–$36,250	$892.50 + 15% of the excess over $8,925
$36,251–$73,200	$4,991.25 + 25% of the excess over $36,250

$73,201–$111,525	$14,228.75 + 28% of the excess over $73,200
$111,526–$199,175	$24,959.25 + 33% of the excess over $111,525
$199,176–$225,000	$53,884.25 + 35% of the excess over $199,175
$225,001 +	$62,923 + 39.6% of the excess over $225,000

In 2013, taxpayers with taxable incomes above $400,000 for singles and $450,000 for joint filers are subject to a new 39.6% top tax bracket, and they owe a 20% tax on long-term capital gains and qualified dividends. Also, the Affordable Care Act (ACA) adds a 0.9% surtax to the 1.45% Medicare tax paid by high-income earners, defined as wages and self-employment income above $200,000 for singles, $250,000 for joint filers, and $125,000 for married filing separately (flow through business income from S-corporations is not subject to the 0.9% surtax). Employers are required to withhold the additional Medicare tax on wages it pays to employees in excess of the $200,000 threshold. In addition, the Affordable Care Act (ACA) imposes a 3.8% surtax on investment income (unearned income) on the same high income earners that are subject to the additional 0.9% Medicare surtax. The 3.8% surtax is calculated on the <u>lesser of net investment income or the amount by which modified adjusted gross income (MAGI) exceeds the $200,000/$250,000 thresholds</u>. **(SEE "Patient Protection and Affordable Care Act," Provisions Effective Beginning in 2013, Tax Provisions)**

These new taxes and the reinstatement of the personal exemption and itemized deduction phase-outs can penalize married taxpayers. For example, two single people, each with taxable incomes of $400,000, would neither be subject to the 39.6% top tax bracket. However, if married, they would pay the 39.6% tax rate on $350,000, which would, in essence, impose a marriage penalty on them of about $30,000. The phase-out of the personal exemption wouldn't affect the same two people if each had a $250,000 AGI. But if married, all of their personal exemptions would be eliminated, and that could increase their tax bill by approximately $1,500 for each person, or $3,000 for both of them. Similarly, the phase-out of the itemized deductions wouldn't affect the same two single individuals, but would increase their taxable income by as much as $6,000 if they were married, adding as much as about $2,400 to their tax bill. The 0.9% surtax and the 3.8% surtax implemented by the Affordable Care Act (ACA) wouldn't have any effect on the same two unmarried people earning $200,000 each, but if married, they would pay between $1,350 and $5,700 in new taxes depending on whether their combined incomes were all wages or all investment income.

A taxpayer does not have the right to reduce Federal income taxes reported on a return based on religious or moral beliefs, such as objections to funding a war or wars.

Filing Requirements

Any individual taxpayer must file a tax return if his gross income equals or exceeds his standard deduction, plus his own personal exemption, even though he may not owe any tax. Example for a single taxpayer (**S**): $6,100 + $3,900 = $10,000 (must file a return). **Gross income does not include social security benefits and tax-free income generated by municipal bonds.**

Filing Thresholds for 2013 (any exemptions available for dependents do not affect these threshold amounts)
- Single **(S)** under 65 - $10,000; over 65 - $11,500
- Married filing jointly **(MJ)** under 65 - $20,000; one over 65 - $21,200; both over 65 - $22,400
- Surviving spouse **(SS)** under 65 - $16,100; over 65 - $17,300
- Head of Household **(HH)** under 65 - $12,850; over 65 - $14,350
- Married filing separately **(MS)** - $3,900 (even if 65 or blind)
- Single dependents under age 65 must file a return if they have:
    - Unearned income of more than $1,000, or
    - Earned income of more than $6,100

An individual is required to file anyway if he owes: self-employment tax (has net earnings from self-employment of $400 or more); social security or Medicare taxes not withheld from tip income; tax on a qualified retirement plan or IRA; received advanced Earned Income Tax Credit payments; or had wages of $108.28 or more as an employee of a church or church organization that is exempt from employer Social Security and Medicare taxes (must file Schedule SE). **(SEE "Carrying on Trade or Business," Sole Proprietor/Self-Employed)**

Dependency Exemption
If you *can* claim another person as a dependent on your tax return, that person may not claim an exemption on his or her tax return for himself/herself. This is true *even if you do not actually claim* that person as your dependent on your tax return.

Uniform definition of a qualifying child for the dependency exemption: (1) specified relationship to taxpayer (son, daughter, stepson, stepdaughter, brother, sister, stepbrother, stepsister, descendent of taxpayer, adopted children, foster children); (2) same principal place of abode as taxpayer for more than ½ of the year (except for temporary absences for school or military service); (3) age under 19 or under 24 for a full-time student (at least 5 months of year); and (4) **child must be younger than the individual claiming him/her as a qualifying child, or the qualifying child must be permanently and totally disabled**. Also, according to the U.S. Tax Court a qualifying child must be a U.S. citizen at some time during the calendar year. Permanently and totally disabled at any time during the calendar year qualifies at any age. But you cannot claim a qualifying child if the child provides more than ½ of his own support. Support includes all amounts spent for food, lodging, clothing, medical expenses, education, recreation, transportation, and similar necessities. Student loans in the name of the student are considered to be support for which the child pays. However, if a child receives a scholarship, it is not considered support. The uniform definition of a qualifying child is applicable to the child tax credit (up to age 17), the dependent care tax credit (up to age 13), the earned income credit, and the head of household (HH) filing status. However the qualifying ages for some of these are different, as shown. A child that is born or dies during the year will be considered as living with the taxpayer for the entire year if the taxpayer's house was the child's home for the entire time he was alive.

- If a dependent who otherwise meets the tests of a qualifying child or relative dies during the year, you can claim an exemption for that dependent.
- Definition of permanently and totally disabled—both of the following apply: (1) he or she cannot engage in any substantial gainful activity because of a physical or mental condition; and (2) a doctor must determine that the condition has lasted or can be expected to last continually for at least a year or can lead to death.
- Married persons are not entitled to the dependency exemption when their children are not U.S. citizens at some time during the year. They are also not entitled to the child care credit, the child tax credit, or the additional child tax credit for the same reason.

Other dependents (Qualifying Relative): (1) taxpayer provides more than ½ of support (food, shelter, clothing, medical, dental, education, etc.—see part 4 of definition of qualifying child, above), **Social Security benefits used for support count toward the half-support test**; (2) specified relationship (grandchild, mother, father, etc.) or if not a relative was a member of your household for the entire year; (3) U.S. citizenship; (4) gross income test – cannot claim if person had gross income of $3,900 or more, which is the personal exemption (gross income for this purpose does not include Social Security benefits) and; (5) joint return test – cannot claim if the supported person filed a joint return with his or her spouse unless the return was only filed to collect a tax refund and neither spouse would have owed tax if they had filed separate returns.

- Gross income test: Gross income includes gross receipts from rental property (do not deduct expenses); partner's share of gross income of partnership (not net income); all unemployment compensation; and certain scholarship and fellowship grants (not scholarships received by degree candidates used for tuition, books, etc.). Gross income does not include Social Security benefits, unless taxable, and tax-free income generated by municipal bonds.
- A person cannot be a dependent of any other person who is not required to file a return for the year or files solely to claim a refund for taxes withheld.

Dependency exemption belongs to the parent with whom the child resides the longest during the year (custodial parent) if divorced, separated under a written separation agreement, or lived apart at all times during the last 6 months of the year. This is determined by using the counting-nights rule (where the child sleeps), whether or not the parent is present, or if the child is in the company of the parent when not at residence (such as on vacation).

- If divorced, the divorce decree can give the dependency exemption to either parent, whether or not the child resides with that parent the most during the year. Also, the custodial parent can use Form 8332 to release the exemption to the non-custodial parent, which allows the non-custodial parent to take the child tax credit and the education credits (no matter who pays the educational expenses), but in this case, the custodial parent is still entitled to the child and dependent care tax credit, the earned income credit, and head of household status. However, **effective for tax years beginning after 7/1/2008, the exemption goes to the custodial parent regardless of what the divorce decree or written separation agreement says**, unless the custodial parent attaches a signed waiver effective for that tax year (Form 8332). This Form can also be used to notify the noncustodial parent that the custodial parent is revoking a signed release of claim.
- If no parent claims a qualifying child as a dependent, another individual may claim the child if that individual: (1) is otherwise eligible to claim the child, and (2) has a higher adjusted gross income for the taxable year than any parent eligible to claim the child.
- Multiple support agreements (Form 2120): If no one taxpayer provides more than ½ of the support for a dependent, any individual who provides more than 10% of support can be treated as meeting the support test, per agreement. More than ½ of support must be provided by persons providing at least 10% of support who sign the agreement. Form 2120 must be filed.
- **If an elderly parent is not a dependent for exemption purposes simply because he/she earned too much, the parent can still be counted as a dependent <u>for medical deduction purposes</u>.**
- You cannot deduct the rent paid to provide a home for an elderly parent; however, the amount paid for the rent counts toward determining the ½ support test.
- **If a dependent parent lives with you and requires continual care, and you work, you can claim the dependent care tax credit for the cost of the care provided.**
- **If more than one person (siblings) provides more than half of the support for a dependent parent, a multiple support agreement (Form 2120) can be used to allow one of the siblings who provides more than 10% of the support to claim the dependency exemption. Who claims the dependency exemption can be rotated from year to year.**

Election to Include a Qualifying Child's Income on Parents' Tax Return

Parents may elect to report a child's income on their tax return if the child: (1) is under 19 or is a full-time student under 24 (at least 5 months in a year); (2) has earned income equal to or less than ½ of his/her support; (3) has unearned income more than $1,000 ($950 in 2012), and less than $10,000; and (4) <u>has no withholding tax</u>. Otherwise, the child is required to file a separate return, and Form 8615 must be attached to the child's tax return. Election to include a qualifying child's income on parents' return is made by attaching a separate Form 8814 for each child to your return. A child's income must be reported on the parent's return with the greater taxable income, if they are married filing separately, unless the parents are not living together, in which case the return of the custodial parent must be used, if unmarried. If the custodial parent has remarried, the stepparent is treated as the child's other parent and their joint return is used.

- If a qualifying child has investment income (unearned income) of **more than $2,000 in 2013** ($1,900 in 2012), part of it may be taxed at the parents' highest marginal tax rate. This is referred to as the "kiddie tax." The kiddie tax is applicable to children under 19, or under 24 if a full-time student (at least 5 months in a year), and is applicable if all of the following conditions are met:
    - The child is required to file a return **(SEE "Filing Requirements")**
    - At least one parent is alive at the end of the year
    - The child does not file a joint return
    - The child is age 18 at the end of the year and his/her earned income was not more than ½ of his/her support. Support includes all amounts spent for food, lodging, clothing, medical expenses, education, recreation, transportation, and similar necessities. Student loans in the name of the student are considered to be support for which the child pays. However, if a child receives a scholarship, it is not considered support
    - The child is between the ages of 19 and 23 at the end of the year and a full-time student (at least 5 months in a year) and his/her earned income was not more than ½ of his/her support
- If a child files a separate tax return, Form 8615 must be attached to his/her return.
- When considering the child's age at the end of the year, a birthday on January 1 does not bring the child to the next age level for that year.
- NOTE: By using some tax planning, a child's earned income can be inflated to an amount that is more than ½ of his/her support, even if it is not actually used for the child's support. This includes reasonable wages that self-employed parents can pay a student/child for services performed by the child. As a result, a contribution by the child to his/her own IRA using earned income could reduce taxable income and thereby reduce or completely eliminate the kiddie tax. Also, the child may be able to take an education tax credit which will offset the kiddie tax. But all of this can only be done when the parent cannot claim a student as a dependent. Students could also invest in tax-free investments, including Section 529 plans, which are not included in income. **(SEE , "Income Exclusions," Distributions From Qualified Tuition Programs)**
- <u>How to overcome the high cost of college if your income is too high to get financial aid</u>: Like in the example above, attempt to make a child independent (income more than ½ of support). If a child is independent for tax purposes by meeting the ½ of support test, the child can claim the $3,900 personal exemption and the $6,100 standard deduction, and can benefit from the 10%

tax rate on the first $8,925 of taxable income, and the 15% tax rate on the next $36,250 of taxable income. In addition, the child will not have to pay the kiddie tax on the child's unearned income above $2,000. In order to accomplish this, the child can work during the summer, take advantage of internships and work study programs, and if his or her parent(s) own a business, the parent can hire the child and shift some of his income to the child. The parent owning his own business can also set-up a tuition assistance program of up to $5,250 per year (which must be available to all employees). Also, a child who is tax independent might be able to take advantage of the "Education Tax Credits." For example, suppose a sophomore in college who earns $14,000 working for his father's business over the summer months and receives $1,700 in interest income from a UTMA account. And suppose the child's grandparents make a $5,000 tuition payment on his behalf directly to the university, and his parents distribute $10,000 from the child's 529 plan (withdrawals from a 529 college savings plan are considered the child's income for purposes of establishing tax independence). Also, suppose he gets $5,250 from his father's company tuition program for a total of $35,950 toward his college expenses. $25,700 counts toward the child being independent for tax purposes ($14,000 + $1,700 + $10,000). The $5,000, $5,250, and the $10,000 are income tax free to the student and his family. Also, the child's father's business gets a deduction for the $5,250. The child's gross income is $15,700, and after applying the $3,900 personal exemption and the $6,100 standard deduction, the student's taxable income is $5,700.

Marital Status and Divorce

You are considered married for filing purposes even if you are separated under a provisional decree of divorce or separate maintenance that has not been finalized, i.e. spouses who have received an interlocutory or temporary divorce decree are deemed to still be married even if you lived apart for the whole year. However, one parent can file as "head of household" (HH) if he/she did not live with the other spouse during the last 6 months of the year, and meets the other provisions to file as HH; and the non-custodial parent must file as married filing separately. When a divorce is finalized at any time during a year, both persons who are party to the divorce are considered unmarried for the entire year.

- Usually the custodial parent can claim the children as dependents; however, the decree of divorce should say who can claim the kids as dependents. If you can't agree with your ex-spouse, you can arrange to alternate years using Form 8332 **(BUT SEE "Filing Requirements," Dependency Exemption, Other Dependents (Qualifying Relatives))**
- If married, must file jointly to claim: (1) the IRA deduction for a non-working spouse; (2) the American Opportunity Credit (formerly the Hope Credit) or Lifetime Learning Credit; (3) the Dependent Care Credit; and (4) Earned Income Credit, unless you lived apart for the last 6 months of the year (can claim head of household in this case).
- Separate returns can be amended to a joint return within 3 years, but a joint return cannot be amended to separate returns.

- If a joint return is filed while a couple is still considered married, the IRS will accept an amended return (Form 1040X) claiming a refund filed by a divorced taxpayer that is signed by only one of the former spouses, and issue a check in the name of the spouse that filed the 1040X, but the amount of the refund will be determined by re-computing the taxpayer's share of the joint liability and the taxpayer's contribution toward the joint liability using the IRS allocation method. NOTE: the community property laws effect how much is the proportional share of each spouse. **(SEE "Married Filing Separately and Community Property" below)**
- It is important to notify the IRS that separate residences have been established (change of address).
- No gain or loss is recognized on transfer of property between spouses during marriage, or any transfer of property between former spouses incident to divorce (even if transfer is a bona fide sale), if the transfer occurs within one year after date the marriage ceases. A transfer of property to a third party on behalf of a former spouse can also qualify for non-recognition of gain, if required by the divorce agreement. The basis of property transferred in a divorce is always the transfer's adjusted basis of the property, which is an exception to the "Gift" rules of lower of fair market value (FMV) or adjusted basis of property.
- For both spouses to qualify for the home sale gain exclusion after divorce, the divorce instrument must require them to co-own the principle residence, even if only one spouse occupies the residence. Otherwise, the non-occupying former spouse may not qualify for the 2 out of 5 year rule. **(SEE "Income Exclusions," Gain on the Sale of a Principal Residence)**
- IRA's can be transferred from one spouse to another in a divorce agreement without any tax consequences.
- Retirement plans transferred or split in a divorce require a formal written agreement per the divorce settlement.
- **If you and your spouse obtain a divorce in one year for the sole purpose of filing tax returns as unmarried individuals, and at the time of divorce you intend to remarry each other in the next year, you and your spouse must file as married individuals.**
- If you obtain an annulment, which holds that no valid marriage ever existed, you must file amended returns for all tax years affected by the annulment that are not closed by the statute of limitations.
- In the nine "community property states", property is owned concurrently between spouses. In the rest, referred to as "common law states," courts must determine an equitable distribution of the spouses' property between them. In the 41 common law states, the courts decide what is fair, reasonable, and equitable division of assets. A court may decide to award a spouse anywhere from none to all of the property value. The courts focus on factors such as how long the marriage lasted, what property each party brought into the marriage, the earning power of each spouse, the responsibilities of each spouse in raising their children, the amount of retraining needed to make a spouse employable, the tax consequences of the asset

distribution, and debt allocation. If the couple signed a prenuptial agreement or an agreement during the marriage, they have more control over how the property is divided. In the end, equitable distribution is considered fair, but not necessarily equal.
- Almost all states require the parties to disclose all material information needed to allow them to negotiate and agree upon the division of marital property. Therefore, for a property settlement, a schedule of assets with tax considerations for each asset should be prepared. To ensure clients comply with the full disclosure requirement, the divorcing couple should inventory all property, including intangible assets such as advanced degrees, goodwill, and patents, that can result in substantially increased income in future years. Consideration of intangible assets in property settlements is becoming more important as courts express an increased willingness to either classify the intangibles as property subject to distribution or to require spouses to pay for reimbursement.

Married Filing Separately (MS) and Community Property – both must either itemize or claim the standard deduction when filing as "Married Filing separately." **In community property states (California, Arizona, Idaho, Louisiana, Nevada, New Mexico, Texas, Washington, and Wisconsin) each person must report ½ of community income (community income includes income earned by both spouses)**, unless they lived apart and did not transfer any income between them, except for payments solely for child support purposes. The general rule is that anything you bring to a marriage is your separate property, and anything acquired by either partner after marriage is community property. The way to preserve an asset's separate status is not easy, but keeping good records helps, and you can have a prenuptial or postnuptial agreement specifying those assets. In community property states, during year of divorce, each spouse is taxed on ½ of community income for the part of year before divorce is final, unless they lived apart for the whole year (use Form 8958 "Allocation of Tax Amounts"). Also, if a spouse is not informed about the other spouse's income, it is not always possible to apply the community property state requirements. **Self-employment income, including a partner's distributive share of partnership income is not considered to be community income.** Generally you are not responsible for paying tax on community income if all five of the following conditions exist: (1) you did not file a joint return for the year; (2) you did not include an item of community income in gross income on your separate return; (3) the item of community income you did not include is one of the following: (a) wages, salaries, and other compensation your spouse (or former spouse) received for services he or she performed as an employee; (b) income your spouse (or former spouse) derived from a trade or business he or she operated as a sole proprietor; (c) your spouse's (or former spouse's) distributive share of partnership income; (d) income from your spouse's (or former spouse's) separate property (use the appropriate community property law to determine what is separate property); (e) any other income that belongs to your spouse (or former spouse) under community property law; (4) you establish that you did not know of, and had no reason to know of, that community income; and (5) under all facts and circumstances, it would not be fair to include any community income in your gross income. **Form 8857 can be used to request relief from liability arising from community property laws**.

If you file as "Married Filing Separately"
- 85% of Social Security benefits are generally subject to tax
- Cannot claim: (1) the IRA deduction for a non-working spouse; (2) the American Opportunity Credit (formerly the Hope Credit) or Lifetime Learning Credit; (3) the Dependent Care Credit; and (4) Earned Income Credit, unless you lived apart for the last 6 months of the year (custodial spouse can claim Head of Household in this case)
- Cannot take advantage of the $25,000 rental loss allowance, the Credit for the Elderly, or the exclusion of interest on U.S. Savings Bonds unless you lived apart for the whole year
- May claim a personal exemption for a spouse only if the spouse has no gross income for the year, and is a dependent of the taxpayer
- If separate returns are filed, you have 3 years to amend to a joint return. But you cannot file a joint return and amend to separate returns
- <u>In general, filing separate returns will not be beneficial. In fact, filing as married filing separately may actually increase tax liability. Yet, it possible that filing as married filing separately may result in a lower combined tax for a married couple, if there is a large disparity (the greater the disparity, the more pronounced the effect) in the spouses' respective incomes and the spouse with the lower income has deductions that are subject to an AGI percentage limitation that would be lost if they chose to file married filing jointly.</u> However, in a community property state it is next to impossible that married filing separately will be beneficial

Head of Household (HH)
To claim HH status, you must be either unmarried (not a surviving spouse), or not live with your spouse during the last 6 months of the year while still considered married, and you must pay more than ½ of the cost of maintaining a home as a household, which is the principal place of abode of a "qualifying child" or a person that can be claimed as a dependent, who must live with you for more than ½ of the year. Maintaining a household includes paying for: mortgage interest; property taxes; rent; utilities; upkeep of home and repairs; property insurance; food consumed on premises; and other household expenses. It does not include the cost of: clothing; education; medical treatment; vacations; life insurance; transportation; and food consumed off-premises. Temporary absences from the home due to education, business, military service, vacation, or illness do not affect the ½ year rule so long as the home is continuously maintained during the absence. If a qualifying person dies, then the ½ year rule does not apply if taxpayer maintains a household for that person until the time of death.
- <u>**Taxpayer does not have to live in a household maintained for an elderly parent (only exception) if otherwise is entitled to claim the parent as a dependent**</u>

Surviving Spouse (SS)
You can file as a surviving spouse, using joint return rates, for 2 years following the death of a spouse if you have a dependent child. Your filing status is Single filing as a Surviving Spouse, not head of household. Also, a Surviving Spouse is entitled to use the $500,000 home sale gain exclusion on the sale of a principal residence for 2 years after the death of a spouse.

Same Sex Couples
The Treasury Department and the IRS have determined that two same-sex persons that are "legally" married in jurisdictions that recognize same-sex marriages will be treated as married for federal tax purposes. This applies regardless of whether the couple lives in a jurisdiction that recognizes same-sex marriage or a jurisdiction that doesn't. <u>Under the ruling, same-sex couples will be treated as married for all federal tax purposes beginning in 2013</u>. The ruling applies to all federal tax provisions where marriage is a factor, including filing status, personal and dependency exemptions, taking the standard deduction, contributing to an IRA, claiming the earned income tax credit, claiming the child tax credit, and receiving employee benefits. The ruling doesn't apply to registered domestic partnerships, civil unions, or similar formal relationships recognized under state law. Legally married same-sex couples generally must file their federal tax returns using either the "married filing jointly" or "married filing separately" filing status. <u>Individuals who were in same-sex marriages in prior years may (but are not required to) file original or amended returns choosing to be treated as married for federal tax purposes for all open years under the statute of limitations</u>. As a result of this ruling, couples in which one same-sex spouse wishes to adopt the other spouse's child may lose out on the Adoption Tax Credit, because the credit isn't available when adopting a spouse's child. **(SEE "Tax Credits," Adoption Tax Credit)**

U.S. Citizens Living Abroad
U.S. citizens and residents living and working abroad are required to file a federal income tax return. This includes people with dual citizenship. Their tax returns should report worldwide income, and in some cases the taxpayers will need to file Schedule B, Interest and Ordinary Dividends, with their returns. Some taxpayers may need to file Form 8938, Statement of Specified Foreign Financial Assets, and Form TD F 90-22 1, Report of Foreign Bank and Financial Accounts (FBAR) with the Treasury Department. U.S. citizens living abroad qualify for an automatic two-month extension to file their tax returns, including those serving abroad in the military. Many Americans living abroad qualify for the foreign income exclusion up to the amount of $97,600, including the "housing exclusion." **(SEE "Income Exclusions," Foreign Income Exclusion)**
- What should you do if you're a dual citizen of the U.S. and another country, living abroad and not compliant with U.S. taxes? Under a new IRS program you may only have to file 3 years of tax returns and 6 FBARs. However, you must not owe more than $1,500 in U.S. taxes per year. You should complete U.S. tax returns (or amended returns) on your worldwide income for the last 3 years. If you owe more than $1,500 per year, you should prepare U.S. tax returns for the

prior 5 years too (meaning 8 years in total). If you are paying tax in the country where you live, you may have foreign tax credits you can claim.

Aliens

Resident aliens meeting the Substantial Presence Test, i.e. the 183 days in U.S. test (183 test = all days in current year {must have at least 31 days} + 1/3 of days in 1st preceding year + 1/6 of days in second preceding year), or holder of a green card, must file Form 1040 instead of Form 1040NR for nonresident aliens. Therefore, all worldwide income is reported on Form 1040; whereas only U.S. income is reported on form 1040NR by non-resident aliens. Certain aliens are "dual status aliens" (usually first year in U.S.), which means they may be treated as <u>not</u> meeting the substantial presence test even though they satisfy the numerical requirements, because they are deemed to have a closer connection with the foreign country.

Alien students, teachers, trainers, and diplomats in the U.S. on "F", "J", or "Q" visas are exempt from the 183 days in U.S. Test to qualify as a resident <u>alien</u>, and therefore must file form 1040NR, unless they have been in the U.S. for five years or more on a student visa; in which case the exemption does not apply, and they must file a regular Form 1040 (this applies to alien teachers and athletes as well). Exemption does not apply if a student has been exempt as a teacher, trainee, or student for any part of more than 5 calendar years, unless he/she establishes that he/she does not intend to reside permanently in the U.S. (Form 8843). Salaries of employees of foreign governments are excluded from U.S. source income.
- o Non-resident alien students must file form 8843, in addition to Form 1040NR
- o Alien students filing Form 1040 are not eligible for the Earned Income Tax Credit ("Not valid for employment" is on their Social Security card).
- o If one spouse is a U.S. citizen or resident alien and the other spouse is a non-resident alien, they can elect to file a joint return and treat the non-resident alien spouse as a U.S. resident.

Interim Tax Identification Number Procedures

Individuals who need an "interim tax identification number" (ITIN) must supply original documents, such as passports or birth certificates, or certified copies of these documents from the issuing agencies. Acceptable identification documents include passports, national identification cards, visas issued by the U.S. State Department, U.S. or foreign military identification, U.S. or foreign driver's licenses, civil birth certificates, medical and school records, and certain other documents (see IRS website for a complete list). Certifying Acceptance Agents (CAAs) can verify the authenticity of identification documents for ITIN applicants and their spouses and do not need to send the original documents to the IRS. But ITIN applications for dependents must still be submitted with original documents. Taxpayer Assistance Centers are supposed to be set up where documents can be reviewed so taxpayers do not have to part with originals. Beginning in January 2013, ITINs will be effective for only five years, after which time taxpayers have to reapply for a new one.

Filing Your Return and Receiving Your Refund

Taxpayers can split their refund among up to 3 accounts in banks, credit unions, and mutual funds (use Form 8888). Also, a tax refund can be paid directly to an IRA. You can check on your refund using the IRS's "Where's My Refund?" tool, or you can call the IRS's Refund Hotline at 800-829-1954.

FICA - OASDI (Social Security) and Medicare Tax

The maximum wages subject to the OASDI (Social Security tax) portion of FICA in 2013 is $113,700 (6.2% tax). In 2012 it was $110,100 (4.2% tax). All wages are subject to the Medicare tax (1.45%). The FICA taxes paid by an employee are matched by his/her employer. **Beginning in 2013, the Patient Protection and Affordable Care Act (ACA) adds a 0.9% surtax to the 1.45% Medicare tax paid by high-income earners** (wages and self-employment income above $200,000 single; $250,000 married filing jointly; and $125,000 married filing separately). There is no employer match for this tax. For self-employed taxpayers, the surtax is added to the 2.9% Medicare tax paid on self-employment income. Employers are required to withhold the additional Medicare tax on wages it pays to an employee in excess of $200,000, even though an employee may not be liable for the additional Medicare tax because, for example, the spouse had no income. Any withheld Medicare tax not owed will be credited against the total tax liability shown on the tax return. If an individual knows they will be above the limit because of their spouse's wages, the additional tax still cannot be withheld until their wages reach $200,000. In this case, the employee can adjust his W-4 to have additional taxes withheld. The stated thresholds are not indexed for inflation. Overpayment of additional Medicare tax for this purpose should not be claimed on Form 843. Employees may only claim a refund of additional Medicare tax on their tax return if they have not received repayment or reimbursement from their employer. Flow-through business income from an S-corporation is not subject to the 0.9% surtax. **(SEE "Patient Protection and Affordable Care Act," Provisions Effective Beginning in 2013, Tax Provisions)**

- A child younger than 18 who performs services as an employee for his parents in a trade or business (sole-proprietorship or partnership) does not pay FICA, and a child younger than 21 who performs domestic work is not subject to FICA. The wages of an individual who works for her spouse are subject to income tax withholding and FICA, but not federal unemployment tax (FUTA). And compensation for domestic services performed by one spouse for the other spouse is not subject to either FICA or FUTA. Also, FICA and FUTA taxes do not apply when a parent performs domestic services for a child.
- If the person working for you as household help doesn't have his or her own company and is not an employee of an agency or other firm, then likely you are the employer and the person is your employee. On the other hand, if the worker provides services for you and others throughout the week or the month, then he/she may not be your employee. However, if you are the employer, you must pay FICA (Social Security and Medicare tax) if your employee earns more than $1,800 for the year, but you're not required to withhold income taxes. You have to give them a W-2, and you have to pay both their share of FICA and your matching share on your tax return, using Schedule H. And you have to submit the information to the Social Security Administration on Form W-3. Even a babysitter who is age 18 or older earning more than $36 a week for 52 weeks meets the $1,800 per year requirement. In addition to FICA, you also have to pay federal unemployment tax (FUTA) and likely state unemployment insurance when wages

you pay are $1,000 or more for any calendar quarter. The FUTA tax is 6% on cash wages up to $7,000 for the year. However, you are not required to pay FICA on wages you pay your own child, any child under age 18, your spouse, and in most cases, your parent.

- **You must earn $1,160 of income in order to earn one quarter of Social Security credit, so earning $4,640 anytime during 2013 will net the full four quarters of coverage. <u>The Base Medicare Part B premium is $104.90 per month in 2013</u>.**
- If you were married or divorced and changed your name, be sure to notify the Social Security Administration (SSA) before you file your taxes with the IRS. If the name change on your tax return doesn't match SSA records, the IRS will flag it as an error and that can delay your refund. You can inform the Social Security Administration (SSA) of a name change by filing Form SS-5, Application for a Social Security Card, and provide a recently issued document as proof of your legal name change. Form SS-5 is available on the SSA's website at http://www.socialsecurity.gov, by calling 800-772-1213, or at local SSA offices. Your new card will have the same Social Security (SSN) number, but will show your new name.
- For adopted children without Social Security numbers, the parents can apply for an Adoption Taxpayer Identification Number (ATIN) by filing Form W-7A, Application for Taxpayer Identification Number for Pending U.S. Adoptions, with the IRS. The ATIN is a temporary number used in place of a SSN on the tax return. Form W-7A is available on the IRS.gov website or by calling 800-TAX-FORM (800-829-3676).
- If you adopted your spouse's children after getting married and their names are changed, you'll need to update their names with the Social Security Administration (SSA). For adopted children without Social Security numbers, the parents can apply for an Adoption Taxpayer Identification Number (ATIN) by filing Form W-7A.

Taxable Income

Wages and salaries are reported on Form W-2 if you are an employee and on Form 1099-MISC if you are considered an independent contractor. <u>If you do not receive your W-2 by Feb. 14, contact your employer. If your employer still does not provide you with your W-2, contact the IRS for assistance at 800-829-1040</u>. You must provide your employer's name, address and phone number, dates of employment, an estimate of wages earned and federal tax withheld, and when you worked for that employer based on information from your final pay stub or leave-and-earnings statement. You can then use Form 4852, Substitute for Form W-2, to file your tax return. Attach Form 4852 to your return, estimating income and withholding taxes as accurately as possible. If you receive your missing W-2 after you file your return, and the information is different from what was reported on your return, you must file an amended return (Form 1040X).

If you move you should notify the IRS by sending Form 8822, Change of Address. You can download the form from the IRS website or order it by calling 800-829-3676. If you get married, or for any other reason, you may need to change your withholding by completing a new Form W-4. You can use the IRS "Withholding Calculator" available on the IRS website, fill out a new W-4, print it out online and then give it to your employer so they can withhold the correct amount from your pay.

Form W-2, Box 14 can show "after tax" amounts withheld from wages for union dues, health insurance premiums, disability insurance premiums, uniform payments, etc. Also, Box 14 can show employer educational assistance payments, employer matching contributions to a pension plan, voluntary after tax contributions deducted from an employee's pay for a pension plan, and nontaxable income.

Tips

Tips are taxable income subject to Social Security and Medicare taxes. The value of non-cash tips, such as tickets, passes, or other items of value is considered income subject to tax. You must include all cash tips you receive directly from customers, tips added to credit cards, and your share of any tips received from tip-splitting arrangements with fellow employees. If you receive $20 or more in tips in any one month, you should report all the tips to your employer who is required to withhold federal income, Social Security and Medicare taxes. An employee is responsible for paying his/her share of FICA taxes on unreported tips by completing Form 4137, Social Security and Medicare Tax on Unreported Tip Income, and filing it with Form 1040. It's a good idea to keep a running daily log of your tip income. Tips are different than service charges. In order to be considered a tip the IRS cites the following factors: the payment must be free from compulsion; the customer must be able to determine the amount of the payment without restriction; the payment cannot be negotiable or dictated by the employer; and the customer should generally have the right to decide who receives the payment.

Noncash Compensation
Noncash compensation for the performance of services is taxable unless the recipient is subject to a substantial forfeiture risk and the noncash compensation is nontransferable, in which case taxation occurs when the risk is extinguished and the property is transferable. The amount of compensation is determined as follows: the property's fair market value (FMV) less any amount paid for the property. A recipient is subject to substantial forfeiture risk if rights to the property's full enjoyment are conditioned upon the future performance of substantial services by any individual.

Unemployment Compensation
Unemployment compensation is taxable income. But in 2009 only, up to $2,400 of unemployment compensation was excluded from income.

Severance Pay
Severance pay is taxable for federal income tax purposes and has usually been treated as wages subject to payroll taxes (FICA). However, if you paid FICA taxes on severance pay, you may be entitled to a refund under a Sixth Circuit Court of Appeals decision in the case of United States vs. Quality Stores. The decision held that severance payments qualifying as "supplemental unemployment compensation (SUB)" are excluded from the Internal Revenue Code's statutory definition of "wages" and therefore are not subject to FICA employment taxes. You should file a refund claim as soon as possible, even though the IRS is not likely to start paying refunds soon, because there is a big controversy over this issue; i.e. the Sixth Circuit case is in conflict with the Federal Circuit decision (U.S. vs. CSX Corporation) that came to the opposite conclusion. The Sixth Circuit decision was based on the fact that the severance payments were not tied to the receipt of state unemployment compensation or attributable to any particular services that employees provided. However, some types of severance payments may still be subject to FICA withholding. If a client falls within the jurisdiction of the Sixth Circuit, file for a refund if the client paid payroll taxes in an open tax year. However, if a client falls outside the jurisdiction of the Sixth Circuit, file a protective claim if the client paid payroll taxes on severance payments in an open tax year. **The Supreme Court will ultimately decide whether severance payments are subject to FICA taxes.**

Interest
Interest reported to a taxpayer on Form 1099-INT is taxable income:
- Interest earned on tax-exempt municipal bonds and tax-exempt bond funds is not taxable for federal income tax purposes, but it is usually taxable on state income tax returns.
- Interest on U.S. savings bonds are not taxable until redeemed. However, a taxpayer can elect to report the interest earned each year. And the election can be revoked at any time.
- Interest on original issue discount (OID) investments is taxable annually based on deemed interest rates as determined in the prospectus of each individual investment instrument.

- Contributions made to a traditional IRA in a year can be withdrawn in the same year without penalty, but you must pay tax on the interest earned. Excess contributions to both traditional and Roth IRAs are subject to a 6% excise tax each year until they are withdrawn or treated as being contributions for a later year.

Dividends

Dividends reported to a taxpayer on Form 1099-DIV are taxable income. Qualified dividends are taxed at capital gains rates—must satisfy a holding requirement of at least 61 days during the 121-day period that began 60 days before the ex-dividend date. These rates apply to both regular tax and the Alternative Minimum Tax (AMT). **(SEE Capital Gains and Losses, below)**
- Mutual fund dividends (including qualified dividends) are reported to taxpayer on Form 1099-DIV.
- Undistributed Capital Gains are reported in Box 1a of Form 1099-DIV. The mutual fund will send Form 2439 "Notice to Shareholder of Undistributed Long-Term Capital Gains" showing the taxpayer's share (Box 1a) and any tax paid by the mutual fund in Box 2. The taxpayer can take a credit for his/her share of the tax paid by the mutual fund because the shareholder is treated as having paid that tax.
- <u>Net investment income</u>, less investment expenses is taxable. The election to treat qualified dividend income as investment income is made on Form 4952.

Royalty Income

Royalty income is taxable. It is reported to taxpayer on Form 1099-MISC, which is then shown on Schedule E of the individual's tax return. 15% depletion is allowed on amounts reported in box 2 of Form 1099-MISC. Royalties paid for use of trademarks must be capitalized.

Distributive Share of Partnership and S-Corporation Income

Distributive share of partnership and S-Corporation income is taxable, whether received or not. It is reported to taxpayers on Schedule K-1, Form 1065, and Schedule K-1, Form 1120S respectively, which is then shown on Schedule E of the individual's tax return. **(SEE "Carrying on a Trade or Business," Partnerships, and S-Corporations)**

Distributive Net Income From Estates and Trusts

Pro rata share of Distributable Net Income (DNI) from estates and trusts is taxable, whether received or not. It is reported to taxpayers on Schedule K-1, Form 1041, which is then shown on Schedule E of the individual's tax return. Classes of income retain their character, i.e. passive income, etc., in the hands of the beneficiaries. When an estate or trust distributes appreciated assets to beneficiaries, they generally keep the same tax basis that the trust or estate had in the property, which in the case of an estate is generally the stepped-up basis of the assets to their FMV at the time of the decedent's death. **(SEE "Estate Income Tax Return," and "Trust Income")**

Capital Gains and Losses (Form 8949)
Capital gains and losses (Form 8949) are taxable. In 2013, taxpayers who are in the new 39.6% tax bracket are subject to a maximum 20% tax on long term capital gains and qualified dividends. Otherwise, the 2012 tax rates on long term capital gains and qualified dividends are made permanent as of 1/1/2013. The 15% rate apples to taxpayers in the 25%, 28%, 33%, and 35% tax brackets. The 0% rate applies to taxpayers is in the 10% or 15% tax bracket. For example, joint filers who have taxable incomes up to $72,500 would pay no tax on long term capital gains. These rates apply to both regular tax and the Alternative Minimum Tax (AMT). All assets, including securities and other property, are capital assets. However, assets used in a trade or business are not capital assets. Also, supplies regularly used in a trade or business, accounts or notes receivable acquired in the ordinary course of a trade or business, copyrights, literary musical or artistic compositions, letters or memorandums created by your personal efforts, U.S. government publications that you obtain from the government for free or less than the normal sales price, securities held by a dealer in securities, and commodities derivatives are not capital assets. For example, your personal residence and car are capital assets, but inventory, accounts receivable, and depreciable property used in a trade or business (property, plant, machinery, and equipment), and rental property are not capital assets. Sale or exchange of capital assets can incur a capital gain or loss, but the sale of personal assets such as a home or car cannot incur a loss. All capital gain transactions are to be reported on Form 8949. The preparer must indicate on Form 8949 if a basis is shown on **Form 1099-B (Proceeds From Broker and Barter Exchange Transactions)**, not shown on Form 1099-B, or no Form 1099-B was issued. There is also a column to report an adjustment to basis/sales price and the reason for the adjustment. The information is then transferred to Schedule D.
- Must hold a capital asset for one year and a day in order to get long-term capital gain treatment. However, if you inherit a capital asset, you automatically are treated as having held it for more than one year
- **Computing net long-term capital gain subject to the 20% capital gain tax rate:** When ordinary income exceeds the threshold amounts, all of your net capital gain is taxed at 20%. However, if ordinary income is below the threshold amount (assuming no gain on collectibles or unrecaptured Sec. 1250 gain is involved), the amount of net capital gain taxed at 20% is the excess of ordinary income and capital gain beyond the threshold. For example, if joint filers have $375,000 in ordinary income, then their first $75,000 in net capital gains is taxed at 15% ($375,000 + $75,000 = $450,000 which is the threshold amount); any excess net capital gains beyond $75,000 is taxed at 20%

- In exchange for providing the service of managing their investors' assets, fund managers often receive a portion—usually 20%—of the fund's profits, or <u>carried interest</u>, which is taxed at the lower capital gains rates of 15% or 20%.
- Beginning in 2011, brokers that show the gross proceeds from the sale of stocks on Form 1099-B must show the date the securities were purchased, the date the securities were sold, the adjusted cost basis, and whether the gain or loss shown is short or long term gain and wash sale status. <u>This requirement was to be carried out in three phases: (1) stocks purchased/acquired on or after 1/1/2011; (2) mutual funds purchased on or after 1/1/2012; and (3) bonds, options and private placements bought on or after 1/1/2013</u>. While phases one and two occurred as planned, the IRS has delayed the effective date of phase three until Jan. 1, 2014, to allow additional time for brokers to deal with the multiple issues involved in accurately reporting the basis of complicated debt instruments and options. And even though typical fixed bonds and most options are covered as of 1/1/2014, reporting on many complicated securities has been further delayed until Jan. 1, 2016. Brokers are required to reduce the gross proceeds on securities sales on Form 1099-B by commissions and transfer taxes. Brokers are to determine the customer's basis under the first-in, first-out (FIFO) method as a default. However, if a customer owns mutual funds, the basis is measured according to the "average basis method." As the name implies, the broker computes the average basis by dividing the aggregate cost of the securities by the number of shares the taxpayer purchased. However, brokers are supposed to offer customers a choice of at least 4 reporting methods on stock sales: first-in, first-out; last-in, first-out; highest-cost, first-out; and specific identification. If a customer doesn't specify, IRS rules specify first-in, first-out as the default—which could increase taxes paid. A customer can switch methods, but only before selling shares, not after. **If possible, you should specify highest-cost, first-out, which can minimize taxes on gains**. For purposes of computing gain or loss before executing year-end trade tax strategies, an investor should confirm the amount of basis that a broker will be reporting to the IRS for any securities that are sold. An investor must decide what method they are using no later than the settlement date.
- Also, beginning in 2011, brokers are required to report on Form 1099-B whether the securities being reported on are "covered" or "uncovered" securities. Essentially, covered securities are any specified securities purchased after 2010, and uncovered securities are all others.
- In stock-option transactions, the Form 1099-B you receive may underreport your cost basis, causing you to overpay taxes unless you adjust the amount. This can happen because the broker likely won't include a compensation adjustment that can serve to lower your gain or increase your loss. In this situation, you may need to make an adjustment on Form 8949.
- A dual holding period applies to incentive stock options (ISO)—you must hold the stock for one year after the shares are transferred to you, and for two years from the date the ISO was granted in order to be eligible for long-term capital gain treatment. **(SEE Incentive Stock Options, below)**

- Gifts, and property acquired from a spouse (or ex-spouse) include their holding period.
- <u>Form 8939</u> is used by an executor of an estate to report the carryover basis of those inherited assets where the estate elected the **2010 estate tax repeal.** This provides the basis information should the heir have sold those inherited assets in 2011 or in the future. Heirs should obtain the backup support from the executor spelling out how basis determination was made. **(SEE "Estate and**

  Gift Tax," Estate Tax Return)
- Capital gains on collectibles (coins, art, antiques) are taxed at 28%. **Gold bullion and gold collectible coins are collectibles. So, LT capital gains on the sale of these are taxed at a maximum rate of 28% rather than the usual 15% maximum rate.**
    1. Here's how it works on gains from sales of precious metal coins and bullion—if you are in the 28%, 33%, or 35% tax bracket you are taxed at 28%. If you are in the 10%, 15%, or 25% tax bracket, you are taxed at your regular rate of 10%, 15%, or 25%.
    2. Instead of physically owning gold bullion and coins, you can buy shares of an exchange traded fund (ETF) that tracks the value of particular precious metals. However, ETFs are also considered collectibles that are taxed at the maximum capital gains rate of 28%.
- Selling securities that have fallen in value since purchase generates a tax loss that offsets realized capital gains as well as up to $3,000 of ordinary income in the current year (any unused losses can be carried forward to future years). Selling securities at a loss to offset capital gains can result in a substantial tax advantage. *For example*: a $17,000 short-term loss will offset a $12,000 capital gain, potentially taxed at 15%, resulting in a $5,000 short-term loss that offsets $3,000 of ordinary income, potentially taxed at 25 – 35%, and you can carry over the remaining $2,000 loss to the next year to offset ordinary income in that year. This is known as "Harvesting Tax Losses."
- Losses are disallowed when you sell securities at a loss, and buy the same or substantially similar securities 30 days before or after the sale. This is known as a "wash sale" and applies only to the sale of losers. Wash sale rules are not imposed on recognizing gains and then immediately purchasing the same shares again.
- <u>Ponzi Scheme Losses</u> are not subject to the $3,000 limitation (discussed below). 95% of your net investment can be deducted as an ordinary loss on Schedule A, Form 1040 (not subject to the 2% floor)—Revenue ruling in 2008. However, you can deduct only 75% of your net investment, if you plan to join a lawsuit against the financial advisors. Your loss includes your unrecovered investment, including any income, that turns out to be fictitious, reported in prior years. But you cannot amend prior year tax returns for any income that may have been reported from such investments in prior years.
- Worthless securities: You can only take a deduction in the year the securities become totally worthless, and then they are treated as a loss from the sale of a capital asset on the last day of that tax year (limited to $3,000 capital loss deduction for the year, and the remainder is carried

over to future years). The stocks' worthlessness must be established by identifiable events **sufficient to establish the worthlessness of the securities, including**: cessation of the corporation's business; commencement of liquidation; appointment of a receiver; and actual foreclosure. However, a corporation and its securities may be worthless even though the corporation has not dissolved, liquidated, or ceased doing business. It depends on the securities' current liquidation value and the potential value the securities may acquire through the foreseeable operations of the corporation. A security is completely worthless only if both elements of value have disappeared.

- Section 1244: Small business stock that becomes totally worthless is deductible as an ordinary loss on Form 4797 (not limited to $3,000 capital loss deduction). To qualify the loss as ordinary, the following requirements must be met: (1) stock must have been originally issued by the corporation to the individual or partnership in which the individual is an investor; (2) the corp. must not have derived over 50% of its gross receipts from passive income sources during the five years immediately preceding the year of worthlessness; and (3) at the time the stock was issued the amount of capital and paid-in surplus did not exceed $1 million. To be treated as worthless stock, the stock may not be traded on an exchange, so a mere 90% decline in value does not make it a deductible loss. A Section 1244 loss is treated as an ordinary loss and is netted against capital gains. However, the ordinary loss deduction is limited to $50,000 ($100,000 for married filing jointly).
- Section 1202: If small business stock is held more than 5 years, you can exclude from income 75% of any gain from stock issued after 2/17/2009. The Small Business Jobs Act raises the exclusion to 100% for gain on stock acquired after 9/27/2010 and before 1/1/2014, and the excluded gain will not count as an AMT preference item. The amount of gain eligible for the exclusion is limited to the greater of 10 times the taxpayer's basis in the small business stock, or $10 million of gain from the stock. When the stock is issued, the aggregate gross assets of the issuing corporation may not exceed $50 million, and the corporation must use at least 80% of the value of its assets in the active conduct of its business. This provision is limited to individual investments and not the investments of a corporation. The non-excluded portion of section 1202 gain is taxed at the lesser of ordinary income tax rates or 28 percent, instead of the lower capital gains rates.
- Section 1231 (Sale of Business Property): Form 4797 is used to report sales of business property. Any gain on business property held more than 12 months, that is more than the part that is ordinary income due to depreciation, is Section 1231 gain which is treated as long-term capital gain. Some Section 1231 gain must be recaptured as ordinary income (depreciation, Section 179 expensing, and bonus depreciation taken). Sec. 1231 makes available the best of both worlds to businesses with both capital gains and losses. Net gains from the disposal of Sec. 1231 business property are taxed at capital gains rates, while net losses are taxed as ordinary losses (including business property disposed of at a loss that is held less than one year). If total

Sec. 1231 gains exceed losses for the year, then the net gains are capital gains. If total losses exceed gains for the year, then the net losses are ordinary losses which are <u>not limited to $3,000 for that year</u>. However, Sec. 1231 losses on business property held more <u>or less</u> than one year, that are not fully applied against Sec. 1231 gain in the same year, are subject to recapture against net Sec. 1231 capital gains in previous years. Non-recaptured Sec. 1231 losses for the previous 5 years that have not been applied against net Sec. 1231 capital gains, by reclassifying the gains as ordinary income, are applied against net Sec. 1231 gains beginning with the earliest loss in the 5 year period. **(SEE "Carrying on a Trade or Business," Sale of Business Property)**

- <u>Unrecaptured Section 1250 gain on real estate is taxed @ 25%</u>. When real property such as building is sold, any depreciation taken that is not taxed as ordinary income is "non-recaptured" Section 1250 gain that is taxed @ 25% instead of being taxed at ordinary income rates.
- Stock traded in the over-the-counter market or a national exchange is considered sold on the trade date, rather than the settlement date, unless it is a short sale. In the case of a short sale, gain is realized on the trade date (the stock price falls and a gain results), but a loss is not realized until the settlement date (the stock price rises and a loss results).
- Capital gain distributions are generally treated as long-term capital gains.
- <u>A copyright, literary, musical or artistic composition, letter or memorandum that is created by your personal efforts or acquired by gift is not a capital asset.</u> (Example: if you write a novel and sell it, it is not a capital asset that will receive capital gain treatment.) Also, it is not a Sec. 1231 transaction if it is sold; instead it is reported as ordinary income in Part II of Form 4797.

A non-business bad debt must be <u>totally worthless</u> and is deducted as a **short-term capital loss** on Schedule D (limited to $3,000 per year). <u>No deduction is allowed if you guaranteed a loan as a personal favor to a family member, relative or friend, with no profit motive and without consideration. In which case, no bad debt deduction is available, and the payment under such guarantee will likely be characterized as a "gift.</u>" If you claim a loss, you must attach a statement to the tax return describing the loan, relationship to debtor, how you tried to collect it, and why you decided it is worthless. The loss is equal to the creditor's basis in the loan. For a debt to be considered a bad debt, the creditor must have no reasonable expectation of collecting it. The lender must be able to demonstrate that the debt is wholly without value and that the debt became worthless during the tax year for which the lender is claiming the deduction.

Passive Activity Income
Passive activity income (Form 8582) is taxable, and deductions or expenses related to passive income are allowed only to the extent of passive income. Passive activity losses are deductible only from other passive activities. Losses disallowed can be carried forward to later years and become deductible only when passive income is realized or the activity is sold. Form 8582 identifies passive income and losses

and helps determine if passive loss items are deductible. Unlike the at-risk rules, which focus on financial contributions to the business, the passive activity loss rules focus on the individual's participation in the business. The passive activity rules apply to: individuals, personal service corporations, closely held C-corporations, partners, and S-corporation shareholders. The rules do not apply to partnerships, S-corporations, or widely held C-corporations.

- Non-passive income includes portfolio income which generally includes interest, dividends, royalties, and annuities, although portfolio income derived in the ordinary course of a passive trade or business may be passive income. In addition, passive activity income does not include income from: personal services and covenants not to compete; a working interest in oil and gas property; intangible property significantly created by the taxpayer; and income tax refunds.
- In order to determine whether income is passive or non-passive, there are two key terms: material participation and significant participation. If you "materially participate" by meeting one of six IRS tests (such as working 100 hours in the activity, etc.), your activity is not a passive activity. However, a taxpayer must be prepared to prove that one of the material participation tests of IRC §469 has been met in order to be able to deduct losses from the activity against non-passive income. A taxpayer materially participates in an activity if he is involved in the operations of the activity on a regular, continuous, and substantial basis. The six safe harbor provisions that deem material participation are the following:
    1. Participated in the activity more than 500 hours during the year;
    2. Provided substantially all of the participation by individuals;
    3. Participated for 100 hours or more, and this equaled or exceeded others' participation;
    4. Participated for more than 100 hours in several activities and total participation adds up to more than 500 hours annually;
    5. Materially participated in the activity for 5 of the 10 previous years; and
    6. Provided personal (professional) services to the business and materially participated in any three preceding years.
- **"Significant or active participation" is a lower standard than material participation and applies to rental activities. Although rental activities are considered "passive", there is an exception for owners of property that significantly participate in managing the rental property—up to $25,000 of rental losses per year can be deducted against regular/non-passive income. (SEE Rental Income, below)**
- A suspended passive activity loss is deductible upon disposition of the taxpayer's interest in the activity. Also, upon disposition of a taxpayer's entire interest in a passive activity, a taxpayer can elect to increase the basis of property used in a passive activity by the amount of any unused (disallowed) credits that reduced the basis of such property. This can only be done upon disposition, because disallowed passive activity credits cannot be used after disposition of the passive activity unless the taxpayer has passive income from other activities (use Form 8582-CR).

- **In general, limited partners are not deemed to materially participate in partnership activities, so their share of partnership income and losses is considered passive.**
- Interests in LLCs and LLPs are not considered limited partnership interests for purposes of the passive-activity loss rules, but such taxpayers may have to prove material participation in order to claim any resulting losses.
- <u>Whether or not an activity is considered passive is determined each year. If a taxpayer has a carryover of a passive activity loss from a prior year, and the same activity generates active income in the current year, the passive activity loss carryover can be used against active income of the activity for the current year.</u>
- One technique for converting otherwise passive activities to non-passive is by grouping them, treating them collectively as a single activity, and thereby combining the participation hours and improving one's ability to achieve the necessary hours for material participation. Generally, activities can be grouped if they constitute an appropriate economic unit for measuring gain or loss. Factors to consider are: similarities in types of trades or businesses; the extent of common control and ownership; geographical location; and interdependencies between or among the activities. However, there are drawbacks to grouping activities, including the inability to free up suspended losses on the disposal of individual activities in the group. **Example of converting a passive activity to non-passive: Rather than renting space, business owners purchase the building in which they operate their company.** The business is a professional service Subchapter S corporation (Entity 1); and the building is a rental activity subchapter S-corporation (Entity 2). The owners of both Entity 1 and Entity 2 are the same. The owners materially participate in the activities of Entity 1. Entity 2 rents commercial real estate property and one of its primary tenants is Entity 1. The question is whether or not a tax loss by Entity 2 is limited by the Tax Code's passive activity loss rules. Entity 2 had a big loss because it had a "cost segregation study" done, which accelerated depreciation of major parts of the building. <u>In this example, income or a loss that would otherwise be passive can be active by applying the self-rental rule and/or the grouping rules</u>. Here, the self-rental rule converts any rental income from Entity 2 to active income, but the self-rental rule does not convert the rental loss from Entity 2 to an active loss. But, if a timely election is made by the owners to group the activities, and the activities constitute an appropriate economic unit, the otherwise passive rental loss from Entity 2 could be an active loss that can be used to offset the active income from Entity 1. This grouping may be possible by applying the special rules for when the rental activity is insubstantial in relation to the business (e.g. the income from the rental activity is less than 20% of the income from the professional service corporation).

Rental Income

Rental income (Schedule E, Form 1040) is taxable. Advance rentals are included in income in the year received, but deposits are not included in income until forfeited. Rental income includes improvements made by lessee, if made as a substitute for rent. Lease cancellation payments are included in income in the year received.

- **For each separate rental property,** you need to provide the physical location, the type of property (single-family, duplex, etc.), and you need to keep a record, by property of the number of days rented and the number of days used for personal purposes.
- Rental activities are **passive activities**, regardless of the taxpayer's level of participation, unless the individual is a real estate professional. However, individuals who own and "actively" participate in the management of rental property can offset up to $25,000 of losses against active income in any year. Active participation is a lower standard than material participation. The offset is phased out by 50% of the amount the taxpayer's AGI exceeds $100,000, up to $150,000. The entire $25,000 loss is available only when the taxpayer's Adjusted Gross Income (AGI) does not exceed $100,000 (phased out between AGI $100,000–$150,000).
- If a second home is classified as a rental property (either does not qualify as a residence and is rented out, or taxpayer moves from home and turns it into a rental property during year), you can deduct all expenses related to the rental property to the extent of generating a loss of up to $25,000 per year against regular, non-passive income (Schedule E). But, short-term vacation home rentals averaging seven days or less do not qualify for the loss allowance.
- You cannot write off rental losses against Subchapter S-corporation income, if you "materially" participate in the S-corporation, i.e. if you work more than 100 hours per year, etc., in the S-corporation you cannot write off rental losses (passive losses) against the income (non-passive) generated from the S-corporation. But if you work less than 100 hours in the S-corporation, you can, because the income from the S-corporation would then be considered passive income. Material participation S-corporation income is not considered passive, even though it is considered passive for other purposes of the tax code. **(HOWEVER SEE the example in Passive Income, above)**
- If a second home is classified as a combination (2nd home qualifies as a residence and is rented out 15 days or more during year)—expenses allocated to rental use are deductible only to the extent of gross income generated. A loss cannot be generated. **Expenses not deductible may be carried over to the subsequent years**. Expenses allocated to rental use must be taken in same order as a hobby. A second home is classified as a residence if it is used by the owner the greater of 14 days in a year or 10% of the number of days it is rented out at FMV during the year, and therefore, a taxpayer can deduct it's property taxes and mortgage interest as itemized deductions. If the home is rented out for 14 days or less, the income received from the rental does not have to be reported for income tax purposes.

1. The number of personal use days and fair rental days is used to determine the tax treatment of expenses incurred and the amount of depreciation allowed. In other words, the denominator is equal to the total of the number of personal use days and the fair rental days, and the numerator is equal to the number of fair rental days. So the expenses for the year would be allocated based on that formula, except for mortgage interest and real estate taxes, which are deductible anyway.
2. Personal use days include: use by the taxpayer or relatives including siblings, spouse, ancestors, and lineal descendants. Personal use days even include days when the property is rented to a relative at fair rental value, if the owner retains free access to the unit. Use under house-swapping arrangements are considered personal use days, whether or not fair rental is charged. However, <u>personal use days do not include days when repairs and maintenance are performed on a substantially full-time basis by the owner, even if other individuals are present who are not repairing or maintaining the property</u>.

- A "timeshare" that you own is treated much in the same way. If you purchase a timeshare as a vacation spot and you sell it for a loss, the loss is not deductible. However, if you bought it as an investment and sell it at a loss, the loss is deductible.
- You can deduct travel expenses necessary to go check on a rental property, unless it qualifies as a second home or a combination (see above). Travel expenses include automobile expenses at the standard business mileage rate or actual expenses. The U.S. Tax Court allowed a couple who bought their own airplane to deduct the condo-related trips in their airplane to check on their rental condo, rather than drive five to seven hours or be tied to the only daily commercial flight available. They were allowed to deduct the cost of fuel and depreciation for the portion of time used for business-related purposes, even though those costs increased their overall rental loss on the condo.
- Exclusion of gain from the sale of a principal residence attributable to periods the dwelling was used as a vacation home or a rental property after 2008 and then converted to a principal residence is not allowed. The portion of the profit that is taxable is based on the percentage of time before the sale, when the home was used as a second home or rented out. A period of absence generally counts as qualifying use if it occurs after the home was last used as the principal residence, but not before it was converted to a principal residence and then sold. <u>Therefore, if you owned a rental house in 2008 or before, and in 2011 convert it to your principal residence and don't sell it until 2014, you would qualify for the home sale gain exclusion because you lived in the residence for at least 2 of the 5 years preceding the date of the sale. But any gain related to "nonqualified use" (rental) after 2008 is not eligible for the exclusion (must pay capital gain on the portion of the gain related to the period 2009–2011). Also, the home sale gain exclusion does not apply to any gain attributable to any depreciation taken on the home after May 6, 1997. Recapture of depreciation resulting from such gain is</u>

subject to the Section 1231 netting rules. If there is a net Section 1231 gain, the gain attributed to the depreciation is entered in the "unrecaptured Section" of the 1250 Gain Worksheet in Schedule D, the gain is subject to a top tax rate of 25%. **(SEE "Income Exclusions," Gain on the Sale of a Principal Residence)**
- **Mortgage debt forgiveness** does not include debt on a second home or rental property. Taxable income cannot offset any loss realized on the foreclosure sale of a rental property or second home (see below).
- If you buy a house for an adult child and her children to live in, pay the real estate taxes and mortgage, and don't charge her rent, the house is not a rental property because you do not charge a fair rental value; therefore, you can deduct the real estate taxes and mortgage interest if you itemize deductions.
- <u>If you refinance the mortgage on a rental house, you probably can't deduct any closing costs, because most closing costs, such as abstract fees, legal fees, recording fees, surveys, and transfer taxes should be added to the basis of the property, thus increasing your depreciation allowance. Points paid are neither currently deductible nor an addition to basis, but instead are deductible evenly over the term of the loan.</u> **(SEE "Itemized Deductions," Mortgage Interest)**
- **A real estate professional** avoids the passive loss limitation ($25,000) if <u>more than ½</u> of the personal services performed by the taxpayer in trades or business during the year are performed in real estate property in which the taxpayer materially participates, and the taxpayer performs more than 750 hours of services during the year in real estate property in which he materially participates. There are seven safe harbor tests you can use. For example, if you work more than 100 hours on a property and no one else spends more time working on it than you, then you may be termed a material participant. However, time records are required and must be maintained to show material participation in your rental activities. <u>Therefore, qualifying to be a real estate professional means it most likely will have to be your only job</u>. Of course if you have multiple properties, it may be impossible to materially participate in each of them, and without material participation, rental losses will be subject to the passive loss limitation ($25,000). But you are allowed to aggregate your properties for this purpose. You can make a 469 aggregation election to treat all rental properties as one activity. The election is properly made by filing a statement with the taxpayer's original return in a form specified by Treasury. Reg. par. 1.469-9(g)(3). The statement must provide the names, addresses, and employer identification numbers (EIN), if applicable, for the activities being grouped as a single activity. In addition, the statement must contain a declaration that the grouped activities make up an appropriate economic unit for the measurement of gain or loss. Without the election, you might be unable to show material participation in all rental activities. The Sec. 469 regulations permit a taxpayer to group trades or businesses or rental activities together to satisfy the material participation standards and avoid characterization as a passive activity. All relevant facts and circumstances are considered in determining an "appropriate economic unit"

for this purpose, and any reasonable method may be used with the following factors given the greatest weight: similarities and differences in types of trades or businesses; the extent of common control; the extent of common ownership; geographic location; and interdependencies among activities. A taxpayer's initial binding cannot be changed unless it is clearly inappropriate or there is a material change in circumstances. However, there are downsides to this election. One downside is that any suspended losses on a single property will not be freed up unless a complete disposition is made of all properties under the election. The ability to make this election underscores how proactive attention to each real estate activity before year's end may help determine whether such an election is advisable. The election is binding for the year it is made and for all future years. **Rental income is excluded from self-employment taxes whether or not you are considered a real estate professional**. (SEE Passive Activity Income, above)
- In TC Sum. Op. 2011-122, a taxpayer was allowed to deduct rental property losses for two years when there were no tenants in the property, because the property was held for income-producing purposes and was available for rent.
- In PLR 201143011, the IRS determined that rentals received for billboard space were taxable as real estate rental income rather than personal property rentals.
- Rental real estate losses are allowed like other passive losses to the extent of gains from passive activities. When a rental property is sold, all previously un-allowed losses are allowed. Plus the excess of the gain over previously un-allowed losses is used to allow the offset of any other passive losses.

The IRS has agreed with recommendations in a newly released government report urging the Agency to increase its examinations of individual tax returns that report losses from rental real estate activity.

Qualified Retirement Plans and Traditional IRAs

Distributions from qualified retirement plans and traditional IRA's (reported to taxpayer on Form 1099-R) are taxable. These include <u>qualified</u> employee retirement and pension benefit plans—401(k), 403(b), and 457(b) plans; SEPs, SIMPLEs; and SARSEPs, as well as traditional IRAs that make equal monthly payments until death, and possibly reduced payments after death to a survivor. You must start receiving payments from these plans and traditional IRAs by April 1 following the year you turn 70 ½. A "qualified" account, including an IRA, is creditor protected under State law and in bankruptcy. However, qualified accounts are not protected from the IRS.
- A portion of traditional IRA distributions may be non-taxable income if taxpayer had non-deductible contributions. Non-taxable portion = Total non-deductible contributions (reduced by any non-taxable distributions in prior years), divided by total IRA account balance at end of prior year + current distribution amount, multiplied by current distribution amount. The non-taxable portion is not subject to the 10% penalty (discussed below). Rollovers are not taxed, if

made within 60 days of distribution, but the IRS can waive the 60-day requirement in cases of disaster or other events beyond an individual's control. IRAs can be rolled over into other IRAs, qualified plans, and 403(b) tax sheltered annuities.
- A portion of "Railroad" retirement and other plans with employee after tax contributions may be non-taxable. The non-taxable amount must be computed using the "simplified method," where the amount of employee after tax contributions are divided by the expected number of payments to determine the non-taxable portion applicable to each payment. For example, railroad employee after tax contributions are shown in box 3 of RRB-1099-R (railroad pensions). The expected number of payments for computing the non-taxable amount is based on the taxpayer's age at the starting date of the "Annuity" (retirement age). The expected number of payments using the simplified method are: ages 55 and under, 360 payments; 56–60, 310 payments; 61–65, 260 payments; 66–70, 210 payments; 71 and over, 160 payments. In the case of an annuity payable based on the life of more than one individual (survivor annuity), the expected number of payments is based on the combined ages of the annuitants: 110 and under, 410 payments; 111–120, 360 payments; 121–130, 310 payments; 131–140, 260 payments; 141 and over, 210 payments.
- There is a 10% penalty for early distributions before age 59 ½ (Form 5329). The penalty can be avoided if the early distribution is **from an IRA** and is due to: total disability; pay medical expenses exceeding 10% of AGI (7.5% if age 65 or over until 2016); pay medical insurance for a person who received unemployment compensation for 12 months in the year; pay qualified higher education expenses for IRA owner, spouse, child or grandchild, including graduate level courses; buy a principal residence up to a $10,000 lifetime limitation (first time home buyer); is a series of equal annual payments over a lifetime (at least five years); employee separates from service if age 55 or over; employee dies; or in case of another "hardship." An example of another hardship could be 12 consecutive weeks of unemployment for which the IRS would probably waive the 10% penalty.
- It is a lot harder to avoid the 10% early distribution penalty from a 401(k), because such a distribution must be for a "hardship" that is an immediate and heavy financial need, such as: inability to pay for medical care expenses; to prevent eviction or foreclosure from principal residence; to pay burial expenses for deceased parent, spouse or children; or to pay repair damages to residence that qualifies for a casualty loss deduction without regard to the over 10% itemized deduction requirement. Employee must have exhausted all other resources, including other distributions and non-taxable loans from pension plans to qualify for the hardship determination. **In that regard, a taxpayer can take a loan from a 401(k) or other pension plan, but not from an IRA**. The loan cannot be for more than ½ of the account balance up to a maximum of $50,000, and it must be repaid in 5 years in equal payments over the 5-year period. However, if taxpayer losses his/her job, the loan must be repaid within 60 days.

- A divorce-related transfer will not trigger the 10% penalty after the IRA owner has started taking a series of equal payments before age 59 ½, even though the transfer lowered the payout amounts to the IRA owner.
- If you alter a series of pre-59 ½ equal payments due to financial need, all prior withdrawals will be hit with the 10% penalty.
- Taxpayers who are 70 ½ or older can make a non-deductible tax-free distributions for charitable purposes from their IRA of up to $100,000 (reported on Form 1040, Line 15a, but do not enter any amount on Line 15b - write "QCD" next to this Line). This provision is **extended through 2013**. <u>For 2012, an eligible taxpayer could make a charitable distribution by Feb. 1, 2013, that applied to the 2012 tax year</u>.
- Reservists and national guard members called to active duty can withdraw money from their IRAs, 401(k), and 403(b) retirement plans without paying the 10% penalty, but the money has to be returned to the plan within two years after active duty ends to avoid paying the penalty. Must be called to active duty for at least 179 days or more to qualify. **If you served on active duty after 12/31/2007, you are eligible for retroactive tax relief if you've already paid a penalty. You can claim a refund from the IRS.**
- **Beginning in 2007, Retired Public Safety Officers (Policemen and Firemen) can exclude up to $3,000 of otherwise taxable distributions from a government retirement plan for amounts withheld and paid directly to a health insurance company to pay premiums for accident or health insurance coverage, or qualifying long-term care insurance.** The amount shown in Box 2a of Form 1099-R does not reflect this exclusion. Instead, the amount withheld is shown in Box 5 of Form 1099-R. Premiums may be for the retired public safety officer, spouse, or dependents.

Required Minimum Distributions

Required Minimum Distributions (RMD) from traditional IRAs and qualified retirement plans are taxable (reported to taxpayer on Form 1099-R). A taxpayer must begin taking distributions from traditional IRAs and qualified retirement plans no later than April 1 of the year following the year in which he/she attains age 70 ½. These distributions are taxable income, except for the non-taxable portion. **(SEE Distributions From Qualified Retirement Plans and Traditional IRAs, above.)** There is a penalty for failure to take minimum distributions (penalty is a tax equal to 50% of the amount the required minimum distribution exceeds the actual distribution). If you reach 70 ½ in 2013, you can either take your first RMD in 2013 or delay it until April 1, 2014. However, you will have to take your 2nd RMD by Dec. 31, 2014, and from then on you must take your RMDs by Dec. 31st of every year. Minimum distributions are calculated in accordance with IRS actuarial tables.
- **Exception** – if you continue working after age 70 ½, and you don't own over 5% of the business that employs you, you can put off taking RMDs from that employer's plan for as long as you

- keep working (but the exception only applies to your current employer's plan, not to IRAs or former employers' plans).
- For calculating your first year's distribution, the IRS specifically states to use your age on your birthday in the year you turn 70 ½. For example, if your birthday is between Jan. 1st and June 30th, the first year of the distribution would be age 70. And if your birthday is between July 1st and Dec. 31st, the first year of the distribution would be age 71.
- The required withdrawal is based on your account balance at the end of the previous year, divided by the IRS life expectancy figure (must use tables or a RMD calculator). If your husband or wife is more than 10 years younger than you and the sole beneficiary of one, but not all, of your IRAs, you'll need to use different life expectancy factors for different accounts.
- If you have multiple IRAs, you're supposed to figure the RMD for each one separately, but you don't have to take a withdrawal from each account. **You can take the required amount from any IRA or combination of IRAs**. In reality, <u>you can simply add the account balances of all your IRAs as of the end of the prior year, and divide it by your life expectancy factor</u>. However, RMDs must be figured separately for each of your 401(k)s, 403(b)s, and other retirements accounts. <u>Do not combine a 401(k) accounts with other 401(k) accounts or with your IRAs</u>.
- Taxpayers who are required to take RMDs can make tax-free distributions of up to $100,000 from traditional IRAs to tax-exempt charitable organizations in lieu of RMDs. **(SEE Distributions From Qualified Retirement Plans and Traditional IRAs, above)**. The money must go directly from the IRA trustee to the charity. However, **taxpayers who have already taken their RMDs cannot return their IRA payouts to be used as a tax-free distribution directly to a charitable organization. However, for 2012 only, a RMD made to a taxpayer can be re-characterized as a charitable distribution if transferred to the charity before Feb. 1, 2013.** A special rule treats transferred amounts as coming first from taxable funds, instead of proportionately from taxable and nontaxable funds, as would be the case for regular distributions. Not all charities are eligible. For example, donor-advised funds and supporting organizations are not eligible recipients. Taxpayers who take advantage of the tax-free distributions from their IRAs are not allowed a charitable itemized deduction for the contribution.
- **For RMDs, the payout period is determined without regard to calendar year 2009, i.e. if decedent died in 2007 and the 5-year payout rule is applicable, payout is required to be made by 2013 instead of 2012.**
- A taxpayer required to take RMDs can take stock instead of cash from his IRA to satisfy the RMD amount (an "in kind" distribution of stock). However, the stock you take has a zero basis, so be sure to hold onto the stock for more than one year to qualify for the tax-favored capital gain rates, because what the IRA paid for the stock and the time you had it in the IRA does not count.
- <u>If you miss an RMD, you can escape the 50% penalty by asking the IRS to waive it</u>. This can be done where there is a reasonable cause for the failure, such as an illness or bad advice from the

financial institution with which you hold your account. Complete Form 5329 (lines 50 and 51), and on line 52 enter "RC" and the amount you want waived. Subtract this amount from the total shortfall. Attach a statement to the form indicating the reason why you think the penalty should be waived. You need only pay the penalty on any portion of the shortfall you do not ask the IRS to waive. The IRS will review your waiver request and inform you of whether it is granted. The IRS generally is liberal in granting such a request.
- You can take distributions from your IRA to satisfy RMDs in cash or in kind, meaning in stock. The option you use depends on what's in your account and what you want to do with it. You don't have to sell stock to meet you obligation, but be sure that if you're taking stock, you use the FMV of it to figure your RMD.

Retirement Plans Inherited by Beneficiaries

Traditional IRA's, Roth IRA's, and qualified retirement plans inherited by beneficiaries are taxable to beneficiaries based on the same amount as they would have been taxable to the original owner. However, taxable distributions received by a beneficiary from a traditional IRA are not subject to the 10% penalty for distributions received before age 59 ½. Inherited Roth IRAs will be tax-free unless the account was established less than five years before, in which case the earnings may be subject to tax.

- A surviving spouse who inherits a traditional IRA or a qualified retirement plan can keep it separate (inherited IRA), or roll-it-over into an IRA or qualified retirement plan in his/her own name. Whether a surviving spouse should keep the IRA separate or roll it over and treat it as his/her own depends on the circumstances. A surviving spouse who is under age 59 ½ and who keeps a traditional IRA separate (in this case, the IRA must be titled as follows: [Deceased-spouse's name], deceased on [date of death], FBO [surviving spouses name], beneficiary) can take penalty-free distributions from it, and for RMD purposes must follow beneficiary rules, meaning he/she usually must start to take RMDs by the end of the year after the year of death and base the RMDs on his/her single life expectancy table. However, if the traditional IRA is rolled over and treated as his or her own, then the account cannot be tapped penalty free until the spouse reaches age 59 ½. In this case the account belongs to the surviving spouse, so he/she can name new beneficiaries and would not start RMDs until attaining age 70 ½. RMDs are based on the joint and survivor table. The rollover election is available whether or not the decedent had begun taking IRA distributions. If the decedent was required to have taken a RMD in the year of death but did not do so, the surviving spouse, although electing to be the owner of the IRA, must calculate the RMD for that year as if it were made by the decedent. **NOTE: The rollover option can be used by the spouse for part of the IRA, i.e. the rollover need not be all or nothing. A partial rollover allows the surviving spouse under the age of 59 1/2 to access the funds in the non-rolled-over account without any early distribution penalty**.
- A non-spouse beneficiary has two options for liquidating an inherited traditional IRA or qualified retirement plan: the first (and less desirable) option is to liquidate it within five years

(the 10% penalty does not apply), i.e. the distribution is taxable to the beneficiary in the year received as "income in respect of a decedent" and must be distributed to the beneficiary by the end of the 5th year following the year of death. During those 5 years no distribution is required, but it probably would be tax advantageous to take annual distributions to keep from having to pay taxes on the total of the distributions all in the same year. The second option is the "stretch option," in which a non-spouse beneficiary can make the choice to take the distributions over his or her life expectancy. A designated or "NAMED" beneficiary (other than a surviving spouse) who inherits an IRA from a relative can roll it over in a trustee-to-trustee transfer to an "Inherited IRA", and utilize the **beneficiary's life expectancy.** However, in order to choose the stretch option, the beneficiary must immediately begin taking yearly RMDs, based on his/her own life expectancy. The beneficiary has to take the first RMD in the next calendar year by Dec. 31 of the calendar year following the year that the deceased died. If the beneficiary misses that date, he defaults back to the five-year rule. The inherited IRA must be set up and maintained in the name of the deceased for the benefit of the non-spouse beneficiary, such as: "Jane Smith IRA, deceased Nov. 16, 2009, FBO John Jones, beneficiary." The election is valid even if the decedent had already begun taking distributions from the IRA or retirement plan. However, the second option was not available for inherited employee retirement plans before 2010 (see below).

- While distributions from Roth IRAs are generally not taxable and are exempt from RMDs during the owner's life, **beneficiaries must start taking RMDs from inherited Roth IRAs over their life expectancy.**
- Beginning in 2010, a non-spouse beneficiary who inherited a qualified employee retirement plan (401(k), 403(b), or governmental 457 plan) must have been allowed to rollover the distribution to an IRA in a trustee-to-trustee transfer (see above). Before 2010, this requirement was optional (not a plan requirement).
- If a beneficiary inherits an IRA from someone whose estate was big enough to be subject to the federal estate tax, the beneficiary can get an income tax deduction for the amount of estate taxes paid on the IRA assets you received, i.e. you inherit a $100,000 IRA, and the fact that the money was included in your benefactor's estate added $45,000 to the estate tax bill; therefore, you get to deduct that $45,000 on your income tax returns as you withdraw the money from the IRA. If you withdraw $50,000 in one year, for example, you get to claim a $22,500 itemized deduction on Schedule A.
- Life expectancy is determined by looking at the IRS tables in Appendix C of IRS Publication 590.

Rollovers From Traditional IRAs to Roth IRAs

Rollovers From traditional IRA's to Roth IRA's are included in taxable income (reported to taxpayer on Form 1099-R) as a distribution for the tax year, and taxpayers are taxed at their highest tax rate on the amount converted in the year of conversion. However the 10% penalty does not apply. In 2009 and prior years, only taxpayers with modified adjusted gross incomes (MAGI) of less than $100,000 were allowed to convert traditional IRAs and qualified retirement plans (401ks, etc.) to Roth IRAs. But **effective 1/1/2010, taxpayers with MAGIs of more than $100,000 are allowed to convert their traditional IRAs to Roth IRAs, with no distinction between single filers and joint filers.**

- The conversion may occur directly, through a trustee-to-trustee transfer, or indirectly, via a distribution to the taxpayer that he deposits into a Roth IRA within 60 days. The distribution must happen in 2013 to qualify as a 2013 rollover or conversion, but the deposit may take place in 2014, as long as it occurs within 60 days of the distribution. Married taxpayers filing separately are not allowed to make a conversion. You can convert directly from 401(k) and 403(b) plans to a Roth if the plan allows it. Also, <u>in 2010 only, you could delay reporting the conversion for one year, and then split the converted amount in half on your 2011 and 2012 tax returns, paying part of the tax in 2011 and part of the tax in 2012</u>. NOTE: You may be eligible to convert to a Roth, but not allowed to contribute to it annually, because the MAGI limits for 2013 are between $112,000 to $127,000 (single), and between $178,000 to $188,000 (married filing jointly).
    1. Some high-income investors have gotten around contribution limits through what's known as a "back-door" Roth IRA, where you contribute to a nondeductible IRA, then immediately convert that IRA to a Roth. As long as you act before any earnings accumulate, you won't owe any tax, unless you have other traditional IRAs. For example, suppose you contribute $5,000 to a nondeductible IRA, then immediately convert it to a Roth. And you have another traditional IRA that holds $95,000 in contributions. Because the $5,000 represents just 5% of the new total of $100,000, only 5% or $250, of the $5,000 conversion will be tax-free.
- The American Taxpayer Relief Act of 2012 lifts most restrictions, and now allows participants in 401(k) plans with in-plan Roth conversion features to make transfers to a Roth account at any time. Prior to this Act, participants who wanted to make such transfers were subject to certain qualifying events or age restrictions.
- <u>Also, if you convert to a Roth, you have until October 15, 2014 to undo your decision and recoup the taxes paid</u>. If you have already filed your 2013 return, you can amend it. For example, if you converted and owe 25% tax on the amount converted and the Roth losses value in the meantime, you can save the tax paid by re-characterizing the Roth IRA back into a traditional IRA by 10/15/2014 (due date of the tax return including extension). You don't want to pay the tax before changing your mind, if possible. No formal election is required for the re-characterization; however, the taxpayer must notify the trustee of each IRA involved in the trustee-to-trustee transfer by the due date of the tax return, including extension. The process is simple: **ask your IRA administrator to re-characterize the account, then file an amended return with the IRS** and you'll get a refund of the taxes you paid. Then, if you still want to get

your battered assets back into a Roth, you can reconvert them back to a Roth after 30 days and report the amount you move to the Roth as 2014 income.
- <u>All conversions for 2013 must be completed by December 31, 2013.</u>
- The Small Business Jobs Act allows eligible state and local government 457(b), 401(k), and 403(b) plans (but not plans of nonprofit organizations) to allow participants to contribute amounts to a Roth account (applies to the Federal Thrift Savings Plan). The provision is effective for distributions after 9/27/2010. NOTE: The plans must be amended to permit these rollovers before they can happen.
- <u>Three factors to consider when contemplating a Roth conversion are</u>: Tax rate differential; Use of outside funds to pay income tax; and the time horizon. Because if the taxpayer's current and future tax rates are the same, and the income tax liability is paid with funds inside the IRA, the taxpayer is in the same economic position when converting to a Roth IRA as if no conversion took place. However, a taxpayer who uses outside funds to pay the income tax liability on a Roth conversion is in a better economic position than if the funds were kept in a traditional IRA. The time horizon is critical, because the longer the funds can grow in a tax-exempt environment, the better the economic result.

>_Reasons not to convert_: you expect to be in a lower tax bracket during the traditional IRA withdrawal period (after age 70 ½) than in the year of conversion; your AGI in the year of conversion will be higher, which could put you in a higher tax bracket and effect the amount of social security benefits taxed; the 10% of AGI floor for including medical expenses as an itemized deduction will be higher, which might result in no medical deductions; and you may be subject to AMT in the year of conversion (10% of AGI floor for including medical expenses as an itemized deduction, etc.). Also, converting to a Roth may increase your Part B Medicare insurance premium—for example, for 2013 the premium is $104.90 per month if your MAGI does not exceed $170,000, however the premium increases if your MAGI exceeds $170,000 up to as high as $335.70 per month if your MAGI is in excess of $428,000. Consider this, converting a $20,000 traditional IRA may not put you into a higher tax bracket, but if the additional $20,000 pushes you over the $170,000 "breakpoint," the combined Medicare premiums (for both spouses) could increase to $1,008 for the year, which equates to an additional 5% tax on that $20,000.

>_Reasons to convert_: converting a traditional IRA to a Roth IRA is a hedge against higher income taxes in the future, due either to a general elevation of the tax rate structure or to the taxpayer moving into a higher tax bracket during the traditional IRA withdrawal phase. Converting is not really a mechanism for taking advantage of diminished investment values in your traditional IRA due to the decline in the stock market, unless the decline has resulted in your investments being depressed to the extent that the current value of your tax-deferred retirement account is less than the contributions originally contributed to the account, **at which point the amount converted to the Roth IRA will never be taxed**. You will have the opportunity

for the retirement account to grow from then on and be distributed free of any future income tax; and you will have the ability to retain the funds in the Roth IRA indefinitely beyond retirement which provides a very effective means for accumulating assets to pass on to your heirs free of future income tax. Heirs will be subject to RMD rules when they inherit Roth IRAs, but they will not owe income tax on the funds they withdraw.

>**Even if your IRA account has not declined to the extent that the current value is less than the contributions originally made to the account, you might decide at some point to convert the total amount of contributions originally made to the traditional IRA to a Roth IRA, and thus, take advantage of the reasons put forth above in favor of conversion.**

Distributions From "Nonqualified" Tax Deferred Annuities

Distributions from "nonqualified" tax deferred annuities are usually taxable. Nonqualified tax deferred annuities are issued by insurance companies. There is a 10% early distribution penalty prior to age 59 1/2 unless payments are made because of disability or other permissible reasons. For example, there is no penalty if the payment is from an annuity contract under a qualified personal injury settlement or from an immediate annuity, which is a single-premium annuity where the starting date is no more than one year from the date of purchase. However, most of these annuities allow annual penalty free withdrawals of up to 10% of the value each year prior to maturity. If the insurance contract was purchased after August 13, 1982, withdrawals are considered interest only, which is taxed as ordinary income. If the contract was purchased before Aug. 14, 1982, the withdrawals are usually considered principal first and, therefore, may not be taxable. Nonqualified tax deferred annuities are generally funded with voluntary contributions that have already been taxed. And the owner of the annuity must start receiving a payout of substantial equal periodic payments over 5, 10, 20 years, etc., before the already taxed contributions, or principal, can be considered in computing the non-taxable portion of payments.

- Unlike qualified employee retirement plans and traditional IRAs, these contracts do not require a person to start receiving substantial equal periodic payments by age 70 ½.
- Loans taken from nonqualified tax deferred annuities are treated as cash withdrawals. If you borrow against the contract, you are taxed in the same way as if you'd taken a distribution. This distribution is taxable to the extent that the cash value of the contract exceeds your investment in the contract (the premiums you paid for the annuity).
- When substantially equal periodic payments begin ("Annuitization"), the nontaxable portion of each payment is computed by using the "General Rule" method—dividing the investment (principal) by the "total expected return" to get a percentage, which is used to compute the nontaxable portion of each annual equal payment. The total expected return is computed by multiplying the amount of each annual equal payment by either the fixed number of years over which payments will be received, or if for life, by the multiple found in the Treasury (IRS) Tables. EXAMPLE: the multiple for age 62 is 22.5. Therefore, if you are receiving equal annual payments

for life, the total expected return is computed by multiplying the amount of each annual equal payment by 22.5.
- **The Small Business Jobs Act allows an owner of a nonqualified annuity to split up the contract by taking a portion of the benefits as a separate stream of annuity payments (must be for 10 years or more, or the lives of one or more individuals) while leaving the remaining balance of the contract untouched. The remaining balance of the contract will continue to accumulate earnings on a tax-deferred basis. <u>This provision applies to payouts after 12/31/2010</u>.**
- If you want to move the deferred annuity to another insurance company, you can do so tax free via a "1035 exchange." However, you cannot exchange on a tax-free basis an annuity contract for a life insurance contract or endowment policy.
- Some annuities cannot be passed on because payments cease at the owner's death. However, other annuities have guaranteed payouts, which means that amounts that have not been paid to the owner will be paid to named beneficiaries. Annuity payments made to beneficiaries are taxable in the same way as they would have been had they been made to the contract owner before death.
- **To avoid or reduce federal taxes paid by beneficiaries (except spouse) who inherit annuities, you can convert your unqualified annuity to an IRS approved tax-free benefit plan owned by a 3rd party, such as an irrevocable trust. This should be done if you do not need the annuity payments to provide income, and you choose to pass these on to your heirs. Unfortunately, these tax deferred annuities are subject to significant income tax, and in some cases, estate tax. However, annuitizing the value of the annuity for life, and purchasing an IRS approved tax-free death benefit plan (which will normally be worth two or three times the value of the annuity depending on the age of the annuity owner) owned by an irrevocable trust not only converts, for example, a $200,000 annuity from a taxable asset into a tax-free asset upon death, but the value is increased to from $400,000 to $600,000 and will not be included in your Estate.**

Net Unrealized Appreciation

Net Unrealized Appreciation (NUA) should be elected if you hold a significant amount of your employer's stock in a 401(k) plan and you receive a lump-sum distribution of such stock when you retire or change jobs. This means that you probably should not roll it over to an IRA, because the money you or your heirs withdraw from the IRA will be taxed as ordinary income. Instead, you should elect net unrealized appreciation (NUA) for sale of appreciated company stock purchased and held in a qualified plan, such as a 401(k) or an employee stock ownership plan (ESOP). This is a special tax treatment that allows an individual who is retiring or changing jobs to take a distribution of company stock and **immediately pay ordinary income tax on just the basis of the stock and not the appreciated value** (must take a lump-sum distribution from the plan). In all cases, the appreciated value is not taxed until the company stock is sold, either immediately or at a later date (taxed at the long-term capital gains rate and not at the higher ordinary tax rate). The election can be made on your tax return for the year in which the distribution is made or on an amended return. The taxpayer makes the election by attaching an election statement to the tax return and by including the applicable amount of ordinary income on the appropriate line of Form 1040 (other income).

Social Security Benefits
Up to 85% of social security (SS) benefits (including Tier 1 Railroad Retirement Benefits) are taxable income. If your <u>provisional income</u> exceeds the base amounts of $25,000 if unmarried and $32,000 if married filing jointly, 50% of your benefits are taxable. If your provisional income exceeds the base amounts of $34,000 if unmarried and $44,000 if married filing jointly, 85% of your benefits are taxable. <u>If you are married filing separately, and you did not live apart for the whole year, each spouse pays income tax on 85% of their social security benefits</u>. Provisional income = MAGI (AGI, less social security payments in current year + higher education deductions + deduction for interest on qualified education loans + tax exempt interest) + ½ of social security payments in current year.
- If you were born Jan. 2, 1943–Jan. 1, 1955, your full retirement age is 66. If you decide to start taking Social Security (SS) benefits at age 62, you will receive 75% of your full benefit payments. If you work and are at full retirement age, you can earn any amount without your Social Security benefits being reduced. If you are younger than full retirement age when you start receiving SS benefits, $1.00 is deducted from your benefits for each $2.00 earned above $15,120 in 2013 ($14,640 in 2012). If you reach full retirement age during 2013, $1.00 is deducted for each $3.00 earned above $40,080 ($38.880 in 2012) until the month you reach full retirement age. However, the benefit reductions are not truly lost, i.e. your benefit will be increased at full retirement age to account for the benefits withheld due to earlier earnings.
- If you work for more than one employer in 2013, and Social Security taxes of more than $7,049 ($113,700 x 6.2%) are withheld from your wages, the excess may be claimed as a credit on Line 65 in the "Payments" section of Form 1040. In 2012, the excess was any amount over $4,624 ($110,100 x 4.2%).
- Social Security disability benefits are taxable to the same extent as regular Social Security benefits. However, if SS disability benefits are paid to a child of the disabled taxpayer, the benefits are probably not taxable.
- Workers' compensation payments that reduce Social Security benefits is treated as a Social Security benefit received during the year and is, therefore, indirectly taxable (Box 5 of Form SSA-1099 is the taxable amount – not reduced by any amount, such as a workers' compensation offset, shown in Box 3).
- <u>Repayment of Social Security as a result of overpayment</u>—The tax treatment of any required repayments depends on the amount. Any repayment of benefits must be subtracted from the gross amount of Social Security benefits received in 2013, regardless of whether the repayment was for a benefit you received in 2013 or in an earlier year. If the repayment is more than your

total benefits in 2013, you may be entitled to a deduction as long as the benefits had been included in gross income in an earlier year. Usually, the deduction is claimed as a miscellaneous itemized deduction subject to the 2% floor. However, when the repayment is more than $3,000 in excess of your current benefits, there is a special computation that may entitle you to a tax credit.

Alimony/Separate Maintenance
Alimony/separate maintenance received is taxable income to the recipient, as opposed to child support, which is not taxable. Alimony payments do not have to be received under a final decree of divorce or separate maintenance, but <u>must be under a written instrument, such as a separation agreement</u> (an oral understanding between the husband and his former wife will not do), requiring one spouse to make payments of support to the other spouse. Thus, alimony can be paid even though the couple continues to be married for tax purposes. However, payments do not qualify as alimony/separate maintenance if both still live in the same household (a one month overlap is OK). Alimony payments are reported as income on line 11 of Form 1040. **(SEE "Deductions for Computing Adjusted Gross Income," Alimony)**
- o The divorce agreement should clearly state that required alimony payments are not child support.
- o When the divorce or separation agreement designates all or a portion of any required payments as a "property settlement", such payments are not includable in the recipient's gross income as alimony. And no gain or loss is recognized on the transfer of property resulting from a divorce.
- o The "recapture provisions" prevent alimony from being disguised as property settlement payments, by stating that a reduction of $15,000 in alimony payments during the first 3 post-separation years results in recapture of property settlement payments as alimony. Recapture can occur only in the 3rd calendar year after payments begin and should be reported on Form 1040, line 11 (Alimony)—cross out "received" and write in "recapture." Exceptions are death or remarriage before end of 3rd year.
- o Payments made pursuant to a temporary support order are not subject to recapture – entire amounts are included as alimony.
- o Whether or not required payments, including part of a payer's pension payments, to a former spouse are considered alimony depends to a large degree on when the payments will cease in accordance with the divorce agreement. If the payments are to cease upon the death of the recipient spouse, then it is probably alimony. If the payments are to continue to be paid to the recipient's estate after death, it is probably <u>not</u> alimony. This is especially important in community property states, such as Texas, when pension payments to an ex-spouse are required to be paid each year before the payer retires (based on the present value of ex-spouse's share).

- Indirect alimony includes making mortgage payments and paying real estate taxes on a residence a former spouse is occupying. Payer spouse must be the owner of the residence; if they are joint owners – ½ is treated as alimony. When payer spouse owns the residence, he/she may be entitled to deduct the mortgage interest and real estate taxes as itemized deductions if the house qualifies as either his/her principal or secondary residence (otherwise may be limited). <u>It qualifies as a second home if at least one of the payer spouse's children is living in the house.</u>
- Indirect alimony also includes: (1) maintaining life insurance payments for a former/payee spouse, or for the payer spouse if the former/payee spouse is the beneficiary and owner of the policy; and (2) paying medical or other expenses of a former/payee spouse (payee spouse must include in income and deduct the medical expenses as itemized deductions). Medical payments made directly to a 3rd party must be documented in writing in order to be considered alimony.
- Legal expenses arising from a divorce are usually considered non-deductible personal expenses, unless they are related to obtaining (collecting) alimony or separate maintenance, or can be shown to be tax advice related to obtaining/paying alimony/separate maintenance. But if one spouse is required to pay the other spouse's legal expenses, that may be considered alimony.
- Payer spouse can deduct alimony payments on Line 31a of Form 1040.

Prizes

Prizes won or awarded are taxable income (reported as "Other Income" on Form 1040). However, any cash awards are not included in income if they are: (1) in recognition of past achievements of the recipient in religious, charitable, scientific, educational, artistic, literary, or civic fields; and (2) recipient was selected without any action on his/her part to enter a contest.

Gambling Winnings

Gambling winnings are taxable, and reported as income on Line 21 (Other income), Form 1040. Gambling losses can be taken to the extent of gambling winnings as a miscellaneous itemized deduction not subject to the 2% floor on Schedule A. Therefore, gambling winnings for the casual gambler will not necessarily be brought to zero by equal gambling losses. **A professional gambler's winnings and losses are shown on Schedule C, but the losses are limited to his/her earnings on Schedule C, and cannot be carried over to the next year.** For most types of gambling at a legitimate gaming facility, the facility will issue you a W-2G if you win $600 or more. The IRS says it's permissible for casual gamblers to simply keep a record of his net win or loss amount for each gambling session. In other words, the determination of the net win or loss amount can be made when the gambler redeems his tokens at the end of each session or determines that he lost all of the tokens he started out with at the beginning of the session. If the casual gambler then reports the sum total of the net winnings from all winning sessions as gross income on page 1 of Form 1040 and keeps track of the sum total of the net losses from all losing sessions for purposes of applying the losses-cannot-exceed-winnings limitation to his Schedule A itemized deduction, the IRS will consider that close enough to the theoretically required recording of each win or loss from each spin of the slot machine, etc. Presumably the IRS will consider this concept of recording all the net wins and losses from all the taxpayer's gambling sessions sufficient recordkeeping for both casual gambling and for professional gambling as well. Reporting an amount of gross income equal to the sum total of the net winnings from all days you had winnings on page 1 of Form 1040 will probably keep you out of trouble with the IRS (assuming the amount reported as income equals or exceeds the sum total of any amounts reported as income on Forms W-2G). Whether an amateur or professional gambler, you must adequately document the amount of your losses in order to claim them. The following information should be kept in a log: (1) the dates of your losses; (2) name and address of the gambling establishment; (3) if possible, the names of other persons present with the taxpayer at the gambling facility; and (4) the amount lost (record the number of the table played and keep statements showing casino credit issued to the player).

- Gambling losses can offset all gains from wagering transactions, not merely gambling winnings, i.e. raffle, lottery, and horse race winnings are treated as gambling winnings that can be offset by gambling losses, and the cost of <u>a losing raffle ticket paid to a charity is a gambling loss, not a charitable contribution</u>. Gambling winnings include cash winnings and the fair market value (FMV) of prizes such as cars and trips. However, **a prize or contest award that is won without an entry fee or other consideration is not gambling income**.
- Complimentary items received from a casino as an inducement to gamble are gambling gains from which the taxpayer can deduct gambling losses.
- For professional gamblers <u>only</u>, gambling losses include related business expenses, such as admission fees, meals, and lodging.
- Gambling losses may only offset gambling winnings from the same year. <u>Excess gambling losses and expenses from one year are lost (cannot be carried over to a future year), even by professional gamblers</u>.
- A gaming facility must give you a W-2G if you receive: $1,200 or more in gambling winnings from bingo or slot machines; $1,500 or more in proceeds (the amount of winnings minus the amount of the wager) from keno; more than $5,000 in winnings (reduced by the wager or buy-in) from a poker tournament; $600 or more in gambling winnings (except winnings from bingo, keno, slot machines, and poker tournaments) and the payout is a least 300 times the amount of the wager; or any other gambling winnings subject to federal income tax withholding.
- The combined gambling losses of a husband and wife who file a joint return can be deducted against the couple's combined gambling winnings.
- Professional gambler status is hard to achieve. Casual gamblers cannot become professional gamblers in the eyes of the IRS simply by gambling frequently. Strict requirements include the ability of the gambler to show activities being treated in a business-like manner using plans, strategies, and schedules.

Social Security Disability Income
Social Security disability income is taxable income. However, <u>Social Security disability income (SSDI) received by a child as a result of a parent's disability is not taxable to the child</u>. Because it can take years to receive SSDI benefits, most people receive a lump-sum amount, which includes back payments. Paying tax on this amount in one year is a mistake—the IRS allows taxes on this lump-sum payment to be spread over previous tax years using the current year tax return, without having to file amended returns. Also, if you hired a representative to help you get your SSDI benefits and you itemize, you can deduct the fee that you paid for your representative when figuring out the taxability of a lump-sum payment.

Cancellation of Debt
Cancellation of Debt (COD) of $600 or more is taxable income, and must be reported in Box 2 of Form 1099-C, which a lender is required to send to the taxpayer. Cancelled debt must be reported as "other income" on line 21 of Form 1040. A number of factual situations can result in the lender canceling the balance of the debt and sending Form 1099-C to the taxpayer. One situation is in the case of a short sale. Canceled debt is considered income to the debtor unless there is a "<u>discharge of indebtedness</u>." Debt is deemed to be cancelled at the time it is determined that it will never be repaid, and the <u>nonpayment testing period is a 36-month period during which a creditor has not received any payment from the debtor</u>, which creates a presumption that the loan has been cancelled; thus triggering the Form 1099-C filing requirement. However, a creditor can rebut this presumption by showing significant, bona fide collection activity or other facts and circumstances that indicate the debt has not been cancelled. Discharge of indebtedness can result from insolvency, bankruptcy, a disaster victim, qualified farm indebtedness, <u>forgiveness of mortgage debt</u>, or discharge of a qualified student loan made by a governmental agency or a qualified public benefit corporation, where a student is required to work for a specific period of time in certain professions (does not apply to private or non-government loans). A cancelled debt does not include a compromise between a debtor and creditor on a disputed debt amount. <u>A creditor's loss on a compromise of a debt owed by a solvent debtor is a loss, not a bad debt</u>.
    o If COD income is not recognized due to discharge of indebtedness, the debtor generally must reduce tax attributes. Some attributes are business related, such as a "net operating loss" (NOL). A common attribute for individuals is the basis of property – sometimes, the property for which the debt was incurred, sometimes other property. Thus, the excluded income is offset by reducing the basis (cost) of property owned by the debtor. This reduction delays the recognition of the cancellation of debt income, but generally ensures that the income will be recognized on the sale of the property (unless the gain is excluded under the "gain on sale of a personal residence" rules). Tax attributes have to be reduced for most exclusions due to discharge of indebtedness, but not on exclusions for qualified student loans. <u>For example, if a</u>

<u>taxpayer losses a rental property, and he/she can show he is insolvent, the taxpayer can fill out Form 982, Reduction of Tax Attributes Due to Discharge of Indebtedness.</u>
- Foreclosure on a home can result in COD income to the owner, if at the time of foreclosure the fair market value (FMV) of the encumbered property is less than the outstanding debt. Also, a "short sale" can result in income to the owner. A short sale in real estate occurs when the outstanding loans against a property are greater than what the property is worth and the lender agrees to accept less than it is owed to permit a sale of the property (home) that secures the note. Abandonment is also disposition of a property and can result in cancelled debt income to the owner. However, **mortgage debt is forgiven on a principal residence up to $2 million, or $1 million if married filing separately, and is not included in income for years beginning Jan. 1, 2007–Dec. 31, 2013**. This benefit covers an agreement or "work-out" with the lender to make payments lower – example: lender forgives $100,000 of taxpayer's current $325,000 mortgage debt + $4,500 of interest in arrears, thus both the $100,000 and the $4,500 are not taxable income. It also includes refinancing up to the amount of the old mortgage principal, but does not include home equity loans not used for home improvements, nor debt on a second home or rental property (taxable income cannot offset any loss realized on the foreclosure sale of a rental property or second home).
- **Is it really cancellation of debt?** While the issuance of Form 1099-C is an identifiable event, it is not necessarily determinative of an intent to cancel the debt. While <u>the IRS has determined that creditors must file Form 1099-C at the end of the 36-month period</u>, it does not mean the debt has necessarily been cancelled. This can cause confusion about whether the recipient of the form must report the amount on the form as COD income if the debt has not actually been cancelled. Form 1099-C is not always prepared correctly, and it is difficult for the taxpayer to get the lender to correct it. For example, in many cases there is a genuine dispute with the creditor as to the amount of the debt, and the debt is resolved for less than was deemed to be owed, but the creditor considers the unpaid amount as cancellation of debt. In this case, the taxpayer should take prompt action in an attempt to have the lender correct the Form 1099-C. Failing that, the best alternative is to file a U.S. Tax Court petition. **NOTE: In a recent bankruptcy court decision (the case of William and Elaine Reed), the court ruled against a bank who had issued the Reeds a 1099-C for COD income, and then filed a lawsuit to try to collect the past due debt, plus interest. In ruling against the bank, the court stated that it is inequitable to require a debtor to claim COD income as a component of the debtor's gross income on which income taxes are paid, while still allowing the creditor, who had reported to the IRS and the debtor that the indebtedness was cancelled, to try to collect it from the debtor. The Reeds argued that the bank had thrown in the towel when it issued the 1099-C. The bank, relying on IRS guidance, argued that the 1099-C was not an admission that the debt was no longer due, but rather an effort to be in compliance with reporting requirements. The court agreed with the Reeds.**

- When a taxpayer's liabilities exceed assets, including retirement accounts, annuities, and home, the taxpayer is considered insolvent and may declare insolvency or bankruptcy. For example, to determine insolvency, you have to compile a list of all of your assets and all of your debts the day before a short sale takes place. Your list of assets must include the FMV of a principal residence, a vacation home, and your pension plan. If you arrive at a negative number after subtracting debt from assets, you are considered insolvent to that extent. For example, your assets, <u>including the home you are short selling</u> total $500,000, and your debts, including the balance of the mortgage on the residence total $720,000. <u>Then, you are insolvent to the extent of $220,000. If the loan forgiveness totals $250,000, you would be required to pay taxes on $30,000 of loan forgiveness unless it is debt on a principal residence which is forgiven in 2013</u>. Bankruptcy requires a taxpayer to be under the jurisdiction of the court (Title 11 bankruptcy). Debt not included in income as a result of insolvency is not under court jurisdiction, and is generally limited to the amount of insolvency. For both bankruptcy and insolvency, certain losses, credits, and the basis of property must be reduced by the amount excluded from income. The order of the required reductions is in accordance with certain "tax attributes." However, a taxpayer may elect to initially apply all or part of the required reductions to the basis in depreciable assets or to real property held as an investment. <u>If the insolvency or bankruptcy indebtedness exclusions are used, the basis reductions do not occur immediately, but instead at the start of the next year, and any gain on the subsequent sale of assets is recaptured as ordinary income. And the home sale gain exclusion is not available to exclude the recaptured income</u>.
    - When a taxpayer receives a 1099-C and does not include the cancelled debt as income, the IRS must issue a statutory notice of deficiency before an assessment can be made. This gives the taxpayer the right to file suit in the U.S. Tax Court to contest the amount of income alleged to result from a discharge of indebtedness. The taxpayer has the burden of proof in establishing insolvency.
- <u>A taxpayer is deemed to have cancellation of debt income where he/she negotiates with a credit card company to reduce the taxpayer's credit card debt</u>. Credit card debt may, sometimes, be included under the insolvency or bankruptcy exclusions.
- Assets in a retirement plan are not protected in bankruptcy if the purpose of the plan is not really for retirement.
- Discharge of indebtedness reduces the basis of the principal residence (but not below zero); however, this does not normally hurt the homeowner, because the sale of the residence is usually sheltered by the "home sale gain exclusion." **(SEE "Income Exclusions," Gain on the Sale of a Principal Residence)**
- Another option to take advantage of mortgage debt forgiveness is called "deed in lieu of foreclosure" in which the homeowner vacates the residence and turns it over to the lender in exchange for debt forgiveness. The Mortgage Debt forgiveness Act allows some of the debt to

- be excluded from taxable income, and allows most of the gain from the sale of the home (whether foreclosure action is now or years later in the case of a "mortgage workout") to escape tax through the home sale gain exclusion.
- **Taxpayers have numerous options for debt relief: a short-sale; foreclosure; mortgage restructuring; and bankruptcy.** Often, banks reserve the right in short-sale agreements to claim a deficiency (the difference between the amount owed on the mortgage and the market value of the home) from the borrower. Most at risk for this type of collection are homeowners who have previously borrowed against the value of their home. Also at risk are homeowners who earn a steady income from a W-2 employer. Then banks have an incentive to recoup as much as they can from borrowers with steady earnings. In this regard, taxpayers should consider the option of bankruptcy, in order to keep their homes and avoid foreclosure. However, if a home is worth half of what a taxpayer owes, a short-sale might be the best option.
- A taxpayer must live in a home 2 out of 5 years in order to take advantage of the home sale gain exclusion related to sales of foreclosure properties (see Gain on Sale of a Principal Residence), but no period of ownership or use is needed to obtain mortgage debt forgiveness.
- <u>Debt on second homes, rental property, business property, credit cards and car loans does not qualify for tax relief under the forgiveness relief act.</u>
- Home owners who took advantage of the run-up in real estate prices to do a "cash out" refinancing in which funds were not put back into their home but instead were used to pay off credit card debt, etc. are excluded from the mortgage debt forgiveness program.
- **The principal reduction alternative offered is the Home Affordable Modification Program (HAMP)** - To help financially distressed homeowners lower their monthly mortgage payments, Treasury and HUD established HAMP. Under HAMP-PRA, the principal of the borrower's mortgage may be reduced by a predetermined amount called the PRA Forbearance Amount if the borrower satisfies certain conditions during a trial period. The principal reduction occurs over three years. More specifically, if the loan is in good standing on the first, second, and third annual anniversaries of the effective date of the trial period, the loan servicer reduces the unpaid principal balance of the loan by one-third of the initial PRA. If the borrower continues to make timely payments on the loan for three years, the entire PRA Forbearance Amount is forgiven. The HAMP program administrator will make an incentive payment to the loan holder for each of the three years in which the loan principal balance is reduced. <u>Mortgage loan holders are required to file a Form 1099-C with respect to a borrower who realizes cancellation of debt (COD) income of $600 or more for the year in which the permanent modification of the mortgage occurs.</u>
- The "Deed for Lease" program allows borrowers to transfer ownership to Fannie Mae and sign a one-year lease, with month-to-month extensions after that. The program eliminates some of the uncertainty of foreclosure, keeps families in their homes during a transitional period, and helps to stabilize neighborhoods and communities.

Abandonment of Property
Abandonment of property by voluntary or involuntary action can result in a taxable gain depending on whether the taxpayer was personally liable for the debt securing the abandoned property. If the debtor is personally liable for the loan it is a recourse debt, and until foreclosure or repossession procedures are completed, there are no tax consequences, whether the property is personal use or business use property. Foreclosure or repossession is treated as a sale, and the debtor may realize a gain or loss. The amount realized from the deemed sale is the lower of the asset's fair market value (FMV) on the date of abandonment or the outstanding debt immediately before the transfer. The amount realized is compared with the debtor's basis in the property to determine gain or loss. Involuntary conversion (Section 1033) is the result of an event beyond the taxpayers' control.
- o Gain is included in gross income whether or not the taxpayer used the property for business or personal purposes. If a business use asset, a gain or loss is either a capital or ordinary gain or loss. Losses on personal use property are nondeductible.
- o If the debtor is forgiven for part of the debt, the forgiven portion is cancellation of debt income and may be included as gross income (see "Cancelled Debt" above and "Mortgage Debt Forgiven on a Principal Residence" below)

If the debtor is not personally liable for the debt (nonrecourse debt) and abandons personal use property, such as a home or car, the abandonment is treated as a sale in the year of the abandonment. The amount realized on the sale—the outstanding loan balance—is compared with the taxpayer's basis in the property to determine gain or loss. Any loss is nondeductible personal expense. If the property abandoned is business or investment property, the amount of gain or loss is determined in the same way, however a loss is deductible. Generally, there is no cancellation of debt because the debtor is not personally liable for the debt. However, if the debtor retains the collateral and accepts a discount from the creditor for early payment of the debt, or agrees to a loan modification that reduces its principal balance, the amount of the discount or principal reduction is considered cancellation of debt (COD) income.

Cash Surrender Value of a Life Insurance Policy
Cash surrender value of a life insurance policy is taxable income. The owner of a surrendered policy must include in income the proceeds that are more than the cost (total premiums paid) of the policy. This applies to universal life insurance policies where the premiums are more than the cost of the insurance, where part, even most of the premiums go to cash reserves, i.e. the owner would not have to pay tax on the part of the premiums that went to cash reserves. Surrender of a life insurance policy is reported to taxpayer on Form 1099-R, which shows total proceeds and taxable portion.
- o Owners of universal life policies can make partial withdrawals, or receive a loan, tax-free from the reserves, unless the withdrawals are more than the cost of the policy. Partial withdrawals are taxable income if the cash surrender value at the time of withdrawal exceeds the net investment in the policy.

- No medical deduction is allowed for payment of medical expenses with money from a withdrawal of the cash surrender value of a life insurance contract. Instead, the amount is not included in income and the investment in the contract is reduced by that amount.
- When an original owner surrenders a policy, the owner's taxable profit is reduced by the amount of any premiums paid. However, if the original owner sells the policy to a third party, the original owner's basis is not equal to the full amount of premiums paid, but instead the cost basis consists of the cumulative premiums paid into the insurance contract plus a subjective "cost of insurance" or "provision of insurance." Example: An owner pays $64,000 in premiums over 8 years, and surrenders the policy for $78,000. During the 8 years, he pays $10,000 in "cost-of-insurance" charges. If he surrenders the policy, he has $14,000 of ordinary income ($78,000 - $64,000). However, if he sells the policy to a 3rd party investor for $80,000, he has $26,000 in taxable income ($14,000 in ordinary income, plus $12,000 long-term capital gain) – calculated as follows: the cost basis drops from $64,000 to $54,000 ($64,000 - $10,000 in "cost-of-insurance"). Therefore, even though the seller received just $2,000 above the cash surrender value ($80,000 - $78,000), the total gain is $26,000 ($80,000 - $54,000 adjusted basis).

Personal Injury Awards Associated with Nonphysical Injuries
Personal injury awards associated with nonphysical injuries are taxable to the recipient. And, even though personal injury awards for physical injuries (say, broken bones from an accident) are generally tax exempt, awards for emotional distress related to a physical injury (Appeals Court decision Murphy, D.C. Cir.) are taxable, except that damages paid for medical care attributable to emotional distress are excludible from income.
- Punitive damage awards associated with physical injury or sickness and interest paid on an injury award are taxable, whether awarded by law suit or agreement. In addition, a portion of contingent fees paid to attorneys may be included in income, if recovery amount includes punitive damages. The amount of contingent fees paid to attorneys is taxable based on the percentage of punitive damages compared to amount of total damages recovered for physical injury, i.e. the tax law treats you as receiving 100% of the settlement, even if the defendant issues a separate check to the lawyer for his cut.
- How you settle can matter – You have more flexibility to reduce taxes if you settle, especially if you negotiate with an eye on the tax rules. A settlement agreement might say all the cash is for a (nontaxable) physical injury, while a court verdict might attribute some of it to taxable punitive damages or interest. Consider the settlement agreement, the complaint, the checks issued to resolve the case, IRS Forms 1099, W-2, etc. You can influence how your recovery is taxed by how you deal with these issues.
- **Funds received from a class action settlement** are generally taxable, because damages received for any type of injury other than personal physical injury or sickness are taxable.

Sale of Demutualized Stock
Sale of demutualized stock is stock that a life insurance policyholder receives when the insurer switches from being a mutual company owned by the policyholders to a stock company owned by stockholders. The IRS's longstanding position was that such stock had no tax basis, so that when the shares were sold, the taxpayer owed tax on 100% of the proceeds of the sale. But after a long legal struggle, a federal court ruled that the IRS was wrong. The court didn't say what the basis of the stock should be, but many experts think it's whatever the shares were worth when they were distributed to policyholders. So, be sure to claim a basis when you sell the stock to hold down your tax bill. As a rule of thumb, use the FMV of the stock on the date received as the basis of the stock.

Incentive Stock Options
A dual holding period applies to incentive stock options (ISO)—you must hold the stock for one year after the shares are transferred to you (exercise date), and for two years from the date the ISO was granted in order to be eligible for long-term capital gain treatment. No income is recognized when stock options are exercised; instead when the stock is later sold, any gain or loss is treated as a capital gain (basis of stock is exercise price). However, part of the gain may be ordinary income, if the exercise price is less than 85% of the market price on the exercise date. A disqualifying disposition occurs if taxpayer sales the stock within one year of the date of exercising (or within 2 years from the date of the grant—known as statutory holding period), which triggers ordinary income equal to the difference between the exercise price and market price on the exercise date, in which case the basis of the stock would be the market price instead of the exercise price. And, any difference between the sale price and the market price would be capital gain.

Earnings on Uniform Transfer to Minors Custodial Accounts (UTMA)
Earnings on uniform transfer to minors custodial accounts (UTMA) are taxable to the minor child to whom contributions are made. The UTMA has replaced the UGMA, but earnings on both are custodial accounts that are taxable to minors in the year the earnings from the account are earned. Parents can make a "gift" of $14,000 per year to each dependent child ($28,000 if a married couple and gift-splitting is used) and deposit it in one of these custodial accounts. However, keep in mind that the "kiddie tax" may affect these accounts, i.e. the earnings may be taxed at the higher parents' tax rates. A custodial account comes under the child's legal control when he/she reaches the age of majority under the applicable state law (usually 18 or 21).

Reimbursements for Medical Expenses
Reimbursements for medical expenses are taxable if beneficial to taxpayer in a prior year, i.e. the medical expenses were deducted as an itemized deduction in a prior year. In addition, reimbursements received in excess of medical expenses are partially taxable, if your employer paid all or part of your health insurance premiums (part of reimbursements must be included in gross income).

State and Local Income Tax Refunds

State and local income tax refunds received in the next year are taxable, if they gave rise to a tax benefit in the prior year (deducted as an itemized deduction in prior year).

Property Transferred to a Taxpayer in Exchange for Services

Fair market value of property transferred to a taxpayer in exchange for services is taxable income, including the cash surrender value of a life insurance contract transferred in exchange for services.

Employer Provided Vehicle

An employer provided vehicle is taxable to the employee if the employee uses the vehicle for personal use. An appropriate amount should be included in the employee's wages and reported on his/her W-2. The amount to be included is calculated based on how much an employee would have to pay for a comparable vehicle in an arms-length transaction. The amount to be included in an employee's W-2 is computed by using one of three methods: (1) If the only personal use of an employer-provided vehicle is commuting to and from work, the employer can use the commuting rule, which provides that the deemed value of each one-way commute is $1.50, and either the deemed value has to be included in the employee's wages or the employee can reimburse the employer for the amount. (2) The cents-per-mile rule is based on the IRS standard mileage rate (56.5 cents per mile in 2013). Employees must either reimburse the employer at this rate for all personal miles driven in an employer-provided vehicle, or the amount has to be added to the employee's taxable income reported on his/her W-2. If the employer does not provide the fuel for the car, the rate is reduced by 5.5 cents per mile. The cents-per-mile rate includes the value of maintenance and insurance. If the employer does not pay for maintenance and/or insurance and the employee is required to pay for those costs, then the cost of the personal use is reduced by the expenses incurred by the employee. (3) The annual lease value method is different from the other two methods, because instead of calculating the employee's personal use of the vehicle, the rule provides that the employer has to calculate how much of the vehicle's FMV can be included in the employee's income as a working condition fringe benefit. This is done by calculating the FMV of the vehicle, calculating the FMV of the business use of the vehicle, and then calculating the difference as the taxable fringe benefit. The fair market value (FMV) has to be determined on the first date it is available for use by an employee. **(See "Employee Travel and Entertainment Expenses" and "Depreciation.")**

- Police officers, firefighters, and public safety officers who are permitted to drive their official vehicles home are exempt from including the benefit in income. However, the vehicles must be clearly marked by insignia or words.

Constructive Dividends

Constructive dividends distributed to shareholders in the form of loans (no intent to repay), forgone interest on a below market loan made by a shareholder, sale of corporate assets to a shareholder for less than FMV, etc. are taxable income to the recipients. These are usually related to small closely held corporations and not labeled as dividends.

Services Rendered to a Person for the Benefit of a Charitable Organization

Services rendered to a person for the benefit of a charitable organization is income to the person performing the services. The amount of income is the amount paid to the organization by the person to whom the services are rendered.

Bartering

Bartering to get products or services results in the fair market value of the goods and services exchanged having to be reported as income by both parties. Barter dollars or trade dollars are identical to real dollars for tax reporting purposes. Income from bartering is taxable in the year it is performed. Rules for reporting barter transactions may vary depending on which form of bartering takes place. Generally, you report this type of business income on Form 1040, Schedule C, or other business returns such as Form 1065 or Form 1120S. Organized barter exchanges function primarily as the organizer of a marketplace where members buy and sell products and service among themselves. Whether this activity operates out of a physical office or is internet-based, a barter exchange is generally required to issue Form 1099-B, Proceeds from Broker and Barter Exchange Transactions, annually to their clients or members and to the IRS.

Net Operating Loss

Net Operating Loss (NOL) is an overall loss from trade or business activities for a tax year that is computed and reported on Form 1045. A NOL can apply to self-employed persons, farmers, individuals whose casualty losses exceed income, and partnerships and S-corporations. Individual taxpayers can have a NOL, including losses from employment, business losses, losses from rental property, and casualty and theft losses. Schedule A of Form 1045 is used to compute NOL. Form 1045 must be filed within one year of the end of the tax year generating a NOL, and is used to carry forward a NOL to subsequent years. NOLs can normally be carried back 2 years and carried forward 20 years (a taxpayer can waive the carry back period and immediately carry forward a NOL). Any loss remaining after the carry forward period is lost forever (expires). To claim a NOL carry back, an individual must file an amended return (Form 1040X) within three years of the due date of the return for the year to which a NOL is carried back. When a partnership or S-corporation incurs a NOL, it passes through to the individual partners or shareholders (owners). Taxpayers can deduct from a current year's income NOLs both carried over to the current tax year from previous tax years and carried back from later tax years.

- The general rule is that a NOL is used in the following order until exhausted: (1) carried back to the second preceding tax year; (2) carried back to the first preceding tax year; and (3) carried forward to the following 20 tax years. A taxpayer may elect to waive the carry back period, which is an all-or-nothing election, by the due date for filing the tax return. A farming NOL may be carried back 5 years. The application of an NOL to prior years is a multi-step, complicated calculation which requires the adjustment and refiguring of a number of things, such as taxes owed and the taxable income in the carry back year, not to mention many of the deductions taken in that year.
- <u>Calculating a NOL for a year is not as simple as plugging figures into Form 1045. You have to know what qualifies in figuring a NOL. A NOL is the excess of allowable deductions over gross income for the year. The starting point for determining whether an individual taxpayer has a NOL is adjusted gross income (AGI), minus itemized deductions or the standard deduction. If the result is a negative number, an individual **may** have a NOL. But further computations and adjustments must be made, including:</u>
    - Personal and dependency exemptions must be added back.
    - If an individual itemizes deductions, only employee business expenses, and casualty and theft losses, even if not incurred in a trade or business, can be used to offset business income (including employment income). This means that all other non-business itemized deductions, such as charitable donations, deductible medical expenses, mortgage interest, real estate taxes, etc. must be added back.
    - Moving expenses for job relocation is the only above-the-line deduction for adjusted gross income that can be used to offset business income. This means that all other non-business above-the-line deductions for adjusted gross income such as contributions to traditional IRAs, alimony/separate maintenance, health savings accounts (HSA), self-employed individual retirement accounts, etc. must be added back.
    - All of the above listed non-business itemized deductions, and above-the-line deductions that must be added back, can be used to offset non-business income, which includes interest income, dividends, annuity income, and <u>non-business capital gains</u>. This means that if the total of all of these non-business deductions is more than non-business income, NOL is increased (must be subtracted).
    - Non-business capital losses (those arising outside your trade or business) can only be used against non-business capital gains, which means that net capital losses must be added back.
    - Expenses of rental property can be used to offset business income, which includes rental income (whether net rental income is a gain or a loss). Therefore, nothing has to be added back.
    - Exclusion of gain from Section 1202 small business stock must be added back.

- Net operating losses (NOLs) carried back or forward from a different year must be added back.

Installment Sale

Installment sale is a sale of property for a gain, with payments after the year of sale, which allows gain to be deferred in direct proportion to the payments that are deferred. Each installment payment under the "note" will include a portion of: return of adjusted basis of the property; gain on the sale; and interest. The objective of an installment sale is to lock in a sale while deferring recognition of income. In reporting gain, two variables are key: basis in the property and the sales price. The basis includes selling expenses and depreciation recapture. "Gross profit" is determined by subtracting the basis from the sales price. Next, gross profit is divided by the contract sales price, which results in the "gross profit percentage." The gross profit percentage is applied to each payment to determine the amount of reportable gain. If the property is a capital asset, the seller recognizes capital gain and ordinary income for depreciation recapture. A sale at a loss does not qualify for an installment sale.
  - Electing out of deferral of gain on an installment sale – Capital gain is usually recognized as cash is received from the buyer, but the taxpayer can elect to recognize the entire gain in the year of sale (not usually advantageous to buyer). **NOTE: Installment payments received after 2012 are subject to the tax rates for the year of payment, not the year of sale. Thus, the capital gains portion of payments made in 2013 and later is now taxed at the 20% rate for higher-income taxpayers.**

Jury Duty Pay

Jury duty pay is taxable income. Many employers continue to pay their employees' full salary while they are on jury duty, and some require them to turn over their jury pay to the company. If this happens, you still have to report the jury pay as income, but you can then deduct it on line 36 of Form 1040. Line 36 is for totaling up all deductions that get their own lines. Add your jury fees to the total of your other write-offs and write "jury pay" on the dotted line to the left.

Damages Received for Discrimination

Damages received for discrimination after loss of a job are taxed as ordinary income, but not as wages subject to payroll taxes (FICA). Payments for emotional suffering from discrimination are also taxable – unless, for example it gives you a heart attack. **Outplacement and help with health insurance premiums (if paid directly to the insurer) aren't taxed**. The tax law treats you as receiving 100% of the settlement, even if the defendant issues a separate check to the lawyer for his cut. However, attorney fees for discrimination awards are deductible above-the-line, so they won't affect your tax bill in this instance.

Bequests Made in Exchange for Services
Bequests made in exchange for services is taxable income.

Requisition of Property by the Government
Requisition of property by the government in exchange for payment is taxable income, i.e. if the government takes part of your land for road widening and you receive a payment, it is taxable income.

Net Investment Income (Form 8960)
"Net Investment Income" (Form 8960) as defined by the Patient Protection and Affordable Care Act (ACA) is assessed a 3.8% surtax <u>beginning in 2013</u>, as required by the ACA. **The surtax is in addition to the income taxes payable on the items that are included in "net investment income."** The 3.8% surtax is on the investment income (unearned income) of high-income earners ($200,000 singles; $250,000 joint filers and surviving spouses; $125,000 married filing jointly; and $200,000 head-of-household). These thresholds are not indexed for inflation. The surtax applies to individuals, estates, and trusts. The 3.8% surtax on individuals is on the <u>lesser of "net investment income" (NII) or the amount by which modified adjusted gross income (MAGI) exceeds the above stated thresholds</u>. "NII" <u>includes</u>: interest; dividends; gains on the sale of securities (any losses that can offset capital gains in computing "taxable income" can also be used to reduce NII, but not below zero); annuities; royalties; <u>rents</u>; all passive activity income including passive business activity income from partnerships and S-corporations; gain on the disposition of property other than property held in a trade or business; and gain over and above the $250,000/$500,000 exclusion from the sale of a principal residence. "NII" <u>does not include</u>: salaries and wages; social security; self-employment income; tax-exempt interest; conversion of traditional IRAs to Roth IRAs; excluded gain from the sale of a <u>principal</u> residence; distributions from qualified plans, IRAs and Roth IRAs (including required minimum distributions (RMDs)); lump-sum distributions from retirement plans; income derived in the ordinary course of a trade or business (partnerships and S-corporations) that is not considered passive activity income; gain on the sale or disposition of property held in a trade or business; and gain on the sale of an active interest in a partnership or S-corporation. In addition, any investment interest and expenses, and state taxes that are itemized deductions allocable to investment income should be deducted in computing "net investment income." **IRS Form 8960, Net Investment Income Tax - Individuals, Estates, and Trusts is used to compute the new 3.8% tax reported on Form 1040**.
  o MAGI means adjusted gross income (AGI) increased by otherwise excludable foreign earned income or foreign housing costs. MAGI does not include: tax-exempt interest; veterans' benefits; and excluded gain from the sale of a principal residence. MAGI <u>does include</u>: gain over and above the $250,000/$500,000 exclusion from the sale of a principal residence; lump-sum distributions from retirement plans; conversion of traditional IRAs to Roth IRAs; required minimum distributions (RMD); and all distributions from qualified plans, IRAs, and Roth IRAs.

- Net investment income includes "rents" unless the rental income is derived from a trade or business. A single rental property can qualify as a trade or business if the taxpayer "materially" participates in the activity. There is a safe harbor for real estate professionals who materially participate in rental real estate activities for more than 500 hours per year. Alternatively, if the taxpayer has participated in rental real estate activities for more than 500 hours per year in five of the last ten taxable years, then the rental income will be deemed to be derived in the ordinary course of a trade or business. Income derived from real estate rentals are not subject to self-employment tax. **(SEE "Taxable Income," Rental Income)**
- An estate or trust is subject to the 3.8% surtax to the extent of the lesser of: the estate's or trust's undistributed net investment income; or the excess (if any) of the estate's or trust's AGI over the dollar amount at which the highest tax bracket begins for the year ($11,950 for 2013). Grantor trust income flows-through to the grantor; therefore, only non-grantor trusts are required to pay the surtax. Non-grantor trusts should consider paying distributions to beneficiaries to avoid the 3.8% surtax, which kicks in for trusts at $11,950 in 2013. The 65-day rule can be used to defer distributions to as late as March 6 of the following year and still have them apply to the current year. Trusts that are subject to the tax include non-grantor trusts, electing small business trusts, non-grantor charitable lead trusts, pooled income funds, cemetery perpetual care funds, qualified funeral trusts, Alaska Native Settlement Trusts, and foreign trusts with U.S. beneficiaries. The tax does not apply to common trust funds, real estate investment trusts, designated settlement funds, wholly charitable trusts, other trusts exempt from tax and foreign trusts without U.S. beneficiaries. **(SEE "Patient Protection and Affordable Care Act," Provisions Effective Beginning in 2013, Tax Provisions)**

Alternative Minimum Tax (AMT)

Alternative Minimum Tax (AMT) is the excess of the Tentative Minimum Tax over regular income tax that is paid in addition to regular income tax. Form 6251, Alternative Minimum Tax, must be attached to any return if the deductions taken on the return are greater than adjusted gross income (AGI), or alternative minimum taxable income (AMTI) is above the exemption amounts applicable to AMT for the taxpayer's filing status. **(SEE "Alternative Minimum Tax")**

Income Exclusions

Interest on Municipal Bonds
Interest on Municipal Bonds and tax-exempt municipal funds earned by individuals is exempt from federal income tax.

Contributions to Qualified Employee Retirement Plans
Contributions to qualified employee retirement and pension benefit plans - 401(k), 403(b), and 457(b) plans (Profit Sharing Plans); SEPs, SIMPLEs; Keoghs and SARSEPs can be made by both employees and employers. These plans are pre-tax or salary reduction retirement plans that are not taxable to employees. Retirement plan contributions are reflected on Form W-2, Box 12 and each plan is allocated a different Code.
- Saving Incentive Match Plans (SIMPLEs) are pre-tax salary reduction retirement plans for employers with 100 or fewer employees with at least $6,000 in compensation. The SIMPLE is the least expensive to install because it is free. You simply set up IRAs for each eligible employee. However, the deferral is limited to $12,000 in 2013 ($11,500 in 2012 & 2011), but for those over 50 the catch up provision adds $2,500 to the deferral limit or $14,500 in 2013 ($14,000 in 2012). All employees are eligible no matter the age or number of hours worked, so even part-time employees can become eligible. Employers must make either matching contributions or non-elective contributions at a maximum of 3%, but can be as low as 1%. All contributions must be fully vested. Employers can establish a SIMPLE by using Form 5304-SIMPLE. Once a SIMPLE plan has been adopted, no other plan can be adopted during the plan year. After terminating a SIMPLE plan, no other plan can be adopted until the following year. SIMPLEs and SEPs allow small employers who can't afford the expense or effort of establishing qualified employee pension benefit plans to set up an employee plan.
    - A sole proprietor using Form 1040, Schedule C, can set-up a SIMPLE IRA. Contributions to the SIMPLE are deductions in determining adjusted gross income (AGI) that reduce taxable income, but do not reduce Schedule C net income that is subject to self-employment tax.
- Simplified Employee Pension IRAs (SEPs) and defined contribution plans have a deferral limit of 25% of compensation or $51,000 in 2013 ($50,000 in 2012), whichever is less. Only employer contributions can be made to SEPs. Employer contributions to SEPs maintained for an employee are not taxable to the employee. Employers can establish a SEP by using Form 5305-SEP. All contributions are immediately vested, and employee withdrawals must be permitted without penalty. All employees who are age 21, and have performed services during 3 of the immediately preceding 5 years and receive $550 in compensation are eligible. Contributions must be made for all employees who qualify (the same percentage of salary must be contributed for each employee).

- Salary reduction SEPs (SARSEPs) could be established by employers with 25 employees or less until 1997. Contributions are pre-tax salary reduction contributions by employees, and are limited to $17,500 or $23,000 in 2013 (same as a qualified employee pension plan). For highly compensated employees, there is a limited deferral percentage of 125% of the average deferral for all eligible non-highly compensated employees. Highly compensated employees are: 5% owners or employees receiving compensation in excess of $115,000 in 2013 & 2012. However, an employer can elect to limit it to the top 20% of compensated employees. New SARSEP's cannot be established after 1996, but existing ones can continue.
- A qualified retirement and pension plan (defined benefit plan) - 401(k), 403(b), and 457(b) allows more flexibility and larger contribution possibilities. Because it is built on a profit sharing platform, a discretionary profit sharing contribution can be considered each year, and is allocated taking into account compensation and age, which could be a big advantage to business owners. The deferral limit is $17,500 in 2013 ($17,000 in 2012). The catch-up contributions for those over 50 is $5,500, or a total of $23,000. Compensation for benefit purposes for qualified plans is $255,000. The required match is 4%, and like the SIMPLE, the match is only for those who actually defer. The significant advantage over the SIMPLE is that the only eligible employees are those who are age 21 and who work 1,000 hours or more in their first 12 months of employment. They become eligible on the following January 1 or July 1, so most part-time or seasonal workers never enter the plan, are not eligible to defer, nor would ever get any profit sharing allocation. The cost to set-up a defined benefit plan is $1,500. The annual administration fee is $975, plus $30 per participant. As long as at least one employee (other than the owner) is eligible, there is a start-up tax credit of up to $500 per year (50% of administration costs) for the first three years of the plan's operation. These plans are generally required to file an annual report disclosing information relating to the plan's qualified status, financial condition, and operations. Annual reports are filed on the Form 5500 series information returns. However, most small plans (sole proprietor and partnership plans) with total assets of $250,000 or less are exempt from the annual filing requirement. A final return/report must be filed when a plan is terminated, regardless of the value of the plan's assets. On termination of employment, a person can contribute unpaid (accrued) sick and vacation leave to qualified employee retirement plans – these are elective contributions that can be included in contributions not to exceed the maximum amounts allowed, and will only be taxed when distributions are made.
    - You can borrow from a 401(k) plan, but the amount is limited to the lesser of 50% of the vested account balance or $50,000. You cannot roll over funds from a 401(k) to a 403(b) nonprofit plan.
    - Your employer may include a Roth 401(k) or Roth 403(b) feature in your retirement plan. However, contributions to Roth IRAs are made with after-tax dollars, so they won't

reduce your current taxable compensation as do traditional retirement plans with pre-tax contributions. The advantage of a Roth feature in your employer retirement plan is that you can withdraw assets later on (generally after age 59 ½) free from federal taxes. You may find this appealing if you expect to be in a higher tax bracket during your retirement years.
- Beginning in 2008, if you are eligible to make a Roth IRA conversion from an employee plan, the new law allows you to rollover your retirement plan directly into a Roth IRA (although you owe federal taxes on the amount converted).
    o Keoghs are tax-deferred retirement plans for self-employed persons (similar to SARSEPs). Self-employed individuals can contribute as much as $51,000 to a Keogh in 2013 ($50,000 in 2012). Contributions are subject to deduction limits, i.e. taxable income.

For all qualified plans, the maximum annual compensation taken into account for contributions is $255,000 ($250,000 in 2012). The annual benefit limit under defined benefit plans is $205,000 ($200,000 in 2012). The threshold amount for definition of highly compensated employees is $115,000 ($115,000 in 2012). The threshold amount for definition of key employees in top-heavy plans is $165,000 ($165,000 in 2012).

Rollovers From Qualified Employee Retirement Plans
Rollovers from qualified employee retirement and pension benefit plans – 401(k), 403(b), and 457(b) plans; SEPs, SIMPLEs; and SARSEPs to traditional IRAs (reported to taxpayer on Form 1099-R) are not taxable. Rollovers can be made to IRAs or designated employer retirement plans. Rollovers can be either direct or indirect. If indirect, a 20% withholding tax is required, and deposits to an IRA or to a new employer plan must be made within 60 days. Rollovers can be made only once in any 12-month period.
   o If you hold a significant amount of your employer's stock in a 401(k) plan, you probably should not roll it over to an IRA at retirement or when you change jobs, because the money you or your heirs withdraw from the IRA is taxed as ordinary income. Instead, you should elect net unrealized appreciation (NUA) for sale of appreciated company stock purchased and held in a qualified plan. **(SEE "Taxable Income," Net Unrealized Appreciation)**

Distributions From Coverdell Education Savings Accounts
Distributions from Coverdell Education Savings Accounts are not taxable if used for qualified higher or lower education expenses (reported to taxpayer on Form 1099-Q, which should show the tax-free earnings portion of each distribution). Qualified education expenses include: tuition and fees; room and board; books, supplies and equipment; and special needs services. Also, non-taxable distributions from Coverdell's can be made to Qualified Tuition Programs (529 Plans – see below). You cannot claim education credits for the same expenses paid for with Coverdell distributions and 529 Plan

distributions. Also, any expenses paid with tax-free scholarships and VA education assistance cannot be claimed with Coverdell distributions and 529 plan distributions. Any distributions not used for education expenses are taxable, plus an additional 10% penalty, that should be reported as "Other Income" on Form 1040. Only earnings are subject to taxation and the 10% penalty. An individual can contribute a maximum of $2,000 to a Coverdell Education Savings Account each year to an unlimited number of beneficiaries, but the contributions are not deductible. Contributions must be made by the tax return filing date. Any contributions are reported on Form 5498-ESA. The Coverdell Education Savings law was **made permanent as of Jan. 1, 2013.**

- A contribution cannot be made to a beneficiary after he reaches age 18, unless he is a special needs beneficiary. Any assets remaining in the account when the designated beneficiary reaches age 30 must be withdrawn within 30 days.
- Contributions for a beneficiary can be made each year to both to a Coverdell plan and a 529 plan (see below).
- For both 2013 and 2012, the maximum contribution of $2,000 is phased-out between AGI $190,000 - $220,000 (married filing jointly); $95,000 - $110,000 (singles). Individuals receiving military death benefits can disregard the contribution limitations for Coverdell Savings Accounts, and can contribute the full amount of the death benefits to a Coverdell.

Distributions From Qualified Tuition Programs

Distributions from Qualified Tuition Programs (QTPs, or 529 Plans) are not taxable if used for qualified higher education expenses. They are subject to the same requirements as distributions from Coverdell Education Savings Accounts, except they can only be used for qualified higher education expenses, including graduate school (tuition and fees, books, room and board, supplies, computers, and equipment). 529 plan distributions are reported on Form 1099-Q, which should show the tax-free earnings portion of each distribution. The best part about a 529 Plan is that no amount accumulated in the plan will be included in the gross income of a designated beneficiary or a contributor to the plan with respect to any distributions or earnings under the program. What's more, there is asset protection for 529 plans, preventing them from being obtained by creditors in the case of an account owner's personal bankruptcy. For financial purposes, a 529 plan is treated as a parental asset. This means only 5.64% of the account's value is included in the financial aid formula (a child's assets are included at 20%). Contributions to these state-sponsored college savings plans are not deductible, and must be made by December 31 each year. 529 assets can be used at any eligible educational institution that meets specific federal accreditation standards. This includes most four-year colleges and universities, many two-year institutions, and some vocational schools.

- Example of possible taxable portion of a QTP distribution: Total qualified education expenses = $8,300; tax-free scholarship = $3,100; QTP distribution = $5,300 of which $950 are earnings.

    Adjusted qualified expenses: $8,300, minus $3,100 = $5,200

    $950 (QTP earnings) x $5,200 = $932 tax-free QTP earnings

    $5,300 $ 18 taxable QTP earnings

- Many states do not cap annual contributions to 529 plans. However, **contributions are eligible for the annual gift tax exclusion, so to avoid paying gift taxes you should limit annual contributions to each beneficiary to the gift tax exclusion allowance ($14,000; $28,000 if gift-splitting is used in 2013)**. One child can be the beneficiary of numerous accounts, and if a beneficiary chooses not to go to college, plan assets can be transferred to another close relative without penalty. You can transfer assets among family members with no tax repercussions. Also, multiple family members and friends can give to the same 529 plan account to help create larger college funds.

- Anyone can be a 529 account owner and anyone can be named a beneficiary. The only requirements for being a beneficiary are that the person must be a U.S. citizen and have a Social Security number. There are absolutely no age restrictions for a participant. For example, if a beneficiary decides to go back to school later in life, the assets are there for them because there is no time limit for keeping funds in a 529 plan.

- If you realize you won't be able to use all of the funds in a 529 account and decide to close it, the income earned on the contributions will be taxed and, in addition, there is a 10% penalty on the income withdrawn.

- Many states allow a state tax deduction for withdrawals from a 529 plan, imposing no waiting period on 529 withdrawals and allowing account holders to deduct contributions from their state income taxes regardless of how long the money is held in the account. This tax loophole can lower your state income tax bill, i.e. let's say a child attending school in the fall plans to pay his/her tuition out of pocket. Rather than paying the school directly, the family instead adds funds to an existing or newly opened 529 account in the student's name and then withdraws the funds shortly thereafter to cover the tuition payment. This allows the family to deduct the amount of the contribution from their state income taxes, assuming their state offers a tax break and their plan has no waiting time limit for withdrawals. For example, Illinois allows residents to deduct up to $20,000 per year in contributions for a couple filing jointly, and has a flat income tax rate of 5%. So if a family contributed $20,000 to one of the state's 529 plans and then withdrew it for tuition in the fall, it would gain a tax break of $1,000 ($20,000 x .05). There is no waiting period for withdrawals in 34 states.

- You should consider rolling over children's UTMA investments into a 529 Plan to avoid paying taxes on those investments at the higher parents' tax rate under the kiddie tax rules. For 2013, the kiddie tax is applicable to dependents under age 19 or under age 24 if a full-time student. There are no tax implications if you are rolling over cash from A UTMA to a 529 plan. However,

- if the UTMA holds appreciated securities, they must be sold (only cash can be contributed to a 529 Plan), and your child will be taxed on the gains, if any, under the kiddie tax rules.
    - Consider using the annual Gift Tax exclusion ($14,000; $28,000 if married) to fund a 529 Plan. And according to the 5-year averaging rule a donor can contribute up to $70,000; $140,000 if a married couple, and average it over 5 years with no Gift Tax consequences (however, a gift tax return must be filed, and the election for the 5-year averaging must be made on the donor's Gift Tax return). <u>NOTE: A 529 plan is the only investment vehicle allowing five years of tax-free gifts in a single year.</u>
    - Contributors to 529 plans, such as grandparents, who don't want to owe estate taxes but also worry they might have unexpected costs, such as health care, have a useful option. Although 529 contributions remove assets from an estate, the giver can take back account assets if the money is needed (although they will have to pay a 10% penalty on funds taken back).
    - <u>If your child wins a scholarship and you cannot use the amount accumulated in the 529 plan to pay for college expenses, normally you would owe income taxes and a 10% penalty on the earnings portion of any 529 withdrawals that are not used for qualified education expenses. But there is an exception for tax-free scholarships, i.e. you can withdraw up to the amount of the scholarship without being subject to the 10% penalty (you still have to pay income tax). However, you should ensure that the money and the 1099 Form reporting the withdrawal is sent to the student who is in a lower tax bracket than you.</u>
    - If you withdraw money from a 529 plan to use for other than education expenses then change your mind and return the money to the same 529 plan, it isn't a tax free rollover because the money was not transferred to a different 529 plan for the same beneficiary or to a different beneficiary's 529 plan. Thus, the withdrawal is taxed, but you won't have to pay the 10% penalty.
    - **Downside of 529 plans – An IRS rule allows only one investment allocation change per year in a 529 plan.** This limits parents from hastily yanking their money during volatile markets. But it prevents a family that adjusted its holdings in March, for example, from switching to a more conservative portfolio if the stock market falls in September. Therefore, in order to maintain flexibility, families should make any desired changes by the end of the year, if possible, to leave the option open again the next year. It might also be prudent to split college savings between a 529 plan and a second type of account, such as an IRA in the child's name. This would allow for investment changes when needed. A child's IRA can be used for college without triggering early-withdrawal penalties and it isn't reported as an asset on financial applications, thus avoiding the risk of a smaller aid package. One option is a Roth IRA, which allows tax-deferred growth for college. <u>However, in order to be able to establish an IRA in the child's name, contributions to the IRA must come from the child's earnings. But parents can pay children for household services as long as the wage is reasonable for the work performed.</u>

- o **NOTE: Parents or grandparents can make tuition payments directly to the college without using up their gift tax exclusion.**

U.S. Savings Bond Redemptions

U.S. Savings Bonds redemptions used for qualified higher education expenses (tuition and fees only) or for contributions to 529 Qualified Tuition Plans and Coverdell education savings accounts are tax free – they must be EE or I U.S. Savings Bonds issued after 1989 to an individual who has reached the age of 24 before the date of issuance. You must file Form 8815 or optional Form 8818 when redeemed. Redemptions can be used for taxpayer, spouse, and dependents. <u>You must know both the total redemption amount and the interest earned to put on Form 8815</u>. For 2013, tax free exemptions are subject to phase-outs between MAGI of $112,050 - $142,050 (married filing jointly & surviving spouse); $74,700 - $89,700 (all others). You cannot exclude any of the interest if your MAGI is equal to or more than the upper limit.

Qualified Scholarship and Fellowship Grants

Qualified scholarships and fellowship grants received by an individual who is a candidate for a degree are not taxable if the money is used to pay for qualified education expenses. This does not include amounts that represent payments for teaching, research, or other services required as a condition for receiving the scholarship, except for teachers' aides and armed services obligations after graduation. Qualified education expenses include tuition and fees required to enroll or attend the institution and course-related expenses, such as fees, books, supplies, and equipment required for the courses. It does not include amounts paid for room and board, travel, research, clerical help or equipment that is not required for the coursework.

- National Health Services Corps and Armed Forces Health Professions Scholarships are excluded from income permanently by the American Taxpayer Relief Act of 2012.

Distributions From Health Savings Accounts

Distributions from Health Savings Accounts (HSAs) are not taxable if used to pay qualified medical expenses. Distributions are reported on Form 1099-SA. For 2013, the additional tax on non-qualified distributions from an HSA is 20% (prior to 12/31/2010 the additional tax was 10%). Unlike distributions from a Flexible Spending Account (FSA), distributions from an HSA are not required to be substantiated by the employer or a third party for the distributions to be excluded from income. The determination is subject to individual self-reporting and IRS enforcement. Over-the-counter medications are excluded from the definition of qualified medical expenses unless prescribed by a health care professional, or is insulin. **(SEE "Deductions for Computing Adjusted Gross Income," Contributions to Health Savings Accounts)**

Contributions to Flexible Spending Accounts

Contributions to Flexible Spending Accounts (FSAs) are employee pre-tax contributions available under an employer sponsored cafeteria plan (see below). **Beginning in 2013, total contributions to FSAs are limited to $2,500 per individual under the Affordable Health Care Act (adjusted annually for inflation for tax years beginning after 12/31/2013). Also, a new provision adopted in 2013 permits employers to allow participants who do not use all of the money in a plan year to carry over up to $500 to the next plan year.** Prior to 2013 there was no limit on the amount of money you or your employer could contribute to a FSA, but there was no carryover provision. Amounts contributed had to be spent on eligible unreimbursed medical expenses and child care expenses by the end of the year or the money was forfeited, unless employers permitted the grace period rule which allowed participants to spend unused amounts in the first two months and 15 days after the beginning of the next plan year. For reservists called to active duty, the law permits, but does not require, amounts left over at the end of the year not to be forfeited, i.e. reservists can get money back, but must pay income taxes and FICA on the amounts recovered. Beginning in 2011, the Affordable Care Act (ACA) excludes over-the-counter medications, <u>except for insulin and over-the-counter medications prescribed by a physician</u>, from qualified medical expenses for purposes of reimbursement and tax-free distributions from a FSA, Health Reimbursement Arrangement (HRA), Health Savings Account (HSA), and Archer MSAs. This applies to purchases made on or after 1/1/2011. No over-the-counter medications were allowed in 2010, even if reimbursed in 2011. Also, items that are not medicines continue to qualify, including bandages, and diagnostic devices such as blood sugar test kits.

Forgiveness of Student Loans for Medical Professionals

Forgiveness of student loans for certain medical professionals under state loan repayment or forgiveness programs was implemented by the Affordable Care Act (ACA) with the intent to provide increased availability of health care services in underserved or health-professional-shortage areas. Forgiveness of the loans is excluded from income effective for tax years beginning after Dec. 31, 2008. **(SEE "Patient Protection and Affordable Care Act," Effective for 2010, Tax Provisions)**

Foreign Earned Income Exclusion

The Foreign earned income exclusion is reported on Form 2555. In 2013, up to a maximum of $97,600 of foreign earned income can be excluded from income ($95,100 in 2012). The total amount of foreign earned income you can exclude in 2013 is the total of the "foreign earned income exclusion" and the "housing exclusion" or $97,600, whichever is less. The "housing exclusion" is computed by deducting the "base housing amount" from your total housing expenses. The base housing amount is 16% of the maximum foreign earned income exclusion (computed on a daily basis). For example, in 2013, 16% of $97,600 is $15,616, which is $42.78 per day. To figure your base amount, multiply $42.78 by the number of your qualifying days in 2013. If you spent all of 2013 abroad, and you spent $17,152 for your housing, then your housing exclusion is $1,536 ($17,152 - $15,616). The housing exclusion applies only to amounts considered paid for by your employer and included on your Form W-2, or to amounts paid with self-employment earnings. In the case of married taxpayers, each spouse may compute the exclusions separately, if both earn foreign income. To qualify, taxpayer's home must be in a foreign country, and must either meet the bone fide resident test or physical presence in a foreign country test: The bone fide resident test requires a taxpayer to be an uninterrupted resident of a foreign country for one entire calendar year (Jan 1 –Dec 31). The physical presence test requires 330 full days of physical presence in a foreign country during 12 consecutive months. After meeting the test, you can leave temporarily and still qualify, and part-years will then qualify. <u>The maximum foreign earned income exclusion includes the "housing exclusion.</u>" You must claim the housing exclusion before claiming the rest as the "foreign earned income exclusion", and both must be considered foreign taxable earned income paid by your employer.

- **Even if you can exclude foreign earned income from U.S. income taxes, you still must pay FICA taxes on the income if you work for an American employer, which includes the U.S. government, a U.S. corporation, or a foreign affiliate of an American employer (10% or more American ownership)**. FICA should be withheld by the employer if you are an employee. If you are a consultant or contractor (compensation reported on Form 1099-MISC), you must pay self-employment tax. **(SEE "Carrying on a Trade or Business," Sole Proprietor/Self Employed, Self-Employment Tax)** If you work in a country with which the U.S. has a social security agreement (Europe, Australia, Japan, etc.), you may have to pay social security taxes to that country, but not to both the U.S and that country.
- HR 6081 stops the practice of some U.S. government contractors from using offshore shell companies to avoid paying FICA and unemployment taxes (FUTA). The bill treats foreign subsidiaries of U.S. companies performing service under a contract for the U.S. government as U.S. employers for purposes of federal payroll taxes.
- **The bona fide residence test or physical presence in a foreign country test can be waived if taxpayers had to leave a foreign country because of war, civil unrest, or similar adverse conditions in that country. Revenue Procedure 2012-21 provides a list of qualifying countries.**

Foster Care Income
Foster care income payments to foster care parents on behalf of foster care children are not taxable.

Child Support Payments
Child support payments are not taxable to recipient, and are not deductible by payer. In order to be considered child support, the divorce agreement must tie the payments to an event related to a child, i.e. reaching a specified age, graduating from school, leaving the household, marriage, etc. If payments are for both alimony and child support, child support takes priority over alimony when the total required amount is not paid.

Gifts and Inheritances
Gifts and inheritances are not taxable to the beneficiaries, but can be taxable to the payers. **(SEE "Gift and Estate Tax," Gift Tax Return (Form 709))** The basis of a gift of property to a beneficiary is the lower of FMV or the adjusted basis of the property. But the basis of inherited property is usually the stepped-up basis to FMV on the date of the decedent's death. Traditional IRAs and tax-deferred annuities are taxable to beneficiaries based on the same amount as they would have been taxable to the original owner. However, taxable distributions received by a beneficiary are not subject to the 10% penalty for distributions received before age 59 ½. **(SEE "Taxable Income," Traditional IRAs, Roth IRAs, and Qualified Retirement Plans Inherited by Beneficiaries)** If you receive a gift or inheritance, start with the assumption that it isn't income to you and therefore, you don't have to do anything. However, if you're concerned about proving that something is a gift or inheritance, file Form 3520. In any case, <u>File Form 3520 if you receive either of the following during the year</u>: (1) more than $100,000 from a nonresident alien individual or foreign estate that you treated as a gift or bequest, or (2) more than $14,375 from foreign corporations or foreign partnerships (including foreign persons related to such foreign corporations or foreign partnerships) that you treated as gifts. Also, <u>you are required to report bequests on Form 3520</u> when you actually or constructively receive them (report a gift in the year you actually receive it or the year you could have acquired title in your name, whichever occurs first). In this regard, the penalty for reporting a gift late is 5% of its value for each month the gift is not reported (capped at 25%). However, no penalty applies if the IRS is convinced the failure to report was due to reasonable cause and not willful neglect.

Qualified Distributions From Roth IRAs
Qualified distributions from Roth IRAs that include <u>any earnings</u> are tax and penalty free if you are age 59 ½ or older. If you are under age 59 ½, and <u>have owned the Roth for at least 5 years</u>, distributions that include any earnings are also tax and penalty free if you have a disability, you are a qualified home buyer (up to a lifetime maximum of $10,000 for the purchase of a home), or you are using the funds to pay for a child's college costs. Otherwise, <u>if you withdraw earnings</u> before the age of 59 ½, you'll pay taxes on the earnings plus a 10% penalty. But to the extent any distributions represent a return of the owner's contributions, the penalty would not apply. Also, each separate account has a separate 5 year waiting period. You can withdraw the amount of your contributions at any time, for any reason, without paying tax and a penalty, and any distributions represent a return of the owner's contributions first.

VA Pensions or Allowances
VA pensions or allowances for personal injuries, sickness, or death resulting from active service in the armed services or foreign service are not taxable. This includes payments to eligible survivors of deceased service members, such as proceeds from government life insurance.

- Payments under the Dept. of Veterans Affairs Compensated Work Therapy (CWT) Program are not taxable.
- Education and training allowances paid by the VA are not taxable. However, deductible education costs or credits must be reduced by VA allowances.
- If a veteran qualifies for retroactive disability compensation, any taxable retiree pay, or a percentage thereof, that he/she has already received is designated as nontaxable disability compensation and the veteran is eligible for a refund of the taxes paid (not limited to usual 3 year statute of limitations). In some cases, a retired service member receiving taxable retirement benefits may later receive a determination that he is eligible for a service connected disability, in which case the portion of retirement benefits attributable to the disability is retroactively excluded from income.

Long-Term Disability Insurance Benefits
Long-term disability insurance benefits are not included in taxable income if you paid the premiums with after-tax dollars. However, they are taxable if you paid the premiums with pre-tax dollars as part of a cafeteria plan, or your employer paid your premiums.

State Paid Veterans Bonuses
State paid veteran bonuses are tax-free.

Employer Paid Assistance Programs
Employer paid assistance programs paid to an employee or directly by the employer are not taxable to the employee:
- Employer Educational Assistance Programs (including graduate school tuition assistance) up to $5,250 annually is excluded from income. This provision was made permanent as of Jan.1, 2013.
- Certain employee fringe benefits (De Minimis fringe benefits).
- Transit Benefits – $245 per month for transit passes and van pooling, and $245 per month for parking ($240 per month for each in 2012). $20 per month is paid to employees who commute by bicycle in 2013 and 2012.
- Qualified employee discounts (up to 20% of retail).
- No-additional-cost services (services provided without charge or at a reduced price).
- Athletic facilities.
- <u>Employer paid benefits under a cafeteria plan</u>, which are excluded from an employee's gross income. Employer contributions to a cafeteria plan are usually made under salary reduction agreements between the employer and the employee in which the employee agrees to contribute a portion of his or her salary on a pretax basis to pay for the qualified benefits. A cafeteria plan must offer participating employees a choice among two or more benefits

consisting of "qualified benefits." A cafeteria plan may include: a health flexible spending arrangement (FSA); accident and health insurance; dependent care assistance program; disability coverage; group term life insurance; health savings account (HSA); health reimbursement arrangement (HRA); adoption assistance; and 401(k) plans. A cafeteria plan must be a written plan and may not discriminate in favor of highly compensated participants. A cafeteria plan discriminates in favor of highly compensated participants if the plan provides greater benefits to those employees in comparison to non-highly compensated employees. Additionally, it may not favor key employees. It favors key employees if more than 25% of the nontaxable qualified benefits provided are provided to key employees. If a plan discriminates in favor of highly compensated or key employees, they will be subject to tax on the benefits they receive under the plan. Such discrimination is often determined under relatively complex rules.

- Employer adoption assistance program for 2013 is limited to $12,970. The amount excludable from an employee's gross income begins to phase out for taxpayers with modified adjusted gross incomes (MAGI) in excess of $194,580, and is completely phased out at $234,580 or more.
- Employer child and dependent care assistance programs up to $5,000. This provision was made permanent as of Jan. 1, 2013.
- Employer paid group-term life insurance coverage up to $50,000. Exclusion is not available to key employees unless the plan meets nondiscrimination tests of eligibility. The imputed value of employer-provided group term life insurance coverage in excess of $50,000 is taxable for withholding (only FICA is required to be withheld).
- Employer contributions to accident and health insurance plans.
- Employer furnished meals and housing, if furnished on the business premises for the convenience of the employer (meals must be served during and after working hours).
- Gifts from employer worth less than $25. Items costing $4.00 or less such as pens, etc. are not considered gifts. These are deductible by employer. Gifts over $25 are not deductible by employer.
- Employee achievement awards that are tangible personal property (such as watches or golf clubs). To be deductible by employer, cannot exceed $400 for nonqualified plan awards, and $1,600 for qualified plan awards. **Cash awards, gift certificates, and similar items are taxable to the employee.**
- **Employer-provided cell phones are an excludable fringe benefit. When an employer provides an employee with a cell phone primarily for non-compensatory business reasons, the business and personal use of the cell phone is nontaxable to the employee. The IRS will not require recordkeeping of business use in order to receive this tax-free treatment. Also, employers that require employees, primarily for non-compensatory business reasons, to use their personal cell phones for business purposes may treat reimbursements of the employees' expenses for reasonable cell phone coverage as nontaxable. This treatment does**

not apply to reimbursements of unusual or excessive expenses or to reimbursements made as a substitute for a portion of the employee's regular wages.

Clergy Furnished Housing

Clergy furnished housing is income tax-free, but self-employment tax must be paid on the FMV of the housing. **(SEE "Carrying on a Trade or Business," Sole Proprietors/Self Employed)**

Stock Dividends

Stock dividends are tax-free, unless the shareholder has the option to take cash or property instead of stock, or it is a preferred stock dividend.

Personal Injury Awards

Personal injury awards as a result of physical injuries or physical sickness are tax-exempt, except for punitive damages. In addition, payments for medical treatment, including counseling (treatment of emotional trauma related to physical injury), are not taxable. Payments for medical expenses are tax-free, and what constitutes "medical expenses" is surprisingly liberal. For example, payments to a psychiatrist or counselor qualify, as do payments to a chiropractor or physical therapist. And many nontraditional treatments count too. But, a portion of contingent fees paid to attorneys may be taxable, if recovery amount includes punitive damages, which are taxable. Damages for emotional injuries <u>are</u> taxable. Physical symptoms caused by emotional distress – say, headaches – are generally taxable, but it's fuzzy and much litigated. The IRS says that in order for physical injuries to be nontaxable, they must be visible. Example: If in settling an employment dispute you receive $50,000 extra because your employer gave you an ulcer, is an ulcer physical or is it merely a symptom of your emotional distress? Many plaintiffs end up taking aggressive positions on their tax returns, claiming damages of this nature are tax-free. But that can be a losing battle if the defendant issues a Form 1099 for the entire settlement. This means it can behoove you to try to get an agreement with the defendant about the tax issues. If you sue your employer for <u>sexual harassment</u> involving rude comments or even fondling, that's not physical enough for the IRS. Taxpayers routinely argue in Tax Court that their damages are sufficiently physical to be tax-free, but the IRS usually wins these cases. **(SEE "Taxable Income," Personal Injury Awards Associated with Nonphysical Injuries)**

Property Damages

Property damages can be tax-free if the settlement merely pays for the cost of fixing your car or house, provided you don't get back more than you paid for the car or house, and you have not claimed a casualty loss deduction for damage to the property. The recovery will be treated as a reduction in your purchase price of the house, etc. If the damage is to your business, the same rules apply – although a recovery in excess of your basis might be taxed at the 15% or 20% capital gains rate.

Workers' Compensation
Worker's Compensation payments for job-related injuries or illness are not taxable. Payments must be made under the authority of a law or regulation that provides compensation for on-the-job injury or illness. However, workers' compensation payments that reduce Social Security benefits is treated as a Social Security benefit received during the year and is, therefore, indirectly taxable (Box 5 of Form SSA-1099 is the taxable amount – not reduced by any amount, such as a workers' compensation offset, shown in Box 3).

Gain on the Sale of a Principal Residence
Gain on the sale of a principle residence is excluded from income if taxpayer qualifies for the home sale gain exclusion of $500,000 (married filing jointly), or $250,000 (single) for sale of a principal residence. Proceeds from a home sale should be reported on Form 1099-S (Proceeds from Real Estate Transactions), which shows date of closing and gross proceeds from sale. Exclusion of gain does not require the home to be used as a principal residence at the time of sale, but only as a principal residence for 2 years (24 full months or 730 days) out of a 5-year period, and you cannot have gone through a sale in which you excluded the gain during the prior two years before the sale of the current home. Otherwise, you cannot exclude any gain unless there is: a change in employment requiring a change in location; change in health requiring money for a cure, diagnosis or care; or unforeseen circumstances, such as death, termination of employment, divorce/separation, or other qualified reasons (hardships). In which case, exclusion of gain is prorated based on the number of days lived in home over a 2 year period, divided by 730 days, times the maximum exclusion ($250,000 or $500,000). Hardship exceptions are available, but must be proved to the satisfaction of the IRS, usually through the letter ruling process. For both spouses to qualify for the home sale gain exclusion after divorce, the divorce instrument must require them to co-own the principle residence, even if only one spouse occupies the residence. Otherwise, the non-occupying former spouse may not qualify for the 2 out of 5 year rule.
- **If you can exclude all of the gain, you do not need to report the sale of your home on your tax return, unless you receive a Form 1099-S - Proceeds From Real Estate Transactions. Then you have to report the sale of your home on your tax return.**
- The exclusion does not apply to any gain attributable to any depreciation taken on the home after May 6, 1997. Recapture of depreciation resulting from such gain is subject to the Section 1231 netting rules. If there is a net Section 1231 gain, the gain attributed to the depreciation is entered in the "unrecaptured Section" of the 1250 Gain Worksheet in Schedule D – the gain is subject to a top tax rate of 25%. If house is sold, any depreciation claimed for a home office must be recaptured as unrecaptured Section 1250 gain (LT capital gain taxed @ 25%).
- You can add the following to the original cost of the home (basis): closing costs from the original purchase and from any refinancing or equity line loans secured by the property that were made over the course of the ownership; capital improvements made to the residence

- such as a new hot water heater, roof, windows, landscaping, etc. You can't include costs for painting or basic maintenance.
- You can deduct the following from the selling price of the home: realtor's commission, closing costs and any agreed upon costs to fulfill the contract. You can also deduct advertising expenses and certain repairs if they were made within 90 days of the sale and clearly for the intent of marketing the property.
- The sale of vacant land is not included in a sale of a home unless: (1) it is adjacent to land where the home is located, and (2) taxpayer owned and used it as part of the main home.
- If you sell a home at a loss, you cannot claim a loss on your tax return. However, if you took home office depreciation, you may be able to take a portion as a loss - Example: purchase price $100,000; sale price $85,000; business use 10%; depreciation taken $10,000; recognized loss $500 ($8,500 – [$9,000]).
- A marriage that results in a large, combined new family is considered an "unforeseen circumstance" that allows a taxpayer to benefit from the capital gain exclusion on the sale of a principal residence, even though he owned the house for less than 2 years (a larger house with more bedrooms is needed).
- A Surviving Spouse (SS) may use the joint return $500,000 home sale gain exclusion for 2 years following the date of death of spouse. A surviving spouse is allowed the stepped-up basis for the deceased spouse's ½ share of the home.
- If a home is foreclosed on, it is reported on Form 1099-A (Acquisition or Abandonment of Secured Property). It is reported just like a sale on Schedule D. (see discussion on foreclosures under "cancelled debt").
- The new Housing Act tightens the "home sale gain exclusion", i.e. it disallows the exclusion of gain from the sale of a principal residence attributable to periods the dwelling was used as a vacation home or a rental property or other nonqualified use, and then converted to a principal residence – effective for sales and **periods of nonqualified use after 2008**. <u>The portion of the profit that is taxable is based on the percentage of time before the sale when the home was used as a second home or rented out. The portion of profit that is taxable does not include a period of absence that occurs after the home was last used as the principal residence</u>.
- A taxpayer can have only one principal residence at a time – usually the one occupied more of the time. Factors in establishing principal residence: place of employment; location of recreational clubs; address used on driver's license; voter registration.
- The five-year ownership and use test period is suspended for certain individuals working outside of the country – members of uniformed services, foreign service, intelligence community, and peace corp. These taxpayers may extend the running time of the 5-year ownership and use requirement for a maximum of 10 years (taxpayer and/or spouse). **Employees of federal contractors do not qualify for the suspension.**

- U.S. citizens living abroad (not the ones discussed above) have to pay capital gain tax when they sell a house in the United States. They do not qualify for the $250,000/$500,000 gain exclusion.
- Unmarried co-owners of a residence can exclude each of their share of gain on the sale of a principal residence (other than gain allocated to nonqualified use of the home) as long as they used the home as their principal residence for at least 2 of 5 years preceding the date of sale. Therefore, one co-owner may qualify to exclude his share of the gain and the other may not. The dollar limit for a single individual is $250,000 of gain.

<u>A lender who acquires a taxpayer's property through foreclosure, repossession or abandonment should send the taxpayer Form 1099-A. Form 1099-A should only be used if there is no cancellation of debt in excess of the value of the property. The form is used by the taxpayer to calculate gain or loss and any ordinary income from disposition of the property.</u> **(SEE "Taxable Income," Cancellation of Debt)**

Mortgage Debt
Mortgage debt is forgiven on a principal residence up to $2 million, or $1 million if married filing separately, for years beginning Jan. 1, 2007 – Dec. 31, 2013. Foreclosure on a home can result in income to the owner that is forgiven, if at the time of foreclosure the fair market value (FMV) of the encumbered property is less than the outstanding debt. Also, a "short sale" can result in forgiven income to the owner. A short sale in real estate occurs when the outstanding loans against a property are greater than what the property is worth and the lender agrees to accept less than it is owed to permit a sale of the property (home) that secures the note. This benefit also covers an agreement or "work-out" with the lender to make payments lower – example: lender forgives $100,000 of taxpayer's current $325,000 mortgage debt + $4,500 of interest in arrears, thus both the $100,000 and the $4,500 are not taxable income. Another option to take advantage of mortgage debt forgiveness is called "deed in lieu of foreclosure" in which the homeowner vacates the residence and turns it over to the lender in exchange for debt forgiveness. In this case, the Mortgage Debt forgiveness Act allows some of the debt to be excluded from taxable income, and allows most of the gain from the sale of the home (whether foreclosure action is now or years later in the case of a "mortgage workout") to escape tax through the home sale gain exclusion. Abandonment is also disposition of a property that can result in cancelled debt income to the owner. <u>Forgiveness of mortgage debt also includes refinancing up to the amount of the old mortgage principal, but does not include home equity loans not used for home improvements. Also, does not include debt on a second home or rental property.</u> **(SEE "Taxable income," Cancellation of Debt)**
- <u>To claim mortgage debt forgiveness, you need to complete Form 982 and check the appropriate boxes to tell the IRS that you're entitled to this exclusion.</u>
- You can have a principal residence short sale that produces a capital gain – say you paid $190,000 for a home that you sell for $250,000; it is a short sale because you have first and

second recourse mortgages that total $280,000; but for IRS purposes you have a $60,000 capital gain ($250,000 sale price, $190,000 basis = $60,000 gain). However, the $60,000 gain is probably tax-free, thanks to the home sale gain exclusion (but not for a rental property or a vacation home).
- o In some states, some personal residence mortgages can be nonrecourse. When these residences are sold in a short sale, the transaction is treated for tax purposes as a sale for a price equal to the nonrecourse loan balance. The actual sale price is irrelevant, so there is no cancellation of debt (COD) income because the nonrecourse mortgage obligation is deemed to be fully satisfied in the short sale. A tax gain is triggered if the nonrecourse loan balance exceeds the property's basis, which is probably tax-free, thanks to the home sale gain exclusion.

Gain on the Sale of Section 1202 Small Business Stock

Gain on the sale of Section 1202 Small Business stock that is held more than 5 years, is either totally or partially excluded from income depending on when it was acquired: 100% is excluded on stock acquired after 9/27/2010 and before 1/1/2014; 75% is excluded on stock acquired after 2/17/2009 and before 9/28/2010; and 50% is excluded on stock acquired before 2/17/2009. When the stock is issued, a qualified small-business corporation's aggregate gross assets may not exceed $50 million. If at any time before the issuance the corporation or any predecessor held gross assets exceeding $50 million, the stock will not qualify. Although qualification of issued stock is not dependent upon keeping under the $50 million asset ceiling subsequent to its issuance, the test will disqualify any subsequently issued stock once the $50 million ceiling is reached. Also, the corporation must use at least 80% of the value of its assets in the active conduct of one or more qualified trades or businesses. Code Section 1202(e)(3) provides a non-exclusive long list of trades or businesses that are **not qualified**, including service businesses in health, law, architecture, accounting, and financial services. It is the shareholders' burden to prove qualification for the exclusion. A taxpayer may hold qualified stock in more than one corporation and apply the limit separately to each. The amount of gain eligible for exclusion of gain from the disposition of qualified stock of any single issuer for any given tax year is limited to the greater of $10 million ($5 million for married taxpayers filing separately) reduced by the total amount of eligible gains taken in prior tax years, or 10 times the taxpayer's adjusted basis in all qualified stock disposed of during the tax year. This provision is limited to individual investments and not the investments of a corporation. To be eligible for the exclusion, the taxpayer must acquire the stock at its original issue (directly or through an under-writer), for money, property other than stock, or as compensation for services provided to the corporation. The non-excluded portion of section 1202 gain is taxed at the lesser of ordinary income tax rates or 28%, instead of the lower capital gains rates.

Like-Kind Exchanges (Section 1031)

No gain or loss is recognized in a Like-Kind Exchange (Section 1031) of business or investment property, except to the extent of "boot" received – money, other property, or a transferred liability (mortgage). If you receive any cash in the deal, this is considered boot and is subject to capital gains taxes. No loss is recognized to any extent. The basis of property acquired is the same as the adjusted basis of property relinquished, less any boot received, plus any gain recognized. Form 8824 must be filed when there is a Section 1031 exchange, and any gain is recognized on Schedule D, Form 4797. Section 1031 exchanges between related parties require a holding period of two years for both parties. A Section 1031 exchange requires a "Qualified Intermediary ("QI") to facilitate the exchange. Since there is no entity that oversees or regulates QIs, it is crucial in selecting a QI that you verify the experience of the company and the security measures they will provide for the exchange funds held in their possession during the exchange period. A Section 1031 exchange is normally implemented for real estate transactions but is also available for vehicles, equipment, livestock and any other business property. However, you cannot apply Section 1031 to any personal use property such as your residence or personal car or truck, and it doesn't apply to stocks or bonds. Also, the new (replacement) property must be equivalent or higher in value and it must be a like-kind property: real estate for real estate (it can be land for an apartment building).

- o In a Section 1031 exchange, the replacement property must be identified within 45 days before or after transfer, and the exchange must be completed within 180 days.
- o The business nature of the transaction must remain intact, i.e. you cannot trade a rental property for a personal residence. Also, you cannot exchange a property into one that is located outside of the United States. If you are a dealer in real estate, such as a house flipper, you do not qualify for 1031 exchange deferral.
- o In a Section 1031 exchange of a vacation home for another vacation home, the gain is deferred on the relinquished dwelling if it meets the criteria of a property held for investment: (1) the relinquished and replacement dwellings must be owned by the taxpayer for at least 2 years immediately before (relinquished property) and immediately after (replacement property); and (2) for each of those years, the dwellings must be rented at FMV for at least 14 days, and your personal use of the property cannot have exceeded the greater of 14 days or 10% of the days the property was rented out at market rates. In this respect, if gain is deferred until the owner's death, the appreciation may escape tax entirely due to the stepped-up basis of the property. Example: you own a vacation home worth $600,000 with a tax basis of only $200,000. You find another home worth $700,000 that you would like to own. So, you swap your old vacation home (the relinquished property) for the new one (the replacement property) and throw in $100,000 cash for the trade. As long as you meet the aforementioned usage guidelines for both properties, you can pull off a tax-deferred 1031 exchange and thereby avoid any current income tax hit. Your basis in the replacement property is $300,000 ($700,000 - $400,000 gain rolled over from the relinquished property).

- o Intangibles may be like-kind property (trademarks, trade names, etc.) – except for goodwill.
- o Transfers of buildings constructed on owned land, sold to investors, and then leased back, cannot be treated as a Section 1031 exchange.
- o The IRS is stricter when it comes to animals: if you want to exchange livestock, it must be of the same sex or a like-kind exchange will not fly.

Life Insurance Proceeds

Life insurance proceeds received by a beneficiary in a lump-sum payment are not taxable. However, if installments are received by the beneficiary, part of each installment may be taxable as interest earned – divide the lump-sum amount payable at death by the number of installments to be paid, and include anything paid over this excluded part per installment in income as interest. But a surviving spouse who receives installments can exclude up to $1,000 per year of interest included in the installments.

- o Life insurance policies with an accelerated death benefit clause allows lifetime distributions for those who are terminally ill (someone with a condition expected to result in death within 24 months) or chronically ill. Such payments to a terminally ill person are tax free, as well as payments to a chronically ill person for long-term care expenses. Payments made to chronically ill individuals on a per diem basis without regard to care costs are excludable up to a set dollar amount ($300 per day). If benefits exceed this limit, the excess is excludable to the extent used to pay for long-term care services.
- o With or without an accelerated death benefit clause, it may be possible to sell a life insurance policy to pay for long-term care. Proceeds from the sale of a life insurance policy paid to a terminally ill individual are not taxable. Proceeds paid to a chronically ill individual are tax free to the same extent as accelerated death benefits.

Military Personnel Combat Pay

Military personnel can exclude combat pay from earned income. Enlisted persons, including non-commissioned officers, can exclude all of their combat pay from earned income. Military officers can exclude part of their combat pay from earned income - limited to the maximum salary of a non-commissioned officer. This covers all compensation for any month the individual served in a combat zone or was hospitalized as result of wounds, disease, or injury in a combat zone.

State Payments for Combat Service

State payments for combat service (in a combat zone) are excluded from taxable income, even if paid to a dependent.

Interest Earned on Tax-Exempt Housing Bonds

Interest earned on tax-exempt housing bonds issued by state and local governments is exempt from federal tax. To help veterans buy homes, Congress authorized states to issue qualified veterans' mortgage bonds under which interest payments are tax exempt. Certain dates for the completion of military service before 1977 are removed, and the eligibility period is reduced from 30 to 25 years after separation from service.

Payments to Volunteer Fire Fighters and Medical Responders

Payments to volunteer fire fighters and emergency medical responders are excluded from gross income for federal tax purposes, and also from FICA and FUTA.

Rebates Received From Tangible Assets

Rebates received resulting from purchases of tangible assets are excluded from income. Also, credit card rebates are not included in gross income, even though they may be claimed as a charitable contribution if so directed. Business-owner reward cards that generate awards for the purchase of equipment used in the business, reduces the basis of the equipment by the value of the awards.

Airline Miles

Airline miles received for making purchases on credit cards or frequent flier miles earned for taking trips are tax-free. **But consumers technically owe taxes on miles they receive for opening a bank or credit card account**. Miles earned for making purchases on a credit card can be used or donated to a charity, and if donated to a charity it is considered a charitable contribution deduction provided substantiation rules for written acknowledgment from the charity are followed for amounts of $250 or more.

- Personal use of airline frequent flier miles or other in-kind promotional benefits attributable to a taxpayer's business or official travel are not taxable to the employee.
- Mutual funds that offer a promotion that awards airline miles for the purchase of shares lowers the basis in the shares that the investor purchases by the value of the miles acquired.
- Airline miles received for opening up a bank account or received as a sign-up bonus for getting a credit card are technically taxable, but unless the recipient receives a 1099-MISC, the reality is that reporting such income is likely to be overlooked. A 1099-MISC is not required to be issued unless the payer has paid a recipient a least $600 during the year in rents, services, prizes and awards, and usually not that many miles are paid to open an account that would exceed the $600 mark.

National Health Service Corps Scholarship and Armed Forces Scholarships

The National Health Service Corps Scholarship Program and the Armed Forces Scholarship Program payments to recipients are permanently excluded from income.

Deductions for Computing Adjusted Gross Income (AGI):

Educator Expenses
For educator expenses, deductions were extended through 2013. Up to $250 in out-of-pocket expenses can be deducted by teachers, instructors, counselors, principals, and teachers' aides in public or private schools who have out-of-pocket expenses, and work at least 900 hours during the school year. The expenses can be for books and supplies.

Student Loan Interest
For student loan interest, deductions were made permanent as of Jan. 1, 2013. A maximum of $2,500 in student loan interest can be deducted each year by a taxpayer. The interest is reported on Form 1098-E when a person pays more than $600 in interest. Deduction is also available for loans used to pay room and board expenses. However mixed loans are not eligible for the deduction. Phase-out ranges for 2013: $60,000 - $75,000 (single and head of household); and $125,000 - $155,000 (married filing jointly). If a parent pays back a child's student loans, the IRS treats it as a Gift to the child, who then pays off the debt; therefore, the child who is not claimed as a dependent by the parent can deduct the interest on his/her tax return.

Tuition and Fees for Higher Education (Form 8917)
For tuition and fees for higher education (Form 8917), deductions were extended through 2013. A tuition and fees deduction of up to $4,000 per student is available for taxpayers with modified adjusted gross income (MAGI) up to $65,000 ($130,000 for joint filers), and a deduction of $2,000 per student for taxpayers with MAGI over $65,000 and up to $80,000 ($160,000 for joint filers). No deduction is available for taxpayers with MAGI over $80,000 ($160,000 for joint filers). The deduction is not available to married taxpayers filing separately. Tuition and fees must be required for enrollment in an accredited post-secondary institution for taxpayer, spouse and dependents. Allowable expenses do not include expenditures for room and board or books, supplies and equipment. You must attach Form 8917 to your 1040 tax return to claim the deduction. Deduction cannot be taken if one of the available Education Credits is taken. Deduction is reduced by the tax-free earnings portion of any distributions from Coverdell savings accounts and 529 plans (reported on Form 1099-Q) that pay for the same expenses. **(SEE "Income Exclusions," Distributions From Coverdell Education Savings Accounts, and Distributions From Qualified Tuition Programs)**

Allowable tuition and fees are reported on Form 1098-T by educational institutions. An eligible educational institution may choose to report payments received (Box 1) or amounts billed (Box 2) for qualified tuition and fees (either one is acceptable for the deduction). The amount of scholarships and grants reported on Form 1098-T, Box 5, may or may not need to be deducted from "payments received" or "amounts billed" to determine allowable expenses (this has to be determined on a case by case basis). **The amount of expenses allowable is the actual expenditures for tuition and fees in a calendar year rather than expenditures for an academic school year.**

Contributions to Health Savings Accounts (Form 8889)

Contributions to Health Savings Accounts (HSA) (Form 8889) – In 2013, persons with **high deductible health insurance coverage (HDHP)**, and not enrolled in Medicare, can deduct maximum contributions to an HSA of $6,450 for family coverage and $3,250 for self-only coverage. Persons age 55 and older can deduct an additional $1,000 a year. An HSA can be established through an employer's cafeteria plan to pay for qualified medical expenses of the account beneficiary. Contributions are reported on employees' W-2 forms, Box 12, Code W. Contributions can be made by eligible individuals or by any other person, including a family member, on behalf of the account beneficiary. Contributions can be made until the income tax filing due date, and interest earned on HSAs is tax-free. Distributions from HSAs are reported on Form 1099-SA, and are not taxable if used to pay for qualified medical expenses. Form 8889 must be attached to your tax return to report contributions to an HSA. A **high deductible health plan (HDHP)** must have at least a $2,500 deductible (families), or a $1,200 deductible (self-only), and the limit on out-of-pocket expenses has to be $12,500 and $6,250 respectively. <u>However, a plan will not fail to qualify as a HDHP if it has no deductible for preventive care</u>. The Archer MSA was replaced by the HSA after 2005. New Archers cannot be established, but contributions can still be made to existing Archers. The terms of an Archer are virtually the same as an HSA.

- Form 8889 is used to report contributions, deductions, and distributions from HSAs, including employer contributions. Employers must make comparable contributions to each employee.
- Excess contributions to an HSA are subject to an excise tax of 6 percent (amounts in excess of the maximum amounts deductible by taxpayers - $6,450 for family coverage and $3,250 for self-only coverage).
- Employees can carry over unused amounts in HSAs from previous years to future years.
- Nonqualified distributions from HSAs are included in taxable income, and there is an additional 20% tax on nonqualified distributions. Unlike distributions from a FSA, distributions from an HSA are not required to be substantiated by the employer or a third party for the distributions to be excluded from income. The determination is subject to individual self-reporting and IRS enforcement. Over-the-counter medications are excluded from the definition of qualified medical expenses unless prescribed by a health care professional, or is insulin. Meds purchased from Canada are not eligible for reimbursement from HSAs.
- In addition to a HDHP, an eligible individual may be covered by another health insurance plan that provides **permitted** coverage. Other permitted insurance covers only accidents, disability, dental care, vision care, or long-term care. Participation in an employer assistance program is OK, as long as the program does not provide significant medical care benefits or treatments.
- Only one person can be the "beneficiary" of an HSA. That person is either the individual who sets up the account or, upon death, the named beneficiary. Spouses cannot share a HSA, so

each spouse must open a separate account. A person may have more than one HSA account, but all accounts are aggregated for purposes of the annual contribution limit. Although only one person is the beneficiary of an HSA, account distributions can also be used to pay medical expenses incurred by the beneficiary's spouse or dependents.
- Self-employed persons may not contribute to an HSA on a pretax basis and may not take the amount of their HSA contributions as a deduction for self-employment purposes. However, they may contribute to an HSA with after-tax dollars and take the above-the-line deduction.
- An individual is allowed to fund a full year as long as the HSA starts by Dec. 1st of that year.

Moving Expenses (Form 3903)
Unreimbursed moving expenses are deductible using Form 3903. Moving expenses that are reimbursed by employer are also accounted for on Form 3903. Non-taxable reimbursements for moving expenses are not included in taxable income, and are shown in Box 12 (Code P) of Form W-2, and are not deductible by taxpayer, because the non-taxable reimbursements offset allowable moving expenses. Box 14 of Form W-2 shows taxable reimbursements for moving expenses that are included in Box 1 (taxable income), and do not offset allowable moving expenses, and therefore are deductible by taxpayer.
- Allowable moving expenses include: (1) cost of moving household goods; (2) storage of household goods for 30 days; (3) cost of transporting a vehicle(s); (4) cost of transporting family members to new location, including airfare and by car at a mileage rate of $.24 a mile in 2013 ($.23 in 2012); and (5) one night lodging at both old and new locations. Meals are not deductible. You can write-off the cost of hiring movers (or renting a moving truck) plus the cost of one-way travel to your new home for everyone in your household – whether it's airfare, train, or by car. You can deduct lodging expenses while traveling to your new home, the cost of packing your stuff and storing the goods for 30 days, and the cost to disconnect utilities at your old residence and connect them at your new residence.
- Distance and time requirements – new place of work must be 50 miles farther from former residence than former place of work; and you must expect to stay in new job for at least 39 weeks. If you quit or get fired before the time period is met, you have to report it to the IRS.
- House hunting trips; temporary living expenses at new location; expenses related to the sale, purchase or lease of a residence; mortgage penalties, etc. are not deductible.
- A delay of up to one year does not jeopardize a deduction for moving expenses. If you move to the new job area within one year, your family may stay in the old residence for a longer period and their moving expenses will still be deductible, even though incurred after one year.
- Job-hunting expenses incurred while looking for your first job, like after graduating from college, are not deductible (as itemized deductions). But moving expenses to get that position are deductible.
- There are special rules for foreign moves.

Traditional IRA Contributions

A deductible contribution to a traditional IRA is the lesser of taxable earnings, or the maximum allowable contribution, which is $5,500 in 2013 ($5,000 in 2012); $6,500 if over age 50 in 2013 ($6,000 in 2012). Taxpayers can make both deductible and non-deductible contributions. A deductible contribution is limited to taxable earned income (salaries and wages, self-employment income, partnership income, and alimony), and a non-deductible contribution cannot be more than the difference between the maximum allowable contribution and the deductible contribution, but it is still limited to taxable earned income. A deductible contribution may be less than taxable earned income, because it can be further limited if you are a participant in an employer retirement plan, even if the plan is available and you decline to participate. If married filing jointly, the allowable contribution amounts are doubled, even if one spouse has no earned income – "nonworking spouse IRA." Contributions can be made up to age 70 ½, including the nonworking spouse contribution. If you make non-deductible contributions, you must file Form 8606. Maximum allowable contributions are phased-out in 2013 between MAGI of $95,000 - $115,000 (married filing jointly) if both individuals are active participants in an employer's qualified retirement plan ($92,000 - $112,000 in 2012). For an individual who is not an active participant in a retirement plan, but whose spouse is, the maximum allowable contribution is phased out in 2013 between MAGI of $178,000 - $188,000 ($173,000 - $183,000 in 2012). For single/head-of-household, the phase-out range in 2013 is between $59,000 - $69,000 ($58,000 - $68,000 in 2012). When an individual files as married filing separately, and the individual, or the spouse, is an active participant in an employer's retirement plan, the phase-out range is $0 - $10,000.

- Contributions must be made by the filing due date (not including an extension).
- On a joint return, each spouse can deduct the maximum amount, so long as the combined compensation of both spouses is at least equal to the allowable maximum amount.
- Only cash contributions can be made to IRAs, including Roth IRAs. You cannot contribute stock to an IRA, but you can buy stock with cash that you contribute to an IRA.
- The maximum allowable contribution also applies to Roth IRAs. However, Roth contributions are not deductible. Whether or not an individual(s) is a participant in an employer's retirement plan is not applicable in determining the maximum contribution to a Roth IRA. However, the maximum allowable contribution is phased-out for married filing jointly in 2013 between MAGI of $178,000 - $188,000 ($173,000 - $183,000 in 2012). For single/head-of-household in 2013 the phase-out range is between $112,000 - $127,000 ($110,000 - $125,000 in 2012). And for married filing separately, the phase-out range is $0 - $10,000. Also, contributions to Roth IRAs can be made after age 70 ½.
- Contributions can be made to both traditional and Roth IRAs in the same year, as long as the total for both does not exceed the maximum allowable contribution for the year. Contributions to Roth IRAs generally benefit younger individuals saving for retirement and those who expect

their tax bracket to increase. **(SEE "Taxable Income," Rollovers from Traditional IRAs to Roth IRAs)**

- If a contribution exceeds the maximum amount deductible, the excess can be carried over and deducted in succeeding years to the extent that contributions in succeeding years are less than the allowable contributions in those years, or you can have the excess returned (withdrawn) by the filing date – April 15. **Contributions made in a year can be withdrawn in the same year without penalty, but you must pay tax on the interest earned**. <u>Excess contributions to both traditional and Roth IRAs are imposed with an excise tax equal to 6% of the lesser of the excess contribution or the fair value of the IRA account at the end of the year</u>. The tax is imposed each year until the excess contribution and its earnings are removed from the account. <u>A taxpayer who has made an excess contribution is required to file Form 5329</u>, and failure to file the form can result in a penalty of up to 25% of the excise tax. The penalty will not apply if the failure is due to reasonable cause.

- Taxpayers who mistakenly contribute to a traditional IRA when they intended to make a contribution to a Roth IRA or vice versa can undo the mistake by electing to re-characterize the contribution. The re-characterization must be made by the due date of the tax return, including extension.

- <u>Military personnel serving in Iraq, Afghanistan and other combat zone localities can count non-taxable combat pay when figuring how much to contribute to traditional or Roth IRAs</u> (retroactive to 2004). Individuals receiving military death benefits are allowed to disregard the Roth dollar amount contribution limitations, and start a Roth IRA with the full amount of the death benefits.

- If you have a self-directed IRA, you can buy rental property with your IRA. However, there are many restrictions when it comes to owning real estate in an IRA. For example, the rental property can't be leased to someone who is related to you; this would be prohibited and would trigger taxation of the IRA, and the 10% penalty if you're under age 59 ½. You will need to find the right custodian for a self-directed IRA.

- <u>A child's IRA can be used for college without triggering early-withdrawal penalties, and it isn't reported as an asset on financial applications, thus avoiding the risk of a smaller aid package. One option is a Roth IRA, which allows tax-deferred growth for college. However, in order to be able to establish an IRA in the child's name, contributions to the IRA must come from the child's earnings.</u>
<u>Parents can pay children for household services as long as the wage is reasonable for the work performed</u>. It might be prudent to split college savings between a 529 plan and an IRA in the child's name. **(SEE "Income Exclusions," Distributions From Qualified Tuition Programs)**

Alimony/Separate Maintenance (Form 3559)
Alimony or Separate maintenance payments to a former spouse are deductible only if you have a written instrument of divorce or separation agreement (an oral understanding between the husband and his former wife will not do), and you must file Form 3559 with your tax return to claim the deduction. The divorce agreement has to require payments to cease upon the death of the former spouse in order to be considered alimony payments. Also, any payments due at death can be alimony. You should be aware of the recapture provisions. **(SEE "Taxable Income," Alimony/Separate Maintenance)**

Self-Employment Tax
50% of Self-Employment Tax is deductible.

Self-Employed Health Insurance Premiums
If you are self-employed, 100% of your self-employed health insurance premiums paid for yourself, spouse, and dependents are deductible. This includes dental insurance premiums, and some long-term care premiums. It also includes premiums paid for coverage for any child of yours who was under age 27 at the end of the year, even if the child was not your dependent. However, you cannot deduct self-employed health insurance premiums if you participate in an employer subsidized health plan. Beginning in 2010, self-employed taxpayers can move Medicare premiums from Schedule A, medical expenses (where they may be wasted anyway), to self-employed health insurance premiums (above-the-line deduction). Flag prior years' returns to be amended to include Medicare premiums as self-employed health insurance premiums. Self-employed persons may not contribute to an HSA on a pretax basis and may not take the amount of their HSA contribution as a deduction for self-employment purposes. However, they may contribute to an HSA with after-tax dollars and take the above-the-line deduction. **(SEE Contributions to Health Savings Accounts (HSA), above)**
- Besides a sole proprietor, a self-employed individual for purposes of the Medicare premiums deduction can be a person who had self-employment earnings as a partner reported on Schedule K-1 (Form 1065), or you were paid wages reported on Form W-2 as a shareholder who owns more than 2% of the outstanding stock of an S-corporation.
- For 2010 only, self-employed persons could deduct self-employed health insurance premiums in determining net income from self-employment - claimed on Schedule SE, Line 3, then deduction claimed on Form 1040, Line 29.

Self-Employed Retirement Contributions
Self-employed persons can deduct amounts contributed to retirement programs. This includes SIMPLE and SEP IRA contributions which are deductible as above-the-line deductions. The deductions do not reduce the amount of income on which self-employed persons have to pay self-employment taxes.

(SEE "Income Exclusions," Contributions to Qualified Employee Retirement and Pension Benefit Plans)

Penalty For Early Withdrawal of Savings

Penalty for early withdrawal of savings is deductible. This is forfeited interest and any principal (Box 2 of Form 1099-INT).

Business Expenses of Statutory Employees

Business expenses of statutory employees, reported on Schedule C, Form 1040 are deductible.

Business Expenses of State and Local Officials

Unreimbursed business expenses of state and local officials paid on a fee basis are deductible.

Overnight Travel Costs of Reservists and National Guard Members

Overnight travel costs of reservists and National Guard members are deductible, such as travel expenses to drills and meetings (must travel more than 100 miles away from home and stay overnight for training). Must use regular federal per diem rates for lodging and meals (M&IE) and standard mileage rates, plus parking and toll fees. Form 2106 must be filed. **(SEE "Employee Travel and Entertainment Expenses," Claiming Travel and Entertainment Expenses, and Vehicle and Other Transportation Expenses)**

Business Expenses of Performing Artists

Business expenses of performing artists are deductible under certain conditions. Form 2106 must be filed. Also, Code Sec. 181 permits an owner of a qualified film or television production to elect to deduct production costs paid or incurred by the owner for the year the costs are paid or incurred, in lieu of capitalizing the costs and recovering them through depreciation. For productions commencing after 1/1/2008, the amount that can be deducted is limited to $15 million. A film or television production is qualified if at least 75% of the total compensation of the production is compensation for services performed in the United States by actors, directors, producers, and other production personnel.

Attorney Fees Paid in Connection With Unlawful Discrimination

Attorney fees paid in connection with a claim of unlawful discrimination or under the Medicare Secondary Payer Statute are deductible, only if any payments received as a result of such claims are included in taxable income.

Domestic Production

Taxpayers are allowed to deduct 9% of the lesser of (1) qualified production activities resulting from specified domestic production activities; or (2) taxable income determined without regard to the deduction. Qualified domestic production activities are the manufacture or production of qualifying property substantially within the United States. Only taxpayers that have the benefits and burdens of owning the property are entitled to claim the deduction for that property. However, determining which party has the "benefits and burdens" of ownership is often a complex process. In general, taxpayers will be required to supply benefits-and-burdens certification statements within 30 days of the date that an information document request is issued by the IRS regarding the deduction. Qualifying property is property in which the "form or function" of the property has been changed. For example, adding accessories to a car does not change the form or function of the car. However, purchasing various automobile parts from suppliers, such as the frame, engine, wheels, etc. and assembling them to create the car itself is undoubtedly manufacturing, because the form or function of the various parts assembled into the car has been changed.

Itemized Deductions

Itemized deductions are generally deductible if they are more than the standard deduction. In 2013, the itemized deduction phase-out is reinstated at a threshold of $250,000 for singles; $300,000 for married filing jointly and surviving spouse; $275,000 for head-of-household; and $150,000 for married filing separately. Itemized deductions are reduced 3% of the amount by which adjusted gross income (AGI) exceeds the applicable threshold. However, the amount of itemized deductions is not reduced by more than 80%. In 2012, there was no phase-out of itemized deductions.

Under the "tax benefit" rule, if you claimed a deduction for an amount that produced a tax benefit to you in the previous year (meaning it reduced the amount of income tax you paid), and you recover that amount or a portion of that amount, you must include the recovered amount in income and pay tax on it in the current year. This usually applies to refunds from state income taxes claimed as an itemized deduction in the previous year. If you deducted an amount in a previous year, and that deduction produced no tax benefit to you, then you can exclude the recovery of that amount from income in the current year.

Medical Expenses
Medical expenses that are more than 10% of adjusted gross income (AGI) are deductible as an itemized deduction in 2013, except individuals who are age 65 and over can still deduct medical expenses that are more than 7.5% of AGI until 2016. Deductible medical expenses include the following:
- Health insurance premiums paid by a taxpayer, <u>unless paid with pretax dollars</u>, are deductible. Medicare Part B premiums are deductible. Premiums that cover more than health and long-term care insurance (i.e. life insurance) are not deductible, unless the separate items can be identified.
- Deductible long-term Care Insurance premiums in 2013: $360 age 40 or less; $680 age 41-50; $1,360 age 51 - 60; $3,640 age 61 - 70; and $4,550 over age 70. Deductible long-term Care Insurance premiums in 2012: $350 age 40 or less; $660 age 41-50; $1,310 age 51-60; $3,500 age 61-70; and $4,370 over age 70. **Proceeds from long-term care insurance are not taxable**.
- The cost of prescription medications that are not reimbursed by insurance are deductible.
- Doctor, dentist, and chiropractor expenses that are not reimbursed by insurance are deductible.
- Expenditures incurred as a medical necessity are fully deductible in the year paid, i.e. glasses, hearing aids, guide dogs, artificial teeth and limbs, wheelchairs, crutches, the cost of a chairlift on the stairs, bandages etc.
- Medical mileage including round trips to the doctor, dentist, pharmacy, dialysis, etc. is deductible. The medical mileage rate for <u>2013 is $.24</u> a mile ($.23 in 2012). In addition, the cost

of any other transportation is deductible, as is lodging @ $50 per night for 2 people while away from home – but not meals. Parking and tolls are also deductible. Travel costs may or may not be deductible, i.e. travel costs to accompany a child who needs medical care and to visit a patient if the visitation is recommended as part of the treatment can be deductible. It is up to you to show that travel was medically necessary and not just your personal choice.

- Expenses of a rehabilitation facility for substance abuse are deductible medical expenses.
- The cost of weight loss programs to treat obesity or hypertension is deductible, and if a doctor puts you on a special diet, even the extra dollars spent for groceries is deductible.
- The cost of stop-smoking programs is deductible.
- If you can get a prescription from a doctor, the cost of some over-the-counter drugs, such as Motrin, are deductible.
- Insulin is deductible, even without a prescription.
- Expenses for a legal abortion are deductible.
- The cost of breast pumps is a deductible medical expense.
- Lasik eye surgery is a deductible medical expense.
- Blood sugar kits for diabetics are deductible.
- Birth control pills, fertility enhancement, and pregnancy test kits are deductible medical expenses.
- <u>Medical expenses of a qualifying child can be claimed, even if you can't claim the child as a dependent</u>.
- Medical expenses of a qualifying relative who is not your child can be claimed, even if you can't claim the relative as a dependent due to the gross income test ($3,900). <u>You must furnish more than ½ of the support of the relative, i.e. mother, in order to claim the deduction</u>.
- You can claim the medical expenses of a supported person who doesn't meet the relationship test, if you live in the same household and the other tests are met.
- Capital expenditures for removing barriers in the home of a physically handicapped person are deductible. A capital expenditure <u>deduction is limited to the extent the improvement does not add value to the home</u>. That is, expenditures that permanently improve a taxpayer's property as well as providing medical care (i.e. swimming pools and spas) are currently deductible only to the extent that the amount of the expenditure exceeds the increase in the fair market value (FMV) of the residence. Also, the cost of heating the pool, pool chemicals, and a proportionate part of insuring the pool area are treated as medical expenses. <u>However, if an expense is to accommodate a disability, a home improvement is treated as not increasing the value of a home</u>.
- Medical services, meals, and lodging in nursing homes, convalescent homes, and special schools for the mentally or physically handicapped are deductible if obtaining medical care is the primary reason for admission. <u>If obtaining medical care is not the primary reason for admission (i.e. an assisted living facility), then institutional care that represents medical or nursing care,</u>

but not the portion that represents living expenses, is deductible. Example: medical care is the primary reason for admission if a person is unable to perform at least 2 of 6 specified daily living activities, such as eating, toileting, transferring, bathing, dressing, and continence, due to a loss of functional capacity or requiring substantial supervision to protect the individual from threats to health and safety due to severe cognitive impairment.
    - Medicare does not pay for long-term care, but will pay for related expenses for a period of at least 90 days. Ways to pay for long-term care are the following: out-of-pocket (personal resources); long-term care insurance; and Medicaid for those who fall below certain income and asset limits.
    - Seniors who move into a retirement community where the entrance fees and the monthly residential fees include assisted living and skilled nursing support as part of what are considered lifetime care benefits may be able to include between 30 to 40 percent of the fees paid as allowable medical expenses. Also, children who provide more than half of the support of their parents moving into these communities may be able include a portion of the fees as allowable medical expenses.
- Qualified long-term care expenses required by a chronically ill person for in-home personal care under a prescribed plan of care by a licensed physician (diagnostic, therapeutic, rehabilitative, and personal care services) are deductible. A U.S. Tax Court decision held that a person was qualified as a chronically ill individual because she required substantial in-home care and supervision to protect her from threats to her health and safety due to her severe cognitive impairment (dementia, impaired speech, and confusion). The court held that the services provided by the caregivers were necessary maintenance and personal care services to assist her with daily living activities and that she required because of her diminished capacity and the risk of falling, and that they were provided pursuant to a care plan prescribed by her physician, and the individuals providing the care didn't have to be licensed. Therefore they were qualified long-term care services, and the payments to the caregivers for their services and the payments to the physician both qualified as deductible medical expenses.
- Transgender surgery **may be deductible**. For example, a man who felt he was a woman trapped in a male body was diagnosed with gender-identity disorder. He tried to deduct $22,000 in medical costs for multiple surgeries, including hormone therapy, sexual-reassignment surgeries, and breast augmentation, in order to become a woman. The U.S. Tax Court allowed the costs of the hormone therapy and sex-change operation - a total of $14,500 - as qualified medical expenses because those procedures helped treat a disease, but the court disallowed the cost of breast augmentation, saying it was nondeductible cosmetic surgery.

Expenses that are not deductible or may not be deductible:
- Cosmetic surgery is not deductible unless necessary to correct a deformity arising from a congenital abnormality, personal injury resulting from an accident or trauma, or a disfiguring disease.
- Teeth whitening is not deductible.
- Infant formula is not a medical expense.
- Costs of in vitro fertilization have generally been held deductible only when necessary to overcome infertility. Expenses incurred in fathering children through unrelated gestational carriers via in vitro fertilization of an anonymous donor's eggs using the taxpayer's sperm are not deductible.
- Surrogate parenting expenses are not eligible for the adoption credit. Thus, the adoption expenses related to the partner who provided biological material (sperm or egg) are not eligible for the credit. **However, expenses related to a second-parent adoption are deductible as medical expenses for the parent with no biological connection, regardless of surrogacy (for instance, in the case of a same-sex couple).**
- No medical deduction is allowed for payment of medical expenses with money from a withdrawal of the cash surrender value of a life insurance contract. Instead, the amount is not included in income and the investment in the contract is reduced by that amount. **(SEE "Taxable Income," Cash Surrender Value of a Life Insurance Policy)**
- **Funeral expenses are not deductible as medical expenses.**

Other related provisions:
- Reimbursements received in excess of medical expenses are not taxable, unless your employer paid all or part of your health insurance premiums, then part must be included in gross income.
- Reimbursements for medical expenses, received in the next year, are taxable if beneficial to taxpayer in prior year (deducted as medical itemized deductions in prior year).
- Life insurance policies with an accelerated death benefit clause allows lifetime distributions for those who are terminally ill (someone with a condition expected to result in death within 24 months) or chronically ill. Such payments to a terminally ill person are tax free, as well as payments to chronically ill persons for long-term care expenses. Payments made to chronically ill individuals on a per diem basis without regard to care costs are excludable from income up to a set dollar amount. If benefits exceed this limit, the excess is excludable to the extent used to pay for long-term care services. **(See "Income Exclusions," Life Insurance Proceeds Received by a Beneficiary in a Lump-Sum Payment)**
- With or without an accelerated death benefit clause, it may be possible to sell a life insurance policy to pay for long-term care. Proceeds from the sale of a life insurance policy paid to a terminally ill individual are not taxable. Proceeds paid to a chronically ill individual are tax-free to the same extent as accelerated death benefits.

Taxes
There is no threshold for claiming allowable taxes, which include the following:
- Real property taxes paid on real estate not used for business is deductible in the year paid – this includes property taxes paid on your principal residence and a vacation home, as well as on unimproved land, if considered a personal asset. For example, if you purchase land because you think it would be a good place to build a home and that is also a good investment, you can deduct the property taxes and mortgage interest. But taxes paid on unimproved land that is considered investment property is a miscellaneous itemized deduction subject to the 2% floor. Property taxes paid by the seller of a house for a buyer, and vice versa, shown on a closing statement are not deductible, but such taxes should reduce the amount realized by the seller and the adjusted basis of the house for buyer. Deductibility of real property taxes is not limited to two properties or houses owned by a taxpayer. In order to be deductible, property taxes must be based on the assessed value of a property. Special assessments or service charges are not deductible. Automobile taxes paid based on the value of a car are deductible, but not other taxes, such as annual license fees that are not based on the value of a car.
    - Unmarried co-owners of a property can allocate real property taxes based on any reasonable method such as: the amount of payments during the year; or the percentage of home ownership, i.e. if the home is owned 50/50, then each owner can deduct half of the property tax payments regardless of which one actually made the payments.
- State and local income taxes are deductible in the year paid. State and local income tax refunds received in the next year are taxable only if they gave rise to a tax benefit in the prior year (deducted as an itemized deduction).
- Sales taxes are deductible in lieu of state and local income taxes in 2012 and 2013. Actual sales taxes paid in a year are deductible, or you can use the "Sales Tax Tables" provided by the IRS, which are based on a taxpayer's adjusted gross income (AGI). If the tables are used, sales taxes paid on large ticket items may be added to the table amounts. Large ticket items are: cars, other motor vehicles, boats, mobile homes, major home improvements, etc. The sales tax deduction usually benefits taxpayers who live in states that do not have state income taxes, such as Texas. Example: the Sales Tax Table for Texas is based on the state tax rate of 6.25%, so the local tax of 2.00% must be added to get the total tax rate of 8.25% paid in Texas. **NOTE**: Non-taxable income items can be added back to AGI in order to determine allowable sales taxes from the Sales Tax Tables: tax-exempt interest; veterans' benefits; nontaxable combat pay; workers' compensation; the nontaxable portion of Social Security/railroad retirement income; nontaxable part of IRA, pension, and annuity distributions; etc.
- Income taxes paid on foreign source income are deductible, if you do not opt for the "foreign tax credit." However, usually the foreign tax credit is more beneficial to the taxpayer. The

amount of foreign tax that qualifies for the deduction is not necessarily the amount of tax withheld by the foreign country, i.e. certain adjustments may be required. **(SEE "Tax Credits," Non-Refundable Tax Credits, Foreign Tax Credit)**
- If you pay the real estate taxes of a relative who is not your dependent, such as a daughter, the relative can deduct the taxes on his/her tax return because your payment is considered a "gift" to your daughter. And if the payments are less than $14,000, you do not have to file a gift tax return.

Mortgage Interest

There is no threshold for claiming allowable mortgage interest. Interest on a mortgage loan is deductible on two residences – principal residence, and a second residence or vacation home. A residence is defined as a house, condominium, cooperative unit, mobile home, house trailer, or a house boat that has sleeping, cooking, and toilet facilities. **There is no requirement that the home be located within the United States.** Deductible mortgage interest is reported by the mortgage company on Form 1098. Maximum qualifying mortgages available for deductible interest are $1 million on a principal residence and a second residence, and $100,000 on home equity loans. The deduction of interest on a home equity loan cannot exceed the appraised value of the home (original loan + home equity loan = appraised value). The IRS has ruled that a taxpayer who purchases a home and has a mortgage larger than the $1 million can treat the first $100,000 in excess of the $1 million limit as home equity indebtedness, because it is other debt secured by the home. This allows a taxpayer to deduct interest on $ 1.1 million of an initial mortgage loan.

- Points paid to purchase a principal residence are deductible in the year of purchase (including loan origination fees). However, points paid to purchase a second home (vacation home) are not currently deductible, but instead must be deducted ratably over the term of the loan. **Also, points paid to refinance an existing mortgage must be deducted ratably over the term of the loan.** But, if a loan is paid off, you can deduct the balance of the points in the year the loan is paid off, with one exception – if you refinance a loan with the same lender, you have to add the points paid on the latest deal to the left over points from the previous financing and deduct that amount gradually over the life of the new loan. This rule also applies to refinancing a loan on a second home if you refinance the loan with the same lender.
- Interest on a **home equity loan** is allowed for a principal residence and one other residence, even if the home equity loan is used for other than home improvement expenses such as to purchase a car, other personal expenses, etc. However, it is not deductible for alternative minimum tax (AMT) purposes if used to purchase a car or for some other purpose other than home improvement. Also, a boat with cooking and bathroom facilities is not considered a second home for AMT purposes.
- If you refinance your home mortgage and increase the amount of the loan and use the extra amount to improve your principal residence, your new mortgage is considered to have two

separate parts for tax purposes – the first part equals the refinanced balance from your old loan and is considered home-acquisition debt; and the second part equals the cash you took out when you refinanced to improve the residence. Thus, you may be able to deduct the points paid on the second part of the loan. But if the extra amount is used to pay-off a credit card balance (for example), you cannot deduct the points on the second part of the loan. Remember that home-equity debt that is not used to pay for home improvements cannot be deducted interest for AMT purposes.

- A taxpayer who files separately is limited to a $500,000 home mortgage interest deduction and a $50,000 home-equity interest deduction on a residence (no exceptions).
- Unmarried co-owners with total mortgages exceeding $1.1 million on their first and second homes must allocate the limit between them and deduct only a proportionate share of the interest paid. The allocation can be based on any reasonable method such as: the amount of mortgage payments during the year; or the percentage of home ownership, i.e. if the home is owned 50/50, then each owner can deduct half of the total mortgage payments regardless of which one actually made the payments. The same allocation rule applies to real estate taxes paid (see above). In Sophy vs. the Commissioner (2012), the U.S. Tax Court ruled that the $1,100,000 limitation on mortgage debt must be applied on a per-residence basis, rather than on a per-taxpayer basis. In Sophy, this issue was surprisingly addressed for the first time in the courts.
- You can also deduct mortgage points paid by the seller on your behalf (stated on the settlement statement) to sweeten the deal. However, this position is **contrary to another position taken which states that the buyer cannot deduct points paid by the seller but instead has to reduce the adjusted basis of the residence by such amount, and the seller cannot deduct the points but instead must treat the points paid as a selling expense**.
- Qualified mortgage insurance premiums are deductible as home mortgage interest from 2007 through 2013 – including premiums paid or accrued on qualified mortgage insurance obtained in connection with acquisition indebtedness on a qualified residence (provided by the VA, FHA, and the Rural Housing Administration) and required as Private Mortgage Insurance (PMI). The mortgage insurance contract must have been issued after 2006. However, for every $1,000 by which the taxpayer's AGI exceeds $110,000, the amount of premiums treated as interest is reduced by 10%. For married filing separately, the 10% phase-out applies to every $500 that AGI exceeds $55,000. If you prepay a mortgage insurance premium that is allocable to periods that extend beyond the year in which it was paid, you must allocate the premium over the shorter of (1) the mortgage's stated term, or (2) 84 months, beginning with the month the insurance was obtained.
- You can deduct mortgage interest you paid, even if you are not the legal owner of the residence, if you occupied the residence and made the mortgage payments.

- A second home is considered a residence if the number of days it is used for personal use <u>exceeds</u> the greater of 14 days, or 10% of the number of days during the year it is rented at fair rental value. Personal use includes any day the property is used for personal purposes by the taxpayer or taxpayer's family (however, does not count if family member pays a fair rental). If a property qualifies as a residence and is rented for less than 15 days during the year, the property is considered completely personal in nature and no rental income is reported nor expenses deducted. Taxpayers can deduct all taxes and mortgage interest paid on a second residence as itemized deductions.
- When a taxpayer owns a residence that his former spouse lives in, he/she may be entitled to deduct the mortgage interest and real estate taxes as itemized deductions if the house qualifies either as his/her principal or secondary residence. The house qualifies as a second home if at least one of the taxpayer's children is living in the house.
- You are allowed a mortgage interest deduction for a house even though it is never built. Interest is deductible on a loan for 24 months after construction begins or for 24 months after the teardown date if you are replacing an existing structure. IRS regulations on deducting interest on a loan for a home under construction don't condition deductibility on the house's completion. After the 24 month period, the interest paid is nondeductible personal interest.
- Reverse Mortgage – No payments are required, so there is no tax deduction. A reverse mortgage is a bank loan secured by the house. The money is received up-front in a lump sum or in increments for life. The money received is tax free and can be used for any purpose (unlike a regular mortgage), including investments. When you move or die, the mortgage is paid off from the proceeds of the sale of the house. If the proceeds are greater than the mortgage balance (which includes the interest that has built up), you or your heirs would receive a check for the difference. If the proceeds are less than the mortgage balance, the bank eats the loss. You must be at least age 62 to obtain a reverse mortgage.

Investment Interest
Investment interest on indebtedness to carry portfolio investments, except for tax-exempt securities, is deductible only to extent of investment income. Any amount not deductible is carried over to subsequent years.

Charitable Contributions
Total charitable contributions are limited to 50% of adjusted gross income (AGI) – any excess over 50% of AGI can be carried forward for 5 years in the same category. Donation of capital gain property (shares of stocks, etc.) to a public charity is limited to the lesser of fair market value (FMV) or 30% of AGI, unless the contribution is limited to its adjusted basis, in which case it is limited to 50% of AGI. Donation of capital gain property to a private non-operating foundation is limited to 20% of AGI. Taxpayers must have written proof of <u>all</u> cash contributions no matter how small – must have a bank

record, credit card statement, or written communication from the charity showing the name of the charity and the date and amount of the contribution (you can write your own receipt and have them sign it). Before 2007, separate cash donations of less than $250 could be backed up with personal diaries or notes (also applied to non-cash contributions). **Any separate contribution over $250 must also have an acknowledgment letter from the charity, and the letter must be dated by the date your return is filed**.

For <u>non-cash contributions</u>, taxpayers must have a paper trail for any donation, no matter how small (receipt from charitable organization). For any <u>separate</u> (separate date) donation of property or any other type of non-cash contribution of $250 or more, a taxpayer needs a signed receipt from the charity showing: description of property donated; and a statement of estimated value (taxpayer can prepare the receipt and have charity sign it). For payroll deductions, the taxpayer should retain a pay stub, a Form W-2 or other document furnished by the employer showing the total amount withheld for a charity, along with the pledge card showing the name of the charity. If non-cash contributions are more than $500 for the year, taxpayer must file Form 8283, providing dates of donations, names and addresses of charities, and descriptions of donated property. In addition, if any <u>one</u> donation (separate date) is $500 or more, you must provide the date acquired, how acquired, and cost or adjusted basis of donated property. Pledges to a charitable organization are not deductible until payment is made to the charity.

- Contribution of capital gain property (shares of stocks held more than one year, etc.) and other non-cash property – taxpayer can deduct the FMV and avoid paying capital gains tax, unless the charitable organization promptly sells the asset, in which case the taxpayer can only deduct the adjusted basis. <u>It is a tax advantage to donate stock rather than to sell it and give the proceeds to a charity because you don't have to pay capital gains tax on the donated stock</u>.
- Fair market value (FMV) is generally the price at which property would change hands between a willing buyer and a willing seller, neither having to buy or sell, and both having reasonable knowledge of all the relevant facts.
- **For individual donations of $250 or more, including cash contributions, Sec. 170(f)(8) contains more stringent substantiation requirements**, i.e. the donor must obtain a contemporaneous written acknowledgment, stating the amount of the donation, in whole or in part, <u>and a good-faith estimate of the value of any goods and services the organization provided in exchange for the contribution. If goods or services received consist solely of intangible religious benefits, the contemporaneous documentation must contain a statement to that effect</u>. Example – in Durden, T.C. Memo 2012-140, the U.S. Tax Court denied the Durdens a charitable contribution deduction because the statement from their church did not contain the required statement regarding whether goods or services were received in consideration for their contributions (<u>most of their individual contributions to the church exceeded $250</u>). The IRS disallowed the deduction even after the Durdens subsequently obtained a second written acknowledgment

from their church with the required language, because the statement was not before the earlier of the date of filing or the extended due date, including extensions, and the Tax Court agreed with the IRS.
- Contribution of ordinary income property (i.e. inventory and short-term capital gain property) is valued at the lesser of FMV or the adjusted basis (essentially your cost).
- Donations of motor vehicles (including automobiles, boats, airplanes, and motorcycles) cannot exceed the gross proceeds, if sold by the charitable organization. **The charitable organization must complete and send to the IRS Form 1098-C**, Contributions of Motor Vehicles, Boats, and Airplanes, with Copy B of the form sent to the donor as written acknowledgment of the donation. And the donor must attach the acknowledgment to his tax return. The donor can deduct the lesser of the FMV of the vehicle, or what the charitable organization sells it for. The limit on the donation of a vehicle is $500 unless more is provable. Form 1098-C includes the following information: (1) date vehicle was sold, (2) certification that it was sold in an arms-length transaction, (3) gross proceeds from sale, and (4) a statement that the deductible amount may not exceed gross proceeds. If the charitable organization actually uses the vehicle (does not sell it), donates it to a needy individual in direct furtherance of its charitable purpose, or sells it for significantly less than FMV to such an individual, the gross sales proceeds limitation does not apply and you should be able to deduct the FMV, but must have proof of use by the organization. Use by the organization includes: makes a significant intervening use of, or material improvement to vehicle (must have a statement to that effect). Example: may claim FMV if church gave the car to a needy family and certifies in a letter that the disposition of the car was in furtherance of the church's charitable purpose.
    - For vehicles with a claimed value of $500 or less, only the general substantiation requirements are required for non-cash contributions. You must have an acknowledgement of the donation from the charitable organization.
    - <u>If the charity sells your vehicle for $500 or less, you can deduct $500 or your vehicle's FMV, whichever is less. For example, if your vehicle is valued at $650 and the charity sells it for $350, you can deduct $500.</u>
    - Vehicles are an exception to the requirement to have a qualified appraisal if the FMV is more than $5,000, as long as the written acknowledgment by the organization states that the vehicle was sold without significant intervening use or material improvement and the donor deducts no more than the amount of the sale proceeds. <u>However, if the vehicle has a claimed value of more than $5,000 and the organization does not sell the vehicle, the appraisal requirements apply</u>.
    - An accepted measure of the FMV of a donated car is an amount not in excess of the price listed in an established used vehicle pricing guide, such as Kelley Blue Book or the National Automobile Dealers Association Used Car Guide for a **private party sale**.

- - There are potentially severe penalties for fraudulent acknowledgments of vehicle donations or for failing to provide a Form 1098-C or other proper acknowledgment to the donor and to the IRS where required.
- For donations of other property (besides cars), FMV is normally deductible, but there are instances where the allowable deduction must be reduced to the adjusted basis, i.e. the charitable organization disposes of property before the last day of the taxable year in which the contribution was made.
- To be deductible, used clothing and household items (furniture, electronics, appliances and linens) donated to charity must be in good used condition or better (should be stated on receipt). There is no fixed formula or method for determining value, but the IRS suggests that you use the value that would be set by a consignment or thrift shop. Both Goodwill and the Salvation Army have online guides. However, a taxpayer may claim a deduction of $500 or more for any single item, regardless of condition, if taxpayer includes a qualified appraisal of the item with the return.
- Taxpayers are required to obtain a qualified appraisal for donations of property with a value of $5,000 or more and attach an appraisal summary to the tax return. For 2007 and later, a qualified appraisal must be conducted by a qualified appraiser in accordance with generally accepted appraisal standards (consistent with the Uniform Standards of Professional Appraisal Practice).
- You cannot deduct the value of volunteer work you perform for a charity, but you can deduct any unreimbursed expenses incurred during such work, such as charity related volunteer work mileage and any other transportation, lodging, and 50% of meals. Charitable mileage rate - $.14 per mile (2013 and 2012). The charitable mileage rates can be used regardless of the method used to compute depreciation for the business use of a car, or you can claim actual expenses attributable to charitable trips - gas, oil, insurance, and repairs (based on the percentage of charitable miles driven compared to total miles driven in the year). Parking and toll fees are in addition to the $.14 per mile charitable mileage rate for a car. Since there is no standard meal allowance for charitable travel, a taxpayer must keep very good records. If you're required to wear a uniform or other special clothing - such as a troop leader for the Boy Scouts - you may deduct the cost as long as it's not suitable for everyday wear. In addition, the cost of cleaning counts. You can't deduct the cost of a cell phone, but additional costs for long-distance phone calls are deductible. Reimbursement for expenses is included in income. (SEE "Employee Travel and Entertainment Expenses," Claiming Travel and Entertainment Expenses, and Vehicle and Other Transportation Expenses)
  - Example: if you travel to Africa on a mission trip for your church and you pay for the airfare, you can deduct the cost of the airfare (along with meals and other trip expenses you incur) as an unreimbursed out-of-pocket expense for the charity if the travel did not have any significant element of personal pleasure, recreation, or vacation. If the cost of

- the airfare (and other expenses) is $250 or more, you must obtain a written acknowledgment from the charity.
    - When you host a gathering at you home to promote charitable fundraising, you can deduct the cost as a charitable expense <u>without regard to the usual 50% limit on entertainment expenses</u>. You can deduct the costs associated with attending a convention on behalf of a charitable organization if you've been designated as an official delegate to the convention. This includes meals and lodging while you're staying at the convention.
    - Fees paid to a baby sitter to enable a parent to get out of the house and do volunteer work for a charity are deductible, even though the money didn't go directly to the charity, according to the U.S. Tax Court. The court expressly rejected a contrary IRS ruling.
    - You can deduct the cost of paper, postage, and other out-of-pocket costs incurred while sending out mailings on behalf of a charity - even amounts spent on paper clips and staples.
    - <u>You cannot deduct: your personal expenses, i.e. the cost of meals while you're volunteering (deductibility of meals is generally allowed only while on trips away from home); contributions to a group created to lobby for law changes; and contributions to homeowner associations, social or sport clubs, civic leagues or chambers of commerce.</u>
- Contributions to domestic tax-exempt, charitable organizations that provide assistance to individuals in foreign countries qualify as tax deductible, provided a U.S. organization has control and discretion over the use of the funds. Certain organizations such as churches or governmental organizations may be qualified to accept charitable contributions even though they are not listed. To ensure the deductibility of donations, confirm that the charity is a U.S. based charity.
- <u>You can deduct $50 a month in qualifying expenses as a charitable contribution for foreign exchange students living with you</u>. The student must be residing in your home under a written agreement with a qualified charitable organization. And if a foreign exchange student lives with you for 15 days or more, that counts as a full month.
- No charitable deduction is allowed for contribution of any interest in property that is less than the entire interest in the property unless the transfer meets the requirements for a charitable remainder annuity trust, a charitable remainder trust, or a pooled income fund. Contributions to "Donor Advised Funds" are allowed if a charity gains legal ownership and control of the contributions.
- Continued for 2013, an IRA owner, age 70 ½ or over, can directly transfer up to $100,000 tax-free from an IRA (that would otherwise be taxable) to an eligible charity. Such transfers are not deductible as charitable contributions. Distributions from employer-sponsored retirement plans, including SIMPLE IRAs and SEPs are not eligible for such transfers.

- Airline miles earned for making purchases on a credit card can be used or donated to a charity, and if donated to a charity it is considered a charitable contribution deduction provided substantiation rules for written acknowledgment from the charity are followed for amounts of $250 or more. Also, credit card rebates are not included in gross income, even though they may be claimed as a charitable contribution if so directed.
- The purchase of a raffle ticket is not a charitable contribution. <u>A losing raffle ticket paid to a charity is a gambling loss, not a charitable contribution</u>.
- Donation of the use of a timeshare as a prize in a charity's auction is <u>not</u> an allowable charitable contribution.
- **If you receive a benefit because of your cash or other contribution, such as merchandise, tickets to a ball game, or other goods and services, then you can deduct only the amount of the contribution that exceeds the FMV of the benefit received.**
- It is common practice for persons who purchase season tickets to college football games to get a charitable donation. Here's how it works. You pay $1,640 to buy tickets to 8 games, but to get the tickets, you are required to donate an additional $3,700. You are allowed to write off 80% of that, or $2,950, as a charitable contribution.
- <u>Cash donations by C-corporations are limited annually to 10% of taxable income.</u>
- If you are thinking about selling your company, a charitable remainder trust is an option that helps reduce your payout to the IRS. Charitable remainder trusts allow you to significantly reduce your tax and ensure that you receive regular income in return for donating cash, securities, or real estate to a charity. Because you are giving assets to charity, you qualify for a charitable deduction on your income tax return.
- Only donations to qualified organizations are tax-deductible. You can check whether an organization is qualified on a searchable online database available on IRS.gov, which lists most organizations that are qualified to receive deductible contributions. In addition, churches, synagogues, temples, mosques and government agencies are eligible to receive deductible donations, even if they are not listed in the database.
- Any contribution you make to reduce the national debt burden is deductible as a charitable contribution. You should make the payment as a separate check payable to the Bureau of Public Debt and send it to: Bureau of the Public Debt, Department G, P.O. Box 2188, Parkersburg, W.Va. 26106-2188, or you can stick the check in your tax return envelope.
- <u>The American Taxpayer Relief Act of 2012 extends for two years, through 2013, the special rule for contributions of capital gain real property for conservation purposes. The special rule allows a charitable contributions of up to 50% of the contribution base. The Act also extends for two years the special rules for contributions by certain corporate farmers and ranchers.</u> **(SEE "Carrying on a Trade or Business," Profit or Loss From Farming)**

Casualty, Disaster, and Theft Losses

Non-business casualty, disaster, and theft losses are deductible in the year discovered. Losses are no longer restricted to natural disasters and include financial losses from theft and other crimes. The aggregate of all losses during the year must be more than 10% of adjusted gross income (AGI), and in addition, each separate casualty or theft loss must be more than $100 to be deductible. A total or partial non-business casualty or theft loss is defined as the lesser of the adjusted basis of a property or item, or the difference in its FMV immediately before and after the loss (decline in FMV is provable by necessary repairs). Theft includes the illegal taking of money or property – it is limited to larceny, embezzlement, and robbery. In the case of misrepresentation, there must be intent to defraud. Also, you can cause your own damage and perhaps still be eligible to take the deduction, i.e. Justin Rohrs, a California resident, successfully claimed a casualty loss deduction for wrecking his car while legally drunk, after taking his case to court. The judge found that his decision to drive after drinking, though negligent, did not automatically rise to the level of gross negligence. All losses whether non-business (personal) or business are computed on Form 4684. Non-business losses are reported in Section B of Form 4684, and then entered on Schedule A, Form 1040. If you have a loss caused by a disaster in a federally declared disaster area, a special rule allows you to claim your rightful deduction either in this year (year in which the disaster happened) or last year. If necessary, you can file an amended return for last year.

- If your loss deduction is more than your income, you may have a "net operating loss" (NOL). The loss can either be a non-business or a business casualty loss. **(SEE "Taxable Income," Net Operating Loss)**
- There is no limitation on the amount that can be deducted for business casualty and theft losses. A total business loss is the adjusted basis of a property or item, even if the FMV of the property is less immediately before the loss. A partial business casualty or theft loss is defined as the lesser of the adjusted basis of a property or item, or the difference in its FMV immediately before and after the loss (decline in FMV is provable by necessary repairs, etc). Business losses (property used in a trade or business) are reported in Section B of Form 4684, and then taken as a loss on Form 4797. <u>However if property is for sale, i.e. income producing property, the loss is reported as a miscellaneous itemized deduction not subject to the 2% floor</u>. You must capitalize amounts paid to restore business property, including amounts paid "for the repair of damage to a unit of property" resulting from a disaster even if your casualty loss is ameliorated by insurance. Example: you have a property damaged by a hurricane that had a 15-year recovery period when placed in service 10 years ago and has been depreciated for 10 years. The cost to repair the property and its remaining basis are both $1 million. In this case, you have two alternatives: (1) you can claim a $1 million casualty loss and depreciate the property's remaining basis of $1 million over 15 years; or (2) You don't claim a casualty loss, but you can deduct the $1 million cost of the repair and continue to depreciate the $1 million

- remaining basis over the remaining 5 year recovery period. **(SEE "Carrying on a Trade or Business," Business Casualty and Theft Losses)**
- Based on Code Section 165(a), taxpayers may not claim a theft loss for a decline in the value of stock purchased on the open market due to misrepresentation of the financial status, fraud, or other illegal misconduct made by corporate officers, investment churning, and broker risk misrepresentations. **However, a loss as a result of a Ponzi scheme is allowed if the stock is worthless or has no recognizable value, but there must be evidence of a closed or completed transaction fixed by an identifiable event and actually sustained during the taxable year –** advantage: not subject to the $3,000 limitation on a capital losses (deducted as a miscellaneous itemized deduction not subject to the 2% floor. **(SEE "Taxable Income," Capital Gains and Losses)**
- Losses resulting from "Tax Shelters" are not deductible. In Vincentini v. Commissioner, the court ruled that an investor who thought he was buying tax benefits couldn't claim a theft loss when the investment imploded and the promoters went to jail. Tax shelters are defined by the tax code to include any plan or arrangement having a significant purpose of avoiding or evading federal income tax. <u>The key is whether the tax ramifications are the reason for entering into the transaction</u>.
- Damage to an individual's residence or appliances resulting from corrosive drywall made in China can be treated as a casualty loss in the year of payment for the repairs if the taxpayer does not have a pending claim for reimbursement (and does not intend to pursue reimbursement). If a taxpayer has a pending claim for reimbursement (or intends to pursue reimbursement), he may take advantage of the safe harbor method and claim a loss for 75% of the unreimbursed amount paid during the year for the repairs. The taxpayer may later have to include the amount of any recovery in gross income for amounts treated as a casualty loss in subsequent years or claim an additional casualty loss in subsequent years, depending on the actual amount of any reimbursement received.
- <u>Proving the amount of a casualty loss</u> – You have to prove two things: (1) that your loss was the result of a casualty event, such as a severe storm, mudslide, or fire; and (2) the amount of your financial loss from the casualty event. You'll need pictures, newspaper clippings, insurance claims, or other evidence that your property was damaged or destroyed by a casualty event. The trickiest part of claiming a casualty loss is proving the amount of the loss. You can't take into account any ascetic or sentimental value to you; it must be based solely on the facts. You can obtain an appraisal made by a qualified appraiser of the FMV. Instead of obtaining an appraisal, the cost of repairs to the damaged property is acceptable evidence of the loss in value – the repairs must relate only to the damage suffered in the casualty, and must be only those repairs necessary to restore the property to its pre-casualty condition.

Miscellaneous Itemized Deductions Subject to 2% AGI Floor
- Employee travel and entertainment expenses – Form 2106. **(SEE "Employee Travel and Entertainment Expenses")**
- A hobby is an activity that is deemed not to be a profit-motivated activity or business. Hobby expenses are deductible from adjusted gross income (AGI) as miscellaneous itemized deductions, but only to the extent of income from the activity. Hobby expenses must be deducted from hobby income in a certain order: (1) deductions you can take anyway, such as mortgage interest and real property taxes; (2) deductions such as advertising, insurance, and wages; and finally (3) depreciation. **(SEE "Carrying on a Trade or Business" - Business or Hobby)**
- Expenses to look for a new job in the same line of work – travel expenses, cost of resume, etc. Job hunting expenses incurred while looking for your first job don't qualify. Deductible job-search costs include, but aren't limited to: food, lodging and transportation if your search takes you away from home overnight; cab fares; employment agency fees; and costs of printing resumes, business cards, postage, and advertising (Form 2106 is required to report travel expenses). You can't deduct job search expenses if there was a substantial break between the end of your last job and the time you began looking for a new job. **(SEE "Employee Travel and Entertainment Expenses")**
- Work related education costs, but not education costs that qualify a person for a new profession, are generally deductible. The costs of educational expenses are generally deductible if the courses taken maintain or improve skills required by the individual's employment or trade or business or meets the express requirements of the individual's employer or the requirements of applicable law. If a college degree or courses taken will qualify an employee for a new trade or business or is required to meet the minimum education requirements for qualification in the individual's employment or trade or business, its costs are generally not deductible. However, a court held that a high school teacher's graduate school expenses were deductible, even though the teacher took a year off from teaching to pursue the studies full time and was not on a leave of absence. A suspension for a period of one year or less, after which the taxpayer returns to the same employment or profession, is considered temporary. NOTE: It is usually more advantageous to deduct education expenses incurred in pursuing a college degree, such as an MBA, as an above-the-line deduction for tuition and fees for higher education, or as an education tax credit rather than to deduct the expenses as a miscellaneous itemized deduction. However, any expenses not allowed by these two options may still be deducted as a miscellaneous itemized deduction. **(SEE "Deductions For Determining Adjusted Gross Income," Tuition and Fees for Higher Education; and "Tax Credits," Education Credits)**
- Dues and subscriptions for professional journals.
- Professional and trade association dues are deductible, but not social organization dues, such as country club dues, etc.

- Appraisal fees for casualty losses or charitable contributions.
- Union dues and costs.
- Special work clothes not suitable to wear off the job – special protective clothing and safety boots. Example: police officers and firemen qualify.
- Small tools necessary for employment
- Income tax preparation fees. NOTE: The portion of tax preparation fees related to Schedules C, E, and F are deductible for AGI on the relevant forms.
- Investment expenses – safe deposit boxes, IRA custodial fees, fees for investment advice, subscriptions to investment and financial planning journals, and clerical help and office rent in caring for investments. Mutual fund expenses are not deductible because they flow through, and the mutual funds report net income (income minus expenses). No deduction is allowed for attending conventions, seminars, or meetings related to income-producing (investment) activities.
- Real estate taxes paid on unimproved land that is considered investment property. Investment property is purchased primarily to realize appreciation in value. You can deduct expenses related to the land that you cannot deduct if considered personal use property, including association dues and maintenance expenses, etc. If you will not receive any benefit by itemizing these expenses, you can capitalize them and add them to the basis of the property.
- Employee home office expenses, if necessary and for the convenience of employer. Employees who are allowed to claim home office expenses are not required to file Form 8829 (a worksheet is provided). Instead the expenses are reported directly as miscellaneous itemized deductions, unless employee has to file Form 2106, in which case the home office expenses (figured on the worksheet provided) are reported on Line 4, Form 2106. **(SEE "Carrying on a Trade of Business," Sole Proprietors/Self Employed, Home Office Expenses)**
- Legal expenses to recover taxable job-related personal damages.
- Attorney fees paid in connection with a claim for disputed social security benefits due to a disability can be deducted as a miscellaneous itemized deduction if the benefits received are taxable, i.e. if only 50% of social security benefits are taxable, you can deduct 50% of attorney's fees.

Miscellaneous Itemized Deductions Not Subject to 2% AGI Floor
- Gambling losses, to the extent of gambling winnings. Excess losses cannot be carried forward into the next tax year.
- Disability or impairment related employee business expenses – business expenses incurred by physically or mentally disabled persons which are necessary to allow them to work. Attendant care services at a place of employment that are necessary for such a person to work are deductible.
- Casualty and theft loses from income producing properties (inventory, etc.).

- Deductions for federal estate taxes, i.e. you get a tax deduction for the amount of estate taxes paid on IRA assets you inherit. For example, you inherit a $100,000 IRA that added $45,000 to your benefactor's estate tax bill. You can deduct the $45,000 ratably as you withdraw money from the IRA.
- **95% of Ponzi Scheme losses (75% if part of a lawsuit against the organizers).** The loss includes your unrecovered investment, including any fictitious income you reported in prior years, but you can't amend prior years' tax returns to recover income taxes paid on fictitious income. <u>You can deduct the loss in the "discovery year", defined as the year in which criminal charges are filed against the lead figure(s)</u>. The deduction of Ponzi scheme losses is not subject to the $3,000 limitation on a capital losses. A Ponzi scheme is one in which a party receives cash or property from investors, reports false investment income amounts to the investors, and appropriates some or all of the investors' cash or property. A qualified loss from a Ponzi scheme is one caused by such fraudulent arrangement and results in federal or state criminal charges for theft (larceny, embezzlement, robbery and similar offenses) or a criminal complaint making such allegations. A complaint must also allege that the perpetrator admitted the conduct, or there must have been a receiver or trustee appointed or its assets must have been frozen. The loss is considered discovered and deductible when charges are brought and guilt is implied. <u>The loss is reported on Form 4684, Section B, rather than Section A</u>. The IRS recently broadened the definition of a qualified loss from a Ponzi scheme in two ways. First, by including schemes in which a <u>civil</u> complaint is brought against the lead figure by a state or federal authority that has not been withdrawn. Second, by making an exception for when a lead figure died and foreclosed all criminal charges. The death of the lead figure must preclude criminal charges against the figure, and assets of the arrangement must be frozen or be placed under a receiver's jurisdiction. **(SEE "Taxable Income" - Capital Gains and Losses)**
- Unrecovered investment in a decedent's pension.
- Deductions for amortizable bond premiums.

Tax Credits

All non-refundable tax credits are allowed against both regular tax and the alternative minimum tax (AMT). Refundable tax credits can offset other taxes, i.e. taxes on early distributions from employee retirement plans and IRAs, etc., and are not limited to an individual's tax liability for a year. Non-refundable tax credits are limited to an individual's tax liability for a year.

Refundable Tax Credits

Recapture of First-Time Homebuyer Credit (Form 5405)

The original first-time homebuyer credit was a maximum $7,500 tax credit available in 2008 that was in essence an interest-free loan that had to be repaid in equal installments over 15 years starting in 2010 ($500 a year over 15 years). However, if the taxpayer sold the home before the end of 15 years, repayment had to be accelerated, i.e. the entire remaining balance of the credit must be repaid in the year in which the sale or change in use occurs (limited to the amount of gain from the sale). If taxpayer dies, repayment is excused. If the home is rented out, then the total unpaid portion of the credit is due immediately. Couples who filed jointly in 2008 (when they received the credit) had to file two Forms 5405 beginning in 2010 to start paying back the credit, one for each taxpayer. Couples who filed jointly in 2010 but had a different filing status in 2008, and only one spouse received the credit, had to file just one Form 5405 in 2010 for the spouse who received the credit.

The second first-time home buyer credit was a maximum $8,000 tax credit for homes purchased after 12/31/2008 and before May 1, 2010, that must be recaptured if the home purchased ceases to be the principal residence of the taxpayer at any time within the 36 month period from the date of purchase. The recapture amount is shown as an addition to the taxpayer's income tax in the year the property is disposed of or ceases to be the taxpayer's principal residence. The recapture amount cannot exceed the amount of gain from the sale of the home to an unrelated 3rd party. However, in computing the gain the adjusted basis of the home must be reduced by the amount of the credit. Exceptions to credit recapture: death of the taxpayer; involuntary conversion if the taxpayer acquires a new residence within 2 years; and transfer between spouses incident to divorce.

Any recapture of the first-time home buyer credit is reported on Form 5405, Repayment of the First-Time Homebuyer Credit. However, for the first time in 2011, Form 1040 includes a separate line for first-time homebuyers to include either a normal installment repayment obligation or a repayment of the entire credit balance, possibly without having to file Form 5405.

Earned Income Credit (EIC)

The earned income credit is in effect through 2017. A taxpayer must be over age 24 and below age 65 to claim the EIC. The maximum Credit in 2013: $487 (no children); $3,250 (one qualifying child); $5,372 (two qualifying children); and $6,044 (three or more qualifying children). In order to claim the EIC, a taxpayer must have earnings from working for someone else or from his/her own business, i.e. you cannot claim the credit unless you have earned income. Unemployment benefits are not treated as earnings for EIC purposes. An election may be made to include tax-free combat pay, otherwise excluded from income, for EIC purposes. A taxpayer is not eligible for the EIC if has **disqualified income exceeding $3,300** in 2013 (both taxable and tax-exempt interest, dividends, net rent and royalty income, net capital gain income, and net passive income that is not self-employment income). Tax preparers must answer due diligence questions on Form 8867 and the form must be attached to clients' tax returns, or the preparer will be subjected to a $500 penalty for failure to comply. Here are the parameters for the EIC:

- No qualifying children – Maximum credit is 7.65% of earnings up to $6,366 = $487. Earnings must be less than $14,340; $19,680 for married filing jointly.
- One qualifying child – Maximum credit is 34% of earnings up to $9,559 = $3,250. Earnings must be less than $37,870; $43,210 for married filing jointly.
- Two qualifying children – Maximum credit is 40% of earnings up to $13,430 = $5,372. Earnings must be less than $43,038; $48,378 for married filing jointly.
- Three or more children – Maximum credit is increased to 45% of earnings up to $13,430 = $6,044. Earnings must be less than $46,227; $51,567 for married filing jointly.

- Qualifying children include foster children under age 19 or under 24 if a full-time student at least 5 months of the year who lives with the taxpayer more than ½ of the year (except for temporary absences such as school). Also, children who are permanently and totally disabled qualify at any age.
- **A child who provides more than ½ of his own support may be a qualifying child for purposes of the earned income credit (this is the only exception to the ½ support dependency exemption definition).**
- Taxpayers must file a joint return, unless lived apart for the last half of the year, in which case the custodial parent can claim the credit as head of household. If both parents are eligible and they do not file a joint return, the parent with whom the child resided the longest during the year may claim the credit. If the child lived with each parent for the same amount of time, the child will be treated as the qualifying child of the parent with the higher AGI. For divorced parents, the parent who has custody of a child for the longer period of time during the year (custodial parent) is entitled to the EIC, regardless of whether he/she can claim the child as a dependent.

Additional Child Tax Credit (Form 8812)

This is the refundable portion of the Child Tax Credit, if taxpayer cannot take advantage of the full amount of the child tax credit due to a limited amount of income tax liability. Form 8812 must be attached to tax return. The additional child tax credit is limited to the lesser of the forgone child tax credit or the larger of either 15% of a taxpayer's earned income above $3,000 or the sum of social security and Medicare taxes paid minus the earned income credit.

40% of the American Opportunity Education Credit

This is the refundable portion of the American Opportunity Education Credit, but no portion is refundable if the taxpayer claiming the credit is a child to whom the kiddie tax can be applied (a person under 19 or under 24 who is a student providing less than ½ of his or her own support, who has a living parent, and does not file a joint return). This refundable credit is extended through 2017.

Credit for Federal Tax Paid on Fuels (Form 4136)

This is a refundable credit for federal taxes paid on fuel used on a farm, for off-highway business use, and for other qualifying nontaxable uses (but not for personal use). No credit is allowed if the fuel or mixture is produced outside the United States for use outside the United States. The amount of the credit is determined by multiplying the number of gallons used by the applicable rate factor.

Health Coverage Tax Credit (HCTC)

The HCTC helps make health insurance more affordable for eligible individuals and their families by paying 72.5% of qualified health insurance premiums. ARRA increases the credit from 65% to 80%, and provides that, beginning in January 2010, qualified family members may continue receiving the credit for up to 24 months after the primary eligible individual experiences certain life events, including enrollment in Medicare, divorce, and death. Eligible individuals must be enrolled in a qualified health plan and be members of the following groups: eligible Trade Adjustment Assistance (TAA) recipients under Act Sec. 231 of the Trade Act of 1974; eligible alternative TAA recipients as defined under Act Sec. 246 of the Trade Act of 1974; and eligible Pension Benefit Guaranty Corporation (PBGC) recipients (IRC Par. 35).

AMT Credit (Form 8801)

The refundable AMT credit was enacted to give relief to individuals who exercised incentive stock options (ISO) that generated AMT credits that lost all or a significant portion of their value in later years due to the loss in value of the stocks. Since the difference between the fair market value (FMV) and the option price is a preference item for AMT purposes, these taxpayers paid an increased amount in tax and generated a credit for use in later years, when, hopefully, the stock was sold for a profit. The loss in value of the stocks resulted in these individuals being unable to use a portion, if any, of the sizable amounts of AMT credit to offset their tax liability, and they would carry the amount forward to the next year with the same results. <u>The minimum AMT credit allowed in a year is not less than the greater of the amount of the AMT refundable credit amount determined for the preceding year or 50% of the unused credit</u>. The unused credit is defined as that portion of the minimum tax credit attributable to the adjusted minimum tax for tax years before the third tax year immediately preceding such tax year. Thus, for 2013 taxpayers may be able to claim an amount for credits generated from paying the alternative minimum tax in 2009. To claim the AMT credit, including the refundable portion, taxpayers must complete Form 8801, Credit For Prior Year Minimum Tax - Individuals, Estates, and Trusts. The refundable credit is limited to the lesser of $30 million or 6% of the AMT credit carry forwards generated in tax years beginning before 1/1/2006 that were not used in tax years ending before April 1, 2008. <u>A taxpayer can claim an additional AMT credit in lieu of bonus depreciation. Taxpayers must agree to forgo the use of bonus depreciation on qualified property placed in service and instead depreciate it using the straight-line method.</u> **(SEE "Alternative Minimum Tax," and "Depreciation," Bonus Depreciation)**

Non-Refundable Tax Credits

Non-refundable personal tax credits are claimed in the following order: (1) foreign tax credit; (2) child and dependent care credit; (3) elderly and disabled credit; (4) adoption credit; (5) education credits; (6) savers credit; (7) child tax credit; (8) mortgage interest credit; (9) residential energy credits; (10) plug-in electric vehicle credits; (11) credit for prior year minimum tax; (12) general business credits.

Foreign Tax Credit (Form 1116)
A taxpayer who pays income taxes to a foreign government on foreign source income that is subject to U.S. taxes can either: deduct those taxes as an itemized deduction; or take the foreign tax credit. The foreign tax credit cannot exceed the amount of U.S. tax liability on the foreign income. Therefore, if a taxpayer receives foreign sourced qualified dividends and/or capital gains (including long-term capital gains, unrecaptured Section 1250 gains, and/or Section 1231 gains) that are taxed in the U.S. at a reduced rate, the taxpayer must adjust the foreign source income that is reported on Form 1116, line 1a. Otherwise, the allowable foreign tax credit may be significantly overstated which can trigger a substantial underpayment penalty. Also, interest expense must be apportioned between U.S. and foreign source income. The amount of foreign tax that qualifies for the credit is not necessarily the amount of tax withheld by the foreign country. If you are entitled to a reduced rate of foreign tax based on an income tax treaty between the U.S. and a foreign country, only that reduced tax qualifies for the credit. Also, if a foreign tax redetermination occurs, a redetermination of your U.S. tax liability is required in most situations. Foreign taxes that exceed the credit limitation can be carried back 2 years and forward 5 years. <u>It is usually better to take the foreign tax credit than an itemized deduction for the foreign taxes paid</u>. The credit is not allowable for taxes paid to countries the U.S. does not recognize. There is a separate AMT foreign tax credit.

Amounts paid to a foreign taxing authority that are attributable to a "structured passive investment arrangement" are not treated as an amount of tax paid for purposes of the foreign tax credit. Structured passive investment arrangements are generally designed to exploit differences between U.S. and foreign tax law by artificially creating a foreign tax liability that allows the U.S. party to claim a U.S. foreign tax credit and a foreign counterparty to claim a duplicative foreign tax benefit.

Child and Dependent Care Credit (Form 2441)
You can claim a credit for expenses incurred to care for a "qualifying child" while you are working, even if the child is not your dependent. The maximum credit available is on a sliding scale based on your AGI. For example, if your AGI is more than $43,000, the maximum credit is $600 for 1 child, and $1,200 for 2 or more children, based on 20% of expenses, up to $3,000 for 1 child, or $6,000 for 2 or more children. If your AGI is $15,000 or less, the maximum credit is $1,050 for 1 child, and $2,100 for 2 or more children, based on 35% of the same maximum expenses. The credit was made permanent as of Jan. 1, 2013.

- The credit is for children under 13, or dependents of any age, including a spouse or parent who lives with you, who are physically or mentally incapable of self-care. Dependents must have the same principal place of abode as the taxpayer for more than ½ the year, and dependents other than qualifying children must not have gross income in excess of the personal exemption ($3,900 in 2013). The Care-taker can be a relative.
- **Taxpayer can claim the credit even if he/she did not provide more than ½ of the cost of maintaining a household for the child. For example, a taxpayer who lived with a qualifying child in the home of another family member can still claim the credit.**
- In order to claim the credit, both parents must be gainfully employed or are looking for work, but you can claim the credit if one parent is a full-time student or is incapacitated. You are not required to allocate expenses for short, temporary absences from work such as vacations or minor illness (2 consecutive calendar weeks is OK). If one parent is a full-time student, his/her presumed income is $250 per month per child. The credit is limited to the lowest income of either parent.
- The credit goes to custodial parent (parent with whom child resides the longest during year), even if the other parent claims the child as a dependent. If divorced, the non-custodial parent is not entitled to any credit even if child resides with him/her for part of the year. The name, address, and taxpayer ID of the provider of child care services must be provided on Form 2441, unless it is an exempt organization in which case only the name and address must be provided.
- Expenses incurred for summer day camps and similar programs (soccer and computer camps) qualify for the credit, but expenses for summer school and tutoring programs do not qualify.
- Parents are not entitled to a credit for any portion of kindergarten or higher grades tuition or costs, even half-day sessions. But if parents pay other child care expenses before or after full or

half-day kindergarten sessions, those expenses are eligible for the credit. However, the cost of preschool does qualify for the credit.
- If taxpayer receives "dependent care benefits" under an employer provided dependent care assistance plan, the amount of employer paid benefits are shown in Box 10 of Form W-2. Taxpayer will owe taxes on those benefits, unless they are used for child care expenses. Taxpayer can only claim a credit for any amount paid for child care expenses that is more than the amount shown in Box 10 of the W-2.
- If you pay your child-care expenses through a pre-tax Flexible Spending Account (FSA) at work, which is limited to $2,500 in 2013, and you spend even more than that for child care, you can only get a credit for the difference between the amount actually spent and the $2,500. **(SEE "Income Exclusions," Contributions to Flexible Spending Accounts)**
- If you use a day care provider, get taxpayer identification information on Form W-10. **You have to have the provider's social security number or employer identification number, and their address in order to claim the credit on your tax return**.
- **If a dependent parent lives with you and requires continual care and you work, you can claim the dependent care credit for the cost of the care provided.**

Elderly and Disabled Credit (Schedule R)
You are eligible for the credit if you are age 65, or at any age if retired and permanently and totally disabled (inability to engage in gainful employment for a continuous 12-month period or have a condition that is expected to lead to death). The maximum credit is 15% of: $7,500 (married filing jointly/both eligible); $5,000 (married filing jointly/one eligible); or $3,750 (single/eligible living apart). Credit is available for low income persons with adjusted gross income less than the following: $17,500 (single); $20,000 (married filing jointly – one qualifies); $25,000 (married filing jointly – both qualify). You cannot take the credit if your non-taxable social security, pensions, and disability income is equal to or more than $5,000 (single and married filing jointly - one eligible) or $7,500 (married filing jointly - both qualify, and married filing separately).

Adoption Credit (Form 8839)
The adoption tax credit is nonrefundable in 2012 and 2013. The credit is available for expenses of adopting a child under 18, but there is an exception to this rule for children who are physically or mentally unable to care for themselves. The maximum credit for qualified adoption expenses in 2013 is $12,970 for a child with special needs, and $12,697 for other adoptions. The adoption credit was made permanent as of Jan. 1, 2013. Form 8839 is used to claim the credit, and the taxpayer has to attach certain documents to the tax return, which means **the tax return cannot be e-filed**. For domestic adoptions, you may be able to claim the credit even if the adoption is not finalized, but usually the credit is allowed in the year the adoption becomes final even if the expenses are paid in the prior year. The credit is allowed in the year after the adoption if the expenses occur then. If the adoption is

unsuccessful, the credit is allowed in the next tax year. For foreign adoptions, the credit is allowed in the year adoption becomes final. Allowable expenses include adoption fees, court costs, attorney fees, travel expenses, and certain other related expenses. <u>For adoption of special needs children you may claim the maximum credit, even if actual expenses are less</u>. The credit is not available to a taxpayer adopting a spouse's child. The credit begins to phase-out for taxpayers with MAGI in excess of $194,580, and completely phases-out for taxpayers with MAGI of $234,580.

- As a result of the ruling that married same-sex couples are recognized as married for federal income tax purposes, couples in which one same-sex spouse wishes to adopt the other spouse's child may lose out on the Adoption Tax Credit, because the credit isn't available when adopting a spouse's child.
- Surrogate parenting expenses are not eligible for the credit. Thus, the adoption expenses related to the partner who provided biological material (sperm or egg) are not eligible for the credit. However, expenses related to a second-parent adoption are <u>deductible medical expenses</u> for the parent with no biological connection, regardless of surrogacy (for instance, in the case of a same-sex couple).
- If your credit exceeds your tax, you may be able to carry forward the unused credit. This means that if you have an unused credit amount in 2013, you can use it to reduce your taxes for 2014. You can carry over an unused credit for up to five years or until you fully use the credit, whichever comes first.

Education Credits (Form 8863)
These can be claimed for taxpayer, spouse, and dependents. A person claiming a student as a dependent can claim the credit, not the student. If a third person pays the expenses, the student can claim the credit if not claimed as a dependent, but if a dependent, the person claiming the student as a dependent can claim the credit. Education credits must be claimed on a joint return, unless the special rules for married persons living apart or separated apply. Tuition and related expenses are eligible, but not room and board. Related expenses include text books, supplies, etc. Student activity fees are included <u>only</u> if they must be paid to the educational institution as a condition of enrollment. Expenses related to sports, games, or hobbies are not eligible unless part of a degree program. "Course Materials" are added as eligible expenses by the new American Opportunity Credit, which means computers and any other necessary expenses other than room and board. Eligible expenses must be reduced by the tax-free earnings portion of distributions from Coverdell savings accounts and 529 plans that pay for the same expenses. **(SEE "Income Exclusions," Distributions From Coverdell Education Savings Accounts, and Distributions From Qualified Tuition Programs)** Allowable tuition and fees are reported on Form 1098-T by educational institutions. An eligible educational institution may choose to report payments received (Box 1) or amounts billed (Box 2) for qualified tuition and fees (either one is acceptable for the deduction). The amount of scholarships and grants reported on Form 1098-T, Box 5, may or may not need to be deducted from "payments received" or "amounts billed" to

determine allowable expenses (to be determined on case by case basis). The Education Credits cannot be claimed, if the above-the-line deduction for tuition and fees for higher education is taken. And the Credits cannot be taken for the tax-free earnings portion of any distributions from Coverdell savings accounts and 529 plans shown on Form 1099-Q that pay for the same expenses. **Education credits are based on expenditures in a calendar year rather than on expenditures for an academic year.**

- American Opportunity Credit – Enhances the Hope Education Credit, and the credit is available through 2017. The maximum credit is $2,500 per year for each student, extending to all 4 years of higher education and adding "Course Materials" to qualifying expenses. Student must be in a degree program and at least a ½ time student to qualify for the credit.
    - Computation of credit – 100% of first $2,000 of expenses and 25% of next $2,000 of expenses.
    - 40% of credit is refundable, but no portion is refundable if the taxpayer claiming the credit is a child to whom the "kiddie tax" can be applicable (any person under 19 or under 24 who is a student providing less than ½ of own support, who has a living parent, and does not file a joint return).
- For 2013 and 2012, the credit phases-out between modified adjusted gross income (MAGI) $160,000 - $180,000 (married filing jointly), and $80,000 - $90,000 (single and head-of-household).
- Life Time Learning Credit – Maximum credit is $2,000 per year for all qualified students (20% of $10,000). A person is eligible for the credit even if enrolled in one course of higher education. For 2012/2013, the credit phases-outs are the same as for the American Opportunity Credit.

Savers Credit (Form 8880)

This credit is for low-income taxpayers who have made **elective contributions** to tax deferred employee 401(k) and 403(b) retirement plans as well as to both traditional and Roth IRAs. You can take the credit in addition to the traditional IRA above-the-line contribution deduction, and you can take the credit regardless of deductibility of the contributions – Roth IRAs and non-deductible traditional IRA contributions. The maximum retirement savings contribution credit is $2,000 (married filing jointly) and $1,000 (all other filing statuses), and any unused credit can be carried forward. Depending on your adjusted gross income, a credit percentage of 50%, 20%, or 10% of the elective contributions apply. To be eligible for the credit a taxpayer must be at least age 18, not a full-time student, and not claimed as a dependent by someone else. The Saver's Credit can be claimed by:

- Married filing jointly (incomes $0 - $35,000); Single ($0 - $17,750) = 50% credit
- Married filing jointly ($35,501 - $38,500); Single ($17,751 - $19,250) = 20% credit
- Married filing jointly ($38,501 - $59,000); Single ($19,251 - $29,500) = 10% credit
- Married filing jointly (over $59,000); Single (over $29,500) = Not Available
- Heads of Household with incomes up to $44,250 are eligible for the credit
- Married filing separately and singles with incomes up to $29,500 are eligible for the credit

Child Tax Credit

You can claim a credit of $1,000 for each "qualifying child" under age 17. The child tax credit was made permanent as of January 1, 2013, and the refundable provisions of the child tax credit have been extended through 2017. A qualifying child includes your child, foster child, stepchild, grandchild, great-grandchild, brother, sister, stepbrother, stepsister, half-brother or sister, or a descendant of any of these who is under 17 and lived with you for more than ½ the year. If divorced, the non-custodial parent may be entitled to claim the credit if entitled to claim the child as a dependent. **The child tax credit goes with the dependency exemption, but the child must live with you for more than ½ the year in order for you to claim the credit**. The credit is subject to phase-outs: beginning at modified adjusted gross income (MAGI) $110,000 (married filing jointly); $75,000 (single and head of household); $55,000 (married filing separately). The allowable credit per qualified child is reduced by $50 for each $1,000 over the MAGI thresholds. Combat pay that is excluded from taxable income is included for child tax credit purposes. Unused credit in a year can be carried forward.

- You can claim the child tax credit for a child who is a qualifying child, even though he cannot be claimed as a dependent because: (1) you or your spouse can be claimed as a dependent by another taxpayer, or (2) the child is married and files a joint return. To claim the credit for a non-dependent child you must complete Form 8901.
- Credit is allowed against AMT, and the refundable portion is not reduced by the AMT.

Mortgage Interest Credit (Form 8396)

With a Mortgage Credit Certificate (MCC), a qualified home buyer is eligible to write off a portion of the annual interest paid on a home mortgage as a special tax credit, not to exceed $2,000 in a year. A Mortgage Credit Certificate (MCC) is issued through special programs established by state or local governments. While all home owners can claim an itemized deduction for mortgage interest, a taxpayer can go a step further with a MCC. A MCC reduces tax liability dollar-for-dollar by a percentage of the mortgage interest paid. A MCC is provided in connection with a mortgage to purchase a principal residence or to improve a home. The MCC must specify the percentage rate and the certified indebtedness available to calculate the tax credit amount. The credit is determined by multiplying the percentage rate (shown on the MCC) by the interest paid by the taxpayer for the tax year, or by the remaining principal of the certified indebtedness amount. Example: The MCC specifies a percentage rate of 15%, and $60,000 of certified indebtedness. So, if the taxpayer pays $4,000 in mortgage interest for the year, then he/she may claim a mortgage interest credit of $600 ($4,000 X 15%), and an itemized mortgage interest deduction of $3,400 for the year. If the MCC specifies a rate that exceeds 20%, then the taxpayer's maximum credit for the year is $2,000. Unused credit can be carried forward to the next 3 years or until used, whichever comes first. The current year's credit is used first and then the prior years' credits, beginning with the earliest prior year.

Residential Home Improvement Credit (Form 5695)

This credit was extended to 2013, but the law returns the credit to its pre-2009 Recovery Act parameters. Therefore, the lifetime credit limit is 10% of the amount paid for allowable improvements up to a maximum of $500 (**no more than $200 for windows and skylights**). You can take advantage of this credit in 2013 only if you did not take advantage of at least $500 of the $1,500 aggregate credit offered in 2009 and 2010, or you have not taken any non-business energy property credits in prior years (since 2005) of $500 or more. The credit can be claimed for energy efficient improvements, including adding insulation, energy-efficient exterior windows and doors, and certain roofs. The credit can also be claimed for the cost of residential energy property, including labor costs for installation. Residential energy property includes certain high-efficiency heating and air conditioning systems, water heaters, and stoves that burn biomass fuel. Qualifying improvements must be placed in service in the taxpayer's principal residence.

- Homeowners should check the manufacturer's tax credit certification statement before they purchase. Taxpayers can normally rely on this certification statement which can usually be found on the manufacturer's website or with the product packaging.

Residential Energy Efficient Property Credit (Form 5695)

This credit is 30% of the cost of alternative energy equipment that you install on or in your home. Qualified equipment includes solar water heating equipment, solar electric equipment (including solar panels installed on a roof), small wind energy turbines, geothermal heat pump equipment, and fuel cell property. The credit applies to any purchase before Dec. 31, 2016, and there is no limit to the amount of credit available for most types of property except the credit for qualified fuel cells are eligible for a maximum credit of $500 per each 0.5 kilowatt of capacity. If your credit is more than the tax you owe, you can carry forward the unused portion of this credit to next year's tax return. You must install qualifying equipment in connection with your home located in the United States. **It does not have to be your main home**.

- Solar water heating equipment must be certified for performance by the non-profit Solar Rating Certification Corporation or a comparable entity endorsed by the government of the state in which such property is installed.
- Expenditures which are properly allocable to swimming pools and hot tubs are not allowable.
- Qualified fuel cell power plants use electrochemical means to convert fuel into electricity, have a generation efficiency of more than 30%, and generate at least 0.5 kilowatt of electricity. The maximum credit for fuel cells shall be $1,667 per each 0.5 kilowatt of capacity if the expenditures are for any dwelling which is a multi-family property.

Plug-in Electric Drive Vehicle Credit (Form 8936)

This credit is available for both hybrid and battery electric plug-in vehicles. The credit is available for new plug-in electric drive vehicles having a battery capacity of at least 4 kilowatt hours, which brings a credit of $2,500. Each kilowatt hour of battery power above this adds $417 to the credit, up to a maximum of $7,500 for vehicles up to 14,000 pounds gross vehicle weight. The amount of the credit begins to phase-out after a manufacturer exceeds a vehicle sales limit, in this case 200,000 vehicles. It appears that the credit is still available for certain vehicles in 2013. The vehicles are: 2012 and 2013 Ford Focus electric; 2013 Ford Fusion; 2013 Ford C-Max; and the Nissan Leaf. <u>A vehicle used in a trade or business will be treated as a component of the general business credit. The personal use of such a vehicle will be treated as a non-refundable personal credit.</u>

Low Speed 2 and 3 Wheel Plug-in Electric Vehicles Credit (Form 8936)

A separate credit is available for low speed and 2- and 3-wheel plug-in electric vehicles and low power electric golf carts in the amount of 10% of the vehicle price, up to $2,500.

Credit for Prior Year Minimum Tax (Form 8801)

This credit, which includes a refundable aspect for an unused long-term credit amount **(SEE Refundable AMT Credit, above)**, can be carried forward indefinitely and is for the amount of the AMT that was attributable to deferral items (timing preferences and adjustments). A taxpayer subject to the AMT accrues AMT credits generated only by AMT timing items. Timing items are those accounted for in different tax years in the regular tax system and the AMT tax system, i.e. accelerated depreciation, etc. AMT credits can only be used in years when the regular tax liability exceeds the "Tentative Minimum Tax" for the year. Unused long-term AMT credits are refundable. The refundable AMT credit was enacted to give relief to individuals who exercised incentive stock options (ISO) that generated AMT credits that lost all or a significant portion of their value in later years due to the loss in value of the stocks. The minimum AMT credit allowed in a year is not less than the greater of the amount of the AMT refundable credit amount determined for the preceding year or 50% of the unused credit. <u>The minimum tax credit (MTC) is the amount of the AMT attributable to deferral-type adjustments (accelerated depreciation, etc.) available to reduce the taxpayer's regular tax liability in a tax year by some or all of the AMT tax paid in previous years.</u> **(SEE "Alternative Minimum Tax")** To claim the AMT credit, including the refundable portion, taxpayers must complete Form 8801, Credit for Prior Year Minimum Tax - Individuals, Estates, and Trusts. <u>A taxpayer can claim an additional AMT credit in lieu of bonus depreciation. Taxpayers must agree to forgo the use of bonus depreciation on qualified property placed in service and instead depreciate it using the straight-line method.</u> **(SEE "Depreciation," Bonus Depreciation)**

Non-Refundable Business Tax Credits

All general business tax credits generated can offset both regular tax and AMT (including the R&D tax credit).

The General Business Tax Credits (Form 3800)
The general business credit is a limited nonrefundable credit that is claimed after all other nonrefundable credits. The general business credit is the sum of: (1) the business credit carried forward to the current year; (2) the amount of the current year business credit; and (3) the business credit carried back to the current year. Some of the general business credits are: the investment credit (rehabilitation credit; business energy credits; qualifying advanced coal project credit; qualifying gasification project credit; work opportunity credit and the heroes and wounded warriors work opportunity credits; R&D credit; disabled access credit; federal HUD zone credit; new markets credit; credit for small employer pension plan startup costs; employer-provided child care credit; energy efficient homebuilder credit; energy efficient appliance credit; alternative fuel vehicle refueling property credit; credit for employer differential wage payments; and small business healthcare credit.

Investment Credit (Form 3468)
The investment credit is the sum of the Rehabilitation Credit; the Business Energy Credits; the Qualifying Advanced Coal Project Credit; the Qualifying Gasification Project Credit; etc.

Rehabilitation Tax Credit (Form 3468)
The credit applies to costs incurred for rehabilitation and reconstruction of certain buildings. Rehabilitation includes renovation, restoration, and reconstruction. It does not include enlargement or new construction. Also, the credit is not allowed for expenditures with respect to property that is considered to be tax-exempt use property. The credit is 10% for buildings placed in service before 1936, and 20% for certified historic structures. The credit was temporally increased for property located in specific disaster areas: 13% for pre-1936 buildings and 26% for certified historic structures. The increase applied to property located in disaster areas impacted by Hurricanes Katrina, Rita, and Wilma before January 1, 2012.

Business Energy Credits (Form 3468)
A number of Energy incentives primarily targeted to businesses are extended through 2013, not including the ones listed below that are already applicable through 2016. They include the Energy Efficient Appliance Credit and the Energy Efficient Home Credit (see below). In addition, there are about 15 other credits that are extended for one or two years.

- The credit for solar energy property is 30% for periods prior to January 1, 2017. Additionally, equipment that uses fiber-optic distributed sunlight to illuminate the inside of a structure is solar energy property eligible for the 30% credit.
- The energy credit applies to qualified fuel-cell power plants for periods prior to January 1, 2017. The credit rate is 30%.
- The energy credit applies to qualified geothermal heat pump property placed in service prior to January 1, 2017. The credit rate is 10%.
- The energy credit applies to qualified small wind energy property placed in service prior to January 1, 2017. The credit rate is 30%.
- ARRA allows taxpayers to make an irrevocable election to have certain qualified facilities that produce electricity to be treated as energy property eligible for the 30% business energy credit.

Qualifying Advanced Coal Project Credit (Form 3468)
This credit is 20% of qualified investments in advanced coal projects using an integrated gasification combined cycle, and 15% of qualified investments in other certified qualifying advanced coal projects.

Qualifying Gasification Project Credit (Form 3468)
This credit is 20% of qualified investments in qualifying gasification projects that employ gasification technology and the investment amount does not exceed $650 million. The credit is 30% where (1) $350 million of credits are to allocated to qualifying projects ("Phase 1 gasification projects"), and (2) an additional $250 million of credits are to be allocated to qualifying projects that include equipment that separates and sequesters at least 75% of such project's total CO_2 emissions ("Phase II gasification projects").

Work Opportunity Tax Credit (WOTC) (Form 5884)
The WOTC is extended through 2013, except for Unemployed Veterans and Disconnected Youth. The credit program is available to employers for qualified wages paid to new employees who are members of 11 targeted groups (see below). The maximum credit for the following targeted groups is equal to 25% of first year wages of $6,000 when the employee works 120 hours =$1,500, or 40% of first year wages of $6,000 when the employee works 400 hours =$2,400:
- Qualified Food Stamp Recipient – Must be 18 – 39 years old and a member of a family receiving food stamps for 3 out of the last 5 months before date of hire.
- Designated Community Resident – Must be 18 – 39 years old and a member of a family with a place of abode in an Empowerment Zone (EZ), Enterprise Community (EC), Renewal Community (RC), or a Rural Renewal Community (RRC).
- Unemployed Veteran – Must have been discharged from the service during the 5-year period ending on the hiring date, and receiving unemployment compensation for at least 4 weeks. **(NO LONGER APPLICABLE)**

- Qualified Ex-Felon – Must have been released from prison within one year before date of hire.
- Disconnected Youth – Must be at least 16 and less than 25 years old and without any skills to be readily hirable, out of work, and not a high school graduate. **(NO LONGER APPLICABLE)**
- Vocational Rehabilitation Referral – Must have a physical or mental disability.
- Qualified SSI Recipient – Must be receiving supplemental security benefits from the Social Security Administration and have a statement of proof.
- Other targeted groups:
    - Qualified Veteran/Disabled Veteran – There is no age cut-off, but must have been released from military service and have a service connected disability. Maximum credit is double the credit of the above targeted groups – 25% of first year wages of $12,000 when the employee works 120 hours = $3,000, or 40% of first year wages of $12,000 when the employee works 400 hours = $4,800.
    - Qualified Summer Youth Hire – Must be 16 or 17 years old and work must be performed between May 1 and September 15. Also must be a member of a family that lives in an Empowerment Zone (EZ), Enterprise Community (EC), or a Renewal Community (RC). Maximum credit is 25% of first year wages of $3,000 when the employee works 120 hours = $750, or 40% of first year wages of $3,000 when the employee works 400 hours = $1,200.
    - Long-Term Family Assistance Recipient – Must be a member of a family that has received Temporary Assistance to Needy Families for at least 18 consecutive months. This is the only targeted group that has an available credit for 2 years. Maximum credit for the first year is 25% of first year wages of $10,000 when the employee works 120 hours = $2,500, or 40% of first year wages of $10,000 when the employee works 400 hours = $4,000. Maximum credit for the second year is 25% of second year wages of $10,000 when the employee works 120 hours = $2,500, or 50% of second year wages of $10,000 when the employee works 400 hours = $5,000. Total maximum credit = $9,000.

- Qualified wages can be paid by more than one employer, i.e. Temp Agencies qualify. Wages can be paid to aliens who are here legally. Employers receive the credit through a State by initially completing Form 8850, Pre-Screening Notice and Certification Request for the Work Opportunity Tax Credit, which must be signed by both employer and employee and sent to the State's Department of Labor (original Form must be sent within 28 days). Form 9061 and supporting documentation must be sent in with Form 8850. Supporting documentation includes birth certificates, drivers' licenses, DD Forms 214, W-4's, parole officer's statements, etc. Then, the State's Dept. of Labor will send the employer Form 9063 (employer cannot take advantage of the credit until they receive this Form). Employers then would use Form 5884 to claim the WOTC. Credit can be carried forward 20 years and back one year.

Heroes and Wounded Warriors WOTC (Form 5884)

This is in essence an addition to the WOTC. It offers employers a tax credit of up to $5,600 for hiring veterans who have been looking for a job for more than six months, as well as a $2,400 credit for veterans who are unemployed for more than four weeks but less than 6 months (Returning Heroes Tax Credit). In addition, it offers a tax credit of up to $9,600 for hiring veterans with service-connected disabilities who have been looking for a job for more than six months, and $4,800 for all veterans with service-connected disabilities or who qualify as food stamp recipients (Wounded Warrior Tax Credit). It also provides expanded training and education opportunities for all veterans. The credits will be available for eligible individuals who begin work for the employer **after November 21, 2011, and before Jan. 1, 2014**. To qualify for the credit(s), employers must establish that the veteran they hired is a member of a targeted group that qualifies for the credit by obtaining a Form 8850, Pre-Screening Notice and Certification Request for the Work Opportunity Tax Credit from a designated local agency (a state employment security agency). The certification can either be received from the agency before the veteran starts work, or the employer can complete a pre-screening notice (also on Form 8850) under penalties of perjury no later than 28 days after the veteran begins work. Tax-exempt organizations can qualify for the credit against their share of the Federal Insurance Contributions Act (FICA) tax they pay on wages to qualified veterans, provided the veterans are performing services related to the organizations' tax-exempt function.

The Returning Heroes Tax Credit:
- Short-term unemployed – credit is 40% of the first $6,000 of wages (up to $2,400) for employers who hire veterans who have been unemployed at least 4 weeks.
- Long-term unemployed – credit is 40% of the first $14,000 of wages (up to $5,600) for employers who hire veterans who have been unemployed longer than 6 months.

The Wounded Warrior Tax Credit: (will double the existing tax credit for long-term unemployed veterans with service-connected disabilities)
- Maintain the existing Work Opportunity Tax Credit for veterans with service-connected disabilities (currently the maximum is $4,800).
- A new credit of 40% of the first $24,000 of wages (up to $9,600) for firms that hire veterans with service-connected disabilities who have been unemployed longer than 6 months.

R&D Tax Credit (Form 6765)

Extended through 2013, the research and development (R&D) tax credit is a 20% wage based credit that can go back 3 open tax years (4 years total). To qualify for the credit, a business has to meet all four of the following requirements: (1) develop a new and improved business component, product, process, software (that can be used either internally or externally), technique, formula, or invention; (2) must be technological in nature; (3) eliminate uncertainty, through (4) process of experimentation.

Marketing strategy and financing methods do not qualify. Eligible costs for the credit are: wages (W-2), supplies, and contract costs (65% of contract research). Net benefit comes out to about 6.5% of all qualified costs, including wages, supplies, and 65% of contract costs. A company needs to have an annual payroll of at least $2 million, 20% passive shareholders, and be paying taxes above the alternative minimum tax (AMT). A company getting the credit for the first time can use 4 years of payroll (current year + 3 prior years) to determine the amount of the credit. Taxpayers are sometimes required to determine their average gross receipts to compute the credit. The average annual gross receipts for a tax year consist of the mean amount of gross receipts generated by the taxpayer during the prior four tax years. "Gross receipts" for this purpose should include all revenues generated by the company except for long term capital gains, returns and allowances, and repayments of loans or similar instruments. The burden of proof is on the company; there is an assumed blanket denial by the IRS. **A company needs to hire an engineering company specializing in computing the R&D tax credit to compute and document the credit before claiming the credit**. Unused credits can be carried back one year and forward 20 years.

- Since the credit expired at the end of 2011 and was not extended until Jan. 2, 2013, the taxpayer does not reflect this tax credit in its 2012 financial statements but rather will record a retroactive discrete benefit for the 2012 credit in 2013.

A taxpayer can claim an additional R&D tax credit in lieu of bonus depreciation. Taxpayers must agree to forgo the use of bonus depreciation on qualified property placed in service and instead depreciate it using the straight-line method. **(SEE "Depreciation," Bonus Depreciation)**

- There are two ways to compute the credit – Regular credit method and the Alternative Simplified method. You cannot amend a prior year's tax return and use the Alternative method. If you haven't taken a credit in a prior year, you must use the Regular method when filing an amended return.

Disabled Access Credit (Form 8826)

If your sales for the prior year were less than $1 million or you had fewer than 30 employees, you may take a tax credit for improvements made to your business property to fulfill the requirements of the Americans for Disability Act. You can take a tax credit of 50% of your expenditures up to a maximum credit of $5,000.

Federal HUD Zone Tax Credit (Form 8844)

Maximum credit is $1,500 and employee's place of employment and abode must be in one of the Empowerment Zones. NOTE: The WOTC and HUD Zone tax credits must be figured together, i.e. cannot double dip on these credits. HUD credit is claimed on Form 8844.

New Markets Tax Credit (NMTC) (Form 8874)
The NMTC is designed to encourage investments, loans, or financial counseling for businesses and real estate projects in low-income communities, and has been extended through 2013. Under Code Sec. 45D, taxpayers may claim the credit by making an equity investment in a community development entity (CDE), which in turn will invest the funds in the low-income community. Both individuals and corporations can invest in a CDE. The investment must be acquired at its original issue, either directly or through an underwriter. The Treasury Department allocates credits to the CDEs. Taxpayers may claim a total credit of 39% of the original amount invested. The credit is claimed over seven years: 5% in the first three years, and 6% over the succeeding four years. Because the majority of investments have involved real estate, Treasury and the IRS have issued regulations to encourage investments, primarily as working capital and equipment loans, in businesses that are not involved in real estate.

Credit for Small Employer Pension Plan Startup (Form 8881)
If you implement a defined benefit plan including a 401(k), SIMPLE, or SEP, you can take a credit of up to $500 for startup expenses. Claim it on Form 8881.

Employer-Provided Child Care Tax Credit (Form 8882)
This credit is 25% of the child care expenditures made by the employer, limited to $150,000.

Energy Efficient Homebuilder Tax Credit (Form 8908)
An eligible contractor can claim a business credit for each qualified new energy-efficient dwelling that the contractor constructs, and is used as a residence. Apartment developers (3 stories or less) and home builders are eligible for the credit, which is either $2,000 for each 50% energy reduction dwelling or $1,000 for each 30% energy reduction dwelling. Dwellings must be certified by a licensed engineer that it consumes 50% or 30% less energy for heating and cooling. Manufactured homes can receive a maximum credit of $1,000. **This credit applies to dwellings sold or leased before 1/1/2014.**

Energy Efficient Appliance Credit (Form 8909)
A manufacturer can claim this credit for production of dishwashers, clothes washers, and refrigerators through 2013. The credits are $25 to $75 per unit for dishwashers; $175 to $225 per unit for clothes washers; and $150 to $200 per unit for refrigerators.

Alternative Fuel Vehicle Refueling Property Credit (Form 8911)
Credit is 50% for commercial and retail refueling stations placed in service (capped at $50,000). The credit for hydrogen refueling property is 30% (capped at $200,000). The credit is extended through 2013.

Credit for Employer Differential Wage Payments (Form 8932)
Small employers with fewer than 50 employees who pay differential pay to reservists called to active duty can claim a tax credit equal to 20% of the differential wages up to $20,000 a year for each employee (provision extended through 2013). The credit can be claimed for amounts paid after 6/17/2008. The differential pay is treated as taxable wages subject to income tax withholding after 12/31/2008, but it is exempt from employment tax (FICA and FUTA). Before 12/31/08, the differential pay was not treated as wages for income tax purposes or employment tax purposes. A qualified employee is a person who was employed by the employer for the 91-day period immediately preceding the period for which any differential wage payment is made.

Small Business Healthcare Tax Credit (Form 8941)
The Patient Protection and Affordable Care Act (ACA) provides a tax credit to small businesses and eligible tax-exempt small employers that provide health insurance coverage to their employees. A qualified small business employer has to have fewer than 25 full-time equivalent (FTE) employees and have average annual compensation of less than $50,000. Self-employed individuals, partners, 2% shareholders of an S-corporation, 5% owners of an employer, and family members and dependents are not counted as employees. In 2010 through 2013, the maximum credit is 35% (25% for tax-exempt organizations) of the employer's premium expenses. Small employers with 10 or fewer employees and average annual wages of less than $25,000 are eligible for the full 35% credit. The credit is reduced on a sliding scale for small employers with 11 to 25 employees and annual average wages of $26,000 to $50,000. The credit is reduced by 6.667% for each full-time equivalent (FTE) employee in excess of 10 employees and is reduced by 4% for each $1,000 that average annual compensation paid to the employees exceeds $25,000. The credit is calculated on Form 8941 "Credit for Small Employer Health Insurance Premiums" and then claimed as a general business credit on Form 3800, which is reflected on line 53 of Form 1040. The credit can be applied against both regular taxes and Alternative Minimum Tax (AMT). Up to 4 million small businesses are eligible for the credit, which can be a lot of money, i.e. the maximum credit is $51,000 in 2010 - 2013 for a for-profit small business ($36,700 for a tax-exempt organization). **(SEE "Patient Protection and Affordable Care Act," Provisions Effective Beginning in 2010, Tax Provisions)**

Other General Business Credits
- American Samoa Economic Development Credit (Form 5735)
- Alcohol and Cellulosic Biofuel Fuels Credit (Form 6478)
- Low-Income Housing Credit (Form 8586)
- Recapture of Low-Income Housing Credit (Form 8611)
- Orphan Drug Credit (Form 8820)
- Renewable Electricity, Refined Coal, and Indian Coal Production Credit (Form 8835)
- Empowerment Zone and Renewal Community Employment Credit (Form 8844)

- Indian Employment Credit (Form 8845)
- Credit for Employer Social Security and Medicare Taxes Paid on Certain Employee Tips (Form 8846)
- Credit for Contributions to Selected Community Development Corporations (Form 8847)
- Biodiesel and Renewable Diesel Fuels Credit (Form 8864)
- Low Sulfur Diesel Fuel Production Credit (Form 8896)
- Qualified Railroad Track Maintenance Credit (Form 8900)
- Distilled Spirits Credit (Form 8906)
- Nonconventional Source Fuel Credit (Form 8907)
- Mine Rescue Team Training Credit (Form 8923)

Employee Travel and Entertainment Expenses

Employee travel and entertainment expenses are miscellaneous itemized deductions subject to the 2% AGI threshold/floor. **(SEE "Itemized Deductions," Miscellaneous Itemized Deductions (Subject to the 2% AGI Threshold/Floor)** Form 2106 has to be filed by an employee when reporting travel, vehicle, meals and entertainment expenses. Form 2106 does not have to be filed when only reporting miscellaneous employee related expense items, such as work related education costs, dues and subscriptions to professional journals, or union costs that are entered on line 4 of Form 2106. Rules and regulations for employee travel and entertainment expenses are also applicable to sole proprietor/self-employed persons who file Schedule C, except <u>sole proprietors are not subject to the 2% AGI floor and they do not have to file Form 2106</u>.

Claiming Travel and Entertainment Expenses
Work related expenses incurred in traveling away from home to another location are deductible. Travel expenses incurred for commuting to work are not deductible. The "Sleep and Rest Rule" determines whether or not a trip takes a taxpayer away from home, where it is reasonable that he/she needs sleep and rest during off time, and it is not reasonable to return home. A taxpayer's tax home is where his major post of duty is located. Three factors that define a taxpayer's tax home: (1) taxpayer has living expenses at claimed tax home that are duplicated when work requires him/her to be away from tax home; (2) taxpayer worked in the area of claimed tax home immediately before present job assignment and continued to have work contacts in that area; and (3) taxpayer's spouse and children live at claimed tax home, or taxpayer continues to use that home for lodging. Work assignments of one year or less are generally considered temporary, and thus travel expenses are deductible unless the original assignment was expected to be for more than one year. Work assignments of more than one year are considered indefinite, and thus travel expenses are not deductible. However, if the assignment is less than two years, a taxpayer can overcome the "one-year presumption" by showing: (1) the job was realistically expected to last less than 2 years; (2) he/she expected to return home after the job ended; and (3) claimed tax home is his/her regular home in a real and substantial sense. If all three factors are met, the assignment may be considered temporary. If two factors are met, there is a strong case for the assignment being considered temporary. If only one factor is met, the assignment would not be considered temporary. You cannot claim another place other than your real tax home as your tax home, such as where your family lives. You also cannot deduct expenses at the other place.

- An Itinerant worker is not entitled to deduct travel expenses due to the lack of a regular place of abode.
- Travel expenses for investment purposes are ordinarily deductible. However, expenses incurred for the acquisition of investment property must be capitalized rather than currently deductible. <u>There is no deduction allowed for expenses incurred for conventions, seminars, or similar meetings attended for investment purposes.</u>

- **Trips combining business and pleasure** – Expenses of traveling to and from a destination in the U.S., i.e. airplane tickets and hotel, are deductible only if the trip is <u>primarily</u> related to a business purpose. This is determined by the percentage of time spent on business and pleasure (51%/49%). Spouses and dependents' travel expenses are not deductible unless business related. If a traveler spends an extra night in a hotel to visit family, he cannot deduct that night. <u>However, if a trip is determined to be primarily for personal reasons (pleasure), a taxpayer can deduct any expenses he/she has that are directly related to business (not airplane ticket, or other travel expenses).</u>
- **Travel outside of the U.S.** – To be fully deductible, foreign travel must be primarily for business purposes (51%/49%). However, if there are <u>any</u> non-business activities, not all of the travel is deductible unless <u>one</u> of four criteria are met, then all expenses are deductible. The four criteria are: (1) the trip lasts less than 8 days; (2) taxpayer had little control over arranging the business trip; (3) taxpayer is an employee not related to his employer (related also means owns more than 10% of business); and (4) a personal vacation or holiday was not a major reason for the trip.
- There are limits on business expenses claimed for trips on cruise ships. The cruise ship must be registered in U.S., and all ports of call must be located in the U.S. in order to claim any business expenses. Deductible expenses on cruise ships meeting the criteria are limited to twice the per diem rate of the highest per diem rate allowed to employees of the executive branch of the U.S. government. Deductible expenses are limited to $2,000 for an individual in any calendar year.
- For foreign conventions, no deductions for expenses outside of the North America area are allowed (U.S. and its possessions; Canada, Mexico; the Republic of the Marshall Islands; the Federated States of Micronesia; the Republic of Palau; Antigua; Aruba; Barbuda; Bahamas; Barbados; Bermuda; Costa Rica; Dominica; Dominican Republic; Grenada; Guyana; Honduras; Jamaica; Netherlands Antilles; Panama; and Trinidad and Tobago) unless the meeting is directly related to the taxpayer's business, and it is reasonable that the meeting be held outside of the North America area. Prominently not on the allowed list are St Lucia, Cayman Islands, British Virgin Islands, and Kokomo. Deductible expenses for foreign conventions, seminars, or other meetings are limited to $2,000 for an individual in any calendar year. The term "North America area" also includes a "beneficiary country" if there is an information exchange agreement between that country and the U.S. and there is no finding by the Secretary of the Treasury that the tax laws of the beneficiary country discriminate against conventions held in the U.S. Guidance lists all U.S. possessions and all beneficiary countries, along with dates after which conventions held in those countries may generate deductible expenses.
- **Lodging, entertainment, meals and incidental expenses** – A log or account book should be used to keep track of lodging, meals, entertainment, and incidental expenses. The log book should show time, place, business purpose, and amount of each separate expense. In addition, documentary evidence is required for any lodging expense over $75.00 (this also applies to

other expenses as well). The federal government issues a standard per diem rate for the continental U.S. (CONUS) annually, **as well as per diem rates for specific cities and localities that may be higher than the standard rate.** The standard per diem rate for CONUS for Oct. 1, 2012 through Sept. 30, 2013 is $129, which is $77 for lodging and $52 for miscellaneous and incidental expenses (M&IE). The standard per diem rate for CONUS for Oct. 1, 2013 through Sept. 30, 2014 is $129, which is $83 for lodging and $46 for M&IE. Here's how it works: in lieu of reimbursing its employees for actual travel expenses, an employer may use the per diem rates allowed for federal government employees within CONUS, as long as the employees substantiate the time, place, and business purpose of the travel. This method is considered an "accountable plan," so reimbursements aren't subject to payroll or income taxes. However, reimbursements can't exceed the annual maximums established by the federal government. Otherwise it will be considered a non-accountable plan, and the reimbursements will be subject to payroll and income taxes. Employees who aren't reimbursed by their employers for meals and entertainment expenses are limited to claiming 50% of such expenses, including M&IE. Exceptions to the 50% rule for claiming meals and entertainment expenses: (1) 100% of meals and entertainment expenses are treated as compensation by employer; (2) business meals and entertainment expenses are reimbursed by employer (accountable plan); (3) items paid for are made available to the general public; (4) entertainment is sold to customers; and (5) certain de minimis fringe benefits such as recreational expenses for employees and charitable sports events. **NOTE: If you incur a large amount of travel expenses and these expenses are treated as compensation by your employer, you should get your employer to establish an "accountable plan", which could be very beneficial for tax purposes. For example, if your W-2 shows taxable income of $250,000 (which includes $120,000 of employer reimbursed travel expenses), an accountable plan will reduce your W-2 wages to $130,000. This could save a single taxpayer in this situation as much as $30,000 in income tax, because the itemized deduction phase-out prevents him/her from deducting employee business expenses and may even trigger the AMT tax and the 0.9% Medicare surtax.**
- Entertainment expenses must be directly related to or associated with the active conduct of a taxpayer's trade or business. Any portion of a business meal considered extravagant is disallowed. However, expenses for laundry, cleaning and pressing clothes, and business telephone calls are in addition to the M&IE allowance.
- Self-employed individuals and those owning 10% or more of a company cannot use the per diem method to substantiate lodging expenses. However, self-employed individuals may use the M&IE per diem method for meals and incidental expenses instead of keeping records (3/4 of the M&IE rate is allowed for partial days), but they must use actual costs for lodging expenses. Employees and self-employed taxpayers can claim only 50% of unreimbursed business meals and entertainment expenses for themselves, clients, and customers. This rule

also applies when the M&IE allowance is used in lieu of actual meals and incidental expenses, i.e. the 50% limitation is applicable to the M&IE allowance.

- **Taxpayers who used the M&IE rate for the first 9 months of 2013 may continue to use that rate instead of the new M&IE rate, effective Oct 1, 2013, for the last 3 months of 2013. However, they must consistently use one or the other of the two rates for the period 10/1/2013 – 12/31/2013.**
- In lieu of using per diem rates for specific business locations (higher than standard per diem rate), employers may rely on simplified "high-low" per diem rates established annually for travel within CONUS (the "high-low" method). Using this method is also considered an "accountable plan." Under this method, if an employer travels to one of a handful of places designated as high-cost areas, trouble-free reimbursements are based on the special rate for high-cost areas (this includes resort areas like Vail and Martha's Vineyard). Otherwise, the employer uses the rate for low-cost areas. For purposes of the high-low method, the per diem rates for the federal government's 2013 fiscal year beginning Oct. 1, 2012, are $242 for travel to any high-cost location, and $163 for travel to any low-cost location within CONUS. The M&IE rates for travel to any high-cost location are $65, and for travel to any low-cost location $52 within CONUS. The rates for the 2014 fiscal year beginning Oct.1, 2013, are $251 for travel to high-cost locations, and $170 for travel to low-cost locations within CONUS. The M&IE rates for travel to any high-cost location are still $65, and for travel to any low-cost location $52 within CONUS. The list of high-cost locations are those with a per diem rate of $202 or more for fiscal year 2013, and $210 or more for fiscal year 2014. Some high-cost areas are only seasonal in nature (these high-cost areas are listed on the IRS website).
- In lieu of using actual expenses in computing the amount allowable as a deduction for ordinary and necessary incidental expenses (includes only fees and tips given to porters, baggage carriers, hotel staff, and staff on ships) paid or incurred for travel away from home, employees and self-employed individuals who do not incur meal expenses for a calendar day (or partial day) of travel away from home may use, for each calendar day (or partial day) an amount computed at the **rate of $5 per day** for any locality of travel. The $5 rate is the same for Oct. 1, 2012, and Oct. 1, 2013.
- The M&IE rates for taxpayers subject to Department of Transportation (DOT) service rules - transportation industry employees (truck drivers, etc.) or self-employed individuals in the transportation industry are: $59 federal rate for any locality in CONUS, and $65 OCONUS (outside of continental U.S.). A transportation employee is entitled to claim only the lesser of an amount paid to him/her by employer as computed on the "cents-per-mile" allowance method that qualifies as an allowance paid under a flat rate or stated schedule, or the M&IE rate for the number of days traveled during a month. For example, a transportation industry taxpayer travels away from home on business for 10 days, and based on the number of miles driven by taxpayer, his employer pays an allowance of $500 for the 10 days of business travel; taxpayer

actually drives for 8 days, and does not drive the other 2 days he is away from home. The amount deemed substantiated is the full $500 because that amount does not exceed $590 (ten days away from home at $59 per day).

- <u>Instead of the 50% limit, taxpayers subject to DOT service rules – transportation industry employees (truck drivers, etc.) who pay their own expenses, can claim 80% of unreimbursed business meals and entertainment expenses, including 80% of the special M&IE allowances for transportation industry employees.</u>
- In order to claim entertainment expenses, the taxpayer or an employee of the taxpayer must be present when food or beverages are furnished. For entertainment tickets, in addition to the 50% limitation, the cost of a ticket is limited to its face value. Entertainment expenses can include out-of-pocket expenses for food, and interest, taxes, and casualty losses on entertainment facilities; but not expenses for maintenance of facilities.
- Expenses incurred for recreational meetings for highly compensated employees (company executives) are not deductible entertainment expenses. Expenses for business meetings with stockholders are deductible entertainment expenses.
- **Home entertainment** – only "additional costs" incurred due to entertaining customers or clients are deductible as entertainment expenses. The mere fact that the guests entertained are "present or potential" customers or clients is not sufficient to allow the deduction.
- **Proposed regulations, which can currently be relied on, explicitly allow employees to treat local lodging expenses as working condition fringe benefits or accountable plan reimbursements. It also frees employers to treat local lodging expenses as deductible travel expenses. In certain circumstances, local lodging expenses to attend business meetings and conferences incurred in carrying on a trade or business can be deducted if: (1) the lodging is necessary for the employee to participate in a bona fide business meeting, conference, training activity, or other business function; (2) the lodging must be on a temporary basis not exceeding five calendar days and not occur more than once each calendar quarter; (3) the employer requires the employee to remain at the activity or function overnight; and (4) the lodging is not extravagant or lavish and does not provide a significant element of personal pleasure, recreation or benefit.** Three examples of local lodging expenses that are deductible are: to attend employer-mandated training at a local hotel; to house athletes for last-minute training and to ensure the players' preparedness; and for housing an employee who is on call outside of normal working hours on a rotating basis with other employees as a condition of employment to respond to business emergencies.
- To take advantage of the "accountable plan" rules, employers must establish a valid, written plan in accordance with Sec. 62(a)(2)(A) and Reg. Sec. 1.62-2. To qualify as an accountable plan, the plan must require that: employee expenses have a business connection; employees adequately account for the expenses within a reasonable time period; and employees return excess allowances within a reasonable period of time – advances are to be received (back)

within 30 days of the time the expenses are paid or incurred; expenses are to be adequately accounted for within 60 days after they were paid or incurred; and any excess reimbursement must be returned within 120 days after the expenses are paid or incurred.

Vehicle and Other Transportation Expenses

A taxpayer may use actual expenses or the standard mileage allowance to substantiate business expenses for the use of a personal vehicle. The standard mileage rate may be used for a vehicle that is either **owned or leased** by the taxpayer. Business usage of a personal vehicle is determined based on business and personal miles driven during a year, i.e. actual expenses and depreciation are allocated based on the percentage of business miles driven compared to total miles driven. Business miles are related to business usage of a vehicle, and also for attending continuing education courses and going to an IRS service center. The standard mileage rate for 2013 is $.56 ½ per mile ($.55 ½ in 2012). The choice to use the standard mileage allowance instead of actual expenses and depreciation must be made in the first year you place a vehicle into service. Claiming either actual expenses or the standard mileage allowance for business use of your car requires you to note the date, destination, purpose, and mileage for each tax-deductible business trip in your vehicle.

- You may not use the standard mileage rate for a vehicle after using any depreciation method under the Modified Accelerated Cost Recovery System (MACRS) or after claiming bonus depreciation or a Section 179 deduction for that vehicle. (**This means that you can only claim the standard mileage rate in a subsequent year after claiming straight-line depreciation based on the vehicle's estimated useful life**). (SEE "Depreciation," Depreciation Methods)
- Claiming the standard mileage allowance in the first year forfeits your privilege to use actual expenses (depreciation [or lease payments], maintenance and repairs, tires, gasoline, oil, insurance, license and registration fees, and state and local property taxes) in any other year.
- Depreciation reduces the basis of a vehicle (but not below zero). If the standard mileage rate is used, an allowance for depreciation called "deemed depreciation" at the rate of $.23 per mile in 2012 and 2013 reduces the basis of a vehicle. Thus, if you drive your car 10,000 business miles, you must reduce the basis of the car by $2,300 ($.23 X 10,000 miles). Parking fees and tolls are deductible in addition to the standard mileage allowance.
- **Interest paid by an employee on a car loan is nondeductible. However, a self-employed taxpayer may claim the interest paid on the business portion of a car as a business expense, in addition to the mileage allowance**. State and local taxes paid in connection with the purchase of a vehicle are considered part of the purchase price of the vehicle.
- You cannot use the standard mileage allowance for more than four vehicles used simultaneously (such as fleet operations).
- **Beginning Jan. 1, 2011, taxpayers are allowed to use the standard mileage allowance for vehicles used for hire, such as taxicabs. However, this is subject to the restriction on fleet operations noted above.**

- Local transportation expenses are deductible when: (1) going directly from one job to another, if employee has more than one job; and (2) going from residence to a temporary job location when employee has a regular work location. However, travel between residence and a temporary work location that is close to regular work location (within same metropolitan area) is considered commuting and not deductible. <u>You may deduct your transportation expenses, but not the cost of personal meals on one-day business trips (not an over-night stay).</u>
- <u>Leasing a car, truck, or van for business use – you can claim the standard mileage allowance, or deduct the lease payments, plus costs of operating the vehicle (must be allocated based on business and personal mileage driven). If you choose to use actual expenses, you can deduct the part of each lease payment that is for the use of the vehicle in your business. You cannot deduct any part of a lease payment that is for personal use of the vehicle, such as commuting. You must spread any advance payments over the entire lease period.</u> You cannot deduct any payments you make to buy a car, truck, or van even if the payments are called lease payments. If you lease a vehicle for 30 days or more, you may have to reduce your lease payment deduction by an "<u>inclusion amount</u>" in your income for each tax year you lease the vehicle. To do this, **you do not add an amount to income; instead, you reduce your deduction for your lease payment** (the inclusion amount has an effect similar to the limit on the depreciation deduction you would have on the vehicle if you owned it).

The inclusion amount is a percentage of part of the fair market value (FMV) of the leased vehicle multiplied by the percentage of business and investment use of the vehicle for the year. The inclusion amount applies to each tax year that you lease the vehicle if the FMV of the vehicle was more than $18,500 for cars, and $19,000 for trucks and vans when you leased the vehicle. Figure the FMV on the first day of the lease term. If the capitalized cost of a car is specified in the lease agreement, use that amount as the FMV. The inclusion amounts are based on a formula and tables prescribed under Reg. Sec. 1.280F-7. The revenue procedure provides an updated table of the amounts to be included in income by lessees of passenger automobiles and another for trucks and vans, in both cases with lease terms that begin in calendar year 2013. The applicable inclusion amount must be prorated based on the number of days of the lease term included in the tax year, which is then multiplied by the percentage of business and investment use for the tax year to get the inclusion amount.

For purposes of leasing a vehicle, the standard mileage allowance may not exceed $28,100 for cars and $29,900 for trucks and vans in 2013 ($28,000 and $29,300 in 2012).

NOTE: The "Cohan Rule" allows taxpayers to prove by "other credible evidence" other than the recordkeeping requirements whether they actually incurred deductible expenses. The Cohan Rule is most classically applied to travel and entertainment expenses, but can apply to virtually any item not specifically subject to heightened substantiation requirements (such as certain travel and meal expenses, and passenger automobiles). The Cohan Rule allows a taxpayer to convince the IRS by oral or written statements or other supporting evidence and reasonable approximation that you are entitled to an expense despite your lack of documentation.

Depreciation (Form 4562)

Depreciation and/or cost recovery can be used for property that is used for both business and investment purposes. **Reduction in the adjusted basis of property based on allowable depreciation is mandatory even if not taken**. A husband and wife filing a joint return are treated as one taxpayer (50% each). According to the regulations, there are seven classes of assets: Class I – cash and general deposit accounts other than certificates of deposit; Class II – actively traded personal property (stocks and securities); Class III – debt instruments; Class IV – inventory items; <u>Class V – all assets other than Classes I, II, III, IV, VI, and VII</u>; Class VI – all section 197 intangibles; Class VII – goodwill and going concern values. **Class V assets are real and personal property that can be depreciated, except for land**. An asset can be depreciated from the date it is "placed in service," which is the date that it is in a condition or state of readiness and "put to use" in a trade or business or for the production of income (an asset may be considered put to use if everything in the taxpayer's power has been done to put the asset to use). **NOTE: Be sure to include land as a separate asset from the building or structure that is on the land, because land is not depreciable (cost or other basis of the land must be separate from the cost or other basis of the building).**

Bonus Depreciation

For 2012 and 2013, a 50% first-year bonus depreciation allowance is provided for certain qualified <u>new</u> property placed in service before 1/1/2014, including most equipment and software and some leasehold improvements (before 1/1/2015 for certain long-production-period property and certain aircraft acquired before 1/1/2014). 100% bonus depreciation was in effect for qualified new property placed in service after 9/8/2010 and before 12/31/2011. There is no dollar limit on this, and even the largest businesses are eligible. If your business adds enough to generate an overall loss (NOL) for the year, you can carry the NOL back or forward and recover some or all of the taxes paid for those years. **(SEE "Taxable Income," Net Operating Loss)** Bonus depreciation is mandatory unless the taxpayer elects out of it. The election out can be by class of asset or for all qualifying assets in a company. First-year bonus depreciation is available for **new** property (used property does not qualify, although current improvements to that property may qualify). Bonus depreciation is also available for investment property, specifically qualifying property in rental properties such as appliances, etc. <u>The property must have a General Depreciation System (GDS) life of 20 years or less. Bonus depreciation should be computed and used before regular depreciation (MACRS), but after 179 expensing.</u> **(SEE Depreciation Methods, below)** Taxpayer can take bonus depreciation and then apply one of the conventional depreciation methods to the remaining basis. **Property converted to business use in 2012 and 2013 by the original owner qualifies for bonus depreciation.**

- 100% first-year bonus depreciation was available for certain long-lived property with a recovery period of 10 years or longer and for transportation property (tangible personal property used to transport people or property) placed in service before 1/1/2013.

- **First-year bonus depreciation is allowed for both regular tax and AMT**.
- **A corporation otherwise eligible for first-year bonus depreciation may claim additional R&D tax credits or AMT credits in lieu of claiming bonus depreciation through 12/31/2013. Taxpayers must agree to forgo the use of bonus depreciation on qualified property placed in service and instead depreciate it using the straight-line method.** The increases in the allowable credits are treated as refundable. Form 3800 and/or Form 8827 plus Form 4562 must be filed claiming straight line depreciation for use of credits in lieu of bonus depreciation.

Section 179 First-Year Expensing

This election can be used for <u>both new and used</u> equipment and <u>computer software</u> in 2013 if the property is used **more than 50% for business purposes** (converted property is not eligible). Also, **cannot be used for property used for <u>investment purposes</u> (such as rental property)**; and Estates and Trusts are not eligible. Unlike first-year bonus depreciation, you cannot claim Section 179 deductions that will create a net operating loss (NOL) for a year, i.e. the Section 179 deduction is limited to the taxpayer's taxable income from the active conduct of any trade or business during the tax year. However, any amount disallowed by this limitation may be carried forward and deducted in future years. **If a person has a Schedule C business, the amount of 179 expense deduction allowed for a year is always limited to taxable income of the filer, including both spouses' wages reported on their Forms W-2**. The 2012 and 2013 maximum 179 expense deduction is $500,000 for each year. The level at which the allowable deduction amount starts to be reduced is $2,000,000, i.e. if you bought $2,020,000 worth of eligible assets in 2013, the maximum 179 expense deduction would be $480,000 ($500,000 - $20,000). Therefore, no 179 deduction is available to taxpayers who place $2,500,000 or more of eligible property into service. You can elect 179 expensing even if there is a lack of income, because it can be carried back and forward to other years – the maximum 179 limits are increased by any 179 carryovers.

The 179 election applies to depreciable personal property such as machinery, equipment, furniture, computers, and <u>off-the-shelf computer software</u> (Section 1245 property). Computer software qualifies for 179 expensing, but if not expensed, it is amortized over a 3-year (36 months) period providing it has a useful life exceeding one year (includes the cost to develop the software). Off-the-shelf computer software qualifies for 179 expensing through 2013. **The Law temporarily expands the 179 election to qualified real property in 2012 and 2013**, which is defined as: (1) qualified leasehold improvement property costs, which covers only nonresidential building interior costs (excluding elevators and any interior structural framework of a building), which must be put to use more than three years after the date the building opened for business; (2) qualified restaurant property costs, which covers both building and improvement costs, if more than 50% of the building's square footage is devoted to the preparation of meals and customer seating; and (3) qualified retail improvement costs, which covers only nonresidential building interior costs for a building that is open to the general public and used in a retail business of selling tangible personal property to the general public (excluding elevators and any interior structural framework of a building), which must be put to use not more than three years after the date the building opened for business. However, taxpayers are limited to 179 expensing of up to $250,000 of the total cost of these real properties. Expensing of Section 179 property other than real property that is disallowed as a current-year deduction because of the taxable income limit can generally be carried forward indefinitely. However, there are limitations on the carryover of qualified Section 179 real property expensing. A taxpayer is allowed to use 179 expensing of real property for 2010 through 2013 and can file amended tax returns to carry over unused 179 real property expensing from 2010 to 2012 and 2013, but not past 2013 (prior to the temporary expansion, a Section 179 deduction on qualified "real" property could not be carried forward to a tax year that began after 2011). A taxpayer may elect to exclude real property from the definition of 179 property.

For Partnerships and S-corporations, the 179 determination is made at that level. However, the maximum dollar limitation and the taxable income limitations apply both at the partnership and S-corporation level, and to the individual partners or shareholders (the basis in 179 property is reduced by the allowable amount, even if the partners or shareholders cannot deduct the full amount).

Depreciation Methods

All property placed in service after 1986 must use the Modified Accelerated Cost Recovery System (MACRS) for depreciation. MACRS consists of two depreciation systems - the General Depreciation System (GDS) and the Alternative Depreciation System (ADS). Generally, these two systems provide different methods and recovery periods to use in figuring depreciation deductions. The GDS provides 3 methods of depreciation: (1) 200% declining balance (DB) method; (2) 150% DB method; and (3) straight-line (SL) method. The ADS provides only a SL method over a longer recovery period than GDS, except for 5-year property which is assigned the same 5-year recovery period (cars, computers, etc.) as GDS. Taxpayers generally use GDS unless they are specifically required by law to use ADS or they elect to use it. Property for which the use of ADS is required includes: certain "listed" property (see below); any tangible property used predominantly outside the United States during the year; any imported property covered by an executive order of the President of the United States; tax-exempt bond financed property; and tax-exempt use property. If ADS is mandatory then bonus depreciation is not available. There is a test to determine if residential and non-residential property is mandatory for ADS: The test is whether there is a disqualified lease – which is a lease whose term is greater than 20 years, including options to renew (ADS applies). The only exception for not including "options to renew" is when the rental is based on the FMV of the property at the time of renewal. Additional examples: a building that is partially financed with tax-exempt bonds will be partially depreciated using ADS and partially with GDS, i.e. a $10 million building financed with $5 million of IDBs would be 50% depreciated using ADS and 50% depreciated using GDS; an office building that is leased to a government agency (tax-exempt use) is depreciated based on the 35% test, which means that if more than 35% of the building (based on square footage) is leased to a tax-exempt entity, the entire building is depreciated using ADS.

Although property may qualify for GDS, taxpayers may elect to use ADS. If property is converted to business use, you must use the lesser of adjusted basis or FMV on date placed in service. The Conventions under MACRS (when a property is considered placed in service during a year) are:
- Half-year – used for all property, except for residential rental property and non-residential real property (unless the mid-quarter convention is required).
- Mid-quarter – used if the aggregate basis of all personal property placed in service during the last 3 months of the year exceeds 40% of the cost of all personal property placed in service during year.
- Mid-month – used for real property.

Personal property is classified into 6 categories and depreciated using the percentages contained in the MACRS (GDS) tables. The tables for 3, 5, 7, and 10 year property use the 200% DB method for personal property, unless an election is made to use the 150% DB method or the SL method, and automatically switch to SL when it results in a larger depreciation for a year. If additions or improvements are made to a property, they are treated separately and are depreciated from the time the additions or improvements are placed in service. Most personal property is classified as either 3-year, 5-Year, 7-Year, or 10-year property (200% DB method).
- 3-Year Class – Certain tools and devices used in manufacturing, race horses more than 2 years old, and qualified rent-to-own property.
- 5-Year Class – Automobiles, light and heavy duty trucks, computers and peripheral equipment, and office equipment such as calculators and copiers. Also, farm machinery. (ADS - also 5 years).
- 7-Year Class – Office furniture and fixtures such as desks, safes and communication equipment; some assets used in agriculture such as certain machinery and equipment and fences; and horses held for breeding purposes. (ADS - 12 years).
- 10-Year Class – Agriculture trees or vines bearing fruit or nuts and water transportation equipment.
- All property that doesn't fit into one of the 6 Classes is considered 7-Year property under MACRS (ADS – 12 years).
- 15 and 20-Year property uses the 150% DB method under GDS. 15 year property includes land improvements such as roads, landscaping, asphalt parking areas, curbs, decorative walls, and shrubbery and plants (ADS – 20 years). 15 year property also includes farm property other than trees or vines bearing fruit. 20 year property includes farm buildings.
NOTE: a taxpayer may elect SL depreciation for a Class, and if elected, all property in that class must be depreciated using SL (GDS), and the election is irrevocable.

- Qualified leasehold improvements – any improvement to the interior portion of a building if made under or pursuant to a lease which must be put to use more than three years after the date the building opened for business (excluding elevators and any interior structural framework of a building) that is non-residential real property. Applies to leasehold improvements made before 1/1/2014. In 2013, allows 15 year SL depreciation (GDS) (ADS – 39 years). In 2013, <u>qualifies for Sec. 179 expensing up to $250,000</u>, **and bonus depreciation** (not for ADS).
- Qualified restaurant building property and improvements if more than 50% of the building's square footage is devoted to the preparation of meals and customer seating (encompasses the entire building structure, including interior costs). Applies to buildings placed in service after 12/31/08 and before 1/1/2014. This is Section 1250 property, which in 2013 allows 15 year SL depreciation (GDS. ADS - 39 years). In 2013, <u>qualifies for Sec. 179 expensing up to $250,000, but does not qualify for bonus depreciation</u> (not for ADS).
- Qualified retail improvement property, which covers only improvements to nonresidential building interior costs of a building that is open to the general public and used in a retail business of selling tangible personal property to the general public (does not include enlargement of a building, interior structural framework of a building, or elevators), and which must be put to use more than three years after the date the building opened for business. Applies to retailers who own their buildings as well as retailers who lease. Property must be placed in service before 1/1/2014. This is Section 1250 property that in 2013 allows 15 year SL depreciation (GDS. ADS - 39 years). In 2013, <u>qualifies for Sec. 179 expensing up to $250,000, but does not qualify for bonus depreciation</u> (not for ADS).

Residential Rental Property
Residential Rental Property (including mobile homes) is depreciated over 27.5 years using the SL method under GDS (ADS – 40 years) – does not include hotels and motels. Improvements or additions are depreciated separately from the time the improvements or additions are made. In some cases, land improvements (see above) can be depreciated over 15 years, and bonus depreciation can be applied.
- If you own residential <u>rental</u> property and buy new appliances for that property, you cannot claim 179 first year expensing for the appliances because the 179 deduction is limited to business property and not to property acquired for the production of income (investment property), such as rental property. However, you can claim first year 50% bonus depreciation as long as the appliances are new as well as with regular depreciation for the appliances purchased and placed in service in 2013.

<u>Non-residential real property is depreciated over 39 years using SL under GDS</u> (ADS – 40 years). Leasehold improvements are depreciated over 15 years (ADS – 39 years) (see above). ADS must be

used for tangible property used outside of the U.S., tax-exempt property, and certain imported property. Short tax years (less than 12 months) have special rules.

For Section 1031 property (like-kind exchange) and Section 1033 property (involuntary conversion), when both the acquired property and relinquished property are subject to MACRS, the depreciation period and method used are generally the same for the acquired and relinquished properties, i.e. the replacement property is depreciated beginning in the year of the replacement and using the same convention, period, and method as the relinquished property. **(SEE "Income Exclusions," No Gain or Loss is Recognized in a Like-Kind Exchange; and "Taxable Income," Abandonment of Property)**

Listed Property
Listed property is Section 1245 personal property that has limitations on the amount of depreciation, bonus depreciation, and 179 expensing that can be claimed in a year. If new listed property is used more than 50% for business purposes, it is eligible for GDS depreciation (200% DB), bonus depreciation, and 179 expensing in the year placed in service. However, listed property used 50% or less for business purposes must be depreciated using ADS, which is straight-line (SL) depreciation, and no bonus depreciation or 179 expensing is allowed. Listed property is often used for both business and pleasure including:
- Passenger vehicles used for transportation – New passenger automobiles placed in service in 2013 have further limitations on depreciation, i.e. they can only be depreciated each year in accordance with a table (including 50% bonus depreciation and 179 expensing): Limitation of depreciation allowed in 1st year - $11,160 (includes $8,000 for bonus depreciation); 2nd year - $5,100; 3rd year - $3,050; and each succeeding year - $1,875. Used vehicles do not qualify for 50% bonus depreciation, so their limited depreciation for the first year is $3,160 and the other years are the same.
    - Trading in a vehicle (or any equipment) for another vehicle defers any gain or loss, and the basis of the new vehicle is the adjusted basis of the old vehicle plus the amount paid after the trade-in, which is used for depreciation purposes because the transaction is considered a like-kind exchange. **(SEE "Income Exclusions," No Gain or Loss is Recognized in a Like-Kind Exchange)**
- Other property used as a means of transportation – includes SUVs, trucks, buses, trains, etc. unless they are qualified non-personal use vehicles (not likely to be used more than a de minimis amount for personal purposes).
    - Limitation on depreciation for new light trucks and vans under 6,000 pounds placed in service in 2013 is not as much as for passenger cars in accordance with the tables: 1st year - $11,360; 2nd year - $5,400; 3rd year - $3,250; every succeeding year - $1,975. 1st year for used trucks and vans - $3,360.

- o New SUV's, trucks, and vans over 6,000 pounds, but no more than 14,000 pounds, placed in service in 2013 escape the annual depreciation caps for passenger vehicles and light trucks and vans. However, <u>the yearly Sec. 179 expense deduction for these vehicles is limited to $25,000</u>. Also, they are still used as a means of transportation and are still subject to the definition of listed property, so two restrictions apply if used 50% or less for business: (1) depreciation is limited to ADS; and (2) bonus depreciation and 179 expensing not allowed.
  - o Certain trucks and vans that weigh more than 14,000 pounds are <u>entirely exempt from the $25,000 Section 179 expense limitation</u> (usually considered non-personal use vehicles) if they:
    a. Have a seating capacity of <u>more</u> than nine passengers <u>behind</u> the driver's seat,
    b. Equipped with a cargo area at least 6 feet in length that is an open area not readily assessable from the driver's seat, or
    c. Have a fully enclosed driver and cargo compartment, with no seating rear of the driver's seat, and is a stub-nosed vehicle.
- <u>Leased passenger vehicles</u> – Sec. 280F(c) limits deductions for the cost of leasing automobiles, expressed as an income inclusion amount according to a formula and tables prescribed under Reg. Sec. 1.280F-7. The revenue procedure provides an updated table of the amounts to be included in income by lessees of passenger automobiles and another for trucks and vans, in both cases with lease terms that begin in calendar year 2013. However, this only applies if you deduct the cost of leasing a vehicle as a business expense. <u>Also, you are allowed to use the standard business mileage rates for leased cars, trucks, and vans.</u> **(SEE "Employee Travel and Entertainment Expenses," Vehicle and Other Transportation Expenses)**

Listed Property Other Than Vehicles
- Property used for entertainment, recreation, or amusement purposes – includes photographic, phonographic, and video recording equipment, <u>unless used exclusively (100%) in taxpayer's trade or business</u>.
- Computer and peripheral equipment, <u>unless used 100% in taxpayer's regular business establishment, which includes an office in a taxpayer's home</u>. Depreciation on a computer used to manage investments can be deducted as an investment deduction (miscellaneous itemized deduction), whether used predominately in business or not; however, they are <u>always considered listed property if used only to manage investments</u>.
- **<u>Cell phones and other similar telecommunications equipment were removed from being classified as listed property in 2010</u>**. Therefore, when employers provide cell phones to their employees or when employers reimburse employees for business use of their cell phones, <u>tax-</u>

free treatment is applied without burdensome recordkeeping requirements. **(SEE "Income Exclusions," Employer Paid Assistance Programs)**

Not Listed Property

If used 50% or less for business purposes, property that is not "listed" property can be depreciated using GDS (200% DB) with no restrictions on the use of 179 expensing and bonus depreciation. Non-personal use vehicles are not listed property, including:
- Ambulances and hearses
- School buses
- Dump trucks
- Fire trucks
- Tractors and combines
- Cement mixers
- Trucks and vans specifically modified, such as shelving and painting a vehicle to display advertising or company name
- Taxies, buses, or vans used for transporting people for compensation
- Vehicles designed to carry cargo and weighing over 14,000 pounds
- Boats used for transportation (if qualified non-personal use vehicle)
- Planes used for transportation (if qualified non-personal use vehicle)

Not Listed Property Other than Vehicles
- Furniture and Equipment
- Photographic, phonographic, communication or video recording equipment used exclusively (100%) in connection with the taxpayer's principal trade or business
- Computers and peripheral equipment used at a regular business establishment, including an office in a taxpayer's home if used 100% for business purposes. **(SEE "Carrying on a Trade of Business," Sole Proprietors/Self-Employed, Home Office Expenses)**
- **Cell phones and similar telecommunications equipment.**

When listed property (car or truck, etc.) formerly used predominately (more than 50%) in a trade or business is converted to personal use (less than 50% business use), any depreciation that exceeds the amount that would have been allowed under the alternative depreciation system (ADS), as well as any 179 expensing and bonus depreciation taken, must be recaptured as ordinary income reported on Form 4797 and added to the basis of the property. The depreciation that must be recaptured is the difference between 200% declining balance (DB) claimed under the general depreciation system (GDS) and straight-line depreciation under ADS. The recapture period for listed vehicles ceases after 6 years, because the normal ADS recovery period for vehicles is 6 years (2 part years, plus 4 full years). However, a taxpayer may continue to depreciate the vehicle after 6 years until it is fully depreciated.

For example, if a taxpayer uses a car 100% for business purposes, he can continue to depreciate it at $1,875 a year or the remaining basis, whichever is less. If the car is used less than 100% for business purposes, e.g. 60%, the taxpayer can claim a depreciation deduction equal to his percentage of business usage (60% of $1,875 = $1,125), but he <u>still has to reduce the basis of the car by the full $1,875 per year</u>. The same holds true for the first 6 years, i.e. the car's basis has to be reduced by the full 100% allowable depreciation, even if the car is used, say, only 60% for business purposes. **(See "Carrying on a Trade or Business," Sale of Business Property (Form 4797)**

If other property (not listed) used in a trade or business is converted to personal use, the property is treated as disposed of in that year, and no gain, loss, or depreciation recapture is recognized upon conversion.

Other Methods of Depreciation
MACRS is generally the required method; however, MACRS does not apply to any property that can properly be depreciated under a method not expressed in terms of years.
- Sum-of-the-Years Digits Method – the Sum-of-the-Years digits method is computed by multiplying the basis of the property (reduced by estimated salvage value) by a <u>fraction</u> which changes based on the remaining useful life. The fraction equals the remaining useful life, divided by the sum-of-the-years digits (sum-of-the-years digits does not change, i.e. 5 years = 15). Can only be used for tangible property having a useful life of 3 years or more.
- Forecast Method (10 taxable years) – can be used for film, sound recordings, copyrights, books, patents, etc. and may be used for any amortizable property.

Energy-Efficient Commercial Building Deduction (Form 3115)
The 179D energy-efficient commercial building deduction provides an immediate depreciation deduction of up to $1.80 per square foot for energy-efficient features of a building's construction, renovation, or retrofit (remodel) that achieves a 50% reduction in total energy and power cost; <u>for buildings placed in service from 2006 through 2013</u>. Qualifying buildings can include commercial and multifamily residential structures so long as they have more than three stories above grade. **The taxpayer must secure an analysis by a qualified professional engineering company or contractor licensed in the jurisdiction where the property is located, who must use software prescribed by the IRS**. The deduction is effectively an acceleration of depreciation deductions that would have otherwise been spread over a 39-year recovery life, and reduces tax basis accordingly. Three primary building components must be analyzed by the engineer, with each available for a deduction of from $.30 to a maximum of $.60 per square foot (partial deductions must show a 25% - 40% reduction in energy cost). The three components are (1) interior lighting systems; (2) HVAC (heating, ventilation and air conditioning) systems; and (3) the building envelope, defined as the outer shell used to protect the indoor environment as well as to facilitate its climate control, such as insulation, windows, upgrades to

walls, reflective coating (low-E coating can be applied to the outside of window panes to reduce heat coming into the building and to the inside pane of glass to help retain heat in the building in colder climates), green roof systems and cool roof systems, insulation and sealant systems, insulated exterior cladding, etc. For government buildings, the building designer (architect) can take the deduction. A 179D deduction should be shown on Form 1040 under "other deductions' with a description "179D."

- IRS Revenue Procedure 2011-14, released in 2012, now makes it possible to take the 179D deduction as far back as the 2006 tax year, by way of an automatic "change of accounting" method instead of amending prior years' tax returns. This is a huge positive for taxpayers who can claim deductions under 179D.

Cost Segregation Study - Other Related Tax Savings Opportunity Separate From 179D
For existing buildings (any building placed in service since 1/1/1987), <u>a qualified engineering company accepted by the IRS can perform a cost segregation study</u> to identify land improvements and property traditionally depreciated over 27.5 or 39 years (real property) that can be reclassified as property that can be depreciated over 5, 7, and 15 years, thus accelerating depreciation of the building. Such property is Section 1245 personal property that includes windows, electrical wiring, track and decorative lighting, wall paneling, counters, freezers, flooring, and wall partitions (depreciated over 5 and 7 years) as well as site or land improvements – sidewalks, sewers, curbs, etc. (depreciated over 15 years).

Deconstruction
Deconstruction is being used by more homeowners who try to avoid the wrecking ball when they remodel or completely tear down an old house and build a new house on the same site. In this process, a crew carefully dismantles an older property by hand instead of using bulldozers. The process costs more than a straightforward demolition, roughly double what would be paid for a wrecking crew. However, you are able to donate home materials such as lumber, roof tiles and even lamps to nonprofit organizations for reuse and get a tax write-off. For example, one family using "deconstruction" donated materials that were "appraised" by an appraisal-and-consulting firm at $159,000, which resulted in a tax savings of $66,000, more than three times the cost of the deconstruction. Spurring the movement is a growing awareness of "green" building, as well as more laws restricting the dumping of building materials into landfills. The growing surge in using deconstruction is currently centered along the West Coast, in areas such as Silicon Valley and cities including San Diego, Los Angeles, Portland, and Seattle.

Repairs vs. Capital Improvements
In September 2013, the IRS issued final regulations on the treatment of costs to acquire, produce, or improve tangible property. Taxpayers will apply these regulations to determine whether they can deduct costs as repairs under Code Sec. 162(a) or must capitalize the costs under Code Sec. 263(a) and

recover them over a period of years. The IRS also re-proposed regulations on dispositions of property under Code Sec. 168. <u>The final regulations do not apply until tax years beginning on or after January 1, 2014</u>. Taxpayers can apply the final regulations to tax years beginning in or after 2012. The final regulations address a universal issue arising over repair and maintenance costs: whether a particular payment "to acquire, produce or improve" tangible property must be capitalized and recovered over time (depreciated), or whether it can be deducted immediately. The final regulations debunk the doctrine that has always required repairs to be capitalized when performed at the same time as improvements that renovate or rehabilitate an asset.

- Improvements, betterments, and restorations generally must be capitalized while repairs can be deducted. While repairs improve a property, the degree of improvement is an important distinction. Permanent improvements, betterments and restorations as well as payments that add to the property's value, prolong its useful life, or adapt the property to a new use must be capitalized. <u>The final regulations allow taxpayers to elect to capitalize repair and maintenance costs as improvements if capitalized for book purposes</u>.
    - **Materials and supplies rule** - Materials and supplies that cost $200 or less are currently deductible as expenses if consumed and used in the operation of the business during the current year. Materials and supplies include a component acquired to maintain, repair, or improve a unit of tangible property that is not acquired as part of any single unit of property. <u>A unit of property consists of all components of the property that are functionally interdependent</u>. Generally, the larger a unit of property, the greater the advantage to the taxpayer, since amounts spent on a portion of the property would be relatively smaller and therefore more likely to not rise to a level of significance sufficient to warrant being considered an improvement required to be capitalized. However, a component of a unit of property can be treated as a separate unit of property if, when initially placed in service (or subsequently due to reclassification), the taxpayer properly depreciated the component using a different class or method of depreciation from the larger unit of property.
    - **Facilitative expenses** – Amounts paid to acquire or produce a unit of property must be capitalized, unless deductible under the materials and supplies rule or the de minimis rule. Such amounts include transaction costs and facilitative expenses, which includes work performed before or after an asset is placed in service. However, <u>employee compensation and overhead related to an acquisition of property are not required to be capitalized under this provision</u>.
    - **Commercial Buildings** – The final regulations view a commercial building as a single unit of property. However, in applying the standards of capitalization, <u>the regulations require nine major system components of a building to be analyzed against capitalization standards separately</u>: the building structure (exterior walls, roof, windows, doors, etc.); heating; air conditioning; plumbing; electrical; elevators; escalators; fire protection; and security systems. Any significant work on any of these components must be capitalized. A taxpayer can recognize a loss on the retirement of a structural component without having to dispose of the entire

building, i.e. rather than continue to depreciate the cost of the component replaced while simultaneously starting to depreciate the cost of the new improvement (replacement component), you can consider the retirement of a structural component of a building as a disposition. You can use Form 3115 to go back and write off the components that were ripped out. Form 3115 is used for an automatic change in accounting method, which must be filed with your tax return. However, this unfortunately can create an unfavorable result, because you are required to take a retirement loss when a component is removed even if the new expenditure (which must be capitalized) would otherwise satisfy the criteria of a repair expense which is probably more than the retirement loss you are required to take. The newly modified rules do provide the option to continue depreciating any asset that is disposed if you make an election to use General Asset Accounting (GAA) rules for your property, which means that you may be able to take a repair deduction rather than capitalize it. For example, if a building and its original roof shingles were in a GAA, you could choose to continue depreciating the old roof shingles and take a repair deduction on the new roof shingles. The GAA rules stipulate that only assets depreciated the same way can be in the same GAA (i.e. assets with the same MACRS tax life, recovery method, convention, and effective placed in service date). The GAA election is made by checking a box on the Form 4562, and taxpayers will need to keep records of which assets are in which GAA. Further, a GAA election must be made on a timely filed tax return (including extensions) for the year the asset was placed in service. In light of these changes, the IRS is allowing two years for taxpayers to file retroactive GAA elections for assets placed in service before 2012 using Form 3115, Automatic Change of Accounting Method Form. If you miss that window, you may be stuck indefinitely with the new procedures.

- **The final regulations provide a new safe harbor for small taxpayers with average annual gross receipts of $10 million or less to deduct annual costs spent on a building, provided the building's unadjusted basis is $1 million or less. Small taxpayers do not have to analyze the building systems. This allows small taxpayers to elect not to apply the improvement rules to a building property if the total amount paid during the taxable year for repairs, maintenance, improvements, and similar activities performed on the building does not exceed the lesser of $10,000 or 2% of the unadjusted basis of the building.**
- <u>De minimis safe harbor</u> – Taxpayers required to file <u>audited financial statements</u> are allowed to claim a <u>current deduction</u> for the cost of acquiring relatively low cost property, including materials and supplies. Taxpayers with an applicable audited financial statement can apply the safe harbor to property of $5,000 or less. The rules extend the safe harbor to taxpayers without a financial statement to property that costs $500 per item or invoice. Taxpayers and examining agents can agree to different thresholds. The safe harbor is an elective rule. This policy is an annual irrevocable election and must be included with a timely filed tax return upon adoption. Following is an example of wording that can be used in making the election:

- "ABC Company elects to adopt for book and Federal income tax purposes the following policy regarding the capitalization of expenses for the year beginning Jan. 1, 2014. In accordance with Internal Revenue Code Sections 167 and 168 and related regulations, ABC company has determined that amounts whose individual cost (including tax, installation and delivery costs) does not exceed $500 will be deducted as incurred as an operating expense. Amounts exceeding this dollar amount will be examined individually to determine if their use or purpose requires capitalization under the betterment, adaption, or restoration rules used by the IRS and will be capitalized or expensed as incurred as a result of the application of those rules." (Companies with audited financial statements should replace $500 with $5,000).

Depletion

Gross income from oil and gas royalties is allowed an annual percentage depletion at 15% per year **(including oil and gas from marginal wells in 2010 and 2011)**. Also applies to mines, timber, and other natural resources, but depletion percentages may be different. In addition, any rents or other expenses is deducted from gross income in addition to percentage depletion in computing net income received by a royalty recipient. **NOTE: percentage depletion for oil and gas from marginal wells is not allowable beginning in 2012 according to the American Taxpayer Relief Act of 2012**.

- Can either use percentage depletion (as above) or cost depletion.
- Any gain realized from disposition of royalty property must be treated as ordinary income to extent deductions for depletion reduced the adjusted basis of the property.
- The amount subject to depletion includes capitalized drilling and development costs, which are added to the basis of the property for the purpose of determining gain on the sale or disposition of property. Recapture of depletion is treated as ordinary income upon sale of property.
- Cost depletion must be used if greater than percentage depletion. Cost depletion is computed by dividing the basis by the number of units of minerals (oil and gas) remaining at the beginning of the year multiplied by the number of mineral units sold during the year.

Amortization of Intangible Assets

Generally, you may amortize the capitalized costs of Section 197 intangibles ratably over 15 years (180 months) if you hold the intangibles in connection with your trade or business or in an activity engaged in for the production of income. The 15-year period begins with the later of the month the intangible is acquired or the month the trade or business or activity engaged in for the production of income begins. You cannot deduct amortization for the month you dispose of the intangible asset. If you pay or incur an amount that increases the basis of an intangible after the 15-year period begins, amortize it over the remainder of the 15-year period beginning with the month the basis increase occurs. The following assets are Section 197 intangibles: goodwill; going concern value; workforce in place;

business books and records, operating systems, or any other information base, including lists or other information concerning current or prospective customers; patents, copyrights, formulas, processes, designs, patterns, literary composition, know-how, formats, or similar items; a customer-based intangible; a supplier-based intangible; license, permit, or other right granted by a governmental unit or agency (including issuances and renewals); a covenant not to compete entered into in connection with the acquisition of an interest in a trade or business; and any franchise, trademark, or trade name.

- Intangibles must have an ascertainable value and a limited life in order to be amortized over a 15 year period (however, see safe-harbor rule). Generally, goodwill, going concern value, etc. must be purchased in order to be amortized. Goodwill is the value of a trade or business based on expected continued customer patronage due to its name, reputation, or any other factor. Going concern value is the additional value of a trade or business that attaches to property because the property is an integral part of an ongoing business activity. It includes value based on the ability of a business to continue to function and generate income even though there is a change in ownership.
- Corporate goodwill is a separate asset that represents the intangible qualities that bring with them continued patronage. It can be sold, and the gain can be taxed as a capital gain. The buyer can amortize the goodwill on a stepped-up basis. This occurs most often within the context of the sale of a closely held corporation.
- "Personal goodwill" is separate from corporate goodwill and can occur when an individual does not have an employment contract, and the individual's personal attributes and relationships constitute a separate asset distinct from corporate goodwill; the sale of which represents compensation to the individual that is taxed as ordinary income.
- **The Safe-Harbor amortization rules apply to self-created intangible assets without readily attainable useful lives. Therefore they can be amortized over 15 years (i.e. a literary composition).**

Carrying on a Trade or Business

Business income and expenses for the different forms of business organizations are reported as follows: Sole proprietorships/self-employed – Schedule C, Form 1040; Profit or Loss From Farming - Schedule F, Form 1040; Partnerships – Form 1065; Corporations – Form 1120; and Subchapter S-Corporations – Form 1120S. Form 990 is filed for Tax Exempt Organizations.

The new Form 1099-K, "Merchant Card and Third-Party Payments" is important if you are in the retail business, restaurant business, etc., and you accept payments with credit cards. It also applies to those selling products on internet sites like eBay and Amazon. Credit card companies are required to provide information about what a business was paid through them by credit or debit cards on Form 1099-K if gross payments exceed $20,000 for the year and when there are more than 200 transactions with the participating payee. If a business accepts credit cards and meets the above criteria, they are going to receive a 1099-K showing the amount of payments they received through charges on the credit card(s), which the IRS originally planned to use to match to tax return information. **As it turns out now, the IRS will not require businesses to reconcile to the Form 1099-Ks in 2013, or as it looks like now, in future years** (the IRS has no plans to match 1099-Ks to business returns). However, it is a good idea for merchants to make sure that there is enough difference between the 1099-K credit card sales and the total sales reported so that a reasonable amount of cash sales are included, considering the type of business. Regarding Form 1099-K, the problem that many businesses face is that their gross transactions are being reported and most small businesses just report the net sales on their tax returns, so by definition this is going to be a mismatch.

Business Expenses Are "Use or Lose"
If you spent the money on your business and have documentation to prove it, you are required to take the expense off against your business income in the applicable year. Therefore, for whatever purpose you may have, shorting your legitimate deductions is not a good idea. Do not manipulate your expenses for Earned Income Tax Credit purposes, as that can lead to trouble with the IRS. Taxpayers have a choice of taking the standard deduction or itemized deductions, even if the itemized deductions are more. This is not the case for business income and deductions. The IRS expects a business to report all their income and take the ordinary and necessary expenses they paid in connection with the business.

Federal Unemployment Tax Act (FUTA)
FUTA is imposed on employers at a 6.2% rate on the first $7,000 paid annually to each covered employee.

Accrual Method of Accounting

Revenue is recognized when payments are received under the cash method of accounting and also for tax purposes. However under the accrual method, the "matching principle" governs the recognizing of income in the books for financial accounting purposes. The tax law is largely unconcerned with the matching principle. For tax purposes, an accrual basis taxpayer is required to recognize income when "all events" have occurred to fix the taxpayer's right to the income and the amount can be determined with reasonable accuracy, which would be the earlier of three dates: the date on which the income is earned, due, or received. However, accrual basis taxpayers can defer "advance" payments to a limited degree. An advance payment is cash you get in year one for a service or product that will not be provided until year two and beyond. In addition, in order to be considered an advance payment for tax purposes, the payment must be treated as deferred revenue on the business's financial statements. Here's the limited part - for tax purposes the advance payment must have been received for: services; the sale of goods; the use (including by license or lease) of intellectual property; the sale, lease or license of computer software; warranty contracts; subscriptions; memberships in an organization; or any combinations of the above. If any of these criteria are met, the taxpayer is allowed to defer the same amount of revenue for the advance payment that is deferred in the business's books. Then in the next year (year 2), all the remaining income related to the advance payment must be recognized, regardless of how much revenue is recognized in year two for book purposes. Also, an employer using the accrual method of accounting may, for tax purposes, take a deduction in the current year for a fixed amount of bonuses payable to a group of employees even though the employer does not know which employees will receive a bonus or the amount of any particular bonus until after the end of the tax year. The employer can establish the "fact of liability" under Code Sec. 461.

Business or Hobby

For tax purposes, a hobby is an activity that is "not engaged in for profit." If an individual, S-corporation, or partnership does not engage in an activity for profit, Code Sec. 183 limits deductions from the activity to the income from the activity. This is commonly known as the "hobby loss limitation" and is aimed at activities primarily carried on as a sport, hobby, or recreational activity. The for-profit restrictions do not apply to C-corporations; they are aimed at individuals. To treat the activity as a business, the taxpayer must have a good faith expectation of making a profit. The burden is normally on the taxpayer to prove that an activity is a business, i.e. has a profit motive. However, a test whereby an activity may be presumed to be a business is when it shows a profit for any three years during a consecutive five-year period (two out of seven years for horse breeding and other horse-related activities) – the burden of proof normally shifts to the IRS when this can be demonstrated. If a taxpayer is questioned before this time frame has elapsed, he/she can file Form 5213 (Election to postpone determination of whether an activity is engaged in for a profit) within 60 days of receiving an IRS notice to delay determination until the end of the fourth year (sixth year for horses). However, filing this form also extends the statute of limitations for the activity, i.e. if the taxpayer fails to demonstrate a business activity, the IRS can go back 5 years and disallow any prior losses, plus penalties. In addition to the 3 out of 5 year rule to show a profit, the IRS has provided guidance on factors it will use to determine whether a business with a loss is a for-profit venture: (1) is there an intention to make a profit; (2) does taxpayer depend on income from the activity, i.e. the fact that the taxpayer does not have substantial income or capital from other sources may indicate an activity is for profit; (3) did the losses occur in the start-up phase of the business; (4) has the taxpayer made a profit in similar activities in the past; (5) does the activity make a profit in some years; (6) carries on activity in a business-like manner (maintains books and records, separate checking account, etc.); (7) has expertise or skills involved with the activity; (8) amount of time and effort expended in the activity; (9) elements of pleasure or recreation may indicate that the activity is a hobby, but not necessarily. In addition, other considerations should be given to the type of activity and whether it is one that happens to take more time than normal to turn a profit, particularly in a recession economy. Also, it is important to know whether a taxpayer acquired a loan to start up the business or for operating capital. Would anyone operating an activity as a hobby get into debt and personally guarantee a loan just to create a loss?

- Hobby income goes on line 21 of Form 1040 (not subject to self-employment tax). Expenses go on Schedule A as miscellaneous itemized deductions subject to the 2% floor (including depreciation), and may not be carried forward if not used in the current year. Some of the expenses may be deductible anyway, i.e. mortgage interest and property taxes. The result is that the miscellaneous itemized deductions will be limited, so hobby income will rarely be completely offset.
- For entities such as limited partnerships, the hobby loss limitation rule applies to tax shelters and may be used to deny deductions to the partners or shareholders if the entity was set-up primarily to generate large tax losses and not to make a profit.

At-Risk Rules

The rules generally apply to a trade or business and to activities engaged in for profit. The at-risk rules apply to individuals, individual partners of a partnership, and individual shareholders of an S-corporation; but do not apply to widely held C-corporations, partnerships, and S-corporations at the entity level. The at-risk rules are applied to partners and S-corporation shareholders before the passive activity loss rules. A loss that is denied under the at-risk rules is not a passive loss. The at-risk rules limit the deduction of losses to the taxpayer's investment in the activity (the amount the taxpayer could actually lose) and denies losses that exceed the taxpayer's investment. If a taxpayer is denied a loss because of the at-risk rules, the loss may be carried over for deduction in subsequent tax years when the amount at-risk increases. **The rules are more lenient for real estate activities**. The amount at risk includes:

- The amount of money (whether a contribution to capital or a loan);
- The adjusted basis (not fair market value) of property contributed to the activity;

- Income from the activity (or from selling an interest in the activity) – all income ever received or made from the activity;
- Loan balances by the taxpayer for which the taxpayer is personally liable or has pledged property as collateral, other than property used in the activity;
- If the taxpayer has a loss or makes a withdrawal from the business, that figure reduces the amount at risk;
- **If a taxpayer engages in a <u>real estate activity</u>, the individual is also at risk for qualified nonrecourse financing for which there is no personal liability that is secured by real property used in the activity, and that is loaned by a government or "qualified person" (an unrelated person who is in the business of lending money and who was not the seller of the property).** This exception does not apply to amounts borrowed from a person holding an interest in the activity or a person related to the interest-holder.

<u>Not considered at risk</u>:
- Personal services, though they have a value, are not treated as a capital contribution;
- Amounts borrowed from related persons or persons having an interest in the activity (other than creditors) are not considered at risk if the activity involves: farming; oil, gas, or geothermal development; or certain other activities;
- Amounts are not considered at risk if they are protected by nonrecourse financing, guarantees, stop-loss agreements, or similar arrangements.

Passive vs. Non-passive Income
Unlike the at-risk rules, which focus on financial contributions to the business, the passive activity loss rules focus on the individual's participation in the business. The passive activity rules apply to: individuals, personal service corporations, closely held C-corporations, partners, and S-corporation shareholders. The rules do not apply to partnerships, S-corporations, or widely held C-corporations. <u>Non-passive income</u> includes portfolio income which generally includes interest, dividends, royalties, and annuities, although portfolio income derived in the ordinary course of a passive trade or business may be passive income. Passive activity income does not include income from: personal services and covenants not to compete; a working interest in oil and gas property; intangible property significantly created by the taxpayer; and income tax refunds. Also, anti-abuse provisions prevent active and portfolio income from being converted into passive income and soaking up passive activity losses. Thus, passive income also does not include income from: <u>"significant participation" passive activities</u> (rental activities); rental and sale of property developed by the taxpayer; rental of property to a trade or business in which the taxpayer materially participates; rental of non-depreciable property; and equity-financed lending activities and interests in pass-through entities that license intangible property if the taxpayer acquires the interest after the entity creates the property. **(SEE "Taxable Income," Passive Activity Income)**

Start-up and Organizational Costs

In creating a trade or business, sole proprietorships, partnerships, limited liability companies, and corporations, often have certain start-up and organizational costs that are incurred before activities of the trade or business actually begin. Start-up costs and organizational costs for a business had to be capitalized and amortized until 10/22/2004. However, for such expenditures incurred after 10/22/2004, taxpayers can elect to deduct up to $5,000 in start-up expenses (sole proprietorships) or organizational expenses (corporations and partnerships). The remainder of the start-up or organizational costs can be amortized over the 180-month period (15 years) beginning with the month in which the active trade or business begins. <u>The deductible amount is reduced by the excess of total start-up costs or organizational costs over $50,000</u>. Start-up expenses are the costs of getting started in business before you actually begin doing business. Start-up costs include expenses for advertising, supplies, travel, communications, utilities, repairs, and employee wages. These expenses are often the same kinds of costs that can be deducted when they occur after you open for business. Start-up costs also include the costs of investigating a prospective business before you get it started. For example, start-up costs may include: a market review of potential business opportunities; an analysis of open office spaces, or labor potential in your community; marketing and advertising to open shop; salaries and wages for employees who are being trained plus their instructors; travel and other necessary costs for signing up prospective distributors, suppliers, or customers; and salaries and fees for executives and consultants or for other professional services. Start-up costs do not include deductible interest, taxes, or research and experimental costs. Organizational costs include costs of legal services to organize a business, such as filing fees with the State to set up a Limited Liability Company or Corporation; setting up accounting services; and drafting a corporation charter, partnership agreement, by-laws, and terms of stock certificates. Commissions paid in connection with issuing and marketing a partnership interest are considered "syndication" fees and are not deductible. **NOTE: For 2010 (one year only), the Small Business Jobs Act raised the deduction limit for start-up costs (sole proprietors, but not corporations or partnerships) to $10,000 and increased the phase-out threshold to $60,000.**

- Effective 9/6/2008, taxpayers are considered to have made the election unless they clearly elect to capitalize the costs.
- Start-up and Organizational expenses must be deducted in the year in which the business becomes active. Therefore, even if you do not have any income to report, you must file a tax return to preserve the tax benefit of these amortizable and otherwise deductible expense items. If you don't report the expenses in the year they are incurred, you will be unable to deduct them against future income in most cases.
- If business operations never begin or are abandoned, the expenses are deductible only to the extent allowable to individual taxpayers (no loss allowable – think hobby rules).

- If a taxpayer disposes of a trade or business before the end of the deduction period, any deferred expenses not yet deducted may be deducted to the extent the closing or disposition of the business results in a net operating loss. **(SEE "Taxable Income," Net Operating Loss)**
- If you are purchasing an active trade or business, start-up costs include only investigative costs incurred in the course of a general search for or preliminary investigation of the business (costs that help you decide whether to purchase a business). Costs you incur in an attempt to purchase a specific business are capital expenses that you cannot amortize.

Requirement to File Information Returns (Form 1099-MISC, etc.)

If you are in business and pay someone for services in the course of your business and the payments total $600 or more during the year, you must issue a Form 1099-MISC to them. Since the $600 is cumulative, you must keep track of all payments to each service provider. Businesses are required to designate on their returns if they should have filed 1099s to back-up deductions and if they did. There are penalties if you don't issue the 1099s as required. Small businesses, including sole proprietorships, are required to send these information returns (Forms 1099-MISC and Forms 1096's) to the IRS by Feb. 28, but you can get an automatic 30-day extension by filing Form 8809. However, payee statements must be furnished to them by Jan. 31. Exceptions to the 1099 reporting requirement include:

- Payments to corporations, except for legal services. **For payments after 12/31/2011, businesses were supposed to be required to file a 1099 for all payments aggregating $600 or more in a calendar year to a single payee, including corporations. But the requirement for corporations was repealed.**
- Payments for merchandise.
- Payments for telephone and similar services.
- Payments for rent to real estate agents.
- Payments for life insurance, etc.

Where the payments are reported on Form 1099-MISC:

- Payments of $600 or more to individuals (not corporations) for cleaning office space (Box 7).
- Payments of $600 or more to individuals and exchanges of services between individuals (not corporations), excluding real estate agents, for rentals of office space, machines, etc. (Box 1).
- Payments of $600 or more to an attorney in connection with legal services – gross payments are reported in Box 14. But if payment is made in the course of taxpayer's trade or business, it is reported in Box 7.
- Royalty Payments from oil and gas royalties, copyrights, trade names, trademarks, etc. of $10 or more to any other person (not corporations, tax-exempt entities, and government entities) – report gross amount before taxes and expenses (Box 2).
- Prizes and awards (Box 3).
- Physicians (Box 6).

- Payers who sell consumer products of $5,000 or more to any buyer (not corporations) on a commission basis for resale other than to a permanent retail establishment must check Box 9 (no dollar amount has to be shown).

Businesses should start keeping adequate records of payments so they are prepared to issue correct 1099s. They should give a Form W-9 to each service provider to which they make payments of $600 or more in order to obtain the name, address, and taxpayer identification numbers of service providers. Penalties for not filing 1099s range from $30 (first-tier) to $250 for intentional disregard of the requirement.

Business Bad Debt

If a debt is in connection with a trade or business, the loss is an ordinary loss and can be deducted against ordinary income. A business bad debt can be <u>totally or partially</u> worthless. However, in order to write off a business bad debt you must have a bona fide business operation (Not a Hobby), and **you usually have to be on the accrual basis of accounting**. If you are on the cash basis, you cannot have a lack of a sale that was supposed to be for $3,000 and take a $3,000 loss on top of it. But if you are using accrual accounting and had already recorded a sale of $3,000, then you can write off a $3,000 bad debt. However, even if you are on the cash basis you can deduct any expenses related to the invalid sale, such as directly related consulting fees and office supplies and expenses but you cannot write off your time spent on making the sale (your time is worth nothing to the IRS). Also, if you have a sale and the item sold is transferred to a customer who fails to pay you or pays you with a bounced check and you exhaust all collection procedures, you may have a bad debt, and in addition you may have to send the delinquent customer a 1099-C (Cancellation of Debt). **(SEE "Taxable Income," Cancelled Debt)** The same thing would apply to an uncollected loan. If you are an employee and make a loan to an employer who fails to pay you back, you may be able to write off a bad debt on Form 2106.

Business Casualty and Theft Losses

There is no limitation on the amount that can be deducted for business casualty and theft losses. A total business loss is the adjusted basis of the property or item, even if the fair market value (FMV) of the property is less immediately before the loss. A partial business casualty or theft loss is defined as the lesser of the adjusted basis of a property or item or the difference in its FMV immediately before and after the loss (decline in FMV is provable by necessary repairs, etc.). Business losses are reported in Section B of Form 4684 and then taken as a loss on Form 4797. <u>However, if the property is for sale, i.e. income producing property, the loss is reported as a miscellaneous itemized deduction not subject to the 2% floor</u>. You must capitalize amounts paid to restore business property, including amounts paid "for the repair of damage to a unit of property" resulting from a disaster even if your casualty loss is ameliorated by insurance. Example: you have a property damaged by a hurricane that had a 15-year recovery period when placed in service 10 years ago and has been depreciated for 10 years. The cost to repair the property and its remaining basis are both $1 million. In this case, you have two alternatives: (1) you can claim a $1 million casualty loss and depreciate the property's remaining basis of $1 million over 15 years; or (2) You don't claim a casualty loss, but you can deduct the $1 million cost of the repair and continue to depreciate the $1 million remaining basis over the remaining 5 year recovery period. **(SEE "Depreciation," Repairs vs. Capitalization)**

Sale of Business Property (Form 4797)

Form 4797 is used to report sales of business property, including rental property and leaseholds. Generally, any gain on real and depreciable personal property used in a trade or business and rental property that is held more than a year (that is more than the part that is ordinary income due to depreciation) is a <u>Section 1231 gain (treated as long-term capital gain)</u>. There are exceptions to the one year rule: cattle and horses held for draft, breeding, dairy, or sporting purposes must be held for 2 years (24 months) to qualify. Section 1231 makes available the best of both worlds to businesses with a certain combination of capital gains and losses. Net gains from the disposal of Section 1231 property are taxed at capital gains rates, while net losses from the disposal of Section 1231 property are taxed as ordinary losses. If total Section 1231 gains exceed losses for the year, then all gains and losses are capital. If total losses exceed gains for the year, then all gains and losses are ordinary.

- Some Section 1231 gain must be <u>recaptured as ordinary income</u> (depreciation, Section 179 deductions, and any bonus depreciation taken).
- Section 1245 – Personal property: cars, machinery, livestock, equipment, etc. Intangible property: patents, licenses, franchises, trademarks. <u>All</u> depreciation and 179 expensing, plus any bonus depreciation taken is recaptured as ordinary income when the property is sold or disposed of.
- Section 1250 – Non-residential real property, residential rental property, and other depreciable real property. Only straight-line depreciation has been allowed on real property since 1986. However, "Unrecaptured Section 1250 gain" on the sale of such real property is taxed @ 25% instead of being taxed as ordinary income or as a long-term capital gain. Unrecaptured Section 1250 gain is all depreciation taken on real property, which is all straight-line depreciation taken (also, will rarely include any 179 expensing and bonus depreciation taken).
- **Net Section 1231 losses on property held more <u>or less</u> than one year that are not fully applied against Section 1231 gains in the same year are deductible as an <u>ordinary loss (not limited to $3,000)</u> in that year.**
- Non-recaptured Section 1231 losses for the <u>previous 5 years</u> that have not been applied against net Section 1231 gains by treating the gains as ordinary income are applied against net Section 1231 gains beginning with the earliest loss in the 5 year period. Example:

How to figure capital gains and losses for 2012:

Previous 5 year period:

Net Sec. 1231 gain or (loss)

2007	0	2012 Net Sec. 1231 Gain	$2,000
2008	0	Treated as ordinary income	$ 700
2009	($2,500)	Treated as LT capital gain	$1,300
2010	0		
2011	$1,800		

Remaining Sec. 1231 Loss ($ 700)

- When <u>listed</u> property (car or truck, etc.) formerly used predominately (more than 50%) in a trade or business is converted to personal use (less than 50% business use), any depreciation that exceeds the amount that would have been allowed under the alternative depreciation system (ADS) as well as any 179 expensing and bonus depreciation taken must be recaptured as ordinary income reported on Form 4797, and added to the basis of the property. The depreciation that must be recaptured is the difference between 200% declining balance (DB) claimed under the general depreciation system (GDS) and straight-line depreciation under ADS. <u>The recapture period for listed vehicles ceases after 6 years, because the normal ADS recovery period for vehicles is 6 years.</u> **(SEE "Depreciation," Listed Property)**
- If you dispose of (sell) your car, you may have a taxable gain or a deductible loss. The portion of any gain that is due to depreciation (including any 179 expensing and bonus depreciation) that you claimed on the car will be treated as ordinary income. However, you may not have to recognize a gain or loss if you <u>dispose of the car because of a casualty, theft, or trade-in</u>. For a casualty or theft of a car, a gain results when you receive insurance or other reimbursement that is more than your adjusted basis in the car. If you then spend all of the proceeds to acquire replacement property (a new car or repairs to the old car) within a specified period of time, you do not recognize any gain. Your basis in the replacement property is generally your adjusted basis in the old property plus any additional amount you pay. When you <u>trade in an old car for a new one</u>, the transaction is considered a like-kind exchange. Generally, no gain or loss is recognized. Your basis in the new car is generally your adjusted basis in the old car plus any additional amount you pay.
- In general, no gain, loss, or depreciation recapture is recognized upon conversion of non-listed business property to personal property, but this would be recognized when the property is sold.
- No depreciation deduction is allowable for property placed in service and disposed of in the same year, and no gain, loss, or depreciation recapture is recognized. **(SEE "Depreciation," Listed Property)**

NOTE: A taxpayer may wish to time the sale of a depreciable asset to coincide with a loss year. Such timing can enable the taxpayer to be hit with a recapture in a year in which the taxpayer's business has an operating loss (which can be used to offset the recapture amount) rather than in a profitable year, when the recapture liability will increase the taxpayer's taxable income and possibly even move the taxpayer into a higher tax bracket.

Payments to Non-Employees

Payments to non-employees are required to be reported on Form 1099-MISC if payments to any individual are $600 or more in a calendar year. Also, Form 1096 must be filed by the payers. There are deadlines and penalties for incorrect reporting. The following are exempt from reporting requirements for payments to non-employees: (See Independent contractors below)

- Reimbursements of expenses under an accountable plan. **(SEE "Employee Travel and Entertainment Expenses," Lodging, Entertainment, Meals and Incidental Expenses)**
- Payments that are for services outside the U.S. to U.S. citizens, if it is reasonable to believe the amounts will be excluded from income as foreign earned income.

Independent Contractors

Employers who classify workers as independent contractors avoid FICA matching, paying federal unemployment taxes (FUTA), and income tax withholding; they also escape providing benefits such as vacation pay, sick pay, health insurance, and workers' compensation. Moreover, workers may be motivated to be misclassified as independent contractors so they can be paid in cash, avoid withholding of taxes, and/or avoid proving immigration status. Regarding immigration status, workers that are hired in the U.S. have a duty to establish they are here legally. An employee must fill out Form I-9 and verify legal working status, while an independent contractor does not have that duty.

- In the next several years, businesses will have <u>another reason to misclassify workers. In 2015, when the Patient Protection and Affordable Care Act (ACA) is fully implemented, businesses with 50 or more full-time equivalent (FTE) employees will be required to provide health insurance to their employees or pay a substantial penalty</u>. This is known as the employer mandate. When workers are classified as independent contractors and are actually employees, the government loses out on employment tax revenue. A study found that 15% of employers misclassified 3.4 million workers as independent contractors, costing the federal government $1.6 billion. **(SEE "Patient Protection and Affordable Care Act," Provisions Effective Beginning in 2015, Tax Provisions)**
- <u>The ACA requirements suggest that the status of part-time workers could see significant scrutiny</u> by the IRS because businesses often hire part-time, temporary, or seasonal workers and classify them as independent contractors when they are actually employees. Classifying such workers as independent contractors is quickly dispelled when evidence indicates that the work performed by them is substantially similar to the work performed by other workers that

are classified as full-time employees. <u>Under the ACA, part-time employees will be included in the computation in determining if a business has 50 or more FTE employees.</u> **(SEE "Patient Protection and Affordable Care Act," Provisions Effective Beginning in 2010, Tax Provisions)**

There is no bright-line test as to whether a worker is an employee or an independent contractor, because the law is not settled and <u>Section 530 of the Revenue Act of 1978 provides a safe harbor</u> for employers to classify workers as independent contractors and prohibits the IRS from issuing revenue rulings or regulations in this area. <u>In making the determination, all factors that provide evidence of the degree of control and independence must be considered</u>. The following are some determinations as to whether a worker is an employee or an independent contractor:

- The business relationship that exists with the person performing the services is important. He may be an independent contractor; a common-law employee; a statutory employee; or a statutory nonemployee. <u>To classify a particular worker as an independent contractor, the employer cannot have treated the worker and others in substantially similar positions as employees for any prior period.</u> **Some businesses automatically treat workers that have a business name and an employer identification number (EIN) as independent contractors, when they should actually be classified as employees.** In the past, the IRS has inadvertently overlooked many of these situations in audits because the auditors commonly look for Forms 1099 issued to individuals with Social Security numbers. The worker's business name and EIN may disguise an employer-employee relationship.
    - <u>Independent contractor</u> – payer has the right to control or direct <u>only</u> the result of the work and not the means and methods of accomplishing the result (example: worker performs a job for a set fee or based on invoices submitted instead of by the hour, and also does the same type of work for other payers). Reimbursement of business expenses is pursuant to a contract. A business should have an independent contractor complete a Form W-9. <u>Common-Law Employee</u> – payer should withhold FICA, pay FUTA, and issue a Form W-2 to the worker. Payer can control what will be done and <u>how</u> it will be done, even when employee has freedom of action. What matters is that employer has the right to control the details of how the services are performed. Employee receives training from the employer and follows a set program or format in performing the services.
    - **Statutory Employee – certain workers who are independent contractors under the common law rules should, nevertheless, be treated as employees by statute. These include traveling salespersons, insurance salespersons, and individuals who work at home ("home worker") on materials or goods supplied by the payer that must be returned to a person named by the payer if the payer furnishes specifications for the work to be done. Statutory employees are subject to FICA and income tax withholding, but may report their expenses on Schedule C.**

- - Statutory Nonemployee – there are two categories: (1) direct sellers, and (2) licensed real estate agents, both of whom are treated as self-employed for federal tax purposes and have a contract stating as such; therefore they have to pay self-employment taxes.
  - Facts that provide evidence of the degree of control and independence fall into three categories: behavioral control, financial control, and the type of relationship of the parties. The IRS has developed 20 factors that are relevant in determining behavioral control, financial control, and the relationship of the parties: control of when, where, and how the worker performs services; training; integration into firm operations; requirement that services are personally performed; control over assistants; length of relationship; work schedule; number of service hours required; location of services; control over technique or sequence; reports to employer; payment method; work-related expenses; tools; work facilities; profit and loss; multiple employers; restrictions on customers and clients; termination of worker; and termination of relationship by worker. **A general rule is that anyone who performs services for a payer (employer) is an employee if the employer can control what will be done and how it will be done. Contractor or employee? – Questions to ask: Does he work for someone else as well, does he come and go whenever he feels like it (set his own hours), does he have all of his own equipment, and does he obtain customers on his own?**

If a person is a worker and receives a Form 1099-MISC from an employer but thinks he's not an independent contractor and should not have to pay self-employment tax because he was previously treated as an employee or is doing the same or similar work as co-workers who are treated as employees, then that person should file Form SS-8 "Determination of Worker Status for Purposes of Federal Taxes and Income Tax Withholding" with the IRS. Employers that do not withhold taxes from "employees" wages may be liable for not only the employer's share of employment taxes but also the worker's share, unless they can prove the worker reported and paid it. Contracts saying workers aren't employees have no tax effect, i.e. the IRS can still reclassify independent contractors as employees. If the IRS reclassifies an employer's independent contractors as employees, they can get some relief on back income taxes not withheld and FICA taxes owed if the misclassification was not intentional. However, if the IRS determines that the employer's conduct was willful, it can be hit with tax deficiencies exceeding 40% of reclassified salaries for the previous three years. Contrast this with the limited penalties levied under the IRS Voluntary Classification Settlement Program (VCSP) in which the employer pays 1.1% of total compensation paid to workers for one year. Following are details of the VCSP:

- **Voluntary Classification Settlement Program (VCSP)** – Under the IRS's VCSP, employers may reclassify independent contractors as employees, which limits the resulting payroll taxes for their most recent tax year and avoids related penalties and interest for prior years because there is no admission of guilt (the employer is not making a representation as to the proper status of the workers for prior years). To participate the VCSP, employers must submit an application and agree to prospectively treat their workers or a class or group of workers as employees for employment tax purposes in future tax periods. In return, employers will pay 10% of the employment tax liability otherwise due for the most recent tax year, which will not be subject to interest or penalties. In addition, the IRS will not conduct an employment tax audit with respect to worker classification for prior years. To be eligible for the Program, a taxpayer can be under an IRS audit other than an employment tax audit. However, a taxpayer is not eligible to participate in the Program if he/she is contesting in court the classification of the class or classes of workers from a previous audit by the IRS or the Department of Labor. Employers whose worker classification has been previously audited must have complied with the results of the audit. Also, employers must have consistently treated workers as nonemployees, for whom they must have filed all required 1099s for the previous three years. <u>Employers can use Form 8952 to apply for the Program</u> at least 60 days before they want to begin treating the workers as employees. Announcement 2012-45 modifies the VCSP and supersedes Announcement 2011-64. Announcement 2012-45 expands eligibility for the Program to taxpayers under audit, other than an employment tax audit, and eliminates the requirement that the taxpayer agree to extend the period of limitations on assessing employment taxes.

- **The Program was expanded through June 30, 2013 to certain employers that were not previously eligible for the Program. The IRS waived the eligibility requirement for employers that were normally barred from the VCSP if they had failed to file required Forms 1099 with respect to workers whom they were seeking to reclassify for the past three years.**
- **The Section 530 <u>safe harbor</u> allows employers to classify certain workers as independent contractors even though they may be common-law employees. It provides that an individual who has not been treated as an employee will not be reclassified if: (1) the employer has consistently treated the worker as an independent contractor, unless the employer had no reasonable basis for not treating the worker as an employee; (2) the employer did not treat any worker in a similar position as an employee; and (3) the employer has filed all required tax returns, including any Form 1099 information returns, in a manner consistent with the worker not being an employee.** The safe harbor rule governs employee status only with respect to employment taxes, and not for other purposes. For example, employees who have been misclassified as independent contractors must be allowed to retroactively participate in a qualified plan. This applies even if the worker has signed an agreement as to his status as an independent contractor and foregoing benefits.

<u>Statutory Employees</u>

Statutory employees are employees that usually have FICA withheld from wages, but can deduct expenses on Schedule C instead of Form 2106 (W-2 will designate as a statutory employee). In VanZant v. Commissioner, T.C. Summary 2007-195, the Tax Court ruled that Laverne VanZant, who received a

1099-MISC from her employer, was a statutory employee and did not have to pay self-employment tax. See Tax Bulletin dated 12/2/2007.

- Under Code Section 3121(d)(3)(C), a statutory employee includes any individual, **other than an officer of a corporation** or a common law employee, who performs services for pay for any person "as a home worker" performing work, according to specifications furnished by the person for whom the services are performed, on materials or goods furnished by such person." An individual is considered to be a home worker if he or she performs services off the premises of the person for whom the services are performed. **An individual is not a statutory employee if the services are performed as a single transaction rather than part of a continuing relationship, or if the individual has a substantial investment in the facilities used in connection with the performance of the services.** In the VanZant case, Laverne VanZant worked for Action Learning Systems Inc. (ALS) as an Educational Consultant for the LA Unified School District – requiring her to visit schools, collect data, and input data into a software template provided by ALS. ALS determined which schools she would service and supplied the material and format for submitting the data. She was also required to attend training at ALS facilities, where she was given a training manual, a CD with a template on it, and instructions on how to collect and input data. She returned the templates to ALS after the data was entered. The IRS argued that Laverne was not a statutory employee because she did not receive materials or goods from ALS. The U.S. Tax Court said that neither the Code nor the regulations provide guidance on the meaning of "materials" or "goods." It therefore looked to a dictionary for the common definition that materials are typically the "tools or apparatus for the performance of a given task." Here, Laverne was required to use the ALS template to perform her duties, which was therefore a material furnished by ALS. Furthermore, her services were not performed as a single transaction. The court concluded that she was a home worker, and therefore a statutory employee exempt from self-employment taxes.

Hiring Your Teenage Children to Work for Your Business

You can hire your teenage children to work after school or on weekends, and this strategy may result in tax savings and other potential benefits if the children are treated as official employees. The children are taxed at their lower tax rate, and assuming you reduce your compensation accordingly the family can save income tax overall. In addition, there are no kiddie tax complications because earned income from employment is exempt from the kiddie tax. The wages paid by the owner to the child are fully deductible by the business, and as an employee the child is also eligible for certain benefits such as including health insurance coverage and participation in retirement plans and other employer-sponsored programs. If a child under 18 is employed by a parent who runs an unincorporated business (self-employed individuals or partners), the child's wages are exempt from federal employment taxes (FICA). This exemption also applies to FUTA for children up to age 21. **(SEE "Filing Requirements,"**

Dependency Exemption, Election to Include a Qualifying Child's Income on Parents' Tax Return; and "Income Exclusions," Distributions From Qualified Tuition Programs)

Employees' Military Service/Retirement Plan

An employer cannot treat a period of military service as a break in service for purposes of participation, vesting, or accrual of benefits under an employer's qualified retirement plan. In addition, the time allowed for the employee to report back to work or apply for reemployment as well as any time (up to two years) required to recover from an illness or injury must be counted for participation, vesting, and benefit accrual purposes. Therefore once the employee is reemployed, the employer is required to contribute "make-up" contributions to the plan to cover those periods. Benefits that are contingent on the employee's own contributions or elective deferrals are required to be made up only if the employee actually makes those contributions.

Mark-to-Market Election

The mark-to-market election is advantageous to securities <u>traders</u> who incur losses. This Section 475 election for a tax year must be made by the due date of the tax return for the prior year. With the election, all securities positions held in the trading business are treated as if sold at the end of the year at FMV, and all of the deemed gains and losses are treated as ordinary gains and losses on Schedule C (not limited to $3,000). <u>Dealers</u> are required to use the mark-to-market method of accounting (no election available). Dealers can obtain capital gain and loss treatment only if they clearly identify securities held for investment as opposed to securities in their inventory for sale to customers. Traders are treated as carrying on a trade or business, but they do not have inventory or customers. Like investors, traders' gains and losses are considered capital gains and losses unless they make the mark-to-market election. An important factor distinguishing a trader from an investor involves a number of factors; although an important factor is the volume of the taxpayer's trades during the year. The IRS frequently challenges whether a taxpayer who chooses the mark-to-market election is a trader.

- Banks are allowed to use the mark-to-market rule and show a "false" gain to boost reported earnings (as their debt lost value it became cheaper for the banks to retire the debt at a price below its issue price resulting in a gain). The rule makes it harder to compare companies because banks have wide discretion on how to apply it. They can use it on financial liabilities with some exceptions, including deposit liabilities or deferred tax liabilities. They can also use it only for certain individual instruments, and not for others. Once a bank chooses to use the rule, it must stick to mark-to-market valuation until the liability in question expires or otherwise disappears.

Cash Transactions Over $10,000
Form 8300 is used to report cash transactions over $10,000 (includes cashier checks, traveler's checks, money orders, and bank drafts) received in a trade or business (large cash payments received in one transaction, or two or more related business transactions).

Small Business Administration (SBA) Loan Limits
Small Business Administration (SBA) 7(a) loan limits increased from $2 million to $5 million; 504 loans from $1.5 million to $5.5 million; and microloans from $35,000 to $50,000. Also, there are increases in government guarantees on 7(a) loans. In addition, 7(a) Express loans have been increased from $300,000 to $1 million, in order to increase working capital to small businesses.

Changing a Tax Year (Form 1128)
To change a tax year, a company must apply under Rev Proc. 2002-39 and show a business purpose for the change. However, a business can apply for an automatic change if has not changed its tax year for 48 months. A business can qualify for automatic approval under the 25% gross receipts test (i.e. gross receipts in the last 2 months of a 12-month period are at least 25% of total gross receipts of requested period for the past 3 years).

Interest on Credit Cards
Interest on credit cards is generally non-deductible. However, if a credit card is used for business purposes, any interest paid is a deductible business expense as is other interest paid on business loans, etc.

Business Outside of the USA
If you own a business outside of the U.S. and you are a citizen or a permanent resident (green card holder) or if you have had substantial presence here over the last few years and thus qualify as a tax resident, you are subject to taxation on your worldwide income and accordingly must file a U.S. tax return related to your overseas business. **("Filing Requirements," U.S. Citizens Living Abroad)**

Best Small Business Tax Practices
- Hire a tax accountant who has experience with your kind of business, whether it's a restaurant or a plumbing business.
- Keep good records about which workers are employees and which ones are independent contractors.
- Keep good records on how much you paid for, and the date you placed in service, all business vehicles and equipment.
- Be aware of the places where you may have a physical presence (even unknowingly) to properly comply with state sales tax rules and procedures.

- Invest in good tax and accounting system software that properly tracks your records and regularly provides updates to new IRS rules and regulations.
- Select a tax year for your business that reflects the natural flow of your business's receipts and disbursements. This way, you won't get caught in a cash crunch when tax time comes.
- Pay estimated taxes on time, calculating them correctly, and know that the safe harbor that can protect you against underpayments is one of the biggest traps for small business taxpayers.
- Miscalculating any of these steps can be a major problem so talk to someone with knowledge, most likely a tax accountant, who knows the rules inside and out.
- If your spouse, child, or other close relative works in your business, make sure he or she adheres to the same employment rules as your unrelated employees.
- Whatever you do, do not consider using funds you have withheld for employee payroll taxes or any taxes as a short-term loan to tide you over during a shortfall in working capital.
- Keep detailed records on how you use your personal or business-owned vehicle for business vs. personal purposes.
- You should retain all relevant tax records for at least three years or have your accountant keep them for you. If your records relate to property and depreciation, keep them until the property is disposed of, plus an additional three years.
- Use a reputable third-party administrator to manage your 401(k) plan and other tax-favored employee benefits.
- Make sure that you and your tax accountant are familiar with the tax rules, including the favorable tax credits and deductions that are unique to your business.
- Don't be fooled into thinking that the IRS will have to prove that you have done something that doesn't comply with the tax laws. The burden of proof is always on you, not the IRS.
- If it becomes necessary for your small business to open a foreign bank account in order to pay vendors or others in another country, make sure you and your tax accountant are vigilantly following the new rules in effect on foreign bank accounts as required by FATCA.
- Familiarize yourself with the tax rules surrounding starting, running, selling and shutting down a business. Make a concerted and logical decision about whether you should begin your business operating as a sole proprietorship, a partnership, an S-corporation, or a Limited Liability Company (LLC). Your tax accountant should be closely familiar with these rules.
- If your plan is to have your business continue operating after you die, under the leadership of another family member or designated heir, take steps to protect the business against a forced sale in order to pay inheritance taxes.
- Have a face-to-face conversation with your accountant about the Affordable Care Act (ACA).
- If you can't pay the taxes you owe the IRS, contact you accountant right away. This situation can only get worse by ignoring it.

- If you get paid in cash, it doesn't mean that the payment is not taxable. The IRS can build a case against alleged tax cheats by using state-of-the-art statistical technology and models based on bank accounts and spending habits.

Sole Proprietors/Self-Employed (Schedules C & SE)

Sole proprietors report self-employment income and expenses on Schedule C, and net income from self-employment is reported on Form 1040. Also, net income from self-employment is reported on Schedule SE where self-employment tax is computed. A husband and wife who jointly operate an unincorporated business who file a joint return, who are the sole owners of a business, and who both materially participate in the business can file a Schedule C instead of filing a partnership return as was required in previous years. Each spouse's share of the net profits is considered to be his/her self-employment earnings for purposes of computing self-employment tax on Schedule SE, which allows both of them to get credit for Social Security and Medicare benefits. **Therefore, spouses who carry on a trade or business together must file separate Schedules SE, reporting their proportionate share of net profit or loss from self-employment.** Sole proprietors should deduct business expenses in the following order: (1) expenses deductible in computing net income from self-employment that are not allocable to a home office; (2) expenses allocable to a "home office," but deductible anyway as an itemized deduction (mortgage interest and real estate taxes); (3) expenses allocable to a home office, but limited to the gross income of the business, i.e. direct expenses such as painting the area of the home office, and indirect expenses (portion of utilities, insurance, and maintenance expenses); and (4) depreciation of portion of home used as a home office. Tax preparation fees related to preparing Schedules C and SE are deductible on Schedule C as a self-employment business expense.

- Self-employed persons have an option of using the Nonfarm Optional Method to compute net earnings from nonfarm self-employment. This method can be used only if net nonfarm profits were less than $4,894 and also less than 72.189% of gross nonfarm income. To use this method, you also must be regularly self-employed. You meet this requirement if your actual net earnings from self-employment were $400 or more in 2 of the 3 years preceding the year that you use the nonfarm optional method. The net earnings of $400 or more could be from either farm or nonfarm earnings or both. The net earnings include your distributive share of partnership income or loss subject to self-employment tax. Use of the nonfarm optional method from nonfarm self-employment is limited to 5 years, which do not have to be consecutive. Under the optional method, net earnings from nonfarm self-employment is the smaller of two-thirds of gross nonfarm income (not less than zero) or $4,520.
- In a difficult lending environment, many self-employed small business owners are unable to finance their businesses through normal commercial lending practices. **However, they may refinance their home or obtain a home equity loan, and by using the interest tracing rules may elect to treat such debt as not secured by their residence and deduct the related interest expense on Schedule C** rather than Schedule A. This "election" is made by the due date of the

- return, including extension, by deducting the interest on the appropriate line of the tax return. It is also recommended that taxpayers attach a statement to the tax return.
- If a sole proprietorship makes a contribution to a local charity, the contribution is deductible, but where? If the payment is viewed as a personal charitable contribution, it is deductible on Schedule A, Form 1040. <u>The payment is only considered a business expense if it is not a contribution and is related to business.</u> For example, if you take-out an ad in a local charity's program booklet costing $50, the primary purpose of the payment is to advertise your business. Thus, the payment is a Schedule C deduction for advertising. <u>If the sole proprietorship simply writes a check to the charity, it is a charitable contribution deductible on Schedule A.</u>

A sole proprietor's fringe benefits generally are not deductible on Schedule C because a sole proprietor is an owner of the business rather than an employee. <u>However, a sole proprietor may set up a retirement plan such as a SIMPLE IRA or SEP IRA to which the owner can make</u> **contributions,** <u>which are deductible as an above-the-line deduction on Form 1040.</u> **This also applies to the sole proprietor's spouse who can also have a SIMPLE or SEP set-up in his/her name**. However, if a sole proprietor has any employees, the retirement plan must also cover them. Also, 100% of a sole proprietor's health insurance premiums paid for himself, spouse, and dependents are deductible as an above-the-line deduction on Form 1040. In this regard, <u>self-employed taxpayers should move his/her Medicare premiums from Schedule A medical (where they may be wasted anyway) to self-employed health insurance (above-the-line deduction).</u> **NOTE: Flag prior years' returns to be amended to include Medicare premiums as self-employed health insurance.** The above-the-line retirement plan contributions and health insurance premium deductions do not reduce the amount of income on which self-employment tax is paid on Schedule SE. If a sole proprietor has employees he/she will need to get a federal employer identification number (FEIN) from the IRS. A sole proprietor may employ family members. Salaries paid to children are their earned income for purposes of contributing to their own IRAs. In addition, no FICA tax is due on salaries paid to family members under the age of 18, and no FUTA tax is due for employee family members younger than age 21. **(SEE "Deductions for Computing Adjusted Gross Income," Self-Employed Health Insurance Premiums, and Self-Employed Persons Can Deduct Amounts Contributed to Retirement Plans)**

- Self-employed persons may not contribute to a Health Savings Account (HSA) on a pre-tax basis and may not take the amount of their HSA contributions as a deduction for self-employment purposes. However, they may contribute to an HSA with after-tax dollars and take the above-the-line deduction.
- <u>According to a court case ruling, a Schedule C business can set-up an AgriPlanNOW or BizPlanNOW plan and deduct the following directly on Schedule C as a business expense:</u>
    - Health insurance premiums (including qualified long-term care insurance and cancer insurance).
    - Dental insurance premiums.

- o Non-insured medical out-of-pocket expenses.
- o Term life insurance (employee only, no dependents of employee. $50,000 maximum).
- o Disability insurance (employee only, no dependents of employee).

Taxpayers whose revenue is reported to them on Form 1099-MISC instead of Form W-2 are considered self-employed independent contractors and must generally report payments shown on Form 1099-MISC as self-employment income on Schedule C. Examples of taxpayers, among others, who are considered independent contractors for tax purposes include: newspaper venders (carriers); U.S. citizens who are employees of foreign governments; and some ministers and other members of religious organizations who are not considered employees. Earnings paid to an independent contractor are required to be reported on Form 1099-MISC if the amount paid is $600 or more from the same payer in a year. **An exception where 1099-MISC earnings do not have to be reported on Schedule C is when: (1) the amount reported did not come from an activity carried on regularly to make a profit; and (2) you did not carry on a trade or business as a self-employed individual or as an independent contractor, i.e. the individual that submitted the 1099-MISC controlled your working hours and the means and methods of accomplishing the work, meaning you were not an independent contractor subject to self-employment tax. NOTE: it is recommended that this exception only be used when, for example, you receive one 1099-MISC for an amount that is not much more than $600.**

Employees of religious organizations have been subject to mandatory FICA coverage since 1984, but this does not always include ministers. A minister's income; fair market value of a parsonage; the value of meals provided to him and his family; and fees for performing marriages, funerals, etc. are subject to self-employment tax even if he is treated as an employee of the church and his wages are reported on Form W-2 for income tax purposes, unless he has received an exemption from self-employment tax by filing Form 4361 (conscientious objector, which generally includes Christian Science practitioners) or Form 4029 ("Application for Exemption from self-employment tax" on which he states that he is opposed to acceptance of any payments from Social Security or Medicare). If for some reason FICA is withheld from his wages, he is still subject to self-employment tax on the fair market value of a parsonage (home), etc. that are not reported as taxable income. Ministers pay no income tax on the rental value of a home provided as part of their pay, and if they are provided with an allowance rather than a home itself, the allowance is income tax-free if used to pay rent, mortgage, utilities, real estate tax, and repair expenses. Ministers can also deduct mortgage interest and real estate taxes as itemized deductions, even if paid with the tax-free housing allowance. **If a minister's wages are reported on Form W-2 but there is no FICA withholding, the minister's wages and the rental value of all non-taxable housing or housing allowances and any taxable payments which he may have received and not paid FICA taxes on are shown on the same line of Form SE. Self-employment taxes are computed on Form SE and reported on Form 1040. A box has to be checked at the top of Form SE if the minister**

has an approved copy of Form 4361 or Form 4029. NOTE: Retired ministers are not subject to self-employment tax on the rental value of a parsonage or parsonage allowance.

Self-Employment Tax (Schedule SE)
In 2013, the self-employment tax is equal to 92.35% of net self-employment income, multiplied by the total FICA tax rate 15.3% (12.4% OASDI and 2.9% Medicare). The cap on OASDI (Social Security tax) for 2013 is $113,700 ($110,100 in 2012). There is no cap on the Medicare tax. **Self-employed individuals paid a reduced rate of 13.3% in 2012.** Net earnings from self-employment less than $400 in a year are excluded from self-employment tax. Employees who have wages of $113,700 on which they pay FICA are not subject to OASDI on any self-employment income. Beginning in 2013, the Patient Protection and Affordable Care Act (ACA) adds a 0.9% surtax to the 1.45% Medicare tax paid by employees who are high-income earners (wages and self-employment income above $200,000 single; $250,000 joint; and $125,000 married filing separately). For self-employed taxpayers, the 0.9% surtax is added to the 2.9% Medicare tax paid on self-employment income above the thresholds so the total amount of self-employment Medicare tax paid on self-employment income above the thresholds is 3.8%. One-half of the amount of self-employment taxes paid in a year is deducted as an above-the-line deduction on Form 1040. The Small Business Jobs Act allowed self-employed individuals to take a deduction for the cost of health insurance premiums for themselves and their families in determining net earnings from self-employment in **2010 only**. The cost of health insurance premiums was deducted in calculating self-employment tax on Schedule SE, Line 3. **(SEE "FICA - OASDI (Social Security) and Medicare Tax," and "Patient Protection and Affordable Care Act," Provisions Effective Beginning in 2013, Tax Provisions)**

- Payments to members of the Board of Directors are considered earnings subject to self-employment tax.
- Payments to executors of estates that include a business, which the executors operate, are subject to self-employment tax.
- Royalties from books, fees for putting on workshops, fees received from speeches, and working interests (not royalties) in oil and gas productions are subject to self-employment tax.
- Exclusions from gross income of certain foreign earned income for income tax purposes are considered net earnings subject to self-employment tax.
- Fees earned by professional executors and trustees of estates, etc. are considered earnings for self-employment tax purposes.
- A partner who does not materially participate in the activities of the partnership will have income that is concurrently subject to self-employment tax and the passive income rules.
- Payments by a partnership to retired partners are not subject to self-employment tax.
- Distributions from an S-corporation to shareholder/owners of the S-corporation are not considered income subject to the self-employment tax.

Home Office Expenses (Form 8829)

Calculating home office expenses can be done in one of two ways: the actual-expense method (regular method) where the home office deduction is based on the actual expenses incurred by the taxpayer related to the use of the home office, or the new safe-harbor method, under which the deduction amount is determined by a formula based on the square footage used as a home office. In January 2013, the IRS released Rev. Proc. 2013-13, which gives taxpayers an optional safe-harbor method to calculate home office expenses, beginning in 2013. Taxpayers are allowed to change which method they use to compute home office expenses from year to year; however, the election for any tax year is irrevocable.

The safe-harbor method is computed by multiplying the allowable square footage of a home used as a home office, not to exceed 300 square feet, by $5. Therefore, the maximum a taxpayer can deduct annually under the safe harbor is $1,500. The IRS may update the $5 allowance from time to time, but it is not inflation adjusted. Because this is a safe harbor, taxpayers who use the safe harbor cannot also deduct actual expenses related to qualified business use of the home. No depreciation is allowed for the years in which the safe harbor is elected. Taxpayers who itemize deductions and use the safe harbor for a tax year may deduct, to the extent allowable, any expense related to the home that is deductible anyway as an itemized deduction (mortgage interest, property taxes, and casualty losses). Like the regular method, the deduction under the safe-harbor method is subject to a gross income limitation, i.e. the amount of the deduction cannot exceed the gross income derived from the qualified business use of the home. Unlike the regular method, taxpayers cannot carry over any excess to another tax year.

The actual-expense or regular method in computing home office expenses is based on the percentage of a home used as a home office, which is computed by dividing the square footage of the home office by the total square footage of the home. Allowable expenses are either direct or indirect expenses. Direct expenses, such as painting a room used as a home office, are reported separately from indirect expenses on Form 8829. Indirect expenses are either expenses that are allowable anyway (mortgage interest, property taxes, and casualty losses) or nondeductible operating expenses (insurance, utilities, miscellaneous deductions, and depreciation of home). Indirect allowable expenses are multiplied by the percentage of the home used as a home office. The nondeductible operating expenses are limited to the net income from the business (not taking into account the nondeductible operating expenses), and cannot add to a net loss for a year. Allowable depreciation expenses are subject to recapture when the home is sold. An area designated as a home office will qualify if it is used by an individual to conduct administrative and management activities, even if some administrative or management activities are performed at places other than the home office, i.e. you can do administrative and management activities in the home office and meet with customers, clients, or patients in another location. Meeting and dealing with customers can qualify, even if not the principal place of business.

Home office expenses are computed on Form 8829 and included on Schedule C for persons who are self-employed, and <u>on Form 2106 for some employees</u> who are qualified to claim home office expenses.

- In order to be allowed to claim home office expenses, you must be able to <u>meet the exclusive and regular use of a home test</u>: a taxpayer must have a specific part of a house, mobile home, large boat; or a garage, barn or other structure attached to such – though not necessarily a complete room – set aside and used regularly and exclusively as the principal place of business, or the individual "meets or deals" with customers in the home in the normal course of business. The area is not limited to a single room; multiple rooms may qualify. <u>If taxpayer uses an area of the home for both business and personal use, no deduction is allowed</u>. Regular use does not imply daily use but may require more than one use per month and must be a designated area used on a continuing basis, not occasional or incidental. You cannot take the deduction if you use your home for a profit-seeking activity that is not a trade or business. For example, if you use part of your home to manage your personal investments, you cannot take a home office deduction.
- Home office expenses computed by the actual-expense or regular method cannot exceed the gross income of the business, but may be carried over to the next year.
- If you deduct the cost of a home office, then any business mileage from and to your home is tax deductible. If there is one telephone line in a home (land line), none of the cost is deductible; however, some of the optional services such as call waiting may be proportionally deductible if a business purpose can be established.
- Costs of landscaping, lawn care, and repairs to non-business areas have usually been considered not deductible. <u>However, a U.S. Tax Court ruling allowed a sole proprietor who regularly met clients in his home office to deduct part of the costs of landscaping the property, on the grounds that it was a part of the home being used for business. The Court also allowed a deduction for part of the costs of lawn care and driveway repairs</u>.
- Depreciation taken as a home office expense is based on the lesser of the adjusted basis or FMV of the home on date the home becomes eligible – **must be depreciated over 39 years**. Depreciation on a home office is computed in Part III of Form 8829 and carried to line 28 of that Form. Also, Form 4562 must be filed if home is first depreciated as a home office in that year. If the house is sold, any depreciation claimed for a home office must be recaptured as unrecaptured Section 1250 gain (gain taxed @ 25%). If you sell your home for a loss, you cannot claim a loss. However, if you took home office depreciation, you may be able to take a portion as a loss (Example: purchase price $100,000; sale price $85,000; business use 10%; depreciation taken $1,000; recognized loss $500 [$8,500 – $9,000]).
- For day care services special rules apply: it is not necessary that an individual meet the exclusive use test. The calculation to determine the percentage of total expenses allowable for day care services is computed as follows: **(1)** total square footage of home available for day

care, divided by total square footage of home (can include laundry room and storage area in garage); **(2)** total hours of business operation in a year, divided by total number of hours in the year. (% determined by **(1)** multiplied by % determined by **(2)** = percentage of total expenses allowed for day care services).
- Storage of business items does not have to meet the exclusive use test either, but the space used must be a space for products sold (inventory) or product samples. Space does not have to be used exclusively for storage, but must be used on a regular basis.
- **If you are an employee, you cannot claim a home office unless your home office is used for the convenience of your employer, i.e. your employer must require you to work at home. The fact that you voluntarily work at home does not qualify. If the employer provides an office or work space elsewhere, a home office is likely considered a matter of the employee's convenience and therefore not deductible.** Employees who are allowed to claim home office expenses are not required to complete/file Form 8829; instead expenses are computed on a worksheet that is provided and then shown as a "miscellaneous itemized deduction" on Schedule A, unless they have to file Form 2106, in which case home office expenses are put on line 4 of Form 2106.

Profit or Loss From Farming (Schedule F)

Farming is another kind of self-employment that is subject to self-employment tax, including income earned by sharecroppers. If you earn money managing or working on a farm, you are in the farming business. Farms include plantations, ranches, ranges, and orchards. Farmers may raise livestock, poultry, or fish, or grow fruits or vegetables. Farming does not include commercial freezing and canning. Farmers who claim home office expenses are not required to file Form 8829. Instead, they claim their entire home office deduction directly on one line of Schedule F. Following are the various kinds of farming income and where reported on Schedule F:
- Sales of livestock or other items bought for resale are shown on Line 1 of Schedule F, and the cost or other basis is shown on Line 2 to determine gain or loss. If you purchased livestock and other items for resale, you may be able to deduct their cost in the year of the sale. This includes freight charges for transporting livestock to your farm. Farmers and ranchers who, due to drought, sell more livestock than they normally would may postpone tax on the extra gains from those sales. To qualify, the livestock must be replaced within a four-year period. This applies to livestock held for draft, dairy, or breeding, and not to livestock raised for slaughter or sporting purposes.
- Sales of livestock, produce, and other products raised for sale are shown on Line 4.
- Farm products not held primarily for sale such as livestock held for draft, breeding, or dairy can be depreciated. Sales of these products are reported on Form 4797 (Sales of Business Assets). However, a farmer has two options on how to treat these assets. They can either be included in inventory or depreciated. Both options have advantages and disadvantages, so the decision is

ultimately based on whether the farmer prefers a current benefit or a future benefit. If farmers decide to depreciate their livestock, depreciation will begin when the livestock is mature (i.e. can be worked, milked, or bred). Most farm business assets are depreciated using the General Depreciation System (GDS). Generally, GDS must be used unless ADS is required by law or is elected. The recovery period for cattle, goats, and sheep under GDS is five years while the recovery period for hogs is three years. Also, all livestock is eligible for Section 179 expensing and 50% bonus depreciation. <u>NOTE: Farmers can deduct the costs of raising livestock during the years in which the animals are being raised. If these costs are deducted, the basis of the livestock is zero and, therefore, these costs cannot be depreciated.</u> **(SEE "Depreciation," Depreciation Methods)**

If farmers chose to inventory their livestock, there are two inventory methods available: (1) the simplest method is called the farm-price method. This method provides for the valuation of inventories at market price less direct cost of disposition; (2) the other inventory method is the unit-livestock-price method. To determine the valuation under this method, livestock are classified into groups with respect to age and kind. Then, a price for each class is established, taking into account the normal cost of raising those animals. Farmers using this method must reevaluate unit prices each year and adjust either upward or downward to reflect changes in the costs of raising livestock.

Sales of livestock are reported on Form 4797. Calculation of the gain depends on whether the animals were raised by the farmer or purchased. The gain on livestock raised is calculated as the difference between the selling expenses and the gross sales price, assuming the basis is zero because the costs of raising the livestock were deducted during the years in which they were being raised. The gain on livestock purchased by the farmer is calculated by subtracting the adjusted basis and selling expenses from the gross sales price. To be qualified under Section 1231, the animals must be held by the taxpayer for draft, breeding, dairy, or sporting purposes for at least 12 months (24 months for cattle). Any livestock that is held primarily for sale to customers in the ordinary course of business does not qualify. If the Section 1231 holding period is not met, any gain or loss from the sale is reported in Part II of Form 4797, Ordinary Gains and Losses. If the holding period is met, the gain or loss is reported in Part I or Part III, depending on if there is recapture of depreciation. **(SEE "Carrying on a Trade or Business," Sale of Business Property)**

- Income from Cooperative Distributions (Form 1099-PATR) received in the form of patronage dividends (refunds) for buying farm supplies through them is shown on Line 5.
- Agriculture Program payments (government payments) such as those for approved conservation practices, including Conservation Reserve Program (CRP) payments, Feed assistance payments from the USDA under the Disaster Assistance Act of 1988, and the value

of fertilizer or lime received under a government program are shown on Line 6. However, some payments are excludable from income under certain cost-sharing conservation programs.
- **Under the 4-H Act (2009), CRP Payments received after 2007 are excluded from self-employment income if the taxpayer is receiving Social Security retirement or disability benefits.** Otherwise, CRP payments must be included in self-employment income.
- Commodity Credit Corporation (CCC) Loans: farmers can elect to treat loan proceeds as income in the year received if they choose to pledge part or all of their crop production to secure the CCC loan. This is shown as income on Line 7 (not the usual treatment for loans received). Farmers must attach a statement showing details of loan amount reported as income, which becomes the basis in the crops pledged. If the farmer forfeits the pledged crops to the CCC in full payment of the loan, the forfeiture is treated for tax purposes as a sale of the crops. If the farmer did not report the loan proceeds as income in the year received, he must include the loan proceeds as income in the year of forfeiture (reported by CCC on Form 1099A).
- Crop Insurance proceeds received as the result of crop damage is income shown on Line 8. However, a farmer may be able to postpone reporting as income to following year if he would have normally included income from the damaged crops in the following year. In this case, the proceeds are report on Line 8, but are not shown as taxable (a statement must be attached).
- Pasture income received from taking care of someone else's cattle for a fee is farm income reported as other income on Line 10.
- Farmers who receive USDA payments intended for them as well as another person should report the total amount received on Line 6 or 8, but should not report the amount not belonging to them as taxable income. They should file Form 1099-G to report the identity of the actual recipient.
- Cost Sharing Exclusion: farmers may be able to exclude from income federal or state cost-sharing payments for certain conservation, reclamation, and restoration programs they get for an improvement (capital expenditure), and the USDA certifies that the payment was for conserving soil, water resources, protecting the environment, etc.
- Storage fees paid by the CCC under a resale agreement to farmers for storing their own grain is other income.
- The part of the dairy termination program that is not treated as an amount realized on the sale of living cattle is other income.

Rental income received for use of farmland is generally rental income, not farm income (reported on Form 4835), which includes leasing a farm to someone else who pays the farmer a share of crop receipts instead of rent. The renter still receives government payments from the Dept. of Agriculture. However, if the renter materially participates in farming operations on the land, he should pay self-employment tax. Material participation includes working 100 hours or more over a period of 5 weeks or more in farming operations, regularly and frequently making management decisions, or pays for at least ½ of the direct cost of producing the crops. **Sharecroppers who rent the land and produce the crops must pay self-employment tax.**

Farming expenses

Some expenses must be allocated between personal and business (rent, electricity, water, telephone, repairs, insurance, interest, taxes, gas, oil, vehicle repairs, etc.). Any reasonable allocation is acceptable. Other expenses such as feed purchased and fertilizer are 100% farm expenses. Farmers can deduct reasonable wages paid to full and part-time workers. <u>Farmers must withhold Social Security, Medicare, and income taxes from employees' wages</u>. You can only deduct the interest paid on a loan if the loan proceeds are used for your farming business. A farmer can claim a mileage allowance for farm business miles driven. You may be able to claim a tax credit or refund of federal excise taxes on fuel used on your farm for farm work. Deductible Soil and Water Conservation expenses include the following:
- Treatment or movement of earth, such as leveling, conditioning, grading, terracing, contour furrowing, and restoration of soil fertility.
- The construction, control, and protection of: diversion channels, drainage ditches, irrigation ditches, earthen dams, and watercourses, outlets, and ponds.
- The eradication of brush.
- The planting of windbreaks.
- You cannot deduct expenses to drain or fill wetlands or to prepare land for center pivot irrigation systems (must be added to basis of land).
- **New law (2009) allows farmers to elect to treat expenses paid for soil and water conservation or prevention of erosion of farm land as <u>expenses</u>, not capital expenditures.**
- **Farm Buildings (other than single purpose agricultural or horticultural structures) can be depreciated over 20 years (SL/GDS).**
- **Farm machinery and equipment is depreciated over 5 years (200% DB/GDS).**
- **Agriculture trees bearing fruit and nuts are depreciated over 10 years (200% DB/GDS).**
- **Farm property other than trees or vines bearing fruit is depreciated over 15 years.**

(SEE "Depreciation," Depreciation Methods)

Farm Optional Method

You can use the farm optional method to figure net earnings from farm self-employment if your gross farm income is $6,780 or less or your net farm profits are less than $4,894. Net farm profits are the total of your net farm income and your distributive share from farm partnerships. There is no limit on how many years you can use this method. Under the optional method, your net earnings from farm self-employment is the smaller of two-thirds of your gross farm income (not less than zero) or $4,520. For a farm partnership, figure your share of gross income based on the partnership agreement. With guaranteed payments, your share of the partnership's gross income is your guaranteed payments plus your share of the gross income after it is reduced by all guaranteed payments made by the partnership. If you are a limited partner, include only guaranteed payments for services you actually rendered to or on behalf of the partnership.

Farm Income Averaging

You may be able to average some or all of the current year's farm income by spreading it out over the past three years (base years). This may lower your taxes if your farm income is high in the current year and low in one or more of the past three years. This method does not change your prior year tax. It only uses the prior year information to figure your current year tax. <u>Schedule J is used to make the computation</u>. The Elected Farm Income (EFI) is the amount of income you choose to have taxed at base year rates.

Net operating losses (NOLs) - If deductible expenses are more than income for the year, you may have a net operating loss. You can carry that loss over to other years and deduct it. You may get a refund of part or all of the income tax you paid for past years, or you may be able to reduce your tax in future years. **(SEE "Taxable Income," Net Operating Loss)**

Sale of Farmland
- Section 1252 Property – If you dispose of farmland held more than one year and less than 10 years at a gain and you were allowed deductions for Soil and Water Conservation expenses for the land, you must treat part of the gain as ordinary income and treat the balance as Section 1231 gain.
    - Ordinary income = Total gain, less total deduction allowed for Soil and Water Conservation expenses, multiplied by the applicable percentage (100% if disposed of within 5 years; 6- 9 years, percentage is reduced by 20% for each year over 5 years; 10 years or more = 0%).
- Section 1255 Property – If you received certain cost-sharing payments on property and excluded those payments from income, you may have to treat part of any gain as ordinary income and treat the balance as Section 1231 gain. Cost-sharing payments from the government that were excluded from income are treated as ordinary income @ 100% if the property was held less than 10 years. After 10 years, the percentage is reduced 10% a year. **(SEE "Carrying on a Trade or Business," Sale of Business Property)**

Farm Act of 2008 (4-H Act)
- **Retired farmers and farmers on disability who participate (receive payments) under land "conservation reserve programs" can exclude such payments from self-employment income, avoiding self-employment tax and preventing reductions in Social Security or disability benefits.**

- Farmers receiving certain government subsidies (i.e. ones from the commodity credit corp.) are limited as to the amount of net Schedule F losses in a year that a farmer may use to offset non-farming business income to the greater of $300,000 ($150,000 filing separately) or net farm income for the prior 5 tax years. In the case of partnerships and S-corporations, this treatment is applied at the partner or shareholder level. Losses may be carried forward to later years. This does not apply to C-corporations.
- Enhanced contribution of capital gain real property for conservation purposes - the American Taxpayer Relief Act of 2012 extends through 2013 the special rule for contributions of capital gain real property for conservation purposes. The special rule allows a charitable contribution of up to 50% (rather than 20%) of the contribution base by farmers and ranchers. The 15-year carryover of contributions of qualified real property for conservation purposes is also allowed. A qualified conservation contribution is a contribution of a qualified real property to a charitable organization or qualified governmental unit that is to be used exclusively for conservation purposes and that is protected in perpetuity. Qualified use is preserving land for recreation; protecting natural habitats; preserving open space for public enjoyment; and preserving an historic land area.
- Enhanced depreciation for race horses – three years regardless of age for property placed in service after 12/31/2008 and before 1/1/2014.
- Deduction for endangered species recovery expenditures – expenditures to achieve site-specific management actions recommended under the Endangered Species Act of 1973 will be eligible for a tax deduction of up to 25% of gross farming income for any particular year (applies to expenditures paid or incurred after 12/31/2008.

Partnerships (Form 1065)

A **general** partnership is an unincorporated organization made up of 2 or more parties that carries on a trade or business and does not pay federal income tax, and instead is a pass-through entity that passes income through to individual partners who pay income taxes and FICA on their individual 1040 tax returns. In a general partnership, all owners have unlimited personal liability for all the partnership's activities. It is an entity separate from its owners; thus, the partnership's income and expenses are determined at the partnership level for tax purposes, and the partnership is required to file a separate tax return (Form 1065). Most states do not require general partnerships to file formation documents with the state. However, the partners should execute a partnership agreement addressing such issues as capital contributions, distributions, profit and loss sharing, management responsibilities, dispute resolution, duration and termination of the business, and transferability of the partners' interests. A general partnership must have a Federal Employer Identification Number (FEIN). <u>Taxable income of a partnership is computed in the same manner as for an individual, except no deductions are allowed for personal exemptions, foreign taxes, net operating loss carry backs or carryovers, charitable contributions, itemized deductions, capital loss carryovers, or deductions for depletion</u>. A partner may be an individual, C-corporation, S-corporation, other partnerships, all types of trusts, decedent's estates, and tax exempt organizations.

A partner can acquire a partnership interest by inheriting it, buying it, contributing services to it, or by receiving it as a gift. A receipt of an interest in a partnership in exchange for services rendered to the partnership is taxable income to the partner. A partnership's tax year must be the same as the principal partners' tax years, unless there is a business purpose for choosing another year. A principal partner has a 5% or more interest in a partnership. The partnership tax return (Form 1065, including Schedule K) is due by April 15th. The partnership must send each partner a Schedule K-1 each year listing the partner's share of partnership income, whether or not the income is distributed to the partners. Form 7004 can be filed to request a 5-month extension to file the partnership tax return. Partners are required to pay self-employment tax on their share of partnership income, whether or not the income is distributed to them.

In determining partnership income for a year, rental income, interest income, dividend income, royalties, and capital gains/losses must be shown separately from the partnership's ordinary income from partnership operations since these are separate items that must be shown separately on the partners' individual 1040 tax returns. Generally, partnership income is computed as follows:

Ordinary business income of the partnership is computed on page 1 of Form 1065:
- Total income (loss) - Line 8 (gross receipts, less cost of goods sold = gross profit + other income = total income).
- Less: Total deductions - Line 21 (wages and salaries, repairs and maintenance, rent, taxes and licenses, interest, depreciation [attach Form 4562], employee benefits, other deductions [from a separate statement], etc.)
- Equals: Ordinary business income (loss) - Line 22

Partners' Distributive Share Items - Schedule K:
Income (Loss)
- **Ordinary business income (loss) - From page 1, Line 22**
- Net rental real estate income (loss) (attach Form 8825)
- Interest income
- Dividends (a. Ordinary dividends; b. Qualified dividends)
- Royalties
- Net short-term capital gain (loss) (attach Schedule D, Form 1065)
- Net long-term capital gain (loss) (attach Schedule D, Form 1065)
- Net section 1231 gain (loss) (attach Form 4797)
- Other income

Deductions
- Section 179 deduction (attach Form 4562)
- Contributions
- Etc.

Credits

The above information is then transferred to each partner's Schedule K-1, Part III <u>based on their ownership percentages</u>. The partners' use Schedule K-1 to include the information on their individual 1040 tax returns:

Schedule K-1 (Form 1065), Part III:
- Ordinary business income (loss) - Line 1
- Net rental income - Line 2
- Interest income - Line 5
- Ordinary dividends - Line 6a
- Qualified dividends - Line 6b
- Royalties - Line 7
- Net short-term capital gain (loss) - Line 8
- Net long-term capital gain (loss) - Line 9
- Net section 1231 gain (loss) - Line 10
- Section 179 deduction - Line 12
- Etc.

Schedule M-3, Form 1065 "Net Income (Loss) Reconciliation for Partnerships" has to be filed if a partner is an entity that is a "reportable entity partner" that owns or is deemed to own an interest of 50% or more in the partnership's capital, profit, or loss, on any day during the tax year of the partnership. <u>A "reportable entity" is a partner that owns a corporate interest or is a corporation</u>. Schedule M-3, Form 1065 is required to be completed only for partnerships with total assets of $10 million or more. Schedule M-3 compares tax information the taxpayer disclosed for financial reporting purposes with the partnership's tax position. Schedule M-3 requires the taxpayer to reconcile the differences between their financial statement net income or loss and reported taxable income. Question 6 on Form 1065 is "Does the partnership satisfy <u>all four</u> of the following conditions." If the answer is YES, then the partnership does not have to complete Schedules L, M-1, and M-2; Item F on page 1 of Form 1065; or Item L on Schedule K-1. The four conditions are:

1. The partnership's total receipts for the year were less than $250,000;
2. The partnership's total assets at the end of the year were less than $1 million;
3. Schedules K-1(s) are filed with the return and furnished to the partners on or before the due date (including extensions) for the partnership return; and
4. The partnership is not filing and is not required to file Schedule M-3 (see above).

Elections made at the partnership level are binding on the partners, i.e. method of accounting, selection of 179 expense deduction, method of computing depreciation, amortization of organization fees, etc. must be treated by the partners in the same fashion as they were treated on the partnership return, except the foreign tax credit vs. deducting foreign taxes as an itemized deduction is made at the partner level.

- A partner's interest in a partnership is a capital asset that must have a basis so that the amount of any gain or loss realized upon sale, liquidation, or other disposition can be determined. The basis of a partner's interest is determined separately from the partner's capital account (ownership percentage). (Example: two 50% partners – one contributes $10,000 cash; the other one contributes property worth $10,000, but the property has an adjusted basis of $6,000 – the 1st partner has a $10,000 basis and the 2nd partner has a $6,000 basis). Also, if the property contributed is subject to a mortgage, the partner's basis is reduced by the amount of the indebtedness (the amount of debt assumed by the other partners is treated as a contribution by them and increases their basis in the partnership). However, a partner's basis cannot be reduced below zero. Therefore, upon the sale or liquidation of a partnership, each partner's gain or loss would be different. **(SEE "Taxable Income," Capital Gains and Losses)**
- After a partner's initial basis is determined, basis is adjusted upward or downward to reflect subsequent events (annually): Increased by – additional contributions; partner's distributive share of partnership taxable income (based on ownership percentage); increase in the partner's share of partnership liabilities; gain recognized by the partner on the transfer of property to the partnership; etc. Decreased by – distributions from the partnership to the partner; partner's share of partnership losses (including capital losses); partner's share of expenditures not deductible in computing partnership income; partner's share of 179 expenses (even if can't deduct entire amount on partner's individual tax return); the partner's debts assumed by the partnership; a decrease in the partner's share of partnership liabilities; etc. NOTE: **Distributions are taxed only to the extent they exceed a partner's adjusted basis because a partner's basis cannot be reduced below zero (i.e. partnership losses allocated to each partner can be deducted on each partner's individual tax return only to the extent of their basis, but losses can be carried forward).**
- **Adequate basis, however, is only one sieve through which a pass-through loss must flow before determining its deductibility. Subsequent to passing the basis test, the next test to be applied is the "at-risk" test. A partner may have sufficient basis for taking a loss, but not have a sufficient amount of risk for the loss to be deductible.** A partner is considered at risk with respect to an activity for:
    - The amount of money and the adjusted basis of other property contributed to the activity;

- - Amounts borrowed for use in the activity if the partner is personally liable for repayment of the borrowed amount or has pledged property other than property that is used in the activity as security for the borrowed amount. If property is pledged as security for a borrowed amount, the partner's at-risk amount is limited to the net fair market value of the partner's interest in the pledged property. **(SEE "Carrying on a Trade or Business," At-Risk Rules)**
- <u>If a partner contributes property in exchange for a partnership interest, there is no recognition of gain or loss on the transaction.</u>
- If a partner sells all or part of his partnership interest, the existence of the partnership is not affected unless the transaction terminates the partnership. A partner recognizes gain or loss based on the receipt of money against his basis – gain is capital gain; loss is recognized only on liquidation of the partner's entire interest in the partnership. If property is received, no gain is recognized until the partner subsequently disposes of the property.
- A partnership will terminate only if there is no continuity of any business carried on by any of its partners, or if within a 12-month period there is a sale or exchange of 50% or more of the total interest in the partnership capital and profits.
- If a partnership interest is inherited, the partner's basis is the FMV of the interest on the date of the decedent's death. If received as a gift, the partner's basis is the same as the donor's basis. If purchased, the new partner's basis is the amount paid for the interest, plus the selling partner's share of partnership liabilities he assumes.
- If non-business personal property (i.e. personal residence) is contributed to a partnership, the basis is the lesser of FMV or the contributing partner's adjusted basis.
- A sell of a partnership interest by a partner is similar to the sale of stock in a corporation. Gain or loss on the sale is capital gain or loss subject to long or short term treatment, depending on how long the partner owned the interest. **(SEE "Taxable Income," Capital Gains or Losses)**
- **If a sole proprietor hires someone and agrees to make him a 50% partner after 3 years, the new partner's 50% share of the business capital (assets) is taxable income that is taxed to him as ordinary income.**
- Upon sale or liquidation of a partnership, each partner's gain or loss is determined based on each partner's "basis".
- A partnership agreement is between partners and does not have to be a formal document. A partnership can be a limited partnership, but it must have at least one general partner with unlimited liability.
- **A partnership can elect to be taxed as a corporation (without formally becoming a corporation) under the "check-the-box" rules by filing Form 8832 (but must still file Form 2553 in order to become an S-corporation).**
- **A partnership that converts to a corporation may make an immediate S-corporation election by filing Form 2553.**

- **Distributions to general partners are subject to self-employment tax, but not distributions of share income or loss to limited partners (except for guaranteed payments for the performance of services).**

Some partnerships were able to defer income from cancelled or forgiven debts in 2009 and 2010 and allowed to start paying taxes on the cancelation of debt (COD) income over 5 years beginning in 2014. The deferrals helped the partnerships get through the recession because usual procedure would have forced the affected partners to report a higher on-paper income in 2009 and 2010 and then to pay taxes on that income when they didn't have the cash or assets to pay the taxes. Beginning in 2014, the taxable amounts will remain the same as they were in 2009 and 2010, and will be spread over 5 years through 2018.

Limited Partnership

A limited partnership must have at least one general partner, and the general partner must run the business. The general partner has unlimited liability for the business's activities; the limited partners' liability is restricted to their capital investment in the business. To retain their limited liability, limited partners may not be involved in managing the business. Therefore, limited partners are considered passive investors subject to the passive activity rules. They do not have to pay self-employment tax on distributions they receive from the partnership. **(SEE "Taxable Income," Passive Activity Income; and "Carrying on a Trade or Business," Passive vs. Non-passive Income)** Limited partners who take an active role in the business may be reclassified as general partners subject to unlimited personal liability for the business's debts and obligations. Forming a limited partnership requires filing formation documents with the state (certificate of formation or other document) in which the general partner(s) and the limited partners are identified. There is usually a fee for filing, and a limited partnership will need to obtain a FEIN. Limited partners' basis is only increased by a share of the partnership debt if they are required to: make contributions to the partnership; pay the partnership debts directly; restore a capital account deficit balance on liquidation; or reimburse another partner who pays a partnership debt under an indemnity agreement. All other increases or decreases are essentially the same as a general partner (see above).

Family Partnership

A family partnership is a common device for splitting income among family members. Unless "capital" is a material income producing factor, a family member cannot give a 50% interest in his/her business as a gift to another family member (mother to daughter) in order to avoid taxes unless that person participates in performing services for the partnership, i.e. has actual control over his/her interest. Capital is not a material income producing factor if substantially all partnership income is derived from personal services, such as a law firm, accounting firm, and doctors. It is easier to make a gift of a limited partnership interest to a person who is not taking an active part in partnership business.

S-Corporations (Form 1120S) – Election Made on Form 2553

The only difference between an S-corporation and a Regular C-corporation is how they are treated by the IRS. Unlike a C-corporation, an S-corporation is a pass-through entity that does not pay income taxes. However, an S-corporation must have a Federal Employer Identification Number (FEIN). Only individuals, S-corporations, and certain trusts and estates may be S-corporation shareholders. Generally, an S-corporation may not have a partnership, a C-corporation, or a nonresident alien as a shareholder. The primary advantage of an S-corporation is that it is not taxed as a separate entity, but rather income and loss are reported by the shareholders on their individual tax returns, thus avoiding double taxation of its income. <u>Also, shareholders do not have to pay self-employment taxes on their pro-rata share of S-corporation income because distributions from S-corporations are equivalent to dividends that are not subject to self-employment tax.</u> However, both employees' and shareholders' salaries reported on Form W-2 are subject to FICA withholding (salaries are deducted in determining an S-corporation's income). For example, a 2% shareholder of an S-corporation may receive a salary reported on Form W-2 on which he/she has to pay both payroll tax (FICA) and income tax, and also have to pay income tax <u>only</u> on 2% of the S-corporation's income passed through to him/her as a shareholder dividend. <u>The S-corporation tax return (Form 1120S) is due by March 15th</u>, but Form 7004 can be filed to get a 6-month extension.

Every S-corporation must file Form 1120S each year (must use the calendar year, unless can establish a business purpose for using a fiscal year) which reports each shareholder's pro rata share of income, loss, deduction, or credit, and must furnish each shareholder a copy of the information on Schedule K-1 (Form 1120S) so each shareholder can report the information on their individual 1040 tax returns and pay any income taxes due on the appropriate items (whether or not actually received by shareholder).

- <u>Taxable income of an S-corporation is generally computed in the same manner as for an individual, except no deductions are allowed for personal exemptions, foreign taxes, charitable contributions, itemized deductions, etc.</u>
- S-corporations are not subject to the corporate alternative minimum tax.
- S-corporation status is lost if it has passive investment income in excess of 25% of its gross income for each of 3 consecutive years or it has accumulated earnings and profits at the end of 3 consecutive years. And if this happens, S-corporation status cannot be elected again for 3 years.
- S-corporation income must be allocated among its shareholders (members in the case of LLCs) based on the number of shares owned or the percentage of ownership.
- **The various types of portfolio income – interest, ordinary dividends, qualified dividends, royalty income, tax-exempt income, income and expenses from rental activities, charitable contributions, net short-term and net long-term capital gains and losses, 179 expensing, AMT**

tax preference items, passive activity items, and other portfolio income must be reported separately on the S-Corporation's Schedule K and the shareholders' Schedules K-1 (similar to a Partnership tax return - see above).

Generally, S-corporation income is computed as follows:

Business income of an S-corporation is computed on page 1 of Form 1120S:
- Total income (loss) - Line 6 (gross receipts, minus cost of goods sold = gross profit + other income = total income).
- Less: Total deductions - Line 20 (salaries and wages [including salaries paid to shareholders/members], repairs and maintenance, rent, taxes and licenses, interest, depreciation [attach Form 4562], depletion, advertising, employee benefits, other deductions [from a separate statement], etc.)
- Equals: Ordinary business income (loss) - Line 21

Shareholders' Pro Rata Share Items - Schedule K:
Income (Loss)
- **Ordinary business income (loss) - From page 1, Line 21**
- Net rental real estate income (loss) (attach Form 8825)
- Interest income
- Dividends (a. Ordinary dividends; b. Qualified dividends)
- Royalties
- Net short-term capital gain (loss) (attach Schedule D, Form 1120S)
- Net long-term capital gain (loss) (attach Schedule D, Form 1120S)
- Net section 1231 gain (loss) (attach Form 4797)
- Other income (loss)

Deductions
- Section 179 deduction (attach Form 4562)
- Contributions

Credits
- Etc.

The above information is then transferred to each shareholder's/member's Schedule K-1, Part III based on their ownership percentages, which is used to include the information on their individual 1040 tax returns.

Schedule K-1 (Form 1120S), Part III:
- Ordinary business income (loss) - Line 1
- Net rental income - Line 2
- Interest income - Line 4

- Ordinary dividends - Line 5a
- Qualified dividends - Line 5b
- Royalties - Line 6
- Net short-term capital gain (loss) - Line 7
- Net long-term capital gain (loss) - Line 8
- Net section 1231 gain (loss) - Line 9
- Section 179 deduction - Line 11
- Etc.

Schedule M-3 (Form 1120S), Net Income (Loss) Reconciliation for Corporations is required to be completed only for S-corporations with total assets of $10 million or more. Schedule M-3 compares tax information the taxpayer disclosed for financial reporting purposes with the corporation's tax position. Schedule M-3 requires the taxpayer to reconcile the differences between their financial statement net income or loss and reported taxable income. **Although the tax rules for S-corporations are similar to those for partnerships, there are some differences: An S-corporation shareholder's basis does not include the S-corporation's debt. Only shareholder loans to the S-corporation are included in the shareholder's basis; the passive activity rules apply to S-corporation shareholders and not to partners; and fringe benefits received by 2-percent S-corporation shareholders must be included in the shareholder's income (however, this does not apply to retirement plans).** Generally, transfers of money and property to a corporation in exchange for stock may be made on a tax-free basis (the rules are the same for both C & S corporations). Generally, transferring assets subject to liabilities to a corporation does not result in boot to the transferor unless the corporation assumes liabilities that exceed the transferor's adjusted basis in the transferred assets. An individual who receives stock in exchange for services for a corporation must recognize income. A stockholder's basis in stock received in exchange for property transferred to a corporation equals the transferred property's adjusted basis, and the corporation's basis in the property transferred equals the transferor's basis plus any gain recognized by the transferor.

The election of S-corporation status is made on Form 2553. This form cannot be filed before the corporation has been approved and is in existence under state law. A state usually does not distinguish between a corporation and an S-corporation. An <u>S-corporation is an IRS designation</u>. If your business is already incorporated, you generally have until March 15 of a particular year to elect to be taxed as an S-corporation. Electing by this date lets you be treated as an S-corporation for the entire year. The election is made by filing Form 2553. If you are already incorporated, you have two months and 15 days from the start of the corporation to make the election. For example, if you incorporate on Jan. 7, you have until March 21 to file the election form with the IRS to become an S-corporation. Otherwise, it will not be effective until the next year (with some exceptions).

Requirements to Become an S-Corporation
- Cannot have more than 100 shareholders, which includes individuals, estates, and some trusts, but none can be corporations or partnerships. A husband and wife (and all family members) may be treated as one shareholder.
- A business entity not classified as a corporation need only incorporate under state law, and elect to be an S-corporation if it meets all requirements to qualify as a small business by filing Form 2553 with the IRS. For example, in the state of Texas, a corporation is created by filing a "certificate of formation" with the Secretary of State. One entity that can be formed by filing a "certificate of formation" is a Limited Liability Company (LLC), which is not a corporation that issues stock but instead an association that has percentages of ownership by individual members. An LLC is not a partnership or a corporation but rather a distinct type of entity that has powers of both a corporation and a partnership. Unlike a partnership, where the element is the individual, the essence of the LLC is the entity in which the owners are called members. LLCs are qualified to apply for S-corporation status with the IRS; otherwise they are taxed as a "disregarded entity." <u>A disregarded entity with one owner is a sole proprietorship and files a Schedule C on the owner's 1040 tax return. A disregarded entity with two or more owners is a partnership and files Form 1065.</u> The deemed election to be classified as an S-corporation will apply upon approval by the IRS within 60 days of submission of Form 2553.
- Beginning in 2011, a C-corporation that converts to an S-corporation generally must hold any appreciated assets for five years following the conversion or, if disposed of earlier, pay tax on the appreciation at the highest corporate tax rate. The 5th year of the recognition period must precede the first year in which the corporation became an S-corporation. This provision provides incentive for more C-corporations to convert to S-corporations. They can hold their assets for five years before emerging from the recognition period free to do what they wish without the fear of corporate level taxes.
- Details of how a corporation and an LLC can become an S-corporation:
    - A corporation must meet all requirements – two or more owners and the filing of articles of incorporation with the state, where state law provides that the corporate existence begins and stock subscribers become "shareholders" upon that event.
    - The taxable year begins on the date the corporation has shareholders, acquires assets, or begins doing business (whichever first occurs).
    - Must timely file Form 2553 with IRS to make the election. All shareholders must consent to the election in writing.
    - The question of whether a person is a shareholder (member) is decided under the IRS code rather than state law; thus a person who is <u>not</u> a shareholder (member) of record under state law may still be considered a shareholder (member) for IRS purposes. **Therefore, an LLC may in reality have only one owner, but a spouse who consents to**

the election by signing Form 2553 as a 50% owner (member) of the LLC qualifies as member, so the LLC will have 2 members for IRS purposes.
- LLC's can elect how to be treated for federal tax purposes because an LLC is not a federal tax entity, and there is no provision in the IRS Code that specifically governs the treatment of LLCs for federal tax purposes. Therefore, <u>both a partnership and an LLC can elect to be taxed as a regular C-corporation under the "check-the-box" rules by filing Form 8832.</u>
- An LLC electing the "default status", i.e. to be treated as a disregarded entity and <u>not</u> to be taxed as a separate entity from its owners, should <u>not</u> file Form 8832, Entity Classification Election. The default status for a single owner or husband and wife LLC is to file Schedule C with their individual tax return (1040); and the default status for an LLC with 2 or more owners is to file a Partnership return (Form 1065).
- **LLCs only need to File Form 2553 "Election by a Small Business Corporation" with the IRS, which is the Form requesting to be treated as an S-corporation. The deemed election to be classified as an S-corporation will apply upon approval by the IRS. Approval or disapproval should be received within 60 days of submission of Form 2553.**

- <u>Ineligible corporations for S-corporation status</u> – Any corporation that is a financial institution and that uses a certain reserve method of accounting for bad debts; an insurance company; an electing (possessions) corporation; or a DISC or former DISC.

Shareholder's Stock Basis

A shareholder's initial stock basis in a newly formed S-corporation is equal to money contributed and the adjusted basis of any property contributed to start the business. Where the stock is actually purchased, its basis is equal to its purchase price. Adjustments to a shareholder's stock basis are made as follows (basis will never be below zero):

- Increases - pro rata share of the S-corporation's income, including tax-exempt income.
- Decreases:
  - Distributions to shareholders – where the distribution exceeds the stock basis, the excess is treated as a gain from the sale of existing property. <u>An S-corporation that was not previously a C-corporation has no earnings and profits; therefore distributions to shareholders are treated as a return of basis.</u>
  - pro rata share of losses and expenses not deductible in computing its taxable income and not chargeable to its capital account (non-capital, non-deductible expenses).
  - If basis is reduced to zero, the remaining loss is carried forward.
- A shareholder can only take a loss up to the total of his/her adjusted stock basis and his/her debt basis (debt basis is the amount a shareholder has lent to the S-corporation via a promissory note, etc.). Any remaining loss may be deducted in future years.

- A passive shareholder is subject to the passive-activity loss limitations; the basis determination comes before the passive-activity limitations.
- Gain or loss is recognized on the sale of S-corporation stock. **(SEE "Taxable Income," Capital Gains and Losses)**
- Shareholders may be required to pay estimated income taxes on their pro rata share of S-corporation income.
- Fringe benefits (health insurance, etc.) of a 2% or more shareholder are included in the shareholder's income, but are deductible by the S-corporation as a business expense. <u>But "retirement plans" are not considered fringe benefits.</u>

<u>S-Corporation Income vs. Distributions</u>

Income that is disguised as S-corporation distributions to avoid self-employment taxes is subject to being (and often is) reclassified by the IRS. **Reasonable salaries paid to S-corporation shareholder/members have not been determined, but such salaries should usually follow industry standards.** Sources of information on comparable compensation for services include the U.S. Department of Labor's Bureau of Labor Statistics, employment agencies, and a market analysis. One key in defending a claimed compensation amount is to document all research to support the amount. Some factors considered by the courts in determining reasonable compensation are: training and experience; duties and responsibilities; time and effort devoted to the business; dividend history; payments to non-shareholder employees; timing and manner of paying bonuses to key people; what comparable businesses pay for similar services; compensation agreements; and the use of a formula to determine compensation. <u>**If the business is primarily a service business with the services performed by the principal shareholder(s), the IRS would tend to expect that the majority of the earnings of the business should be treated as compensation (salary)**</u>. **A service S-corporation with large dividend payouts compared to the amount treated as compensation could be a potential candidate for an IRS audit.** When an S-corporation has used compensation comparisons with other businesses in the industry and stable, steady compensation to justify relatively low compensation compared to dividends, one issue that sometimes arises is the obligation to pay that compensation in years without profits. In C-corporations, compensation is usually paid regardless of profits and subsequently results in increased losses in bad years. To justify low compensation for S-corporations, this also might need to apply to them. Loans made by S-corporations to employee/shareholders have also been attacked successfully by the IRS and reclassified as compensation, as has paying personal expenses out of corporate accounts, and distribution of assets to employee/shareholders rather than cash. If the IRS is successful in making such reclassifications, they can not only collect back employment taxes but can also assert significant penalties exceeding 100% of the employment taxes due to failure to timely deposit the taxes, failure to timely file employment tax returns, failure to withhold income taxes on compensation, and even negligence. However, <u>if you do not take any funds out of an S-corporation in a year, you are **not** required to pay yourself and other owners (shareholders) a reasonable salary in that</u>

year **(the owners/shareholders do not take any funds for their personal use out of the S-corporation bank account)**. Also, if the S-corporation is not profitable in a year, you are not required to pay yourself and other shareholders a reasonable salary. Regardless of the issue over salaries of shareholder-employees of S-corporations, the National Federation of Independent Business and the S-corporation Association released a study showing that S-corporations pay the highest effective rates of any business type. The study shows that in 2013, S-corporations will pay an average effective tax rate of 31.6% of their income, followed by partnerships at 29.4%, C-corporations 17.8%, and sole proprietorships 15.1%.

Watson Case – Revenue Ruling 59-221 was the IRS's incentive to start taking aim at taxpayers who abuse the employment tax advantage of S-corporations by minimizing salaries. In February 2012, the Eighth Circuit affirmed the district court's decision in the Watson Case. Watson, in many respects, was a precedent-setting case in the S-corporation reasonable compensation arena as it shed much needed light on the methodology the IRS and the courts will employ to determine **an amount** of reasonable compensation to follow when guiding clients. David Watson – like many of the subjects of reasonable compensation scrutiny who are in a service oriented business – was a CPA. He was also the sole shareholder and employee of the S-corporation that in turn was a 25% shareholder in a very successful accounting firm. Watson's share of the revenue generated by the accounting firm was allocated to his S-corporation, which would then pay Watson a salary and distributions. Any amounts not paid out in salary by the corporation were reported by Watson as his share of the S-corporation's income on his personal tax return, where it was not subject to payroll tax. In Watson, the court held that an S-corporation shareholder-employee (Watson) who paid himself $24,000 in salary per year in 2002 and 2003 while receiving $203,651 and $175,470, respectively in distributions, in those years was not reasonably compensated for his services. The court further upheld the district court's determination of an annual reasonable compensation amount of $93,000, requiring Watson to re-characterize $69,000 of distributions in each year as salary. As a result, the S-corporation and Watson were held liable for over $23,000 in payroll taxes, penalties, and interest. **The result was that Watson was required to pay himself about 50% of the S-corporation's profits in salary**.

Tax Exempt Organizations (Form 990)

The IRS has to determine whether an organization meets the legal requirements for tax-exempt status. One requirement relates to the amount of political campaign intervention ("political activity") that that the organizations may engage in. Sec. 501(c)(3) organizations are prohibited from engaging in any political activity. Other organizations, including Sec. 501(c)(4) organizations, may only engage in a limited amount of political activity. The IRS has introduced a greatly expanded Form 990, Return of Organization Exempt From Income Tax. Following are steps that an organization needs to understand before completing and filing Form 990:

- A tax exempt organization needs to understand which form to file. Although any organization may file Form 990, it is only required to file Form 990 if gross receipts exceed $200,000 or assets exceed $500,000. Otherwise, charitable organizations should file Form 990-EZ, or, if gross receipts normally do not exceed $50,000, Form 990-N (which is a postcard-size form) should be filed. There are significant differences in the compliance burden, so the decision of which form to file should be made carefully because some rating organizations will evaluate only charities that file the full-length Form 990.
- Filing Form 8868, Application for Extension of Time to File an Exempt Organization Return, provides an automatic three-month extension to file a tax return. Organizations can request a second three-month extension, but it is not automatic and requires IRS approval. Significant penalties are imposed when an organization does not timely file its tax return. Generally, if an organization has gross receipts of $1 million or less, the penalty is $20 per day (maximum of $10,000). If gross receipts are greater than $1 million, then the penalty is $100 per day (to a maximum of $50,000). The ultimate penalty is the revocation of tax-exempt status.
- A tax exempt organization needs to be sure that it files an accurate and complete tax return. It is very important to have a competent professional who understands the complexities of Form 990 to prepare it. Some significant errors include: not properly identifying the executive director as a top management official who is a person that is treated as an officer for Part VII purposes; reporting no conflict-of-interest policy or indicating that the organization has one but it is not enforced; failing to properly identify key employees; and not adequately describing the organization's charitable activities in Part III per the instructions.
- A not-for-profit organization has a significant audience due to the vast public disclosure of Form 990. Other than ensuring that its filing is completely accurate, the organization should use every part of the Form 990 to include information relevant to its audience. Schedule O, Supplemental Information to Form 990, and Part III, "Statement of Program Service Accomplishments," are both important to complete. Form 990, Part III asks the organization to describe its charitable mission and the programs or activities it undertook during the year for the three largest programs, measured by expenses. Part III should contain specific information, such as the number events held, number of clients served, and anything else that describes that particular program. Another way to use this part is to explain that the financial measurements, standing alone, do not fully describe the success of the programs. Schedule O is a continuation sheet which is used to answer specific questions on Form 990 as well as to provide additional important information. Thus, organizations can use this schedule as an addendum to provide detailed descriptions of their accomplishments in the previous year. Schedule O can also be used to explain any area of the core form or schedules that may not be clearly understood from reading the main part of the form. For example, one organization whose CEO left in the middle of the year used Schedule O to explain why the CFO's salary was more than the CEO's salary.

- Part VI, "Governance, Management and Disclosure," should be used to prompt the organization to make governance changes. In preparing Part VI, the organization should be made aware of the need to implement changes to its governance policies. One way is for the organization to adopt a conflict-of-interest policy so the organization can check "yes" to Question 12 in Part VI. This is a chance to improve the organization and show perspective donors and other stakeholders that proper governance is an absolute priority.
- Every possible space on Form 990 should be completed to the maximum.

Failure to file returns will revoke tax-exempt status. Sports booster organizations are not tax exempt, because they provide no public benefit. Calendar year tax-exempt organizations have a May 15th filing deadline.

E-Commerce Taxation

E-commerce raises tax issues, such as the sale of digitized goods which is not adequately addressed by laws written before the advent of e-commerce. An online selling activity that becomes a trade or business must be sure to: (1) register for business license taxes; (2) register for sales tax in states where the business has a physical presence; and (3) maintain records of sales and expenses. The business may have to address the self-employment tax issue. The IRS is focusing on small businesses using the internet because it is estimated that the annual tax gap for such businesses is about $5 billion. There is no clear guidance in the federal tax laws regarding costs incurred to develop and maintain a website. A vendor who has a physical presence in State B can avoid collecting sales taxes in any state by advertising that it ships from State B, but does not ship to State B. However, when a vendor arranges for a supplier to ship goods directly to customers, the supplier may have to collect sales taxes if the vendor does not have nexus in the state where the customer is located; also, if a vendor has an agent for product returns or sales in another state, the vendor likely has sales tax collection obligations where the agent is located. An important court case (Quill Corp. v. North Dakota, 504 US 298 – 1992) held that a business must have a physical presence in a state before the state can make the business collect sales tax from customers in that state.

Some of the Forms 1099 required to be filed under IRC Section 6050W will help the IRS and state tax agencies find businesses that have not properly reported profits from selling goods on internet auction sites. Digital goods such as downloaded music and books are subject to sales tax in a growing number of states. **Tax Preparers** should ask clients: (1) if they sold anything on the internet; (2) if they or their children have a website that generates any income such as from sponsored links or ads; (3) participated in any online tournaments that included prizes; or (4) loaned money to someone through an internet lending business or non-profit group.

Alternative Minimum Tax (AMT) (Form 6251)

The favorable tax benefits available under the regular tax are curtailed by the Alternative Minimum Tax (AMT) with a system of tax "preferences" and "adjustments." **The Alternative Minimum Tax (AMT) is the excess of the Tentative Minimum Tax over regular income tax** that is paid in addition to regular income tax. Starting in 2012 all **non-refundable tax credits** are "permanently" available to offset AMT, including all general business tax credits generated (including the R&D tax credit). However, tax credits carried back cannot offset AMT. The exemption amounts for the AMT are made permanent and indexed for inflation as of January 1, 2013. For 2013, the exemption amounts applicable to AMT are $80,800 for married filing jointly and $51,900 for single filers, and these exemption amounts are made "permanent" and indexed for inflation beginning Jan. 1, 2013. **Form 6251 must be attached to any return if the deductions taken on the return are greater than AGI**, or alternative minimum taxable income (AMTI) is above the exemption amounts applicable to AMT for the taxpayer's filing status.

The primary distinction between tax "preferences" and "adjustments" is that preferences can only increase AMT, but adjustments may increase or decrease AMT relative to regular income tax. **Alternative Minimum Taxable Income (AMTI) is computed by starting with regular taxable income and increasing it by tax preferences not allowed for AMT purposes, and increasing or decreasing it by adjustments.** Many AMT adjustments are deferred items which reflect a difference in the timing of an item of income or deduction between the regular tax and the AMT, thus having an impact not only on current year's taxes but on future years' taxes. The characteristics most likely to give rise to an AMT liability for ordinary taxpayers are a large number of personal exemptions, high deductions for state and local taxes, a large amount of miscellaneous itemized deductions, and incentive stock options. **Bonus depreciation and Section 179 expensing are not tax preference items** and do not have to be added back to regular taxable income in computing AMTI.

Tentative Minimum Tax is computed by multiplying AMTI (less AMT exemption amount) by AMT tax rate and then subtracting the AMT foreign tax credit, which is limited to the foreign tax on foreign source AMTI instead of foreign tax on regular taxable income (a separate Form 1116 must be prepared). Even though capital gains qualify for the preferential capital gain tax rates for AMT, total capital gains are included in AMTI and, therefore, can reduce or eliminate the effect of the exemption amounts. Any decrease in the exemption amounts makes more of the taxpayer's income subject to the AMT.

Example computation of Tentative Minimum Tax:

Alternative Minimum Taxable Income (AMTI)	-	$ 250,000
Exemption amount (married filing jointly)	-	(80,800)
		$ 169,200
AMT tax rate	X	26%
Tentative Minimum Tax	= $	43,992

AMT tax rates and Exemption Amounts:

Rates: All except married	up to $175,000	X	26%
Filing separately	Above	X	28%
Married filing	up to $87,500	X	26%
separately	Above	X	28%

Exemptions:

Married filing jointly & Surviving spouse	$80,800 (2013)	$78,750 (2012)
Single & Head of Household	$51,900 (2013)	$50,600 (2012)
Married filing separately & Trusts & Estates	$40,400 (2013)	$39,375 (2012)

*Exemption amounts are reduced by 25% of AMTI exceeding:

Married filing jointly	$150,000 - $382,000 (phase-out)
Single & Head of household	$112,500 - $273,500
Married filing separately & Trusts & Estates	$75,000 - $165,000

Tax Preferences (added to regular taxable income in determining AMTI)
- Interest on tax-exempt investments.
- Personal exemptions.
- Standard deduction (if used for regular tax, cannot recalculate using itemized deductions for AMT purposes).

- State and local taxes (including real estate taxes), and sales taxes (claimed as an itemized deduction).
- Miscellaneous itemized deductions subject to the 2% AGI limitation. **Miscellaneous itemized deductions not subject to the 2% floor are not added back in determining AMTI.**
- Difference between 10% and 7.5% (2 ½%) of medical expenses over AGI claimed as an itemized deduction (only applicable to individuals age 65 and over in 2013).
- Any mortgage interest claimed as an itemized deduction for regular tax purposes that is not for a principal residence and one other acceptable residence for AMT purposes, i.e. a boat with cooking and bathroom facilities is not considered a second home for AMT purposes, so any interest claimed for the boat must be added back. Also, if a home equity loan is used for other than home improvements, such as to purchase a car, it is not deductible for AMT purposes. **Example: If you deduct interest on a home equity loan for regular tax purposes and it is used to purchase a car, it must be added back to regular taxable income in computing AMTI.**
- Points deducted for regular tax purposes when refinancing a home loan are not allowed for AMT purposes and must be added back.
- Exclusion of gain on the sale of small business stock if held more than 5 years – 50% is excluded for regular tax purposes on stock acquired before 2/18/2009, or after 12/31/2011; 75% is excluded for regular tax purposes on stock acquired after 2/17/2009 and before 9/28/2010; and 100% is excluded for regular tax purposes on stock acquired after 9/27/2010 and before 1/1/2014. **The 100% exclusion is unique in allowing it to apply for both regular tax and AMT purposes.** However, for small business stock sold through 12/31/2012 (except for the 100% exclusion exception): 42% of the gain excluded from regular taxable income from the sale of small-business stock acquired before 1/1/2001 is an AMT tax preference item (must be added back to regular taxable income); and 7% of the gain excluded from regular taxable income from the sale of small-business stock acquired after 1/1/2001 is an AMT tax preference item. For all small-business stock **sold** after 12/31/2012, 28% of the gain excluded from regular taxable income is an AMT tax preference item (must be added back to regular taxable income).
- Exclusion of tax-exempt interest on specified private activity bonds (less any related expenses) issued after Aug. 7, 1986 is an AMT tax preference item (must be added back to regular taxable income). Private activity bonds do not include bonds issued after July 30, 2008 that are: exempt-facility bonds that are part of a bond issue in which 95% or more of the proceeds are used for qualified residential rental projects; qualified mortgage bonds; or qualified veterans' mortgage bonds. Any bond issued after 12/31/2008, and before 1/1/2011 is not treated as a private activity bond.
- Deduction for excess intangible drilling costs for integrated oil companies – the AMT preference is the amount that exceeds 65% of the net income from oil and gas (does not affect producers and royalty owners).

- For taxpayer's other than independent oil and gas producers, the amount by which a depletion deduction for an interest in a property exceeds the adjusted basis of the interest at end of the year must be added back to regular taxable income.

Adjustments (added or deducted from regular taxable income in determining AMTI)
- Incentive Stock Options (ISO): for AMT purposes, ordinary income is recognized when ISOs are exercised (difference between exercise price and the market price) and the basis of the stock is the market price. When the stock is later sold, the difference between the selling price and the market price is recognized as a capital gain or loss. For regular tax purposes, no income is recognized when Incentive Stock Options (ISO) are exercised. Instead when the stock is later sold, any gain or loss is treated as a capital gain (basis of stock is exercise price). However, part of the gain may be ordinary income if the exercise price was less than 85% of the market price on the date of exercise. For regular tax purposes, a **dual holding period applies** to ISOs, i.e. you must hold the stock for one year after the ISO is exercised (shares transferred to you) and for two years from the date the ISO was granted in order to be eligible for long-term capital gain treatment. Therefore, for regular tax purposes a disqualifying disposition occurs if you sell the stock within one year of the exercise date or within two years from the date the ISO is granted, which would trigger ordinary income for regular tax purposes equal to the difference between exercise price and the market price on the date of exercise. In this case, the basis of the stock would be the market price, and any difference between selling price and the market price would be capital gain or loss. If this happens, it is the same way that ordinary income and gains and losses are computed for AMT purposes so no adjustment would be required in determining AMTI.
    - Example requiring an adjustment: An ISO is granted on 1/1/2013 for 100 shares of stock, and is exercised on 1/31/2013 when the exercise price is $10 per share and the market price is $15 per share. The stock is not sold until 2/1/2015 (more than 2 years after the ISO grant date). Therefore, in 2013 no income is recognized for regular tax purposes. For AMT purposes, $500 of ordinary income would be recognized ($1,500 - $1,000). So in 2013, $500 is added to regular taxable income in determining AMTI.

Depreciation
MACRS depreciation is allowed on Sec. 1245 capital assets at a maximum 200% declining balance (DB) rate for regular tax purposes and at a maximum 150% DB rate for AMT purposes. No adjustment is required if 150% DB or straight-line depreciation is used for regular tax purposes.
    - Example requiring an adjustment: In 2013, you have depreciable Sec. 1245 capital assets with a basis of $100,000 and you use MACRS 200% DB to claim $15,000 in depreciation expenses for regular tax purposes. However, for AMT purposes MACRS 150% DB is required for computing allowable depreciation, which would be $10,000 in depreciation

expenses allowed for AMT purposes. So in 2013, $5,000 is added to regular taxable income in determining AMTI.
- o **A taxpayer who expects to incur AMT in future years might benefit from leasing depreciable property, because lease payments do not generate an AMT adjustment since they are fully deductible for both regular and AMT tax purposes.**

Rental Properties

Rental properties (houses, etc.) usually require an AMT adjustment for deduction items not allowed for AMT purposes, i.e. depreciation, mortgage interest and real estate taxes on rental houses. You must complete separate Forms 8582 "Passive Activity Loss Limitations" for regular tax purposes and AMT tax purposes. The At-Risk rules that limit the deductibility of taxpayer's losses from passive activities for regular tax purposes also apply with some modifications for AMT tax purposes.
- o Example requiring an adjustment: In 2013, you own a rental house on which you take these deductions: mortgage interest -$5,000; property tax - $7,000, and straight-line GDS depreciation - $8,000. The mortgage interest and property taxes are not allowable for AMT purposes and only straight-line ADS depreciation is allowable, reducing allowable depreciation to $6,000 for AMT purposes. So in 2013, $14,000 is added to regular taxable income in determining AMTI.
- Losses from passive farming activities (no material participation) that are available for regular tax purposes are not deductible for AMT purposes, and must be added in determining AMTI.
- The limitation on itemized deductions for regular tax purposes in 2013 does not apply for AMT tax purposes. This could result in an adjustment requiring a deduction from regular taxable income in determining AMTI.
- Recoveries of state income taxes paid in a prior year that are included in income in the current year, because the taxes resulted in a tax benefit in a prior year that are not included in calculating AMT. This would result in an adjustment requiring a deduction from regular taxable income in determining AMTI.
- An investment interest expense deduction on tax-exempt investments is allowed for AMT purposes, because tax-exempt interest income is included in calculating AMTI. However, no adjustment is required because investment expenses on tax-exempt investments are a miscellaneous itemized deduction subject to the 2% floor, which are not allowed for AMT purposes.
- A Domestic production activities deduction (above-the-line deduction) is allowed for both regular tax and AMT purposes but is computed separately for each, so an adjustment would probably be required.
- R&D expenditures are deductible in the current year for regular tax purposes, but must be amortized over a 10 year period for AMT purposes (you can also elect to amortize over ten years for regular tax purposes, thus avoiding an adjustment). However, if a taxpayer materially

participates in the activity, he is exempt from an AMT adjustment when R&D expenditures are deducted in the current year. The same rules apply for mining exploration and development costs.

- Net operating losses are computed separately for regular tax and AMT, thus requiring an adjustment. There is a 90% limit on the 5-year NOL carry backs for AMT purposes (farming).
- Passive activity rules for regular tax purposes apply to AMT with some modifications, i.e. a taxpayer who is not a material participant in a farming business but uses a farming tax shelter to avoid regular tax may not deduct passive activity losses in computing AMT, so an adjustment would be required adding back the passive activity losses to regular taxable income in determining AMTI.

AMT Credit

Including the Refundable Portion (Form 8801, Credit For Prior Year Minimum Tax - Individuals, Estates, and Trusts) – This credit, which includes a refundable aspect for an unused long-term credit amount, can be carried forward indefinitely and is for the amount of the AMT that was attributable to deferral items (timing preferences and adjustments). A taxpayer subject to the AMT accrues AMT credits generated only by AMT timing items. Timing items are those accounted for in different tax years in the regular tax system and the AMT tax system, i.e. accelerated depreciation, etc. AMT credits can only be used in years when the regular tax liability exceeds the "Tentative Minimum Tax" for the year. Unused long-term AMT credits are refundable. The refundable AMT credit was enacted to give relief to individuals who exercised incentive stock options (ISO) that generated AMT credits that lost all or a significant portion of their value in later years due to the loss in value of the stocks. Since the difference between the fair market value (FMV) and the option price is a preference item for AMT purposes, these taxpayers paid an increased amount in tax and generated a credit for use in later years, when the stock was sold for a profit. The loss in value of the stocks resulted in these individuals being unable to use a portion, if any, of the sizable amounts of AMT credit to offset their tax liability, and they would carry the amount forward to the next year with the same results. The minimum AMT credit allowed in a year is not less than the greater of the amount of the AMT refundable credit amount determined for the preceding year or 50% of the unused credit. <u>The minimum tax credit (MTC) is the amount of the AMT attributable to deferral-type adjustments (accelerated depreciation, etc.) available to reduce the taxpayer's regular tax liability in a tax year by some or all of the AMT tax paid in previous years</u>. The unused credit is defined as that portion of the minimum tax credit attributable to the adjusted minimum tax for tax years before the third tax year immediately preceding such tax year. Thus, for 2013, taxpayers may be able to claim a refundable amount for credits generated from paying the alternative minimum tax in 2009. To claim the AMT credit, including the refundable portion, taxpayers must complete Form 8801, Credit For Prior Year Minimum Tax - Individuals, Estates, and Trusts. The additional (refundable) credit is limited to the lesser of $30 million or 6% of the AMT credit carry forwards generated in tax years beginning before 1/1/2006 that were not used in tax years ending before April 1, 2008. **(SEE "Tax Credits," AMT Credit and Credit for Prior Year Minimum Tax)** A taxpayer can claim an additional AMT credit in lieu of bonus depreciation. Taxpayers must agree to forgo the use of bonus depreciation on qualified property placed in service and instead depreciate it using the straight-line method. **(SEE "Depreciation," Bonus Depreciation)**

Tax Return of Deceased

When a person dies, a "final return" through the date of death must be filed if required according to the gross income test. However, a surviving spouse may file a joint return that includes the income of the decedent up to the date of death and the income of the surviving spouse for the entire year. Also, if the surviving spouse is the decedent's beneficiary, all of the income that the decedent would have received for the entire year may be included on the joint return filed by the surviving spouse. If a surviving spouse remarries before the end of the year in which the decedent died, the filing status of the decedent is married filing separately. The final return of a decedent is due by the regular filing due date (April 15th). All income that the decedent would have received had death not occurred is "income in respect of the decedent" (IRD) and must be included in the income of one of the following: (1) **The beneficiary, if the right to the income is passed directly to the beneficiary and the beneficiary receives it;** or (2) The decedent's estate, if the estate receives it.

- Joint return filed – surviving spouse should sign the return and write in the signature space for the deceased "Filing as surviving spouse". The word "DECEASED," name of decedent, and the date of death should be written across the top of the return.
- Joint return not filed – either a court-appointed personal representative or another person can sign the return as the personal representative. A court-appointed personal representative will have a certificate from the court. A personal representative (including a court-appointed representative) who is signing the return has to submit Form 1310 with the decedent's final tax return.
- In a community property state, when one spouse dies, the IRS's position is that income from community property should be included ½ in the surviving spouse's income and ½ in the decedent's estate. This does not apply to income from joint accounts where the spouse has the right to the income. It also does not apply if all income and the underlying assets are passed directly to a beneficiary (including the surviving spouse) and the beneficiary receives it.

When IRD is included in the decedent's estate, an Estate Income Tax Return (Form 1041) must be filed if income for a year is more than $600, which is the standard exemption for an estate. However, the exemption is not allowed in the final tax year of the estate, when all items pass through to the beneficiaries. (SEE "Estate Income Tax Return") An estate only pays income tax on income generated by its underlying assets that are not distributed to beneficiaries. **If IRD is received by a decedent's estate, the estate must have a tax identification number (TIN) and a final estate income tax return must be filed to close-out the estate, even if there is no income to report.**

- **Forms 1099, reporting dividends, interest income etc., should show interest, dividends etc. earned before and after the date of death and to whom paid – beneficiaries or the estate.**
- All deductions for medical expenses should be taken on the decedent's final return, as long as they are paid within one year of the decedent's death and the decedent has no Estate Tax

liability. However, if the decedent has an estate tax liability, any unpaid medical expenses that are not deducted on the decedent's final return should be deducted on **Form 706 - Estate Tax return** (not to be confused with the estate income tax return - Form 1041).
- If a decedent engaged in business had a net operating loss (NOL) prior to death, it cannot be carried forward to the estate income tax return but instead must be taken on the decedent's final tax return or carried back to prior years.
- A capital loss sustained by a decedent during his last tax year (or carried over) can be deducted on the decedent's final income tax return only to the extent of the capital loss limit ($3,000). Any left-over capital losses cannot be deducted on the decedent's estate income tax return(s). However, if a joint return is filed, the surviving spouse can carryover any capital losses in excess of $3,000 and deduct the losses on his/her tax returns in future years. Also, if the right of income is passed directly to a beneficiary, the beneficiary is entitled to carryover any of the decedent's capital losses in excess of $3,000.
- When annuity payments end because of a taxpayer's death and there is an **unrecovered non-taxable investment**, that amount is deducted on the taxpayer's final return.

Estate Income Tax Return (Form 1041)

Deductions and credits allowed to individuals are also allowed to estates. In addition, estates are allowed to deduct distributions to beneficiaries. Estates have unfavorable tax rates. The 2013 tax brackets are as follows:

0 - $2,450 = 10%; $2,450 - $5,700 = $368 + 25% of the amount over $5,700; $5,700 - $8,750 = $1,180 + 28% of the amount over $8,750; $8,750 - $11,950 = $2,034 + 33% of the amount over $11,950; over $11,950 = $3,090 + 39% of the amount over $11,950

All income of a decedent in the year of death that is not included in the "final return" of the decedent or in the income of beneficiaries must be included in the decedent's estate. An estate for tax purposes is treated as a separate entity and must have a separate tax identification number (TIN), and **a tax return (Form 1041) must be filed each year for a domestic estate that has taxable income more than $600, which is the exemption amount**. However, the $600 exemption is not allowed in the final year of the estate when all items pass to the beneficiaries. The estate consists of all assets held in the decedent's name after these exclusions: one-half of assets held jointly with the right of survivorship; all assets received by a surviving spouse as the decedent's sole beneficiary; retirement assets that passed automatically or directly to designated beneficiaries, such as traditional and Roth IRAs, annuities, etc.; assets with specific payable at death directions; and certain property held in trust, such as property held in a revocable trust created by the decedent. The exclusion of these assets is important because it means that they do not have to go through probate. Probate is generally required only when the value of the assets exceed a threshold dollar amount, depending on the state. For estates under the threshold, an "affidavit of heirship" or similar document or procedure can usually be used or followed, so the will does not have to be probated and no separate entity has to be established for the estate (no separate TIN required).

If a separate estate entity is established and Form 1041 is required to be filed, Form 1041, Schedule K-1 is used to report distributions to beneficiaries, which must be reported on their individual tax returns, whether received or not. All distributions retain the same character – passive income, etc. Estates can select a tax year other than the calendar year. The executor or administrator chooses the estate's tax period when the first income tax return is filed. It may be any period of 12 months or less that ends on the last day of a month. If the last day of any month other than December is selected, you are adopting a fiscal tax year. An estate of a deceased person is a taxable entity separate from the decedent, and it continues to exist until the final distribution of assets of the estate is made to the heirs and other beneficiaries. The income earned from the property of the estate during the period of administration or settlement must be accounted for and reported by the estate. However, the estate only pays tax on income that is not distributed to beneficiaries. If a fiscal year begins in 2012 and ends in 2013, the information reported on the Form 1041 and the K-1 is reported on the beneficiary's 2013 tax return. A tax return (Form 1041) must be filed by the 15th day of the fourth month following the end of an estate's tax year (including the final return), but the executor of the estate can obtain an automatic 6-month extension by filing Form 7004. Estimated taxes for the estate have to be paid unless the decedent has no tax liability. **The gross and taxable income of estates are computed as they are for individuals (deductions and credits allowed to individuals are also allowed for estates) except the following deductions are allowed in computing adjusted gross income for an estate, which are deductions for determining AGI:**

- Estates are allowed to deduct distributions to beneficiaries in determining adjusted gross income.
- Expenses incurred in connection with the administration of an estate are allowable in arriving at adjusted gross income.
- The $600 exemption is allowed in determining adjusted gross income (but not on the final return).

There are other distinctions between individual tax returns and estate income tax returns, including the following:

- There is no standard deduction for estates.
- No deductions are allowed for medical expenses, because all deductions for medical expenses must be taken on the decedent's final return as long as they are paid within one year of the decedent's death. However, if the decedent has an estate tax liability, any unpaid medical expenses that are not deducted on the decedent's final return can be deducted on Form 706 - Estate Tax return.
- No deduction is allowed for funeral expenses. Funeral expenses must be taken as a deduction from the decedent's gross estate for estate tax purposes (Form 706) if there is an estate tax liability.
- If a decedent engaged in business had a net operating loss (NOL) prior to death, it cannot be carried forward to the estate income tax return, but instead must be taken on the decedent's final tax return or carried back to prior years.
- Estates cannot take the Sec. 179 expense deduction on depreciable assets.
- Any left-over capital losses from before the death of the decedent cannot be deducted on the decedent's estate income tax return.
- **At the election of the executor or trustee, a revocable trust can be treated as part of the estate for income tax purposes rather than as a separate entity. Form 8855, "Election to treat a revocable trust as part of an estate" must be filed. (SEE "Trust Income")**
- An Estate may have a net operating loss (NOL) on the final return if Line 22 on Form 1041 is a loss due to excess deductions. To determine if there is a NOL, do not include any deductions claimed on Line 13 (charitable deductions), Line 18 (income distributions to beneficiaries) or

Line 20 (the $600 exemption - <u>remember you can't take the $600 exemption on the final return</u>). If there is a NOL, enter the beneficiary's share of the excess deductions in Box 11 of Form 1041 Schedule K-1 using Code A. <u>Figure the deductions on a separate sheet of paper and attach it to the return</u>. The NOL can include net capital losses. **(SEE "Taxable Income," Net Operating Loss)**
- **An Estate that has been established by obtaining a TIN from the IRS must file a final return in order to properly close-out the estate, even if there is no income to report.**

Beneficiaries who receive distributions from decedents' estates or who obtain income and assets passed directly to them are required to file tax returns that include the inherited assets and all income that the decedent would have received had death not occurred. These beneficiaries must include these assets and income on their tax returns in accordance with certain laws and regulations, which include the following:
- Capital gains are not recognized by beneficiaries on appreciated assets distributed to them by the estate because the beneficiaries are allowed to take the <u>stepped-up basis</u>, which is the fair market value (FMV) of the inherited assets at the decedent's death.
- Gain on the sale of inherited property is **always long-term capital gain** regardless of how long the decedent or heirs held onto it. The tax law gives an automatic long-term holding period to inherited property. It is a capital gain and not ordinary income, unless the asset inherited is excluded from the definition of capital gain property.
- Upon termination of the decedent's estate, beneficiaries are allowed to deduct their share of any net operating losses (NOLs) - which are excess deductions reported on their 1041 Schedule K-1s - on Schedule A, line 23 of their tax returns. The NOLs can also be carried back to the beneficiaries' prior 2 tax years.
- If the NOL includes net capital losses of more than $3,000 (say $10,000), <u>the $10,000 of net capital losses are either shown on line 3 (short-term losses) or line 4a (net long-term losses) of the beneficiary's 1041 Schedule K-1, and then should be put on Form 8949 of the beneficiary's 1040 tax return which is then transferred to Schedule D</u>. A beneficiary can only deduct $3,000 of the net capital losses on his current year tax return, but the remaining $7,000 is carried over to the next year. Any excess deductions that are not capital losses such as tax preparation and legal fees, fiduciary bond fees, out-of-pocket expenses for the administrator of the estate, etc. that may be a portion of the NOL are shown in Box 11, Code C "final deductions" on the 1041 Schedule K-1 and a separate written list is attached detailing the excess deductions. These excess deductions are then shown on Schedule A of the beneficiary's 1040 tax return.
- **You may deduct a capital loss on the sale of a house acquired by inheritance or as a gift if you personally did not use it and offered it for sale or rent immediately or within a few weeks after acquisition.** The basis of the property is the stepped-up basis when inherited, which would be the appraised value in the year inherited.

Trust Income (Form 1041)

Deductions and credits allowed to individuals are also allowed to trusts. In addition, trusts are allowed to deduct distributions to beneficiaries. Trusts have unfavorable tax rates. The 2013 tax brackets are as follows:

0 - $2,450 = 10%; $2,450 - $5,700 = $368 + 25% of the amount over $5,700; $5,700 - $8,750 = $1,180 + 28% of the amount over $8,750; $8,750 - $11,950 = $2,034 + 33% of the amount over $11,950; over $11,950 = $3,090 + 39% of the amount over $11,950

A trust is a separate taxable entity that can be created pursuant to a trust agreement executed during a person's lifetime or upon a person's death pursuant to his or her will; therefore a separate TIN has to be obtained for the trust. A trustee takes title to property for the benefit of another person in order to protect or conserve the property of the grantor or beneficiary as expressed in the trust agreement or will. Two or more trusts are treated as one trust for tax purposes if they have substantially the same grantor/grantors and substantially the same primary beneficiaries. You can classify trusts in different ways. If a grantor does not have powers over the trust and all the assets in it, then it is an <u>irrevocable trust (non-grantor trust)</u>. If the grantor has powers over the trust, it is deemed a <u>grantor or revocable trust</u>. When the grantor renounces powers, then it becomes a non-grantor trust. The gross and taxable income of trusts is essentially determined like it is for an estate. **(SEE "Estate Income Tax Return)** Beneficiaries who receive distributions of income and assets passed to them from trusts via Form 1041 K-1s are required to include the assets and income on their 1040 tax returns in accordance with certain laws and regulations. The gross and taxable income of trusts are computed as they are for individuals (deductions and credits allowed to individuals are also allowed for trusts). Except:

- Trusts are allowed to deduct distributions to beneficiaries in determining adjusted gross income.
- Administration costs in connection with a trust are allowable in arriving at adjusted gross income of the trust.
- Trusts cannot take the Sec. 179 expense deduction on depreciable assets.

<u>Grantor/Revocable Trust</u>

As a separate taxable entity, a trust reports all income received on assets owned by it and deducts all expenses paid by it that are otherwise deductible. However, if the grantor has sufficient control of trust income or principal, <u>the income is taxed directly to the grantor</u>. **This is a so-called "grantor trust" that becomes a separate entity for tax purposes upon the grantor's death**. A grantor trust may have more than one grantor which are each treated separately as the owner of their portion of the trust. Chances are that if you have significant assets that will be subject to estate taxes (Form 706) you will want to use a grantor trust, with the intention of eventually transferring the assets to children and other beneficiaries. The grantor retains substantial control over the trust, or power to revoke the trust and, therefore, a grantor trust does not have to file tax returns because everything still belongs to the grantor who must report all income, deductions, and credits on his own income tax return (example: a living trust, which is a revocable trust). The grantor's spouse also has the same powers. Following the death of the grantor, the trustee must obtain a separate TIN for the trust and treat it as a separate entity for tax purposes. A qualified revocable trust, upon the grantor's death, can elect along with the estate to be treated as part of the estate for income tax purposes. Making this election qualifies the trust for favorable tax treatment, including the ability to report on a fiscal-year basis. The election is made by filing Form 8855 and, once made, the election cannot be revoked. Making the election still requires the trustee to obtain a separate TIN for the trust. The election allows the electing trust to be treated and taxed as part of its related estate during the election period, which begins at the decedent's death and lasts for a minimum of two years. If an executor is appointed to the related estate after the election is made, the executor must agree to the election or it will terminate. If an election isn't made to be treated as part of the estate, the trustee has to file tax returns for the trust (Form 1041) and start distributing income and assets to the beneficiaries. The trust is entitled to an **annual exemption of $300** if it is required under its terms to distribute all income currently (i.e., a simple trust).

- Living Trust - A living trust is created to hold title to an individual's assets. The benefits of a living trust include: avoidance of probate; continuity of management of assets if the individual becomes incapacitated and unable to take care of his/her financial affairs; privacy as to one's assets upon his/her death; and possible reduced cost, time, and aggravation in settling one's estate. House(s), cars, life insurance, bank accounts, and investments should be put into a "living trust," but not tax deferred annuities and IRAs (because they are passed directly to designated beneficiaries).
- Asset Protection Trust - One of the best types of an asset protection trust is the **Intentionally Defective Grantor Trust (IDGT), which is designed to avoid paying estate taxes upon the grantor's death.** Even though the exclusion amount for estate tax is $5.25 million, which in most cases eliminates the need for a trust for estate tax purposes, a trust is still necessary for asset protection. An IDGT can be used to hold and protect many types of assets and to hold and protect life insurance proceeds from creditors. Litigation and fraud are on the rise, thus making asset protection in estate planning even more critical. An IDGT is advantageous over the traditional Irrevocable Life Insurance Trust (ILIT) because an ILIT can only hold a life insurance policy. Also, the IDGT has Dynasty Trust provisions which prevent the corpus from being distributed to the beneficiaries at the death of the grantor. A grantor still reports and pays tax on the current income in an IDGT. However, any transactions between the trust and the grantor do not result in a taxable event. Upon the grantor's death, the trust is not included in the grantor's estate. There is also another grantor trust called a Grantor-Retained Annuity Trust,

which is the perfect vehicle to transfer a great deal of wealth when you want to avoid estate and gift tax. The grantor sets up the trust and gives yet unappreciated assets to the trust.
- Credit Shelter Trust - The portability election provides no inflation adjustment to account for the time value of money between the first and second death. The answer to that is to establish a Credit Shelter Trust at the death of the first spouse to die. It can be set up in a will as a revocable trust. This allows the remaining assets to grow between the first and second death, whereas the portability election does not. **(SEE "Estate and Gift Tax")**
- Charitable Trust - Charitable trusts are for individuals who intend to leave large parts of their estates to charity. It is important for a client to spell out their charitable intentions so if they die unexpectedly, the money goes to the charity before it gets taxed with the estate.
- For a married couple, each spouse can create a trust for the primary benefit of the other spouse. The children and grandchildren would be discretionary beneficiaries of the trusts. Each spouse would have access as a beneficiary to trust assets at the discretion of a trustee (an unrelated party). At death, the assets would escape estate taxation in both spouses' estates. The terms of the trusts should be substantially different, i.e. give certain powers to one spouse in his trust but not give the other spouse the same powers in her trust, and have different delays in timing and creation of the trusts.

Non-Grantor/Irrevocable Trust

A non-grantor trust is treated as a separate entity for tax purposes (must have a separate TIN). A non-grantor trust is taxed on its income only to the extent it is not distributed. Form 1041 must be filed on a calendar year basis by the trustee or fiduciary of the trust, and Form 1041 Schedule K-1 is used to report distributions to the beneficiaries, which must be reported on their individual tax returns. All distributions retain the same character – passive income, etc. The trustee can obtain an automatic 6-month extension to file the tax return by filing Form 7004. Non-grantor trusts are treated somewhat like a partnership as to distributed income, and like a corporation as to undistributed income. Essentially, there are two kinds of non-grantor trusts:
- Simple Trust – Form 1041 must be filed if gross income for the tax year is $300 or more. A Simple trust is required to distribute income currently.
- Complex Trust – Form 1041 must be filed if gross income for the tax year is $100 or more.
- **To avoid or reduce federal taxes paid by beneficiaries (except spouse) who inherit annuities, you can convert an unqualified annuity to an IRS approved tax-free benefit plan owned by a 3rd party, such as an irrevocable trust. This should be done if you do not need the annuity payments to provide income, and you choose to pass these on to your heirs. Unfortunately, these tax deferred annuities are subject to significant income tax, and in some cases, estate tax. However, annuitizing the value of the annuity for life and purchasing an IRS approved tax-free death benefit plan (which will normally be worth two or three times the value of the annuity depending on the age of the annuity owner) owned by an irrevocable trust not only**

converts, for example, a $200,000 annuity from a taxable asset into a tax-free asset upon death, but the value is increased to from $400,000 to $600,000 and will not be included in your Estate.

Estate and Gift Tax

Estate Tax Return (Form 706)

An Estate tax return is required only if a taxpayer's gross estate plus adjusted taxable gifts after specific exclusions exceeds the exemption amount, which is $5,250,000 in 2013 ($5,120,000 in 2012). An Estate tax return is due nine months after the date of death. The exemption amount is the same for both Estate tax and Gift tax purposes, hence making the wealth transfer tax truly a "unified tax." However, beginning in 2012, any unified credit allocated to gifts in prior periods must be re-determined using the current gift tax rate, not the rates in effect for the years when prior gifts were made (the instructions provide a worksheet for making this calculation, and the result is reported on Form 709, Schedule B, Gifts From Prior Periods). **The $5.25 million exclusion (indexed for inflation) was made "permanent" as of Jan. 1, 2013, but with a top tax rate of 40% instead of 35%.** An alternative regime applies to certain individuals who are non-resident non-citizens by virtue of having relinquished their U.S. citizenship or long-term residency (special rules for income, gift, and estate tax purposes apply for 10 years following their expatriation to alleviate avoidance of taxation).

A decedent's gross estate is not the same as the probate estate when used to compute estate income tax. The gross estate includes property, such as life insurance and retirement benefits, that are not part of probate. A decedent's gross estate includes interests he or she holds in all property (real, personal, tangible or intangible). Included in the decedent's gross estate are: life insurance proceeds received by a beneficiary; retirement assets that pass directly to designated beneficiaries (traditional and Roth IRAs, annuities, etc.); and those assets held in some revocable trusts created by the decedent. In the case of jointly owned property held by a husband and wife, only ½ of the property is included in the decedent's gross estate. A married person's estate is allowed a deduction for property passing directly to the surviving spouse (reported on Schedule M of Form 706). Assets that generally pass tax-free to a spouse include: jointly owned property; life insurance; retirement benefits; and bequests in the will or property passing in trust. If the decedent transfers property within three years before the date of death, then the property is included in the gross estate. For example, if the decedent transfers a life insurance policy to someone else within three years of death, the policy proceeds are included in the decedent's gross estate. Also, the decedent's gross estate includes the amount of gift tax owed on any gifts made within three years of the date of death. Property included in the gross estate is generally valued at the date of death but the executor can elect to value it on a date that is 6 months after the date of death, but only if this will decrease both the value of the gross estate and the taxes payable as well as any generation skipping transfer tax (GST) payable as a result of the taxpayer's death. Certain expenses are deductible from a gross estate for determining the taxable amount of the estate: unreimbursed funeral expenses; administration expenses not deducted from Estate income tax returns, including executor expenses; attorney and accountant fees; fees for maintaining and storing estate property; selling expenses if necessary to pay estate tax liabilities and expenses; unlimited deduction for charitable contributions; claims against the estate; unpaid mortgages on any indebtedness on property included in the gross estate; and other claims and expenses against the estate, which may not be known at the time of filing Form 706.

- Exemption for Lifetime Taxable Gifts and Estates:
  2005 - $1,500,000; Applicable Credit $555,800
  2006 – 2008 - $2,000,000; Applicable Credit $780,000
  2009 - $3,500,000; Applicable Credit $1,455,800
  2010 – (See below)
  2011 - $5,000,000; Applicable Credit $1,730,800
  2012 - $5,120,000; Applicable Credit $1,772,800
  2013 - $5,250,000; Applicable Credit $2,045,800
- <u>Unified Estate and Gift Tax Rates</u>:
  2005 – 47%
  2006 – 46%
  2007, 2008, 2009 – 45%
  2010 – (See below)
  2011 & 2012 – 35%
  2013 - 40%

* The "Applicable Credit" is the amount deductible from any Estate tax determined as payable on Form 706.

The Estate and generation-skipping transfer (GST) tax was originally not in effect for persons who died in 2010, but the <u>Gift tax was imposed at the top individual tax rate of 35% in 2010 and the gift tax exclusion amount was $1 million</u>. However, on Dec. 17, 2010, President Obama signed a law that reinstated the Estate and Generation-Skipping Transfer Tax (GST) retroactive to 1/1/2010. The law gave taxpayers who died in 2010 a special tax break: executors of 2010 decedents' estates could opt out of the Estate tax (with a 35% tax rate and a $5 million exemption) by filing Form 8939. However, filing this Form meant opting out of the stepped-up basis for all assets and opting into a "<u>modified carryover basis</u>" for property acquired from the decedent. A carryover basis generally means that assets keep the same basis as was in the hands of the decedent (Note, however, that when the carryover basis is greater than the FMV, the basis in the hands of the recipient is limited to the fair market value). The modified carryover option allowed executors the stepped-up basis of some assets – limited to $1.3 million in assets passing to a recipient(s), plus an additional $3 million passing either in trust or outright to a surviving spouse. However, both of these provisions could be applied to property passing to a surviving spouse. **Therefore, up to $4.3 million in assets could be allocated to property at the stepped-up basis to a surviving spouse.** <u>In order to opt into the modified carryover basis, Form 8939 had to be filed by the executor of an estate of a 2010 decedent with an estate in excess of $4.3</u>

million and the Form had to be filed on a timely basis no later than Jan. 17, 2012. No extension of time to file the election was permitted by the IRS.

Portability of the Estate Tax exemption
The Tax Relief, Unemployment Insurance Reauthorization, and Job Creation Act of 2010 introduced the concept of portability of the estate tax exemption for the first time. Portability allows a surviving spouse's estate to use the portion of the estate tax exemption that was not used upon the death of the first spouse (after 12/31/2010). **However, executors of estates who want to make the portability election have to file an Estate tax return (Form 706) for individuals who die in 2012 and 2013 even if the deceased person does not owe any estate tax.** The new provision allows both spouses' exemptions to be utilized without having to set-up trusts or engage in other tax planning maneuvers that were previously necessary. For example, John and Elizabeth are married – Elizabeth dies in 2012 and has $1million in her estate. An Estate tax return (Form 706) should be filed for Elizabeth, even though she owes no Estate tax, so that the $4.12 million of her remaining exclusion is transferred to John, who will then have a total exemption of $9.37 million in 2013. After Elizabeth dies, John marries Mary. If John then dies in 2013 with a $4 million estate and leaves the remaining $5.37 million to Mary, a Form 706 should be filed for John even though he owes no Estate Tax. Mary will then have a $10.62 million total exemption amount available. A few reasons in favor of filing a Form 706, even if not needed, come to mind. It is possible that the surviving spouse will get remarried to a wealthy person and the unused exclusion will be needed. In addition, the exclusion has economic value. A single person with a very large estate may see a financial benefit in marrying someone with little or no assets and two available exclusions. If the situation arises where you have a taxable estate and are required to file Form 706 but do not want to make the portability election, you will have to attach a statement to the Form 706 indicating that the estate is not making the election under I.R.C. section 2010(c)(5) or write "No Election Under Section 2010(c)(5)" on the top of the first page of the Form 706. **The portability provision was made "permanent" as of Jan. 1, 2013.**

Basis of Property Acquired by Beneficiaries
The basis of property acquired by beneficiaries is generally the fair market value (FMV) at the decedent's date of death, which is known as the stepped-up basis. In community property states, a surviving spouse is entitled to the stepped-up basis in the entire property (in contrast to the allowable ½ stepped-up basis for property in non-community property states). The stepped-up basis is not allowed for appreciated property acquired by the decedent as a gift within one year of the date of death. If a Form 706 is required to be filed, executors can elect to value the estate on an "alternate valuation date" that is six months after the date of death. Any property distributed, sold, exchanged or otherwise disposed of during the six months is valued as of the date of disposition. However, any interest whose value changed by merely the lapse of time is valued as of the date of death, with an adjustment allowed for any difference in value due to any factor other than the lapse of time. But, as

stated previously, the alternate valuation date can only be used if it will decrease both the value of the gross estate and the taxes payable as well as any generation skipping transfer tax (GST) payable as a result of the taxpayer's death. The stepped-up basis rule does not apply to "Gifts" made during the decedent's lifetime. For Gifts, the basis is generally the donor's adjusted basis in the property (carryover basis). However, the recipient's basis for computing a loss is the lesser of the donor's adjusted basis or FMV. The recipient's basis is increased by any Gift tax and GST attributable to the gift, but not more than the FMV of the property at the time of the gift.

Gift Tax Return (Form 709)

Taxable gifts made in any one year include all gifts made, reduced by the applicable exclusion. To avoid owing gift taxes in any one year, you should limit the amount of gifts made to any one person to the gift tax exclusion amount, which is $14,000 in 2013 ($28,000 if gift-splitting is used with your spouse). However, even if a gift tax is owed, no gift tax is actually payable until the total amount of accumulated gift taxes owed exceeds the applicable credit allowed for life time Estates and Gifts, which is $2,045,800 in 2013. A gift tax return must be filed on Form 709 by April 15th (an extension is available) for gifts made to any one person other than your spouse that exceed $14,000, which is the annual exclusion amount in 2013 ($13,000 in 2012). Also, if gift splitting is used with your spouse you must file a gift tax return, but no gift tax is owed if the amount of the gifts to any one person is $28,000 or less. The Gift tax is a cumulative lifetime tax, i.e. the tax imposed for each calendar year at the unified rate, which is 40% in 2013, on the sum of taxable gifts for the current year and for all prior years, reduced by the total gift taxes previously owed for all prior years.

- Gifts to charitable organizations are not subject to the Gift tax or reporting requirements. There is an unlimited gift tax exclusion for gifts to charitable organizations (no gift tax return has to be filed). However, if a Gift tax return is required to report non-charitable gifts, all gifts to charities then also must be reported on the return.
- The $14,000 exclusion applies to each person to whom a gift is made by a taxpayer in 2013.
- Each spouse must file a separate gift tax return for their own individual gifts. However, only the donor spouse must file if the married couple consents to split gifts of over $14,000 to any one person, but it must be reported to the IRS on Form 709. No gift tax is owed under the annual exclusion if the "split" gift is $28,000 or less.
- Any gift tax owed in a year is off-set by the unified lifetime estate and gift tax credit of $2,045,800 (which provides the $5,250,000 life time exemption for taxable gifts in 2013). This credit applies to both the Gift tax and the Estate tax, i.e. any unified credit used in one year reduces the amount of credit that you can use against your Gift tax and Estate tax in later years.
- There is an unlimited marital deduction for transfers made between spouses, unless a non-citizen spouse is involved.

- There is an unlimited Gift tax exclusion for transfers to pay for tuition and medical expenses made <u>directly</u> to educational institutions or providers of medical care (no gift tax return has to be filed).
- The annual Gift Tax exclusion ($14,000; $28,000 if a married couple) can be used to fund a 529 Plan (QTP). And according to the <u>5-year averaging rule a donor can contribute up to $70,000; $140,000 if a married couple, and average it over 5 years with no Gift Tax consequences (however, a Gift tax return must be filed, and the election for the 5-year averaging must be made on the donor's Gift tax return</u>.
- A Gift tax return (Form 709) must be filed if it is a gift of a future interest (regardless of value) in property, because the $14,000 annual exclusion is not allowed for future interests in property. Although an interest in property may vest immediately in the recipient, it is a future interest if the recipient cannot immediately use or enjoy the property.
- If you pay off your son's mortgage of $30,000 it is a gift to him, and you must file a gift tax return.
- Transfers to "trusts" fail to qualify as a gift of a present interest if the recipient does not have an unrestricted right to the immediate use, possession, or enjoyment of the property, or the income from the property. In order to have transfers to a trust qualify as a gift of a present interest, a provision must be included giving the beneficiary notice of "withdrawal rights" with respect to transfers to the trust. It is advisable that such a notice must be given if the gift tax annual exclusion is being claimed.

Generation-Skipping Transfer Tax (Form 709, Form 706-GS(D), and Form 706-GS(T))

The purpose of the Generation-Skipping Transfer Tax (GST) is to prevent families from avoiding estate tax in younger generations by skipping a generation and transferring property to the next generation. A GST tax return must be filed <u>only</u> in any year in which a GST tax is owed. This is a tax imposed in addition to the Estate and Gift tax on certain transfers from a grandparent generation to a grandchild's generation. The same annual exclusion as the Gift Tax applies to the GST ($14,000 in 2013; $13,000 in 2012). However, for gifts to trusts, the annual exclusion may not be available unless the trust provides the beneficiaries the right to withdraw an amount that does not exceed the gift tax annual exclusion amount. The same exemption amount applies to the GST tax as the Estate tax and the Gift Tax ($5.25 million). The tax return is due on April 15th following the year of transfer. The donor's cost basis and holding period generally carry over to the recipient. The portability provisions do not apply to the GST. There are three types of transfers subject to the GST:
- A direct skip is a gift from a grandparent to a grandchild. In a direct skip during the life of the transferor, the transferor is responsible for filing Form 709 and paying the GST tax.
- A taxable distribution is when the trust of a grandparent makes a distribution of principal to the grandchild. In this case, the transferee (grandchild) is required to file Form 706-GS(D) and pay the GST tax. For example, suppose Bill Jones dies with a $15 million estate and leaves all of his

property in trust with income payable to his child, and upon his child's death the trust assets go to the grandchild. Upon his death, Bill's estate is subject to the estate tax. On the subsequent death of his child, none of the trust property is taxable to the child's estate. The family would have "skipped" a generation of estate taxes.
- See the same example above, but instead the assets in the trust would go to the grandchild upon the termination of the trust, which would be a "taxable termination." This would require the trustee of the estate to file Form 706-GS(T) and pay the GST tax.

Patient Protection and Affordable Care Act (ACA)

Goals: increase the quality and affordability of health insurance; lower the uninsured rate by expanding public and private insurance coverage; and reduce costs of health care for individuals and the government. The ACA uses three primary mechanisms to implement the law: mandates, subsidies, and Exchanges. The law is expected to spend a little over $1 trillion in the next 10 years. The law's spending cuts and tax increases are expected to either save or raise more than that, cutting the deficit by around a trillion dollars in its second decade. The IRS has launched a new ACA Tax Provisions website at IRS.gov/aca to educate individuals and businesses on how the health care law might affect them. The home page of the site includes three sections explaining the tax benefits and responsibilities for individuals and families, employers, and other organizations, with links and information for each group. The site also provides information about tax provisions that are in effect now and those that will go into effect in 2014 and beyond.

The Affordable Care Act (ACA) is not intended to replace an individuals' health insurance plans if they already have insurance through their employers. Despite the rollout of the ACA, employer-offered health insurance plans, in most cases, will be the most cost-effective option for the majority of workers. However, companies have been tinkering with coverage in response to continued increases in health care costs and the expected impact of the ACA. 60% of employers say the new tax on high-cost health insurance plans that goes into effect in 2018 will affect their plan design within the next two years. While 38% of employers planned to decrease or keep steady employees' premiums, 40% planned to increase their premiums by up to 5% this year. Even if individuals' premiums don't go up, out-of-pocket costs are likely to be higher as deductibles are expected to rise. Some companies are requiring spouses that have the option of other coverage to take it. More commonly, companies are using spousal surcharges or creating different rates for different family combinations (employee and spouse, employee plus children, etc.). Also, family deductibles are going up more than employee-only deductibles. In addition, employees could see higher co-pays to visit specialists. Overall, the cost of family coverage could increase as much as three times what it was a few years ago. Employees should take time to compare plans since their 2013 choice may no longer be the most cost effective for them this year.

It's hard to compare the cost of health plans in 2013 to the cost of plans in 2014 because it's like comparing apples and oranges. <u>The type of coverage under the ACA is much more valuable, because consumers are getting better coverage under the ACA. Under the ACA, insurance plans offered in the Exchanges and the individual and small group markets, as well as by employers to their employees, will be required to cover a particular set of benefits and services called the **"essential health benefits" package**.</u> These plans must cover services in 10 categories, including prescription drugs; emergency services; hospitalization; mental health disorder services; ambulatory patient services; maternity and newborn care; substance abuse disorder services; behavioral health treatment; rehabilitative services and devices; laboratory services; and preventive and wellness services. Wellness services include: 100% of screening and counseling for adults for obesity; 50% of smoking-cessation programs; and 30% of certain other wellness programs. Some of these benefits haven't been previously covered by health plans. Additionally, consumers can't be denied coverage because of their health status as they can now in some states.

Provisions Effective Beginning in 2010

Compliance Provisions
- Insurance companies are not allowed to discriminate based on pre-existing conditions.
- The law prohibits insurers from charging women substantially more than men and requires insurers to offer preventive services – including contraception – at no additional cost.
- Insurance companies may not discriminate against children who have pre-existing medical conditions.
- Effective March 30, 2010, health insurance plans are required to cover any adult children who have not reached age 27 by the end of the year. The adult children do not have to be dependents and can even be married. In accordance with this requirement, cafeteria plan rules are relaxed to encourage more small employers to offer tax-free benefits to employees, including health insurance coverage. Employers with cafeteria plans are immediately allowed to permit employees to begin making pre-tax contributions to pay for this expanded benefit. This expanded benefit also applies to self-employed individuals who qualify for the self-employed health insurance deduction.
- Individuals who are uninsured due to a pre-existing condition may obtain coverage through a temporary high-risk health insurance pool (effective through 2013).
- To assist businesses that provide health benefits to early retirees, there is a temporary reinsurance program that provides health insurance coverage to retirees over age 55 who are not eligible for Medicare. Under this program, the federal government reimburses employers or insurers for 80% of retiree claims (effective through 2013).
- Effective March 30, 2010, the law established temporary national high-risk pools that are providing health coverage to the sickest Americans with pre-existing conditions who cannot find insurance on the individual market (effective through 2013). In 2014, they will be able to enroll in insurance through the "Exchanges" that will be established.
- Pharmaceutical manufacturers are required to provide a 50% discount to seniors for prescriptions filled that fall within the Medicare Part D coverage gap. In 2013 and 2014, beneficiaries get a 52.5% discount on brand-name drugs in the doughnut hole.
- Effective for transactions entered into after March 30, 2010, there is a limited deduction for executive pay by certain health insurance providers for services performed by officers, directors,

and employees. Applicable to tax years after Dec. 31, 2009, the deduction is limited to $500,000 per employee.
- The special tax deduction from regular tax that Blue Cross and other health insurance organizations are allowed under Code Sec. 833 is modified to provide that these organizations will only be entitled to this special tax treatment if 85% or more of their insurance premium revenues are spent on clinical services – applies to tax years beginning after Dec. 31, 2009.
- The Department of Health and Human Services is to encourage the creation of qualified nonprofit health insurance issuers to offer health insurance through federal grants or loans. Insurers receiving federal grants or loans under the program would be exempt from federal tax for periods when the insurer complies with the terms of the program.
- Effective for transactions after March 30, 2010, the Economic Substance Doctrine states that a transaction will be treated as having economic substance only if the transaction changes the taxpayer's position in a meaningful way (apart from the tax benefits) and the taxpayer has a substantial purpose (apart from the tax benefits) for entering into the transaction. Failure to meet the Economic Substance test subjects violators to penalty under IRC 6662 and imposes an increased penalty amount for non-disclosed transactions that lack economic substance. Personal transactions by individuals are exempt from the economic substance requirements.
- Charitable hospitals need to conduct community health needs assessments at least once every three years and adopt implementation strategies to meet the community health needs identified. The IRS has issued temporary and proposed regulations for charitable organizations on how to report any excise taxes they owe for failing to meet the community health needs assessment requirements of the ACA. The temporary regulations state that a charitable hospital organization liable for the excise tax must file a return on Form 4720, Return of Certain Excise Taxes under Chapters 41 and 42 of the Internal Revenue Code. The form must be filed by the 15th day of the fifth month after the end of the charitable hospital organization's tax year during which the liability was incurred. Under the ACA, hospital organizations that want to remain or become tax-exempt are required to periodically perform a community needs health assessment and adopt an implementation strategy at least once every three years. They also need to establish a written financial assistance policy and emergency medical care policies. They are expected to limit the charges for emergency room visits or other medically necessary care for individuals who are eligible for assistance under the hospital's financial assistance policy. They also are expected to make reasonable efforts to determine whether an individual is eligible for assistance under the hospital's financial assistance policy before engaging in extraordinary collection actions against the individual.

Tax Provisions
- A 50% tax credit was available for companies with investments in qualified therapeutic projects approved by the IRS, effective for amounts paid after Dec. 31, 2008 in tax years beginning after

that date and <u>expiring after 2010</u>. A taxpayer eligible for the credit must have employed no more than 250 employees at the time of application for the credit. The credit could also have been taken in the form of a grant rather than a tax credit.
- After July 1, 2010, there is a new 10% tax assessed on amounts paid for indoor tanning services (tanning salons). Providers of indoor tanning services collect the tax at the time the purchaser pays for the tanning service. The provider then pays quarterly with IRS Form 720 (Quarterly Federal Excise Tax Return). The first payment was due Nov. 1, 2010. Amounts paid for indoor tanning services includes any amount paid by insurance. Tanning providers do not have to collect the tax on other goods and services if the charges are separable. Qualified physical fitness facilities that include access to indoor tanning facilities as part of a membership fee do not have to pay the tax.
- The adoption tax credit was increased from $12,170 to $13,170 in 2010 which the ACA also made a <u>refundable tax credit</u> in 2010 and 2011, and the increased limits also applied to employer-sponsored adoption assistance programs. Also, the ACA enhanced the incentives for adopting children with special needs. The adoption tax credit had lower allowable expenses in 2012, and it was <u>no longer considered a refundable credit in 2012</u>. The adoption credit was <u>made permanent as of Jan. 1, 2013</u>, <u>but is still nonrefundable in 2013</u>. The maximum credit for qualified adoption expenses in 2013 is $12,970 for a child with special needs, and $12,697 for other adoptions. Form 8839 is used to claim the credit, and the taxpayer has to attach certain documents to the tax return which means **the tax return cannot be e-filed**. For domestic adoptions, you may be able to claim the credit even if the adoption is not finalized but usually the credit is allowed in the year the adoption becomes final, even if the expenses are paid in the prior year. The credit is allowed in the year after the adoption if the expenses occur then. If the adoption is unsuccessful, the credit is allowed in the next tax year. For foreign adoptions, the credit is allowed in the year adoption becomes final. Allowable expenses include adoption fees, court costs, attorney fees, travel expenses, and certain other related expenses. <u>For adoption of special needs children, you may claim the maximum credit even if actual expenses are less</u>. The credit is not available to a taxpayer adopting a spouse's child. The credit begins to phase-out for taxpayers with modified adjusted gross income (MAGI) in excess of $194,580, and completely phases-out for taxpayers with MAGI of $234,580.
- A <u>one-time</u> $250 rebate was available to Medicare Part D beneficiaries who reached the coverage gap (donut hole) in 2010, and the coinsurance rate for costs within this gap are gradually reduced to 25%. The gap begins when $2,830 in out-of-pocket payments have been spent on prescription drugs and lasts until the patient has spent $4,550 in out of pocket expenses. The "doughnut hole" continues to shrink, and in 2013 and 2014 beneficiaries get a 52.5% discount on brand-name drugs in the doughnut hole; the federal subsidy for generic drugs in the doughnut hole rises from 21% to 28% in 2014.
- <u>Small Business Healthcare Tax Credit (Form 8941)</u> - A tax credit is available to small businesses and eligible tax-exempt small employers that provide health insurance coverage to their employees. A

qualified small business employer has to have fewer than 25 full-time equivalent (FTE) employees and have average annual compensation of less than $50,000. Self-employed individuals, partners, 2% shareholders of an S-corporation, 5% owners of an employer, and family members and dependents are not counted as employees. In 2010 through 2013, the maximum credit is 35% (25% for tax-exempt organizations) of the employer's premium expenses. Small employers with 10 or fewer employees and average annual wages of less than $25,000 are eligible for the full 35% credit. The credit is reduced on a sliding scale for small employers with 11 to 25 employees and annual average wages of $26,000 to $50,000. The credit is reduced by 6.667% for each FTE employee in excess of 10 employees and is reduced by 4% for each $1,000 that average annual compensation paid to the employees exceeds $25,000. <u>The credit is calculated on Form 8941 "Credit for Small Employer Health Insurance Premiums," and then claimed as a general business credit on Form 3800, which is reflected on line 53 of Form 1040</u>. The credit can be applied against both regular tax and Alternative Minimum Tax (AMT). Up to 4 million small businesses are eligible for the credit. The credit can be a lot of money, i.e. the maximum credit is $51,000 in 2010 - 2013 for a for-profit small business ($36,700 for a tax-exempt organization).

- A full-time equivalent (FTE) employee is determined by dividing the total hours of service during the year (but not more than 2,080 hours for any employee) by 2,080. The result, if not a whole number, is rounded to the next lowest whole number. The IRS has provided three methods that employers may use to calculate the total number of hours of service that must be taken into account for an employee for the year: actual hours of service; days-worked equivalency; or weeks-worked equivalency.
- <u>Other ways to determine FTE</u>: An employee who on average is employed for at least 30 hours of service per week. One hundred and twenty hours of service in a calendar month is also treated as full-time. FTEs are also determined by calculating the aggregate hours of service worked in a month by non-full-time employees (up to 120 hours per employee) and dividing the total by 120. Determination of hours of service for employees employed on a non-hourly basis may be determined under several methods that use daily or weekly equivalencies, unless it understates actual hours to the extent that an employee is not treated as full-time. <u>Full-time status, in turn, for ongoing employees generally may be determined under a measurement period looking back to not less than three but not more than 12 consecutive months</u>.
- Businesses applying for the credit in 2010 could include premium payments made prior to March 10, 2010, the date of enactment of the legislation (The credit is retroactive to 1/1/2010). Businesses that have already filed and did not claim the credit and later determine they are eligible for the credit can always file an amended 2010 return. Businesses that couldn't use the credit in 2010 are eligible for the credit in 2011 through 2013.
- Franchises are considered individual small businesses.

- Forgiveness of student loans for certain medical professionals under state loan repayment or forgiveness programs is implemented with the intent to provide increased availability of health care services in underserved or health-professional-shortage areas. Forgiveness of the loans is tax-exempt (excluded from income) effective for tax years beginning after Dec. 31, 2008.

Provisions Effective Beginning in 2011

Compliance Provisions
- Tax-free distributions from flexible spending arrangements (FSA), health reimbursement arrangements (HRA), health savings accounts (HSA), and Archers are only permitted for prescription medications, unless the taxpayer has a prescription from a physician for an over-the-counter medication, or it is insulin. This applies to purchases made on or after 1/1/2011 and not to purchases made in 2010, even if reimbursed in 2011 (no tax-free distributions were allowed for over-the-counter drugs in 2010).

Tax Provisions
- The penalty for using flexible spending arrangements (FSA), health reimbursement arrangements (HRA), health savings accounts (HSA), and Archers is increased from 10% to 20% for unauthorized use, such as any tax-free distributions made for over-the-counter medications.
- Effective Dec. 1, 2011, the "medical loss ratio" (MLR) provision requires health insurance companies to spend 80% of the consumers' premium dollars they collect – 85% for large group insurers – on actual medical care rather than overhead, marketing expenses, and profit. Failure on the part of the insurers to meet this requirement will result in insurers having to send their customers a rebate check representing the amount for which they under-spent on actual medical care. If a tax benefit was previously gained on the premiums rebated, the rebate is taxable; otherwise the rebated premiums are tax-free.

Provisions Effective Beginning in 2012

Compliance Provisions
- Businesses are required to file 1099 Forms for payments aggregating $600 or more to each service provider, excluding corporations, unless the payments are to corporations providing legal services.
- Employers that have more than 250 workers have to report the cost of healthcare benefits provided on employees' behalf. This amount should appear on Form W-2 in Box 12, using code DD. This reporting is mandated for 2012 W-2s sent in January 2013. The IRS provided relief for smaller employers (those filing fewer than 250 W-2 forms) by making this requirement optional for them at least for 2012, and continuing this optional treatment for smaller employers until further guidance is issued.

Provisions Effective Beginning in 2013

Compliance Provisions

- **Qualifying employers <u>must notify</u> their employees by October 1, 2013 informing them about the insurance "Exchanges" (Marketplaces) that will debut in 2014.** This requirement applies to employers with at least $500,000 of annual gross revenue and at least one employee; government agencies; hospitals, and facilities for care of the elderly, ill, etc. The notice must inform employees as to: the existence of the Exchange(s); how to contact the Exchange for assistance; the employee's potential eligibility for subsidized coverage on the Exchange if the employer's group health plan doesn't provide affordable minimum coverage (<u>the plan's share of the total allowed costs of benefits provided under the plan is less than 60%, doesn't provide services described in the "essential health benefits package," and costs the employee more than 9.5% of household income</u>); and the fact that the employee may lose the employer contribution (if any) toward coverage if he or she chooses to purchase individual coverage on the Exchange(s). Employers may provide the notification by first-class mail. Alternatively, notice may be provided electronically, but only if the employer follows the Department of Labor's (DOL) electronic disclosure safe harbor - generally, employees must have access to a work computer that is integral to their job duties, and all other employees must affirmatively consent to electronic disclosures. **The employer notification requirement will be enforced by imposing a penalty on employers that don't comply, and the penalty could be as much as $100 per worker per day.**
    - Qualifying employers must send the notices to their employees regardless of whether they provide health insurance to them or not.
    - All current full-time and part-time employees and new employees hired before October 1, 2013 must be notified by that date. For employees hired after Oct. 1, the employer must provide notice within 14 days of the employee's start date. Notices will have to be <u>sent every year by October 1</u>, beginning in 2013.
    - Open enrollment begins October 1, 2013. The state and federal insurance Exchanges are accessed through websites on which individuals and small businesses can shop for health insurance plans. The Exchanges are managed by the states or the federal government; offer government regulated and standardized healthcare plans in the U.S.; provide the only mechanism available to individuals to purchase insurance eligible for federal subsidies; includes the Small Business Health Options Program (SHOP) for small businesses; and are <u>the only way for employees and employers to get insurance tax credits starting in 2014</u>. The Exchanges are designed to allow people buying individual coverage to purchase affordable health insurance from a pool of competing insurers. **The program is not meant to replace all existing insurance plans. It is simply meant to augment what exists today**. The Exchanges will be particularly attractive to the self-employed, the employed whose companies do not offer

health insurance plans, and those with pre-existing conditions. <u>There is a bronze plan, a silver plan, a gold plan, and a platinum plan</u>. The program should better control premiums and create a larger healthy pool in the private system. This dynamic may arrest the growth in the cost of insurance premiums. SHOP is designed to bring down costs in that increasing the size of the insured pool spreads out the risk for small businesses.

  o To assist employers, the DOL has issued two "model" notices. One is for employers that sponsor a group health insurance plan and the other is for those that don't. Employers are advised to use one of the models, and there are two parts to each model notice. Part A provides general information about the Exchange(s); eligibility requirements for subsidies available for exchange coverage; **and the initial open enrollment period, which is <u>October 1, 2013 through March 31, 2014</u>**. The model notice for employers that sponsor a plan also includes a blank entry for employers to provide how to contact the plan for more information about the employer-sponsored coverage. Part B instructs employers to provide additional plan information that employees will need if they choose to apply for coverage on the Exchange. In the model notice that applies to employers with group health plans, this part includes vital employer contact information, basic plan eligibility provisions for employees and dependents, a statement as to whether the employer coverage is intended to be affordable and provides minimum required coverage, and valuable information on the coordination of the ACA with COBRA.

- A patient-centered outcome research trust fund is created to review pharmaceutical medicines to determine if they are of sufficient quality and are relevant to patients' needs. Funding for this organization comes from a $2 fee imposed on each health insurance policy or self-insured plan whose plan year ends after Sept. 30, 2012. The fee is then multiplied by the average number of participants covered in the plan, and will extend to Sept. 30, 2019.
- Even though the employer mandate has been delayed until 2015, the Department of Labor (DOL) requires all employers subject to the Fair Labor Standards Act (FLSA) to send to employees a Notice of Health Insurance Coverage and Marketplace.

<u>Tax Provisions</u>

- The threshold for claiming medical expenses as an itemized deduction rises from 7.5% of adjusted gross income (AGI) to 10%. For individuals 65 and over it remains at 7.5% until 2016.
- Flexible spending arrangement contributions (FSAs) are capped at $2,500, indexed for inflation. The limit is per employee, so if a husband and wife both work for the same employer, each may make a contribution of $2,500 per year. A new provision adopted in 2013 permits employers to allow participants who do not use all of the money in a plan year to carryover up to $500 to the next plan year. The cap does not apply to health savings accounts (HSA). Employers with non-calendar year plans are not required to comply until plan year renewal in 2013.

- **0.9% surtax** - A 0.9% surtax is added to the 1.45% Medicare hospital insurance tax paid by high-income earners (wages and self-employment income above $200,000 single; $250,000 joint return and surviving spouse; $125,000 married filing separately; and $200,000 head-of-household - these thresholds are not adjusted for inflation). For self-employed taxpayers, the surtax applies to self-employment income in excess of the threshold amounts. There is no employer match for this tax. Employers are required to withhold the additional Medicare tax on wages it pays to an employee in excess of $200,000 even though an employee may not be liable for the additional Medicare tax because, for example, the spouse had no income. Any withheld Medicare tax not owed will be credited against the total tax liability shown on the tax return. If an individual knows they will be above the limit because of their spouse's wages, the additional tax still cannot be withheld until their wages reach $200,000. In this case, the employee can adjust his W-4 to have additional taxes withheld. The stated thresholds are not indexed for inflation. Overpayment of additional Medicare tax for this purpose should not be claimed on Form 843. Employees may only claim a refund of additional Medicare tax on their tax return if they have not received repayment or reimbursement from their employer. Flow-through business income from S-corporations is not subject to the 0.9% surtax. **(SEE "FICA - OASDI (Social Security) and Medicare Tax)**
- **3.8% surtax (Form 8960)** - A 3.8% surtax is imposed on investment income (unearned income) of high-income earners ($200,000 single; $250,000 joint and surviving spouse; $125,000 married filing separately; and $200,000 head-of-household - these thresholds are not adjusted for inflation). The surtax applies to individuals, estates, and trusts. The 3.8% surtax on individuals is on the lesser of "net investment income" (NII) or the amount by which modified adjusted gross income (MAGI) exceeds the above stated thresholds. "NII" includes: interest; dividends; gains on the sale of securities (any losses that can offset capital gains in computing "taxable income" can also be used to reduce NII, but not below zero); annuities; royalties; rents; all passive activity income including passive business activity income from partnerships and S-corporations; gain on the disposition of property other than property held in a trade or business; and gain over and above the $250,000/$500,000 exclusion from the sale of a principal residence. "NII" does not include: salaries and wages; social security; self-employment income; tax-exempt interest; conversion of traditional IRAs to Roth IRAs; excluded gain from the sale of a principal residence; distributions from qualified plans, IRAs and Roth IRAs (including required minimum distributions (RMDs)); lump-sum distributions from retirement plans; income derived in the ordinary course of a trade or business (partnerships and S-corporations) that is not considered passive activity income; gain on the sale or disposition of property held in a trade or business; and gain on the sale of an active interest in a partnership or S-corporation. In addition, any investment interest and expenses and state taxes that are itemized deductions allocable to investment income should be deducted in computing "net investment income". **IRS Form 8960, Net Investment Income Tax - Individuals, Estates, and Trusts is used to compute the new 3.8% surtax and then to report the tax on Form 1040.** (SEE "Taxable Income," Net Investment Income)

- MAGI means adjusted gross income (AGI) increased by otherwise excludable foreign earned income or foreign housing costs. MAGI does not include: tax-exempt interest; veterans' benefits; and excluded gain from the sale of a principal residence. MAGI does include: gain over and above the $250,000/$500,000 exclusion from the sale of a principal residence; lump-sum distributions from retirement plans; conversion of traditional IRAs to Roth IRAs; required minimum distributions (RMD); and all distributions from qualified plans, IRAs, and Roth IRAs.
- Flow-through business income from S-corporations is not subject to the 3.8% surtax.
- The business of trading in financial instruments or commodities is subject to the 3.8% surtax no matter whether the activity is considered a passive or a non-passive activity.
- Net investment income would usually include "rents" unless the rental income was derived from a trade or business carried on by a taxpayer who meets the stringent requirements of being classified as a real estate professional. But for the purpose of the ACA, a single rental property can qualify as a trade or business if the taxpayer materially participates in the activity. Usually, qualifying as a real estate professional isn't easy, but the ACA specifically provides a "safe harbor" for a taxpayer who materially participates in rental real estate activities for more than 500 hours per year. Alternatively, if a person has participated in rental real estate activities for more than 500 hours per year in five of the last ten taxable years, then the rental income will be deemed to be derived in the ordinary course of a trade or business. Income derived from real estate rentals is not subject to self-employment tax. **(SEE "Taxable Income," Rental Income)**
- An estate or trust is subject to the 3.8% surtax to the extent of the lesser of: the estate's or trust's undistributed net investment income; or the excess (if any) of the estate's or trust's AGI over the dollar amount at which the highest tax bracket begins for the year ($11,950 in 2013). Grantor trusts pay the tax at the level of the grantor, not at the trust level. Non-grantor trusts are subject to the surtax at the trust level. You determine whether a trust materially participates and, therefore, does not have passive income by looking at what the trustee does. Make sure the trustee is one of the officers of the company, which in a family business is likely anyway. Grantor trust income flows-through to the grantor; therefore, only non-grantor trusts are required to pay the surtax. Non-grantor trusts should consider paying distributions to beneficiaries to avoid the 3.8% surtax. The 65-day rule can be used to defer distributions to as late as March 6 of the following year and still have them apply to the current year. Trusts that are subject to the tax include non-grantor trusts, electing small business trusts, non-grantor charitable lead trusts, pooled income funds, cemetery perpetual care funds, qualified funeral trusts, Alaska Native Settlement Trusts, and foreign trusts with U.S. beneficiaries. The tax does not apply to common trust funds, real estate investment trusts, designated settlement funds, wholly charitable trusts, other trusts exempt from tax, and foreign trusts without U.S. beneficiaries.

- One technique available to reduce investment income and the amount of the surtax is to convert otherwise passive activities to non-passive activities by grouping them, i.e. treating them collectively as a single activity, and thereby combining the participation hours and improving one's ability to achieve the necessary hours for material participation. Generally, activities can be grouped if they constitute an appropriate economic unit for measuring gain or loss. Factors to consider are: similarities in types of trades or businesses; the extent of common control and ownership; geographical location; and interdependencies between or among the activities. However, there are drawbacks to grouping activities, including the inability to free up suspended losses on the disposal of individual activities in the group.
- **2.3% excise tax** - A 2.3% excise tax on manufacturers, producers, or importers of medical devices is imposed on gross sales to wholesale distributors. The tax is on the use and lease of medical devices after December 31, 2012 and applies to most devices used by health care professionals, ranging from X-ray and MRI machines and experimental cancer treatment devices all the way down to tongue depressors. Certain items such as biologics, devices intended solely for use by animals, software updates or sales of software, and most home medical equipment devices aren't subject to the tax. Retail products consumed by the general public such as eyeglasses, contact lenses, and hearing aids are exempt from the tax, as are prosthetic or orthotic devices. Also, consumers who use the internet or telephone to buy a firm's medical equipment fall under the retail category, thereby making their purchases exempt. A wholesale distributor is defined as a firm involved in the business of selling products to people or firms who resell such products. Retailers are considered to be those who sell to end users. <u>A device is treated as an exempt retail item if it is regularly available for purchase and use by individual consumers who aren't medical professionals</u>.
  - Although the excise tax will not apply to the sale of domestically produced convenience kits that includes a taxable medical device, the tax will be assessed against a manufacturer or importer when the medical device is sold.
  - Certain lease contracts for medical devices are grandfathered, i.e. payments made under written binding contracts for lease or installment sales entered into before March 30, 2010 are not subject to the medical device tax.
- It's not clear if companies selling "dual-purpose" products to regular customers as well as medical professionals will be taxed on those products – one good example of a dual-purpose product is latex gloves.

Provisions Effective Beginning in 2014

Compliance Provisions

- One of the main ways that the ACA pays for coverage of those who cannot afford it is with a tax on insurers and reinsurers. The tax in 2014 is $63 per person insured, including dependents. While the tax is levied on insurers, as a practical matter it will probably be paid indirectly by those who are insured.
- "Qualified Health Plans" may be offered through cafeteria plans by qualified employers. For tax years beginning after December 31, 2013, a reimbursement (or direct payment) for the premiums for coverage under any "qualified health plan" through a Health Insurance Exchange is a qualified benefit under the cafeteria plan if the employer is a qualified employer (the small business requirement rules Code Sec. 125(f)(3)(B)).
- The Dept. of Health and Human Services (HHS) will establish a program to determine whether individuals are eligible to enroll in qualified health plans in the Exchanges and are eligible for other benefits, including Medicaid, children's health insurance programs (CHIP), and basic health programs (BHP). In order to carry out this requirement, the IRS will disclose to HHS certain tax return information to help the Exchanges determine taxpayer eligibility where income verification is required. This includes the taxpayer's identity and filing status, the number of personal exemptions claimed, the taxpayer's adjusted gross income (AGI), the amount of taxpayer's Social Security benefits included in income, tax-exempt interest, the fact that the taxpayer did not have a filing requirement for the year, and the fact that the taxpayer did not file a tax return reconciling advance payments of a "premium tax credit" (see below) with the actual allowable premium tax credit.

Tax Provisions

- **Individual Mandate - Beginning in 2014, all individuals who can afford health insurance must carry some form of health insurance or pay a shared responsibility payment/"Penalty" on their federal income tax return.** <u>The federal Exchange and the state Exchanges opened on October 1, 2013, and individuals have until March 31, 2014 to purchase insurance on the Exchanges</u>, if required, before having to face a possible penalty. Individuals have to begin the application process by Dec. 24, 2013 in order to get coverage beginning Jan. 1, 2014. And as it stands now, individuals have to begin the application process by Feb. 15, 2014 in order to avoid a possible penalty. However, as a result of the extensive problems with the federal website where individuals can shop for insurance, it's possible that these dates will be pushed back, penalties abated, etc. The penalty applies to the taxpayer and up to two additional dependents. The individual mandate requires those who can afford health insurance coverage to have it – defined as insurance costing less than 8% of their annual household income – but choose to forgo it. The penalty in 2014 is $95 per adult and $47.50 per child (up to $285 for a family) or 1% of taxable income, whichever is greater. The penalty in 2015 is $325 per adult and $162.50 per child (up to $975 for a family) or 2% of taxable income, whichever is greater. The penalty in 2016 and beyond is $695 per adult and $347.50 per child (up to $2,085 for a family) or 2.5% of taxable income, whichever is greater. For example, an individual with taxable income of $100,000 in 2014 who is required to have insurance, but doesn't have it, will have to pay a penalty of $1,000. <u>The penalties are not deductible on individuals' tax returns</u>. An individual is liable for the shared responsibility payment (penalty) for a person without minimum essential coverage if that person is the taxpayer's dependent, regardless of whether the individual claims the dependent. Penalties are prorated by the number of months without coverage. Coverage gaps are allowed one time per year up to 3 months. But if an individual is without coverage for November through December in one year and January through February in the next year, a penalty tax will be assessed. This is known as "straddling rules." <u>At companies with less than 50 full-time equivalent (FTE) employees, **the responsibility to get health insurance coverage falls on the employees themselves**, because employers with less than 50 FTE employees do not have to pay a penalty if they don't provide insurance to their employees.</u> **However, employees do not have to pay a penalty if they are exempt from having to have insurance. Exemptions are handled through the Exchanges, not the tax return**. Those who are exempt are:

- Those below the poverty level or those who don't file tax returns are not subject to the individual mandate penalty. <u>In 2013, the federal poverty level is incomes from $11,490 to $49,560</u> (depending on status). So, individuals who fall within this income range do not have to pay a penalty if they don't have health insurance coverage.
- Those who qualify for Medicaid but live in states that opted out of the expanded Medicaid program are exempt from the penalty (Texas, Pennsylvania, Wisconsin, etc.).
- Members of recognized religious sects opposed to acceptance of benefits from health insurance.
- Those who are undocumented immigrants, incarcerated, or a member of an American Indian tribe.
- Those with family income below the threshold for filing a tax return ($10,000 for an individual, $20,000 for a family in 2013).
- Those who have to pay more than 8% of their income for health insurance after taking into account any employer contributions or tax credits. For individuals with employer coverage, the test applies to the cost of the lowest self-only coverage. NOTE: affordability for purposes of the individual mandate should not be confused with affordability related to the employer mandate, which is dependent upon whether an employee is eligible for a Code Section 36B premium tax credit when purchasing insurance through an Exchange. There, the standard for determining the penalty imposed on the employer is whether the cost of employer coverage is greater than 9.5% of household income.
- Those who have hardship exemptions.

- Americans who live abroad at least 330 days of the year will be treated as if they have qualifying insurance coverage and won't owe any tax penalty. That's true regardless of whether the U.S. citizen actually has health insurance in the country where he or she lives.
- Individuals who purchase coverage through a federal or state insurance Exchange will receive a premium tax credit only if their employer, if required, does not provide essential minimum and affordable coverage. Minimum essential coverage includes individual health insurance coverage, eligible employer-sponsored plans, and government-sponsored coverage such as Medicare, Medicaid, TRICARE, and veterans' health care. <u>The requirement to have health insurance is satisfied and no penalty is assessed if you are insured for the whole year through a combination of any of the following sources</u>:
  - Medicare.
  - Medicaid or the Children's Health Insurance Program (CHIP).
  - TRICARE (for service members, retirees, and their families).
  - The veteran's health program.
  - Defense Department's Non-appropriated Fund Health Benefits Program.
  - Student health plans.
  - Eligible employer sponsored plan. This is pretty much any employer-sponsored plan <u>that meets the requirements: the plan must cover at least 60% of health care expenses, provide coverage of the services described in the "essential health benefits package" (see below), and it must be "affordable", which means the insurance has to cost the employee less than 9.5% of household income</u>. The plan can be a group health plan or group health insurance coverage offered by an employer to the employee which is either a government-sponsored plan or any other plan or coverage offered in the small or large group market.
  - Insurance bought on your own in the individual market that is at least at the <u>bronze level</u> (see below).
  - **A grandfathered health plan in existence before the Health Reform Law was enacted. A grandfathered health plan <u>must comply</u> with the requirements of the Public Health Services (PHS), Employment Retirement Income Security Act (ERISA), and the Code applicable prior to the changes enacted by the ACA.**
  - Employers' health insurance plans that are not on a calendar year. Generally, employees will not be liable for the penalty through the month the 2013 - 2014 plan year ends.
- Individuals making less than 133% of the poverty level, or about $29,000 for a family of four will be covered through Medicaid unless they live in states that opted out of the Expanded Medicaid Program (Texas, Pennsylvania, Wisconsin, etc.). An individual who lives in a state that is expanding its Medicaid Program will likely qualify for Medicaid coverage if he/she has income of about $15,800 a year for one person ($32,500 for a family of 4) and can apply for coverage as soon as October 1, 2013. Coverage can begin as soon as January 1, 2014.

- If an individual has lower income and lives in a state that isn't expanding Medicaid, one of two situations applies: (1) If income is more than about $11,500 a year as a single person (about $23,500 for a family of 4, or 100% of the federal poverty level), he/she will be able to buy health insurance in the Exchanges and get lower insurance costs based on household size and income; or (2) If income is <u>less</u> than about $11,500 a year as a single person (about $23,500 for a family of 4), he/she will be able to get insurance in the Exchanges, but won't be able to get lower insurance costs based on income, i.e. will have to pay full price. A person who falls into this insurance coverage gap might be able to go to a community health center, which provides primary care for millions of Americans. The health care law has expanded funding to these community health centers that provide services either for free or on a sliding scale based on income. Children and adults under 30 are eligible to purchase "catastrophic" coverage and pay out-of-pocket expenses up to $12,700, but their preventive services are covered. NOTE: None of these individuals will have to pay a penalty if they don't have health insurance coverage.
- Individuals with incomes between 100% and 400% of the poverty level (about $24,000 to $94,000 a year for a family of four) will receive "premium tax credit" subsidies which will reduce the monthly insurance premiums they have to pay each month. The premium tax credit subsidies, which are on a sliding scale, are based on the individual's household income for the tax year ending two years prior to the enrollment period. **Modified adjusted gross income (MAGI) is used to determine household incomes including, in addition to AGI, foreign earned income and housing expenses, tax-exempt interest, untaxed Social Security benefits, and the modified adjusted gross income of any dependents claimed who are required to file a tax return**. Amounts individuals have to pay for insurance will range from 2% to 9.5% of their incomes. For example, those with incomes between 150% and 200% of the poverty level won't have to pay more than 6.3% of their income in premiums. If married, individuals will have to file jointly to qualify. The premium tax credits, or subsidies, are only available to those purchasing insurance through the "Exchanges." <u>The subsidies are paid directly to the insurers and directly reduce the amount individuals pay each month</u>.
  - An individual may apply for and be approved in advance for a premium tax credit/subsidy. However, the advance premium tax credits applied to insurance premiums that individuals will pay monthly during the year will have to be <u>reconciled at the end of the year on their federal income tax return</u>. This means they could possibly get either a tax credit (refund) or have to pay additional taxes on the health insurance premiums. There are no penalties for miscalculation of the advance premium credit.
  - Individuals must declare if they are tobacco users, which could increase their premiums up to an additional 50% (surcharge for tobacco use). The premium tax credits they receive will not apply to the tobacco surcharge.

- According to a study, the average premium tax credit in 2014 will be $2,672 for a family of four purchasing a silver plan on the Exchange. That's a 32% discount from the plan's average cost of $8,250. Medical expenses are covered: 60% (bronze plan); 70% (silver plan); 80% (gold plan); and 90% (platinum plan).
- The ACA requires that health plans cap the maximum out-of-pocket insurance costs (including co-pays, coinsurance and deductibles) at $6,350 for individuals and $12,700 for families. But the Obama administration is delaying that provision for some plans for another year. Some insurers are allowed to wait until January 1, 2015 to comply, but the one-year postponement applies only to a group of health plans such as those offered by employers and unions and only to plans which use independent managers to handle pharmaceutical or other benefits. With the delay, the out-of-pocket limits will remain at $6,250 for individuals and $12,500 for families in 2014, and if an employer uses different providers for health insurance and prescription drug coverage, each provider may impose these limits. However, starting in 2015, regardless of the number of providers individual and family out-of-pocket charges can be no more than $6,350 and $12,700, respectively. Individual policies sold in the Exchanges still must comply on schedule with the overall limits on the out-of-pocket costs.

- **IRS responsibilities: When a person applies for coverage on an Exchange, the information he provides will be cross-checked with income, job, and coverage information from the IRS. That cross-check will determine whether someone is eligible for a premium credit, or if he's eligible for Medicaid. At the end of the year, insurers must provide the IRS and policy holders a form verifying coverage status, and individuals must include those forms with their federal tax return. Also, starting in 2014, the IRS has to determine who must pay a penalty based on the requirements. However, the penalty may not exceed the national average premium of the lowest cost policy on the health insurance exchanges. In the same way the IRS verifies wages and tax withholding, it is supposed to verify whether someone has insurance coverage, if required, or owes a penalty. The law prohibits the IRS from putting liens or levies on your property to collect the penalty. It may, however, be able to withhold your future refunds if you don't pay.**
- Employers with less than 50 full-time equivalent (FTE) employees are not subject to the Employer Shared Responsibility Payment (ESRP) provisions. They may still offer coverage they purchase on their own, or through the Small Business Health Options Program (SHOP). Also, beginning in 2014, they are eligible for the Small Business Healthcare Tax Credit (Claimed on Form 8941) only if they purchase their insurance through SHOP. The tax credit for 2014 - 2015 is 50% of premiums paid (35% for tax-exempt organizations). SHOP is the new program that simplifies buying health insurance for small businesses. It is open to employers with fewer than 50 FTE employees. Open enrollment for SHOP was originally scheduled to start on October 1, 2013 but was delayed until November. However, if employers and employees enroll by December 24, 2013, coverage will begin on January 1, 2014. SHOP will open to businesses with 100 or fewer FTE employees in 2016.

Employers can use brokers to obtain insurance for their employees, but the only way they can get a tax credit is to purchase insurance through SHOP.
- How SHOP works: employer selects a plan; employer notifies its employees; employees either enroll or decline coverage; and employers can sign off on policy after employees chose plans.
- In many states, 70% of employees offered coverage must enroll in order for the employer to be able to buy insurance through SHOP. Employees with coverage through other avenues (spouses plan, Medicare, etc.) are not included in the calculation of the 70% threshold. However, employees with individual non-group private coverage are included in the calculation. Employers without 70% participation may apply from 11/15 - 12/23, 2013.
- <u>Self-employed individuals do not have to use SHOP to purchase insurance through the Exchange</u>. S-corporation shareholders and partners in service provider entities are considered self-employed for this purpose.

Provisions Effective Beginning in 2015

Tax Provisions
- **Employer Mandate** - The employer mandate was delayed from beginning in 2014 to beginning January 1, 2015. <u>No employer is required to provide healthcare coverage</u>. But the employer mandate requires employers with 50 or more FTE employees to offer health care insurance coverage to its employees or pay an Employer Shared Responsibility Payment (ESRP), which in essence is a penalty. If employers offer health care coverage to less than 95% of their full-time employees during a given month, they will have to pay the penalty. And the ESRP will apply to all full-time employees, not just the 5% who weren't offered coverage if the employer falls under the 95% requirement. The tests to determine the 95% are month to month. The ESRP amounts are different depending on the circumstances. If an employer <u>does not</u> offer any health insurance to its employees, then the annual ESRP payment is $2,000 per FTE employee (excludes the first 30 employees). Unlike health insurance premiums, ESRP is <u>not tax deductible</u>. If an employer <u>does</u> offer insurance to its employees, it must meet the affordability and minimum value requirements in order to avoid the penalty. If the insurance offered by the employer doesn't meet the affordability and minimum value requirements, then the ESRP payment is $3,000 per FTE employee <u>who decides to buy insurance on the government Exchanges and receives a tax credit or subsidy</u>. In this case, <u>Employers will pay ESRP if at least one FTE employee gets lower costs on their monthly premiums when buying insurance on the Exchanges</u>, and the ESRP will be based on the total number of full-time employees. The affordability and minimum value requirements are: <u>the plan must cover at least 60% of health care expenses, provide coverage of the services described in the "essential health benefits package," and must be "affordable", which means the insurance has to cost the employee less than 9.5% of household income</u>. However, a safe harbor allows employers to apply the 9.5% standard to an employee's W-2 wages rather than household income.

Therefore, if an employer does not offer any healthcare coverage to its employees, the annual minimum penalty is $40,000 and increases with the size of the firm's workforce by $2,000 for each additional worker past 50. <u>An employer will not be subject to a penalty if their employees' required contribution is less than 9.5% of the employee's W-2 wages, the plan covers at least 60% of health care expenses, provides coverage of the services in the "essential health benefits package," and coverage is offered to at least 95% of its full-time employees</u>. Some employers that have been offering health insurance coverage to their employees have decided to turn to "private" insurance markets which will provide employees with more choices. The employees can then use premium supplements provided by their employers to purchase coverage through the private insurance markets. Employers will have to file a return with the federal government documenting whether or not they have complied with providing affordable and required insurance coverage to their employees. This documentation will have to include an employer's determination of the number of FTE employees it has:

- A full-time equivalent (FTE) employee is determined by dividing the total hours of service during the year (but not more than 2,080 hours for any employee) by 2,080. The result, if not a whole number, is rounded to the next lowest whole number. The IRS has provided three methods that employers may use to calculate the total number of hours of service that must be taken into account for an employee for the year: actual hours of service; days-worked equivalency; or weeks-worked equivalency. <u>Other ways to determine FTE</u>: An employee who on average is employed for at least 30 hours of service per week. One hundred and twenty hours of service in a calendar month is also treated as full-time. FTEs are also determined by calculating the aggregate hours of service worked in a month by non-full-time employees (up to 120 hours per employee) and dividing the total by 120. Determination of hours of service for employees employed on a non-hourly basis may be determined under several methods that use daily or weekly equivalencies, unless it understates actual hours to the extent that an employee is not treated as full-time. Full-time status, in turn, for ongoing employees generally may be determined under a measurement period looking back to not less than three but not more than 12 consecutive months. **The calculation of the number of FTE employees includes part-time, temporary, and seasonal employees, which could be a problem due to businesses misclassifying employees as independent contractors that will not be included in the calculation. In the next several years, the ACA will provide employers with yet <u>another reason to misclassify workers</u>.** This suggests that the status of part-time workers could see significant scrutiny by the IRS, because <u>under the ACA, part-time, temporary, and seasonal workers that meet the definition of employees should be included in determining if a business has 50 or more FTE employees</u>.
- **IRS responsibilities:** If employers don't provide affordable, qualified coverage to employees, the IRS must establish rules and guidance for employers in this regard and collect the penalty from them.

Provisions Effective Beginning in 2018

Tax Provisions

- A 35% tax is imposed on high-cost employer-provided health plans that exceed $10,200 for individual coverage and $27,500 for family coverage. The idea is to give employers that much more reason to avoid expensive insurance policies and thus give insurers that much more reason to hold costs down.

Other Important Tax Provisions

Mandatory E-Filing

Starting with tax year 2012, tax return preparers who file more than 10 <u>individual</u> tax returns are required to e-file all returns, including those filed on behalf of estates and trusts. A tax return preparer can apply to opt out of e-filing due to hardship by filing Form 8944. A taxpayer may choose to paper-file a return, but the preparer must obtain a signed written statement saying that the client prefers to file a paper return and that he/she was not influenced by the preparer to do so. The statement must be dated before the return is filed and returned to the preparer, who must keep the statement on file. A statement for a joint return must be signed by both spouses. Also, **Form 8948** must be attached to the paper filed return (the taxpayer's signed statement is retained by the preparer and not submitted with the paper-filed return). In addition, if an e-filed return is rejected and cannot be e-filed, Form 8948 must be attached to the paper-filed return. **Authorized e-file providers are prohibited from submitting electronic returns prior to the receipt of all Forms W-2, W-2G, and 1099-R forms from the taxpayer.** If the taxpayer is unable to provide all of these correct forms, the return may be filed electronically after Form 4852 is completed in accordance with the use of that form. This is the only time that pay stubs or leave and earning statements are allowed. **(SEE "Taxable Income")**

Requirement to Report Foreign Bank and Financial Accounts (FBAR & Form 8938)

Under Title 31, U.S. persons must annually report their financial interests in or signatory authority over any type of financial account in a foreign country to the Treasury Dept. via filing of a Report of Foreign Bank and Financial Accounts (FBAR), TD F 90-22 on or before June 30 of the following year (it is not filed with your tax return). **After July 1, 2013, all FBARs are required to follow the mandatory e-filing requirement.** <u>In addition to the FBAR filing obligation, Form 8938 requires "Foreign Assets" to be reported if those assets have a total value of more than $50,000 ($100,000 if married filing jointly).</u> Form 8938 is required to be attached to tax returns beginning with the filing of their 2011 tax return. "Foreign Assets" have a broader definition than FBAR reporting of foreign accounts by including stock or securities issued by someone other than a U.S. "person," any interest in a foreign entity, and any financial instrument or contract that has an issuer or counterparty other than a U.S. "person." Form 8938 is required when the total value of specified foreign assets exceeds certain thresholds: Married filing jointly living in the U.S. when their total specified foreign assets exceed $100,000 on the last day of the year or more than $150,000 at any time during the year; Single or married filing separately living in the U.S. - $50,000 and $75,000, respectively. The thresholds for taxpayers living abroad are higher: Married filing jointly and residing abroad when their total specified foreign assets exceed $400,000 on the last day of the year or more than $600,000 at any time during the year; Single or married filing separately - $200,000 and $300,000, respectively. The Form 8938 filing requirement does not replace or otherwise affect a taxpayer's obligation to file a FBAR. Failure to file Form 8938 also comes with a separate set of penalties from those associated with failure to file FBARs. Failing to file Form 8938 when required could result in a $10,000 penalty, with an additional penalty up to $50,000 for continued failure to file after IRS notification. Form 8938 is not required of individuals who do not have an income tax return filing requirement.

- The IRS's 2009 Offshore Voluntary Disclosure Initiative (OVDI) prompted nearly 7,000 taxpayers in 2009 and over 10,000 taxpayers in 2010 with hidden offshore assets and income to disclose them in exchange for a reduced penalty.
- The IRS announced a third OVDI in February 2011, effective for tax year 2012, with somewhat stiffer penalties. Under the new "Amnesty Program," individuals are required to pay a penalty of 27.5% of the highest aggregate balance in foreign bank accounts during 8 full tax years prior to disclosure, up from 25% under the prior program. Taxpayers whose offshore accounts are $75,000 or less in any calendar year will be eligible for 12.5% penalties (same for new and prior program). Participants in the OVDI must file all original and amended returns and include payment for back-taxes and interest for up to 8 years as well as paying accuracy-related and/or delinquency penalties. However, if you get a letter from the IRS saying you're under audit, you won't qualify for the program or for the lower penalties. Requirements to comply with the new Amnesty program are: (1) File amended tax returns for 8 prior years, if applicable, and include all income from foreign accounts; (2) Pay taxes on all income; (3) Pay a 20% accuracy penalty on taxes due; (4) Pay interest on taxes past due; (4) Pay a penalty of 27.5% on the highest aggregate balance in foreign bank accounts during 8 full tax years prior to disclosure.
- <u>Effective Sept. 1, 2012, the IRS offered new procedures that will allow taxpayers residing abroad who haven't been filing tax returns and who are low compliance risks to get current with their tax filing requirements without facing penalties or additional enforcement action. Eligible taxpayers have simple tax returns and owe $1,500 or less in tax for any of the covered years. Such taxpayers will be required to file delinquent tax returns along with appropriate related information returns for the past three years, and to file delinquent FBARs for the past six years.</u>

Foreign Account Tax Compliance Act (FATCA)

Under the Foreign Account Tax Compliance Act of 2010 (FATCA), foreign financial institutions, including banks and hedge funds, are required to report on the holdings of U.S. taxpayers to the IRS or face stiff penalties. The objective of collecting information from these foreign financial institutions (FFIs) is to gather information on U.S. account holders of these FFIs. The IRS has opened a new online registration system for financial institutions that need to register with the IRS under FATCA. Financial institutions that must register can begin the process of registering by creating an account and providing required information. The IRS and the Treasury Department have been moving ahead slowly with the law while negotiating intergovernmental agreements with other countries. The new registration system is a Web-based application with around-the-clock availability. The secure system enables financial institutions to establish online accounts; customize home pages to manage accounts; designate points of contact to handle registrations; oversee member and/or branch information; and receive automatic notifications of status changes.

Starting in January 2014, financial institutions <u>were expected</u> to finalize their registration information by logging into their accounts, making any necessary changes, and submitting the final information. As registrations are finalized and approved in 2014, registering financial institutions will receive a notice of registration acceptance and will be issued a Global Intermediary Identification Number. However, the Treasury Department is delaying some important FATCA requirements until July 2014 as it tries to persuade more foreign governments to sign agreements with the U.S. for mutual exchange of information. The Treasury Department stated that due to the overwhelming interest from countries around the world it will extend by six months the start of the withholding and account due diligence requirements of FATCA, until July 1, 2014, to allow more time to complete agreements with foreign jurisdictions. The IRS announced in January 2013 that seven countries had entered into agreements with the U.S.: Norway; Spain; Mexico; the United Kingdom; Ireland; Denmark; and Switzerland, with <u>discussions with more than 50 countries ongoing</u>. The Treasury Department has been negotiating with foreign officials to aid with FATCA compliance and the timelines for expected agreements, especially for those funds domiciled in the Cayman Islands. The delay in FATCA requirements may ease some of the pressure on financial firms for now, but FATCA is not being held up completely. Originally the IRS planned to electronically post the first FFI list in June 2014, which would have required FFIs to finalize their registrations by April 25, 2014. There are three model agreements that the foreign governments are considering:
- Model 1: The FFI reports to the domestic government, which reports to the IRS in a reciprocal arrangement.
- Model 1B: The FFI reports to the domestic government, which reports to the IRS in a non-reciprocal arrangement.
- Model 2: The FFI reports directly to the IRS.

Under FATCA, U.S. withholding agents are required to withhold tax on certain payments to foreign financial institutions (FFIs) that do not agree to report certain information to the IRS regarding their U.S. accounts, including the accounts of certain foreign entities with substantial U.S. owners and on certain payments to certain nonfinancial foreign entities (NFFEs) that do not provide information on their substantial U.S. owners to withholding agents. A FFI may agree to report certain information about its account holders by registering to be FATCA compliant. As of now, withholding agents will not be required to begin withholding payments until after June 30, 2013.

The IRS has developed draft versions of various forms used in implementing FATCA, including a draft version of Form 8966, FATCA Report. The form asks for the identification of the filer, a Global Intermediary Identification Number that has been developed for FATCA enforcement, and the name of the sponsored foreign financial institution or other intermediary. Part II of the form also requests information on the account holder or recipient and their taxpayer information number. A third part of the form asks for the identifying information of U.S. owners who are specified U.S. persons, including their TIN information. Part IV of the form asks for financial information, including the account balance, account number, currency code, interest, dividends, gross proceeds or redemptions, and leaves space for other information.

Some of the key deadlines for implementing FATCA are as follows:
- Dec. 2, 2013: List of registered FFIs to be posted on IRS Website.
- July 1, 2014: IRS to obtain from FFI required documentation on accounts that prima facie involve U.S. account holders or treat payee as a nonparticipating FFI.
- March 31, 2015: FFIs to report name, address, TIN, account number, and account balance on 2013 and 2014 U.S. accounts to the IRS. U.S. withholding agents to report U.S. owner reporting and updated Form 1042-S (revised form to allow withholding reporting) reporting on income payments for year beginning Jan. 1, 2014. Reporting to continue each year thereafter.
- Jan. 1, 2016: IRS to obtain from FFI required documentation on accounts that do not prima facie involve U.S. account holders or treat payee as a nonparticipating FFI.
- 2018: U.S. withholding agents to begin Form 1042-S reporting on gross proceeds and foreign pass-through payments for year beginning Jan. 1, 2017.

Deductible Legal Fees
Usually legal fees related to individuals are not deductible. To be deductible, legal fees must be related to: (1) producing or collecting income (business related); (2) managing, conserving, or maintaining property held for producing income (rental property, etc.); and (3) determining, contesting, paying, or claiming a refund of any tax. **If you use a contingent fee lawyer, you'll usually be treated (for tax purposes) as receiving 100% of the recovery even if the defendant pays your lawyer his contingent fee directly**. That's why many clients say they are paying tax on lawyer's fees they never received. With high legal fees and costs and the AMT, some clients actually lose money after taxes by winning a lawsuit. The following legal expenses are deductible:
- Tax planning advice related to your income or income producing property (including estate planning that is related to tax planning) and some tax controversy work. Tax advice is not restricted to that provided by attorneys and CPAs, so expenses for advice provided by your accountant and investment advisor may also be deductible.
- Legal fees paid in connection with the preparation of tax returns or in connection with any proceedings involved in determining the extent of tax liability or in contesting tax liability.
- Business legal fees are deductible. However, some fees must be capitalized and added to the basis of assets. For example, if you are trying to sell your business and spend $50,000 in legal fees, you'll usually have to add the legal fees to the basis of your company.

- Some legal fees related to divorce are deductible as an itemized deduction. Specifically, you can deduct legal fees related to collecting child support and alimony. However, the payer of spousal support may not deduct the cost of legal fees in fighting against paying spousal support or child support. Other divorce related attorneys' fees are not deductible.
- If legal fees are only related to investments, they are deductible as miscellaneous itemized deductions subject to the 2% floor.
- Tax-related legal expenses may also be deductible if they are tied to doing or keeping your job. This includes fees paid to defend yourself against criminal charges arising out of your trade or business.
- Attorney fees paid in connection with a claim of unlawful discrimination or under the Medicare Secondary Payer Statute are deductible <u>for AGI</u>, only if any payments received as a result of such claims are included in taxable income (<u>taxable income includes the attorney's cut if you use a contingent fee lawyer</u>). Damages received for discrimination (after loss of a job) are taxed as ordinary income, but not as wages subject to payroll taxes (FICA). Payments for emotional suffering from discrimination are also taxable. However, attorney fees for discrimination awards are deductible above-the-line, so they won't affect your tax bill in this instance.
- Attorney fees paid in connection with a claim for disputed Social Security benefits (SSDI), due to disability, etc. can be deducted as a miscellaneous itemized deduction (subject to 2% floor) if the benefits received are taxable, i.e. if only 50% of social security benefits are taxable, you can deduct 50% of attorney's fees.
- If you hire an attorney to help you get your SSDI benefits and you itemize, you can deduct the fee you paid for your attorney when figuring out the taxability of a lump-sum payment.
- Punitive damage awards associated with physical injury or sickness and interest paid on an injury award are taxable, whether awarded by law suit or agreement. In addition, a portion of contingent fees paid to attorneys may be included in income if recovery amount includes punitive damages. The amount of contingent fees paid to attorneys is taxable based on the percentage of punitive damages compared to amount of total damages recovered for physical injury, i.e. the tax law treats you as receiving 100% of the settlement, even if the defendant issues a separate check to the lawyer for his cut. However, the attorney fees are not deductible unless the punitive damages received are related to your business.

Tax Benefits for Persons With Disabilities
Because it can take years to receive Social Security Disability Benefits (SSDI), most people receive a lump-sum amount, which includes back payments. Paying tax on this amount in one year is a mistake. The IRS allows taxes on this lump-sum payment to be spread over previous tax years using the current year tax return without having to file amended returns. Also, if you hired a representative to help you get your SSDI benefits and you itemize, you can deduct the fee that you paid for your representative when figuring out the taxability of a lump-sum payment. Other tax benefits include:

- Workers' compensation benefits and compensatory damages for injuries aren't taxed, but punitive damages are taxable.
- Long-term disability insurance benefits are not included in taxable income if you paid the premiums with after-tax dollars. However, they are taxable if you paid the premiums with pre-tax dollars as part of a cafeteria plan, or if your employer paid your premiums.
- People with disabilities are eligible for the Earned Income Tax Credit. However, many people with disabilities who don't file a tax return because their income is too low could be out thousands of dollars for not claiming the Earned Income Tax Credit. **(SEE "Tax Credits," Earned Income Tax Credit)**
- You are eligible for the Elderly and Disabled Credit if you receive taxable disability income from a former employer's accident, health, or pension plan and meet the income requirements. Your adjusted gross income (AGI) must be under $17,500 for single filers, under $20,000 for joint filers with one spouse eligible for the credit, and under $25,000 for joint filers with both spouses eligible. **(SEE "Tax Credits," Elderly and Disabled Credit)**
- If you pay someone to care for a dependent or spouse with physical or mental impairments, you may be able to claim the Child and Dependent Care Tax Credit while you are working or looking for work. **(SEE "Tax Credits," Child and Dependent Care Credit)**
- If you take an early distribution from an IRA (before age 59 1/2), you don't have to pay the 10% penalty if you are disabled but you must be able to show that you have a physical or mental condition that can be expected to last indefinitely or result in death and that the condition prevents you from engaging in any substantial gainful activity similar to the type of work you were doing before the condition arose.

<u>Military Service Connected Benefits</u>

Following are various military service connected benefits: (1) moving expenses (same as those for everybody); (2) the filing deadline for U.S. citizens and resident aliens living overseas or serving in the military outside the U.S. is June 15th; (3) if you are in a combat zone or deployed away from your permanent duty station, you have an automatic 180 day extension to file your tax return, beginning with the last day of deployment. If you are hospitalized, you are also given this extension. If you are not available to sign a joint return, a power of attorney may be used; (4) if you travel more than 100 miles away from home to perform reserve duties, you can deduct mileage expenses using Form 2106 (keep a log); you may also deduct airfare, lodging, and meals expenses - this is an above-the-line deduction; (5) if you are an ROTC student and receive subsistence allowances while participating in advanced training, this compensation is not taxable; but if you are in a summer advanced camp and receiving active duty pay, then the income is taxable; (6) if military regulations prohibit you from wearing certain uniforms when off duty, you can deduct the cost and upkeep of those uniforms as well as any job-related education and professional membership dues which are not reimbursed (Form 1040, Schedule A); (7) transitioning back to civilian life – job search expenses, travel and lodging to interviews, outplacement agency fees, and moving expenses are deductible, and don't forget to mention the tax credits available to employers who hire a veteran; and (8) the military cannot deny spousal benefits to a lesbian veteran in a same-sex marriage. Also, **if a veteran receives benefits for a disability from the Veterans Administration (VA), the benefits are generally tax-free**. However, if the veteran is retired from the military and is receiving military retirement benefits, then any disability benefits received from the VA is offset against his/her military retirement pay and is considered a tax-free portion of his/her total retirement benefits.

Dealing with the IRS

If you need an exact copy of a previously filed tax return and all attachments, you have to complete Form 4506 or 4506T-EZ, Request for Copy of Tax Return, and mail it to the IRS address listed on the form for your area. Copies are available for the current year and the past six years. Allow 60 days for delivery. There is a $57 fee for each tax year requested. However, usually all you need is a "tax return transcript" which shows most line items contained on a return, and you can get a "transcript" free of charge: go to IRS website and click on Order a Transcript under the Online Services option, or call 800-908-9946. You can also use the new Form 4506T-EZ or Form 4506-T (for businesses, partnerships, and individuals who need a tax account transcript) to order a transcript through the mail. There are two kinds of transcripts: (1) a tax return transcript shows most line items from the tax return as it was originally filed, including any accompanying forms and schedules. It does not reflect any changes made after the return was filed; (2) a tax account transcript shows any later adjustments either the taxpayer or the IRS made after the tax return was filed. This transcript shows basic data including marital status, type of return filed, adjusted gross income, and taxable income.

Taxpayers' can prove the timely delivery of physical documents to the IRS or the U.S. Tax Court only by using registered or certified U.S. mail. If you receive a refund check that is smaller than expected, you can cash it and then work with the IRS to resolve the difference. If, however, the check is larger than expected, don't cash it. Instead, follow the instructions on the notice accompanying the check.

Record Keeping

Individuals should keep records that support items on their tax return for at least three years after the tax return has been filed. Examples include bills, credit card and other receipts, invoices, mileage logs, canceled, imaged or substitute checks or other proof of payment and any other records to support deductions or credits claimed. You should keep records relating to property at least three years after you've sold or otherwise disposed of the property. Examples include a home purchase or improvement, stocks and other investments, IRA account transactions and rental property receipts. Small business owners should keep all employment tax records for at least four years after the tax becomes due or is paid, whichever is later. Also, keep records documenting gross receipts, proof of purchases, expenses and assets. Examples include cash register tapes, bank deposit slips, receipt books, purchase and sales invoices, credit card charges and sales slips, Forms 1099-MISC, canceled checks, account statements, petty cash slips and real estate closing statements. Electronic records can include databases, saved files, e-mails, instant messages, faxes, and voice messages.

Power of Attorney and Declaration of Representative (Form 2848)

Tax professionals must obtain the taxpayer's signature on Form 2848 in order to obtain power of attorney from the taxpayer. Tax preparers need to obtain power of attorney if they intend to represent a taxpayer before the IRS, and to get a taxpayer's documents quickly from the IRS, because the law states that the IRS can disclose tax information only to the taxpayer or the taxpayer's representative. Tax professionals are allowed to obtain tax transcripts for their clients using online tools on the IRS website.

As of March 1, 2012, the IRS will no longer accept old versions of Form 2848 and will accept only the new version released in October 2011. The new version requires a husband and wife who filed a joint return to each file a separate power of attorney on separate Forms 2848 to designate the representative he or she chooses, even if it is the same person. Another change in the form is that the representative must provide his or her preparer tax identification number (PTIN). Husbands and wives who already had a power of attorney on file as of 3/1/2012 do not have to file new separate forms.

Filing an Amended Return

If you fail to report some income, you'll want to file an amended return as soon as possible to minimize interest and penalties. Also, if you fail to claim a deduction or credit, you should file an amended return. If you are owed a refund, you should wait to receive that refund before filing an amended return. An amended return (Form 1040X) has to be filed within 3 years from the date you filed your original return or within 2 years from the date you paid the tax, whichever is later. There are three reasons not to file an amended return:
- You made a math error. The IRS computers will find this and make the correction for you.
- You failed to attach your W-2 form.
- You want to claim a net operating loss (NOL). You can choose to file amended returns for the carry back years, but you can instead file for a quick refund using Form 1045, which is simpler than filing amended returns.
- You claimed a moving expense deduction for which you were not eligible. If you took the deduction because you expected to meet the time test, but failed to do so (and the reason for failure is not an IRS-acceptable excuse), you can avoid the need to file an amended return by simply adding the deducted amount as income to your current return.

Identity Theft Program

When a tax return is flagged as possibly fraudulent due to identity theft, the IRS sends Letter 5071C or Letter 4883C to affected taxpayers to request additional information to continue processing the tax return. The taxpayer is instructed to: (1) obtain a copy of the past two years' tax returns to provide specific information to the IRS; and (2) call the Taxpayer Protection Line (TPL) at (800) 834-5084 or visit irs.gov to verify identity. The IRS representative or the website questionnaire will request specific information about the taxpayer's return, such as filing status, dependent information, employee information, adjusted gross income, and other personal and financial information that will help the IRS confirm the taxpayer's identity. After the taxpayer has verified his or her identity with the IRS, the IRS should process the return and send any refund within four to six weeks. In 2012, 7.8 million potentially fraudulent returns were detected. Most of the taxpayers affected by this new initiative had prepared their own returns and were expecting refunds.

- Best Practices for Individuals to Prevent Identity Theft - Identity thieves employ a variety of techniques to glean information to defraud the IRS and unknowing taxpayers including: pilfering through trash (whether paper or electronic); phishing scams (including bogus "IRS" inquiries; or deceit by familiar faces (such as a business associate, an ex-spouse or a particularly financially hard-pressed relative). Taxpayers should take certain steps to minimize the risk that they will be victims of ID theft, including: filing tax returns early (identity thieves generally file early in the season to ensure that the IRS will process their fraudulent returns and distribute the refunds before the legitimate taxpayer has the chance to file); protecting Social Security numbers; safeguarding internet passwords; installing firewalls and antivirus protection; safeguarding mail; shredding important documents; and checking credit reports regularly.
- Taxpayers should place a fraud alert on their accounts with the IRS as soon as they suspect that they are been victimized by identity theft, such as when they have received a notice from the IRS that their tax return has been rejected because one has already been filed with their social security number. To do this, taxpayers should file IRS Form 14039, Identity Theft Affidavit. Taxpayers are allowed to file IRS Form 14039 even if no tax problem has yet occurred. However, although no penalty will attach to being wrong about a situation, filing the Form will slow normal dealings with the IRS as they will take additional precautionary steps because of such notification.

Interest Rates

Interest rates are determined on a quarterly basis. For taxpayers other than corporations, the overpayment and underpayment rate is the federal short-term rate plus 3 percentage points. In the case of corporations, the underpayment rate is the federal short-term rate plus 3 percentage points and the overpayment rate is the federal short-term rate plus 2 percentage points. The interest rates will remain the same for the calendar quarter beginning Oct. 1, 2013. The rates are 3% for overpayments (2% in the case of corporations); 3% for underpayments; 5% for large corporate underpayments; and 0.5% for the portion of a corporate overpayment exceeding $10,000.

Avoiding Tax Penalty for Underpayment or Failure to Pay

Income tax withholding and estimated taxes paid (quarterly) must equal either 90% of tax owed on 2013 (current year) return, or 100% of tax paid on 2012 (prior year) return in order to avoid a penalty (110% if your adjusted gross income in the prior year was $150,000 or more; $75,000 if married filing separately) – different percentages apply to farmers and fisherman. **However, ARRA provides that the required annual payment of** <u>qualifying small business owners</u> **beginning in 2009 is not greater than 90 percent of the tax liability shown on the tax return for the preceding tax year. A qualified individual means any individual whose adjusted gross income shown on the tax return for the preceding tax year was less than $500,000 ($250,000 if married filing separately) and who certifies that at least 50% of the gross income shown on the return for the preceding taxable year was income from a small trade or business. For purposes of this provision, a small trade or business means any trade or business that employed no more than 500 persons, on average, during the calendar year ending in or with the preceding taxable year.**

Under the new IRS "Fresh Start Provisions," a six-month grace period on failure-to-pay penalties will be made to certain wage earners and self-employed individuals. <u>The request for an extension of time to pay will result in relief from the failure to pay penalty if the tax, interest, and any other penalties are fully paid by October 15th</u>. Two categories of taxpayers qualify: (1) wage earners who have been unemployed at least 30 consecutive days, and (2) self-employed individuals who experienced a 25% or greater reduction in business income due to the economy. **On May 22, 2012, the IRS announced that it is making the terms under which it will accept offers in compromise more flexible by expansion of its Fresh Start program that is designed to help financially distressed taxpayers clear up tax problems more quickly.** In calculating whether a taxpayer is eligible for an offer in compromise, the IRS will now look at only one year of future income for offers paid in five or fewer months (down from four years). It will look at two years of future income for offers paid in six to 24 months (down from five years). All offers must be fully paid within 24 months of the date the offer is accepted.

- Taxpayers meeting the eligibility criteria have to complete new Form 1127-A, Application for Extension of Time for Payment Due to Undue Hardship, and the form must be filed by the tax return due date (April 15th).
- This penalty relief is subject to income and tax due limits. A taxpayer's income must not exceed $200,000 if he or she files as married filing jointly or $100,000 if filing as single or head of household and the balance due does not exceed $50,000.
- The failure to pay penalty is generally .5% per month with an upper limit of 25%.
- <u>Installment Agreements</u> – The Fresh Start provisions also mean that more taxpayers will have the ability to use streamlined installment agreements to catch up on back taxes. The threshold for using an installment agreement without having to supply the IRS with a financial statement has been raised from $25,000 to $50,000. Only individuals and out-of-business sole proprietors qualify for the $25,001 to $50,000 threshold. Other types of businesses that are out of business can qualify for the $25,000 or less threshold. The maximum term for streamlined installment agreements has been raised to 72 months from 60 months previously (See below). The easiest way to apply for a payment plan is to use the Online Payment Agreement tool at IRS.gov. If you don't have Web access you may file Form 9465, Installment Agreement, to apply. Taxpayers in

need of installment agreements for tax debts more than $50,000 or longer than six years still need to provide the IRS with a financial statement. In these cases, the IRS may ask for one of two forms: either Collection Information Statement, Form 433-A or Form 433-F. <u>If you can pay your taxes within 120 days</u>, you should not use Form 9465, but instead you should apply for an installment agreement online or call the IRS at 800-829-1040.

- <u>Tax Liens</u> - The Fresh Start Program increased the amount that taxpayers can owe before the IRS generally will file a Notice of Federal Tax Lien. That amount is now $10,000. However, in some cases the IRS may still file a lien notice on amounts less than $10,000. When a taxpayer meets certain requirements and pays off their tax debt, the IRS may now withdraw a filed Notice of Federal Tax Lien. Taxpayers must request this in writing using Form 12277, Application for Withdrawal. Some taxpayers may qualify to have their lien notice withdrawn if they are paying their debt through a Direct Debit Installment agreement. Taxpayers also need to request this in writing by using Form 12277. If a taxpayer defaults on the Direct Debit Installment Agreement, the IRS may file a new Notice of Federal Tax Lien and resume collection actions. <u>If your need short-term help and expect to be able to pay what you owe within a few months, ask the IRS for a 120-day extension of time to pay your taxes. However, if you wait too long and the IRS sends you a final notice of its intent to levy on your assets, you'll only be able to get a 60-day extension.</u>

- <u>Offers in Compromise (OIC)</u> - An Offer in Compromise is an agreement that allows taxpayers to settle their tax debt for less than the full amount. Fresh Start expanded and streamlined the OIC program. The IRS now has more flexibility when analyzing a taxpayer's ability to pay. This makes the offer program available to a larger group of taxpayers.

- <u>The Individual Mandate Penalty Under the Affordable Care Act (ACA)</u> – Although the IRS will be the collector for the individual mandate penalty, they don't have the authority to lien or levy to collect this penalty. The IRS can only collect the penalty if you send it in or they can offset a refund. It will be hard to collect this penalty from those who don't voluntarily pay. The maximum penalty in 2014 is $285 or 1% of taxable income, whichever is greater. The maximum penalty in 2015 is $975 or 2% of taxable income, whichever is greater. The maximum penalty in 2016 and beyond is $2,085 or 2.5% of taxable income, whichever is greater (indexed for inflation). It remains to be seen if these penalty amounts are going to motivate young people to buy insurance that costs more.

Avoiding a Late Filing Penalty
If you fail to file your personal income tax return on time (April 15th), you are subject to a late filing penalty which is 5% of the tax due for each month you're late up to a maximum of 25%. <u>If the return is more than 60 days late, the minimum penalty is the lesser of $135 or 100% of the tax due.</u> For partnerships and S-corporations, the late filing penalty is $195 for each month or part of a month the return is late multiplied by the total number of owners during any part of the year, up to a maximum of

12 months. You can avoid the late filing penalty by requesting an extension by the return's due date. Important forms and requirements for avoiding a tax penalty include:

- Form 4868 – Application for Automatic Extension of Time to File (6 months – up to Oct. 15th), which must be filed by April 15th – for individuals and sole proprietors including one-person LLCs. Payment of tax must be made with a voucher – an <u>estimated tax payment or an extension payment (Form 4868)</u>. You cannot just send in a check for it to be considered a tax payment. If you send in a check without a voucher it is considered a deposit.
- Partnerships can request a 5-month extension (to Sept. 15th) on Form 7004. The filing deadline for C and S-corporations is March 15. Corporations can request a 6-month extension to Sept. 15th on Form 7004.
- There is a penalty for <u>not paying on time</u> (late payment penalty) even if an extension is filed. The late payment penalty is .5% of the tax due; the maximum penalty is 25%. In addition, there are interest charges for late payments. If you can't pay the taxes owed by April 15 but think you can do it by October 15, you may be able to avoid the late payment penalty if you were: (1) unemployed at least 30 consecutive days during the year; or (2) self-employed and experienced a 25% or greater reduction in business income due to the economy. File Form 1127-A to seek this penalty relief. This option applies if the taxes are no more than $50,000. Income limits apply.
- You can postpone a tax payment in a disaster area for one year.
- NOTE: <u>the minimum penalty for failure to file a tax return within 60 days of the due date is the lesser of $135 or 100% of the amount of tax due (even if no tax is due)</u>.

Installment Agreements

See "Avoiding a Tax Penalty for Underpayment or Failure to Pay" (Above). When you request an installment agreement, you are still required to pay interest at a certain rate, penalties, and the fees for setting up an installment agreement which are $105 ($52 if payments are made by electronic funds withdrawal). Taxpayers can file Form 13844, Application for Reduced User Fee for Installment Agreements, to get a reduced fee of $43. If you owe $10,000 or less the IRS cannot turn down your request if you meet the requirements, i.e. during the past 5 years you have timely filed all income tax returns and paid all income taxes without entering into an installment agreement, and you agree to pay the full amount owed within the applicable timeframe and comply with all filing requirements and payment of taxes while the agreement is in effect. Before an installment agreement is approved, it is a good idea for you to begin making voluntary payments to show good-faith. Once an installment agreement is established, the client is free of the threat of levy or other collection actions as long as payments are made as agreed.

First-Time Penalty Abatement (FTA) – The penalties for <u>failure to file</u> (delinquency) and <u>failure to pay</u> can be waived or abated for individuals with a past history of compliant behavior. For businesses, this relief also applies to the failure-to-deposit penalty for payroll taxes. In effect, the IRS rewards taxpayers with a history of compliant behavior with a one-time penalty amnesty. For both individuals and businesses, FTA does not apply to the estimated tax and accuracy-related penalties. To qualify for FTA, the taxpayer must meet the clean compliance criteria rules:

- Clean three-year penalty history – cannot have penalties of a "significant" amount assessed in the prior three years on the same type of tax return. For this purpose, the IRS's definition of significant amount generally means any amount. If the IRS rejects the request for FTA because of a small penalty amount assessed in the past three years, practitioners should object. Also, the estimated tax penalty is an exception and would not disqualify your client from receiving FTA.
- Required returns filed – must have filed all tax returns for the past three years, as required.

Keep in mind that there is an "unpublished ceiling" on the penalty amount that the IRS will abate under FTA by phone. If your client's penalties are substantial, you can request FTA in writing – provide other relevant penalty relief arguments, including any reasonable cause arguments. This will increase your client's chances of penalty abatement. <u>FTA has been traditionally used by tax professionals who know internal IRS procedures</u>.

What Happens to Non-Filers

If a taxpayer does not file a tax return and pay the taxes owed when due, the IRS can take several steps including:

- <u>Substitute tax return</u> – The IRS can file a substitute tax return for the taxpayer based on information it has from other sources. The substitute tax return will not include exemptions or expenses to which the taxpayer may be entitled. So, it may overstate the actual tax liability.
- <u>Levies and liens</u> – Next, the IRS will start a collection process. This can include a tax levy or tax lien. With a tax levy, the IRS can seize your property to pay your taxes if you failed to make arrangements to settle your debt. One method is levying the taxpayer's wages, and employers who do not comply can be held personally liable for the value of the property not surrendered and may additionally be subject to a penalty equal to 50% of that property's value. Employees may appeal to the employer's sympathies for the hardship the levy will cause or threaten legal action. An employer who complies with a levy "shall be discharged from any obligation or liability to the delinquent taxpayer and any other person." A tax lien is a claim used as security for a tax debt and can have a direct impact on a taxpayer's credit rating. The federal government presumably has an automatic lien against any person who does not pay federal tax for which they are liable after the government demands payment. If a tax liability remains unpaid after the IRS issues a notice and demand for payment, a tax lien is automatically filed to

record a claim by the IRS to all property owned by the taxpayer. The lien extends to all the person's property and rights to property. The regulations specify that a federal tax lien will not be valid against purchasers of personal property sold in a "casual sale" for less than $1,380 (for 2010 and to be indexed for inflation thereafter). The property subject to this provision includes household goods and various personal effects. The regulations also specify that a federal tax lien will not supersede a valid mechanic's lien against a personal residence in certain cases. Under new IRS procedures to help struggling taxpayers pay back taxes and avoid tax liens, <u>liens will not be filed until a taxpayer owes more than $10,000 in taxes (up from $5,000)</u>. Additionally, the new tax rules make it easier for a taxpayer to have a tax lien withdrawn from their record after paying their tax debt. However, they need to make a formal request to the IRS for the withdrawal. Also, if the taxpayer enters into a direct debt installment agreement with the IRS, they can have the tax lien withdrawn while they are paying off the debt. The IRS has also created easier access to Installment Agreements for more struggling small businesses; and expanding a streamlined Offer in Compromise program to cover more taxpayers.

Individuals who are required to file and have not filed tax returns for several years are in a unique position. If they have not heard from the IRS, most likely it means that based on the information the IRS has, they are due refunds. The bad news is that once refunds are older than three years, they can no longer be claimed and can't be applied to other years' income tax liabilities. Here are some tips for these non-filers:
- Call the IRS. They won't threaten a cooperative person with jail, and they will provide you time to file your unfiled tax returns. If you don't want to talk to the IRS, hire a tax professional – sign Form 2848 Power of Attorney, which enables the tax pro to speak on your behalf. There may be "Substitute Filed Returns (SFRs)" that the IRS has filed for you based on W-2s, 1099s, etc. that they have for you.
- If your account is in "collections," the tax pro may be able to speak with that department about suspension of collection activity while the returns are being prepared. If you owe a large sum, file the tax returns in question. It doesn't matter if you can't pay when you file – you will never go to jail for inability to pay. But there is always the possibility of landing in jail for failing to file.
- In order to file your late returns, you or your tax pro can request transcripts (see above) of all third party documents that the IRS has on file over the years – every W-2, 1099, K-1, 1098 (mortgage interest), etc. Your bank records may fill in the blanks to come up with valid tax returns for past years.
- If you are self-employed and have no records and need to file a business return or a Schedule C, the IRS recommends using industry standards. There are several websites that have listings by type of business of income and expenses by locale and are fairly reasonable standards that can be applied to your business, especially if you can provide a key element such as total sales for the year.

- If the IRS has filed "Substitute Tax Returns (STRs)" for you, the amount you owe based on the STRs is usually ridiculously high. Once you file correct tax returns for the years in question, the STRs and the accompanying tax liabilities may disappear or be reduced substantially or be replaced with refunds.
- Failure to file penalties can be removed (abated) for reasonable cause, such as a divorce that sunk you into a severe depression. However, interest accumulated on tax liabilities cannot be abated.
- Approximately eight weeks after filing, you will receive a bill that will detail the interest and penalties as well as the tax owed. The 10-year statute of limitations on collections will begin running from the date the tax is assessed. There are solutions for dealing with insurmountable balances: (1) being deemed uncollectible; (2) creating an installment agreement; or (3) if you qualify, an offer in compromise. (SEE BELOW)

Tax Penalties and Interest

The regulations state that if an individual taxpayer files a federal income tax return on or before the due date for the return, including extensions, and the IRS does not provide **timely notice** to the taxpayer of specific liability and the basis for the liability, then the IRS has to suspend any interest, penalty, or addition to tax. Timely notice means before the end of the 36-month period "beginning on the later of the date the return is filed or the due date of the return without regard to extensions." The suspension period begins after the 36-month period and ends 21 days after the IRS provides the notice, and applies separately with respect to each item or adjustment.

- Failure-to-file penalty - 5% of the tax due for every month or fraction of a month that the return is overdue, capped at 25%. Additionally, failing to file a federal tax return is a misdemeanor and carries a maximum fine of $25,000 for individuals or a one-year prison term. The failure-to-file penalty is generally more than the failure-to-pay penalty. You should file your tax return on time each year, even if you're not able to pay all the taxes you owe by the due date. You can reduce additional interest and penalties by paying as much as you can with your tax return.
- Late-payment penalty - 5% of your unpaid taxes for each month, or part of a month, after the due date that the tax is not paid. If you filed for an extension, the extension is only for filing, not paying. You will not be penalized during the automatic six-month extension if you paid at least 90% of your actual tax liability on or before the due date of the return, and pay the balance when you file the return. If you enter into an installment agreement and file your tax return on time, you will still incur late-payment penalties, but the rate will be only .25% of the unpaid balance.
- Filing and paying late – if you experience both late filing and late payment in any given month, the failure-to-file penalty is reduced by the failure-to-pay penalty. If you are more than 60 days late in filing and paying, the minimum penalty is the smaller of $135 or 100% of the remaining tax owed at the time of filing.

- Accuracy-related penalty and underpayment of taxes – there is a 20% penalty due to negligence or disregard of tax rules and regulations, substantial understatement of income, and certain over-and under valuations. The penalty is 20% of the underpayment. The penalty is 40% of any portion of the underpayment attributable to an undisclosed noneconomic substance transaction or an undisclosed foreign financial transaction. The penalty will not be figured on any part of an underpayment on which the fraud penalty is charged. Taxpayers can avoid the "Accuracy-related penalty" by showing reasonable cause for their failure and that they acted in good faith. Some people have tried to use the "Turbo Tax" defense with some success. This defense argues that the taxpayer relied on their tax software which did not ask about the type of income omitted, etc. But this defense is not at all reliable. For non-tax-shelter items, if the amount of understatement of tax on a return is more than 10% of the correct amount of tax or $5,000 (whichever is greater), then it is a **substantial understatement**.
- Frivolous tax return (avoidance schemes) - There is a $5,000 penalty for filing a frivolous tax return. This means that you paid less than the larger of 10% of the correct tax liability or $5,000, and you could also face fraud penalties. In some cases, a spouse (or former spouse) is relieved of tax, interest, and penalties (joint return filed) under the innocent spouse rules – spouse must not have materially participated in the disputed proceeding. One-Time Abatement of the $5,000 Frivolous Filing Penalty – The IRS announced that taxpayers who have abandoned any frivolous positions and meet other requirements will qualify for the one-time abatement of the $5,000 frivolous filing penalty, effective Nov. 5, 2012. The relief provides for a one-time frivolous filing penalty reduction to $500 for taxpayers who otherwise have filed all required tax returns and paid all outstanding tax liabilities, including all other penalties and related interest, and who have abandoned any frivolous positions and meet all other requirements in the revenue procedure. A request for the relief must be made on Form 14402 IRC 6702(d) Frivolous Tax Submissions Penalty Reduction, which must be signed under penalties of perjury. Taxpayers must pay at least $250 of the reduced penalty with the form, except for taxpayers who have installment agreements. Taxpayers must file the request before the IRS files suit to collect the full penalty or to reduce any assessment of the penalty for judgment. The penalty relief does not apply to any Sec. 6702 penalty that has already been paid. The IRS must give written notice whether the request has been accepted. If denied, it will not be subject to administrative appeal.
- Penalty for failure to file partnership and S-corporation returns - Increased from $89 to $195 per shareholder or partner for each month, or fraction of a month, and the failure continues up to a maximum of 12 months. This is effective for returns filed for tax years beginning after 12/31/2009.
- Statute of limitations on omission of income – The IRS can assess taxes within three years of the original due date of the tax return. It doesn't matter if the tax return was filed before the due date. If a return is filed late without an extension, the statute runs three years following the

actual (late) filing date. Code Section 6501(e)(1)(A) provides that if a taxpayer "omits from gross income an amount properly includible therein which is an omission of 25% or more of the amount of gross income stated in the return ("substantial understatement of income"), the IRS has six years, rather than three years, from the date on which the return was filed to assess a deficiency. The IRS has argued that any claim that effectively results in an omission of 25 percent or more of tax liability – such as using an inflated tax basis – adds an extra three years to the clock.

- <u>Higher failure-to-file penalties on information returns (1099s etc.)</u> – The Small Business Jobs Act of 2010 substantially increases the penalties for failing to timely file information returns required to be filed after January 1, 2011. First-tier penalties (filing after the filing deadline but not more than 30 days after) – penalty increases from $15 to $30. The calendar year maximum increases from $75,000 to $250,000 (for small filers with average gross receipts of not more than $5 million the maximum increases from $25,000 to $75,000). Second-tier penalties (filing more than 30 days after filing deadline but before August 1) – penalty increases from $30 to $60. The calendar year maximum increases from $150,000 to $500,000 (for small filers the maximum increases from $50,000 to $200,000). Third-tier penalties (failing to file after August 1) – penalty increases from $50 to $100. The calendar year maximum increases from $250,000 to $1.5 million (for small filers the maximum increases from $100,000 to $500,000). The minimum penalty for each intentional failure-to-file increases from $100 to $250.

- <u>Interest</u> – When the IRS proposes adjustments to your account, interest on the liability runs from the date the tax return was due to the date the IRS receives your payment of the **entire amount** including taxes, penalties, and interest. If you convince the IRS they are wrong, there is no interest due. But, if you are wrong in whole or in part and owe taxes, interest mounts quickly – <u>interest compounds daily and runs at the short-term federal rate plus 3%</u>. In order to completely stop the interest from running but still fight the underlying tax that the IRS says is due, you must pay it all, including all interest that has accrued up to that point as well as penalties. Otherwise interest will continue to build on any tax, penalties, and interest assessed. If you win your dispute you will get it back. If you want to pay up and continue disputing the additional taxes accessed you have to make a <u>deposit</u> for everything due up to that point, and you must **specifically call it a deposit** and follow IRS procedures or the IRS may think you are agreeing. You must make your check payable to "United States Treasury" and send a written statement designating it as a "DEPOSIT." Also, include the tax year, type of tax, and why you disagree. The nature and grounds of your disagreement must be specific. Calling the payment a DEPOSIT is important because it allows you to withdraw it upon request. A request to withdraw the money must be in writing and will be honored by the IRS unless it determines that the payment of any tax deficiency would be in jeopardy. Also, if you do withdraw the deposit and it later turns out you owe the additional tax, the IRS will charge you interest from the original due date of the tax return as if you never made a deposit.

Innocent Spouse Relief

Under the original statute, in order to obtain innocent spouse relief taxpayers had to prove to the IRS that they didn't know, or have reason to know, that their spouse underpaid income taxes. When the 2-year limit on innocent spouse relief requests was removed, the new statute now states that the request for relief must be made on or before the Collection Statute Expiration Date, or the date the period of limitation on collection of the income tax liability expires. This is generally 10 years after the assessment of tax but may be extended by other provisions of the Internal Revenue Code. The new statute also provides that if the non-requesting spouse abused the spouse requesting relief and maintained control over the household finances by restricting the requesting spouse's access to financial information, and the requesting spouse was not able to challenge the treatment of any items on the joint tax return or to question the payment of the taxes reported for fear of retaliation, then this satisfied the factor needed to file a request for innocent spouse relief even if the requesting spouse knew or had reason to know of the items giving rise to the tax understatement or deficiency. Innocent spouse relief is available only to someone who files a joint return. The IRS will reject a claim if it believes the taxpayer benefited from the tax avoidance. For example, a taxpayer who shared in unreported lottery winnings would probably be ineligible for innocent spouse status.

The requesting spouse has to be divorced, legally separated, or living apart from the non-requesting spouse. Factors that will be considered by the IRS include: the requesting spouse would suffer economic hardship if forced to pay the tax liability; requesting spouse was abused by non-requesting spouse; requesting spouse received no significant benefit from the underpayment; requesting spouse subsequently complied in good faith with tax laws; and requesting spouse was not under a legal obligation pursuant to a divorce decree or agreement to pay the outstanding liability. The IRS will also consider factors such as the taxpayer's education and the couple's financial situation. Originally, innocent spouse relief was supposed to be denied if the spouse knew the other spouse was not paying taxes, and the IRS initially imposed a deadline of two years after the date of the IRS's first collection activity with respect to the taxpayer for innocent spouse relief requests. But that deadline, which is not specified in the statute, was subject to much litigation and even though the IRS won cases upholding the two-year limit, it abandoned it in 2011. **The U.S. Tax Court first gave relief from the two-year limitation if the spouse did not know anything about husband's affairs (no time limit on claiming equitable relief, according to U.S. Tax Court). The U.S. Tax Court said that the two-year rule did not apply. Also, in July 2011 the IRS granted relief to people who have been burdened with old tax debts of their estranged spouses by eliminating the two-year limit on requests for innocent spouse relief.**

Disclosure Statement (Form 8275)

Form 8275 is used by taxpayers and tax return preparers to disclose items or positions, except those taken contrary to a regulation, that are not adequately disclosed on a tax return to avoid certain penalties. Both taxpayers and preparers are exposed to risk when submitting tax returns. If you think you're OK with a position but not positive, disclose it by attaching Form 8275 to the return. Form 8275 must be discussed and the client must be informed about the use of it in their tax return. It's imperative to note that if there is disagreement on this matter but the preparer believes the use of Form 8275 is necessary, then the return should be delivered to the client with Form 8275 attached. If that task is performed, the preparer has complied with their disclosure responsibility and should document it accordingly. The return is then in the client's hands to include or not include Form 8275 with the submitted tax return. In summary, Form 8275 has emerged as an important weapon in the arsenal of competent tax professionals. When properly used, Form 8275 can protect both the client and the preparer from certain penalties related to difficult tax return issues.

- Rev. Proc. 2012-51 lists specific forms and schedules for which additional disclosure is not necessary (providing the forms and attachments are completed clearly and in accordance with their instructions). All money amounts entered on the forms must be verifiable on audit.
- Form 8275 should be used if the potential amount of an understatement of tax (for non-tax shelter items) on a return in more than 10% of the correct amount of tax or $5,000, whichever is greater (this is a substantial understatement). The amount of an understatement is reduced by any portion of the understatement attributable to items, other than tax shelter items, that were adequately disclosed on the return if there is a reasonable basis for the taxpayer's treatment of the item.
- A tax preparer can be penalized for an unreasonable position if he knew or should have known of the position. A position is unreasonable if there is no substantial authority for it, or it was not properly disclosed and there was no reasonable basis for the position. Positions relating to tax shelter items or reportable transactions are treated as unreasonable.

Reportable and Listed Transaction Disclosure (Form 8886)

Taxpayers must disclose their participation in reportable and listed tax shelter transactions (tax shelter promoters and investors) by submitting Form 8886, which is due when the original or amended return is filed. The taxpayer must also send a copy of the disclosure statement (Form 8886) to the IRS Office of Tax Shelter Analysis (OTSA). Failure to do so is subject to a penalty of $10,000. Promoting a tax shelter is not protected by Sec. 735 (privilege provision).

- Form 8886 is required for reportable transactions which include: individual taxpayers claiming Par. 165 losses of $2 million in a single year or $4 million in any combination of tax years; corporations (including S-corporations) and partnerships – losses of at least $10 million or $20 million, respectively; foreign currency transactions – losses of at least $50,000 in a single year for individuals or trusts, whether or not it flows through an S-corporation or partnership.
- Losses that are not reportable on Form 8886: casualty and theft losses; ponzi scheme losses; losses from the sale or exchange of an asset with a qualifying basis; and losses arising from a mark-to-market treatment of an item.

- **The Small Business Jobs Act (2010)** provides some relief to small businesses that fail to disclose "reportable transactions." The law provides that a participant in a reportable transaction that fails to disclose the transaction is subject to a penalty equal to 75% of the decrease in tax shown on the return as a result of the transaction or which would have resulted if the transaction was respected for federal tax purposes. The maximum penalty is $10,000 for an individual who fails to disclose a reportable transaction; $50,000 for all other taxpayers, $100,000 for an individual failing to disclose a listed transaction; and $200,000 for all other taxpayers. The minimum penalty is $5,000 for an individual taxpayer failing to disclose a reportable transaction or a listed transaction. The minimum penalty for all other taxpayers (partnerships and corporations) is $10,000.
    - A reportable transaction is one that the IRS has determined requires disclosure because it has a potential for tax evasion (can be "like" a listed transaction).
    - A listed transaction is a reportable transaction specifically identified by the IRS as an improper tax avoidance transaction. These can be found on the IRS website.

Uncertain Tax Positions (Schedule UTP)

There was a phased-in reporting requirement for UTPs – in 2010, a taxpayer with assets of $100 million or more if they or a related entity filed audited financial statements; in 2012, $50 million; in 2014, $10 million. Controversial or "uncertain tax positions" (UTP) must be disclosed, i.e. there must be a "reasonable basis" for a tax position taken on a return (greater than 30% chance of sustainability is a reasonable basis), or the return could be considered a disregard of tax laws or an avoidance scheme. Such UTPs must be fully reported and submitted with the tax return even if there is a "reasonable basis" for the tax position taken on the return. Penalties apply upon failure to file Schedule UTP when required. In Announcement 2010-30, the IRS indicated it will treat taxpayers who file Schedule UTP as having filed Form 8275, Disclosure Statement, and Form 8275-R, Regulation Disclosure Statement, because the IRS has recognized that the information reported on these forms duplicates information required on Schedule UTP.

- Any return containing these schedules or forms will undergo a compliance assessment by a Centralized Review Team prior to release to the field. According to the IRS, the mere presence of a return with a Schedule UTP should not prompt an examination.
- NOTE: The IRS is looking into other potential areas of duplicative reporting. For example, Form 8886, Reportable Transaction Disclosure Statement is similar to Schedule UTP. The IRS has also observed that Schedule M-3 (Form 1120), Net Income (Loss) Reconciliation for Corporations with Total Assets of $10 Million or More, may be duplicative to Schedule UTP. This form is somewhat similar to Schedule UTP in that it compares tax information the taxpayer disclosed for financial reporting purposes with the corporation's tax position. Schedule M-3 requires the taxpayer to reconcile the differences between their financial statement net income or loss and reported taxable income.

Economic Substance Doctrine

Effective for transactions after March 30, 2010, the Economic Substance Doctrine states that a transaction will be treated as having economic substance only if the transaction changes the taxpayer's position in a meaningful way (apart from the tax benefits) and the taxpayer has a substantial purpose (apart from the tax benefits) for entering into the transaction. Failure to meet the Economic Substance test subjects violators to penalty under IRC 6662 and imposes an increased penalty amount for non-disclosed transactions that lack economic substance. A 40% strict-liability penalty would apply to tax understatements attributable to undisclosed non-economic substance transactions. The penalty would be 20% if a transaction is adequately disclosed. **Personal transactions by individuals (but not their business or investment dealings) are exempt from the economic substance requirements.**

Tax Refund Offsets

The IRS can use part or all of your federal tax refund to satisfy certain unpaid debts: (1) federal or state income taxes; (2) child support payments; or (3) student loan debt submitted for offset. You will receive a notice from the IRS if an offset occurs. The notice will include the original refund amount, your offset amount, the agency receiving the payment and its contact information. If you believe you do not owe the debt or are disputing the amount, you should contact the agency shown on the notice, not the IRS.

- If you filed a joint return, you may be entitled to part or all of the refund offset. This applies if your spouse is solely responsible for the debt. <u>To request your part of the refund, file Form 8379, Injured Spouse Allocation.</u> Attach Form 8379 to your original return or file it by itself after you are notified of an offset of the refund to pay for part of the debt. Form 8379 can be filed electronically, or if you file a paper return you can write "INJURED SPOUSE" at the top left of Form 1040, 1040A or 1040EZ. The IRS will process your allocation request before an offset occurs. If you are filing Form 8379 by itself, it must show both spouses' social security numbers. You, the "injured" spouse, must sign the form. Do not attach the originally filed Form 1040 to the Form 8379. Carefully follow the instructions on Form 8379. If you don't receive a reply, contact the Financial Management Service at 800-304-3107.

Tax Preparer Responsibilities and Penalties

Tax Preparer Standards

Circular 230, Regulations Governing Practice Before the Internal Revenue Service, is the IRS bible for preparer responsibilities and standards. Under the final rules, a practitioner cannot willfully, recklessly, or through gross incompetence sign a return or advise a client to take a position on a tax return or claim for refund containing a position that lacks reasonable basis, is an unreasonable position under tax code Section 6694(a)(2), or is a willful attempt to understate tax liability or a reckless disregard of the rules and regulations as described in Section 6694(b)(2). Firm managers must take reasonable steps to ensure compliance with Circular 230. The IRS also clarified that a practitioner liable for a penalty under tax code Section 6694 is not automatically subject to discipline under Section 10.34. The IRS will make an independent determination as to whether the practitioner engaged in willful, reckless, or grossly incompetent conduct that would be subject to discipline under Section 10.34.

- All required Forms must be filed and all questions should be answered, unless an exception applies.
- Preparer can rely on the information provided by a client, but there is a responsibility for reasonable scrutiny. If the information appears incorrect, the <u>preparer has a duty to investigate questionable items</u>. Tax preparers must perform adequate due diligence and make reasonable inquiries when information furnished by a client appears to be incorrect, inconsistent, or incomplete. The IRS Office of Professional Responsibility (OPR) states that "willful blindness" and "don't ask, don't tell" approaches are not acceptable. Tax preparers should consider taking extra due-diligence steps for the following four client profiles:
    - Small retail businesses - The IRS knows that small business is the largest segment that underreports income. This is largely because these businesses receive few or no information statements, resulting in little or no audit trail for the IRS. According to the IRS tax gap study released in 2012, 56% of taxpayers who receive few or no information statements misreport income on their tax returns.
    - Noncash contributions - For clients that have noncash charitable contributions, make sure that Form 8283 is accurate and that the client provides all required documentation. If your client donated a vehicle, make sure your client receives Form 1098-C, Contributions of Motor Vehicles, Boats, and Airplanes from the charitable organization, attaches the form to the return, and does not overvalue the donation.
    - Rental property - When preparing returns with rental property activity, ask clients to substantiate expenses, because 35% of taxpayers with rental property deduct a non-allowable personal expense or can't substantiate a reported expense. 19% do not fully report an expense that would have been allowed.
    - Losses taken on personal returns from partnerships and S-corporations - The IRS finds significant errors when it audits these entities. A more considerable concern for the IRS in this area is the deduction of flow through losses from these entities, because many times partners or shareholders recognize a loss in excess of the amount allowed due to basis limitations.
- When a tax preparer discovers an error in a prior-period return prepared by another preparer, he should inform the client promptly upon becoming aware of that error or any error in a previously filed return, an error in a return that is the subject of an administrative proceeding, or a taxpayer's failure to file a required return. The practitioner should advise the client about

the potential consequences of the error and recommend corrective measures. The practitioner may give the recommendation either orally or in writing.
- Preparer should talk to a client about the need to file Form 8275 "Disclosure Statement." You can't force a client to attach Form 8275 to a return if they don't want to do it, but if they refuse you should reconsider your relationship with the client. For disclosure of controversial tax positions, a preparer must advise the client that they must file Form 8275, and advise the taxpayer of all the penalties that are applicable for not filing Form 8275 and all the opportunities to avoid penalties under Code Sec. 6662. Advising the client must be contemporaneously documented in the files. A preparer must advise a client promptly of an error or omission in a tax return and the consequences of not correcting the error or failure to file Form 8275, Form 8886, etc. <u>If Form 8275 is not filed when required, it opens both the client and preparer up to all the consequences (penalties, etc.)</u>. Form 8275 must be filled-out completely.
- Preparer should advise the client that they cannot rely on "reasonable basis" with respect to the new Economic Substance law. <u>Saving taxes is not an acceptable reason for taking a tax position</u>.
- Client privilege does not apply to tax returns. Client privilege may apply to certain tax advice, if a separate engagement letter is prepared for the advice.
- It's OK to use estimates in certain situations if properly disclosed.
- Preparers are not required to continue a position agreed to in an IRS settlement in regard to a previous exam.
- In deciding on the form of advice provided to a taxpayer, the preparer should exercise professional judgment and should consider such factors as: (1) importance of the transaction and amounts involved; (2) specific or general nature of the taxpayer's inquiry; (3) time available for development and submission of advice; (4) technical complexity involved; (5) existence of authorities and precedents; (6) tax sophistication of taxpayer; (7) need to seek other professional advice; (8) type of transaction and whether it is subject to heightened reporting or disclosure requirements; (9) potential penalty consequences of tax return position for which advice is rendered; (10) whether any potential penalties can be avoided through disclosure; and (11) whether you intend for the taxpayer to rely upon your advice to avoid potential penalties.
- Preparer should consider preparing an engagement letter for all tax return preparation engagements.
- A single person in a firm must have responsibility for a tax return.
- **In most cases, a preparer should have nothing to do with reportable and listed transactions (Form 8886).**
- A tax practitioner's written tax opinions would need to meet the following five requirements: (1) written advice should be based on reasonable factual and legal assumptions (including assumptions as to future events); (2) reasonably consider all relevant facts that the practitioner

knows or should know; (3) use reasonable efforts to identify and ascertain the facts relevant to written advice on each federal tax matter; (4) not rely upon representations, statements, findings, or agreements (including projections, financial forecasts, or appraisals) of the taxpayer or any other person if reliance on them would be unreasonable; and (5) not, in evaluating a federal tax matter, take into account the possibility that a tax return will not be audited or that a matter will not be raised on audit. In addition, a practitioner may only rely on the advice of another practitioner if the advice was reasonable and the reliance is in good faith considering all the facts and circumstances. <u>Section 10.35 of Circular 230 has been interpreted to require practitioners to include a disclaimer when communicating with clients regarding tax advice, whether in e-mails or whatever means of written communication, even if there is no tax advice included in the communication, for example – an invitation to a lunch meeting. This has led practitioners to use Circular 230 disclaimers in all written communication to clients, often highlighted in bold and upper case letters, to the affect that **"this cannot and should not be considered tax advice and cannot be relied upon to avoid penalties**." However, there is a proposal to remove Section 10.35 which would eliminate the requirement that practitioners fully describe the relevant facts and assumptions relied upon in giving written tax advice, and the use of Circular 230 disclaimers in documents and transmissions including e-mails. But for the present it is still in effect.</u>

- **In December, 2011, the IRS released new Form 14157 to be used by consumers to file complaints against their tax return preparers.**

<u>Rules on Providing Client Records</u>

Suppose a CPA who prepared a client's tax return(s) receives a request from the client to transfer all of the client's tax records to a new firm. What are the CPA's responsibilities and obligations? Circular 230 states that a "practitioner must, at the request of a client, promptly return any and all records of the client that are necessary for the client to comply with his or her Federal tax obligations." Records of the client are defined as "all documents or written or electronic materials provided to the practitioner or obtained by the practitioner in the course of the practitioner's representation of the client, that preexisted the retention of the practitioner by the client." Records of the client include materials that were prepared by the client or a third party, such as an investment manager or bank or a brokerage firm, and provided to the practitioner to prepare the requisite tax returns. The term "records" also covers any return, schedule, appraisal, or any other document prepared by the practitioner that was presented to the client with respect to a prior representation if such document is necessary for the taxpayer to comply with a current federal tax obligation. The term does not include any return, schedule, or any other document prepared by the practitioner if the practitioner is withholding the document pending the client's performance of a contractual obligation to pay fees with respect to the document. When a client of former client requests that his or her records either be sent to the client or forwarded to another CPA, a member's failure to comply would be a violation of the CPA's responsibilities and obligations.

Tax Preparer Penalties

Tax preparer penalties have changed. Previously, the IRS was contemplating requiring the preparer to have a reasonable belief that the position would more likely than not be sustained (greater than 50%). 1st tier penalty would have been the greater of $1,000 or 50% of the income derived from the tax return preparation; 2nd tier penalty would have increased to $5,000 or 50% of the income derived from the tax return preparation. However, under the final rules, the "more likely than not" standard has been replaced with the "substantial authority" standard (50% or less of being sustained), which is the same as the taxpayer's standard – not more or less stringent. But, the "more likely than not" rule does still apply to tax shelters and reportable transactions (See Above).

- The penalties on a preparer for undisclosed return positions without substantial authority are now the same standard as that for the client (taxpayer).
- Revenue procedure 2008-35 prohibits the use of the taxpayer's information for any purpose other than tax preparation without the client's consent in writing on a separate sheet of paper. Section 7216(a) of the Tax Code imposes criminal penalties on tax preparers who knowingly or recklessly make unauthorized disclosures or uses information from their clients' tax returns without their consent. The civil penalty is $250 for each disclosure up to a maximum of $10,000. The criminal penalty is a misdemeanor, but nevertheless carries a penalty of up to one year in prison or a fine of up to $1,000 for each violation, or both, together with the costs of prosecution for knowingly or recklessly making an unauthorized disclosure.
- Preparer penalties apply to those who prepare Forms 941 (contractor vs. employee) – must have substantial authority.
- Paid preparers failing to meet their due diligence requirements on Earned Income Tax Credit (EITC) claims face higher penalties for returns filed after 12/31/2011. The penalty is increased from $100 to $500, which is an incentive for due diligence compliance, ensuring more accurate EITC claims. In addition, paid preparers will be required to complete and submit Form 8867 with all returns with EITC claims.
- Section 6694(a) imposes a penalty on a tax preparer who prepares a return or claim for refund that understates the amount of tax because of an **unreasonable position** if the preparer knew or should have known the position was unreasonable. Except for tax-shelter-items, a position is unreasonable if there is **no substantial authority** for it or it was not properly disclosed, and there was no reasonable basis for the position. Positions related to tax-shelter items or reportable transactions are treated as unreasonable unless it is reasonable to believe they more than likely not will be sustained on their merits.

IRS Audits

The IRS has a big audit-by-mail program, and they have increasingly relied on these correspondence audits that focus on one or two narrow issues. Taxpayers are sent a letter that, for example, says their charitable or unreimbursed employee business deductions will be denied and a certain amount of extra taxes assessed unless they provide acceptable documentation supporting the deductions within 30 days. Mail processing delays, etc. have resulted in taxpayers who respond within the required time to be assessed extra taxes even though the requested documentation is provided. Taxpayers may eventually get those taxes abated, but it is a big hassle. Examinations of individual tax returns increased 77% from 2001 to 2006 and enforcement revenues grew 44% (liens and levies were the driving force). Also, The IRS now relies more on penalties, liens, and levies rather than seizures (which are more confrontational and visible). There are **IRS Notices** and 3 main types of IRS audits: Correspondence; Office Examination; and Field Examination, although most audits incorporate a mixture of all three. However, the prevailing trend is for the IRS to handle most problems via Notices and correspondence audits.

The IRS usually has three years after you file your tax return to audit you. However, if you omit more than 25% of your income, the IRS gets to double that time to six years. But statutes are often extended, sometimes voluntarily. Frequently, the IRS says it needs more time to audit and asks you to sign a form extending the statute, usually for a year. Most tax advisors generally advise clients to agree. However, you may be able to limit the time or scope of the extension. What if you file a false return under-reporting income or willfully fail to file? The rules for how long you must worry and the stakes go up materially, including potential criminal charges and prison. Section 6531(2) of the tax code says the statute is six years commencing once the return is filed, or from the time you willfully failed to file a return.

IRS Notices
In the 1990's the IRS approached compliance through traditional methods such as audits and in-person tax collection. However, during the past 10 years the IRS has improved its ability to target potential noncompliance through technology. The IRS mail audit program was responsible for 78% of all IRS audits in 2010. This audit program is mainly through notices, which are going out to taxpayers more than ever before. In fact, since 2001, notice volume has increased 670%. This is the IRS being smarter about tackling problems. This year, it's likely that the IRS will exceed the 201 million notices issued in 2009. For practitioners and their clients, this means more contact with the IRS. The IRS sends certain types of notices, for example: CP01H – The IRS cannot process your return; CP04 – The IRS believes you may be eligible for the additional child tax credit, which may entitle you to a tax refund; CP10 – The IRS made corrections to your return because of miscalculations. This affected the amount of estimated tax you wanted to apply to next year's taxes; CP11 – The IRS made changes resulting in an underpayment.

You can accept the IRS corrections or write back that you disagree; CP11A – The IRS made corrections because of miscalculations in the refundable earned income credit and you owe taxes to the government; CP12/CP13 – Math Error Notices (IRS adjusted a filed return due to miscalculation, changing the refund); CP14 – Balance Due; **CP2000 – Unreported Income Adjustment**; CP21B – The IRS made corrections that you requested and they result in a tax refund; CP23/24 – Estimated Tax Discrepancies; CP88 – Refund Hold Due to Missing Tax Return; Letter 3850/1-B – Appointment Letters for Employment Tax Audit for the National Research Program. <u>Practitioners can expect more clients to look to them for support, which means reacting to notices</u>. Here's what to do when you receive an IRS notice:

- Review the letter you've received or take it to your tax advisor to decipher.
- Don't assume it's correct. Review the return you filed and source documents to compare with the information in the notice. For example, sometimes the income they say is missing may be included in a place on the return other than where the IRS is looking.
- After carefully reviewing everything and if you agree with the IRS, be sure to respond by the date indicated in the letter or you will incur more interest.
- **Ask for an extension if you are within 10 days of the deadline and you don't have time to respond. Tax practitioners can call the <u>Practitioner Priority Service hotline at (806) 860-4259 and select Option 6, which will direct you to the Automated Underreporter Unit (for CP2000 notices)</u>. The IRS will grant 30 additional days without much resistance.**
- <u>Format your response – It is important to compile one organized response. Start with a cover letter clearly stating that you are responding to a CP2000 notice (or whatever kind of letter) which includes the taxpayer's name, identification number, and year and form in the reference section of the letter. In the letter, state your position and clearly reference the attachments that prove your position as well as supporting documentation. Also attach a corrected tax return, if applicable, to help the IRS compute the tax liability. Label the corrected tax return "Corrected – for CP2000 response purposes only – Do not process."</u> DO NOT FILE AN AMENDED RETURN.
- Be sure to respond within the designated timeframe shown on the letter even if you disagree in whole or in part. Failure to do so may create problems even more difficult to unscramble. Alternatively, you can call the toll-free number listed in the letter and talk with the IRS agent about the situation. You may be able to resolve the matter by phone, without even replying formally. Make sure that if you respond in this manner and the agent says your case is closed that you receive confirmation of this in the mail (it can take a few weeks for a follow-up letter from the IRS).
- If you are certain you don't owe any additional tax, or owe less than what the IRS is claiming, explain your position and include any supporting documentation you may have.

- Be persistent; make follow-up calls (later in the day generally experiences shorter wait times) to be sure the submitted documentation has been received and acknowledged by the Machine. This will help prevent pre-mature defaults to assessment.
- Don't give up if you receive another letter or the IRS doesn't accept your documentation or explanation the first time you submit it. Unfortunately, many people experience problems with the IRS receiving documents they believe were submitted.
- Even if the mismatched income appears correct, re-calculate the proposed tax to be sure the appropriate method has been used and the amount is correct.
- <u>Include the following statement in all responses you send to the IRS, "In the event the IRS disagrees with this response, the taxpayer requests an appeals hearing with the IRS Office of Appeals."</u> If the IRS sends a premature notice of deficiency on a CP2000 notice, ask them to "back up" the notice of deficiency because of processing delays.

<u>Form 1099-K Notice</u>
If a taxpayer receives a notice related to Form 1099-K, the IRS says that it may be because the taxpayer underreported their gross receipts. The Form 1099-K may show an unusually high portion of receipts from card payments and other reportable transactions. It is very important that taxpayers respond to a 1099-K Notice. You should read the notice thoroughly and complete any worksheets; gather your tax records including the 1099-Ks that you have received and determine if you agree with the notice about the underreporting of gross receipts; if you have questions, use the contact information provided on the notice; and if appropriate, consult your tax professional for assistance. The IRS noted that it uses the information reported from third parties to ensure individuals and businesses meet their tax obligations. The agency said it is integrating the new information supplied on the Form 1099-K into various areas, including its compliance efforts, to address non-compliance and ensure fairness.

<u>Correspondence Audit (this also applies to notices and regular field audits)</u>
The IRS uses correspondence audits to obtain additional information about a few <u>limited</u> issues on the taxpayer's return, and they are conducted by mail or written communications which make them cheaper and less labor intensive for the IRS. Tax preparers should advise taxpayers to notify them immediately if they receive a "notice" of additional taxes due from the IRS. If the notice of deficiency is correct, the tax preparer should advise the taxpayer to sign the agreement sent with the letter and pay the deficiency. However, if an adjustment to the deficiency notice is appropriate, the tax preparer should respond to the IRS service center with correspondence explaining the taxpayer's position and submitting the necessary documentation to support the explanation for the adjustment. Also, you should consider asking that the matter be transferred from the IRS service center to a local office, where it can be resolved by one auditor, if the assessment in the initial contact letter from the IRS is incorrect. This might be prudent because often in a correspondence audit, taxpayer correspondence is not assigned to the auditor who reviewed the earlier documents. Correspondence from the IRS bears

only the name of a supervisor, and if you call the supervisor, the IRS typically refers the call to whatever employee happens to be available at the time. Also, correspondence tends not to be reviewed for several months, resulting in the IRS sending letters advising the taxpayer that it needs additional time to review it. When the IRS finally does answer correspondence, in some cases your proposed adjustments are incorrect because they have not properly considered and evaluated documents and substantiation by the taxpayer or his/her representative. The IRS tends to not want to transfer cases to a local office because it is usually more economical for them to handle the matter by correspondence. Usually, IRS service centers take the view that correspondence examinations will be transferred only in instances of hardship. If there are problems, you can contact the local office of the Taxpayer Advocate Service and request assistance in having the matter transferred to the local IRS office or for assistance in getting the right people at the IRS service center to help resolve the matter.

Field Audit
A field audit is initiated by a "Notice of Audit," or an Exam Field Support Notification, via Letter CCU-CCO (Rev. 1-99) which describes the tax year(s) being examined and the IRS Form being examined. It then takes 60-90 days for the case filed to be transferred from the National Center to the local IRS auditing team, which is done with an Assignment Letter.

- Opening Conference – a request to start the audit will be made by phone or by a formal letter, usually both; which will set: (1) the expectations for the examination; (2) the timelines and expectations during the opening conference; (3) any issues that the Agent will be focusing on during the audit; and (4) the type of audit that will follow this process.
- Power of Attorney (IRS Form 2848) – In order for 3rd party representatives such as CPAs/attorneys to represent a taxpayer during the audit, the taxpayer must sign a Power of Attorney, which includes all representatives privy to the audit and allowed to communicate with the IRS Agent. The form should be sent immediately to the IRS Agent as soon as initial contact has been made scheduling an opening conference.
- Issues encountered during audit – Some issues will be grouped into what is known as "Issue Tiering." Within each issue tier, decision making during the audit will reside at different levels:
    1. Tier 1 Issue – Significant compliance risk which impacts multiple industries;
    2. Tier 2 Issue – Includes potential areas of high non-compliance or significant compliance risk to one or more industries; and
    3. Tier 3 Issue – This is known as an area with the highest compliance risk issues for a particular industry, requiring unique treatment within the industry.
- Information Document Request (IDR) – If the taxpayer is facing a Tiered issue, there is typically a mandatory IDR that will be sent, setting forth questions that are located in the IRS Audit Technique Guide for the specific Tier issue. Take care in looking at the questions being asked and know the issues you are working with. Taxpayers should get representation from someone that has a proven track record working with the IRS, even if they prepared and did their own

taxes. Some of the questions in the IDRs are designed to catch mistakes and a wrong or unclear answer may be the cause of an adjustment to the original return filed. Be sure to try to work with the IRS Agent to address the issues. Be honest and polite to the Agent and try to give them the information they are asking for. Withholding information is never a good practice and the IRS has rights to subpoena information from taxpayers. Don't be difficult – it may be tempting to try to make the field agent's life a little more difficult by providing a shoe box full of receipts, for example. Remember that your goal is to establish a good rapport with the audit Agent so that an issue resolution can be reached with minimal consequences to the taxpayer. <u>Remember, the IRS can go back seven years, so keep detailed tax records that can support every deduction, credit and exemption for that long</u>.
   - Keep thorough documentation of travel mileage, medical expenses, and meals-and-entertainment expenses. Keep logs of mileage driven (write down the odometer readings when you start and when you end). Entertainment expenses should be documented to the "N"th degree. Do not fudge the numbers.
   - Answer the questions put to you as best you can. Don't lie. Answer only that which is asked of you. Do not volunteer any information.
   - Bank statements should be kept along with copies of cancelled checks, which should be accepted by the IRS auditor.
- Typical timeline for audit – Expect 3-8 months, depending largely on the issues involved as well as the size of the case. Some audits can take well up to 1-2 years, especially if it is a Tiered issue that requires review and concurrence by a specialized audit team. This is why it is important to try to establish a timeline at the outset of the audit. <u>Be sure to document all communications and agreements with the IRS in writing</u>.
- Problems that may arise – An unfair or abusive Agent, and not following proper protocol. Remedies exist to protect taxpayers. First, exhaust issue resolutions at the exam level, and if all else fails, contact your local Taxpayer's Advocate Service.
- <u>Taxpayer Advocate Service</u> – An independent organization inside the IRS that advocates taxpayers' rights. It is free, confidential, and tailored to the taxpayers' specific needs. There is a local advocate located in each major city. To contact, check the following: IRS Publication 1546; local phone book; IRS online contact form; phone number: 1-877-777-4778 (case intake).
- End of Audit – There are 2 different types of outcomes: No change; and Un-agreed. A notice of determination can be negotiated with the field agent and then appealed to a manager and then to the appellate level before going to tax court.
- A 30-day letter will notify taxpayers of their Appeal Rights and further guide them as to what they need to do in order to file a protest to the IRS Appeals Division (Letter 950 Series; Letter 569 Series; Letter 953 Series). A <u>Closing Conference</u> should always be made available to the taxpayer once a 30-day letter has been issued. The closing conference should be held before a formal protest is made requesting the audit Agent to send the issue to the Appeals Office for an

un-agreed issue. The closing conference is the taxpayer's final opportunity to resolve the case at the examination level. Key players in a closing conference often include: the IRS Territory Manager; the Area Director; Director of Field Operations; Audit Agent; Audit Agent's Manager; any key players on the audit team that may have review and concurrence on particular issues; the taxpayer; and the taxpayer's representatives.

Surviving an IRS Audit
In a business audit, you will have to gather records and documents. Bear in mind that the IRS isn't just looking for proof that you spent the money shown on the expense lines of your tax return. They are looking for two more major things: that the expenses you reported really were business-related; and that you have actually reported all your income. The IRS examiner routinely adds up all the deposits to all the taxpayer's bank accounts. Naturally, this total will prove that small business taxpayers have far more deposits in their bank accounts than their tax return shows as income. This is a trap. Beware. After all, when you use several bank accounts, you routinely transfer funds between them, have to redeposit bounced checks, or deposit cash advances and other loans. To avoid being ambushed, you should consider assembling a spread sheet to show the IRS which deposits were not income. The most important thing you can do in your audit is to identify all the non-income deposits in all the bank accounts. This is especially important for a business showing losses. What did you live on during the year? Show proof of credit card balance increases, cash advances, loans, or funds drawn from your own savings, investments or home-equity line. If you have a full-time job, the IRS will try to prove it's a hobby. A business showing losses year after year will have a hard time proving it's anything more than a hobby or a tax shelter designed simply to generate deductions. Find the original receipts for depreciable assets, because the IRS has a right to demand the purchase documents for any asset still on your depreciation schedule. You need to have logs for your vehicle usage. You must prove the total miles you drove the car during the year, as well as your business mileage. Anytime you use mapping software to locate your destination, save the file as a PDF file and attach it to your calendar. At least write down the total miles. That will help you prove the mileage later. The three key things you need to prove are: that you don't have unreported income; that your business is not a hobby; and that your expenditures were business, not personal. And finally, if you are missing important documents to support your facts or deductions, find them, reconstruct them, or get written affidavits from people who can objectively verify the information.

Fast Track Settlement Program
The taxpayer or the IRS audit representative may initiate the Fast Track Settlement (FTS) Program for eligible small business/self-employed cases, usually before a 30-day letter is issued. The FTS program is designed to help small businesses and self-employed individuals who are under audit by the Small Business/Self Employed Division of the IRS. The FTS program uses alternative dispute resolution techniques to help taxpayers save time and avoid a formal administrative appeal or lengthy litigation.

As a result, audit issues can usually be resolved within 60 days rather than months or years. In addition, taxpayers who choose the FTS option lose none of their rights because they still have the right to appeal even if the FTS process is unsuccessful (see below). Jointly administered by the Small Business/Self-Employed Division (SB/SE) and the IRS Office of Appeals, FTS is designed to expedite case resolution. Under FTS, taxpayers with issues in dispute work directly with IRS representatives from SB/SE's Examination Division and the Office of Appeals to resolve those issues, with the Appeals representative serving as a mediator.

Avoiding the CP2000 Notice (Unreported Income)

In order to avoid receiving a CP2000 Notice, practitioners can ensure that all of the taxpayer's income has been reported before the return is filed by requesting IRP documents from the IRS: (1) get an authorization (Form 8821, Tax Information Authorization, will do); (2) call the IRS Practitioner Priority Service (PPS) line and ask for the taxpayer's wage and income transcripts (IRP) for 2012, or whatever year, and remember to ask for both spouses on a joint return. The IRS agent can fax it to you immediately. The process takes 10 minutes and provides you with the complete picture of the taxpayer's information statements on file with the IRS. The IRP document will contain all Forms 1098, 1099, W-2 and 5498 on file under the taxpayer's Social Security Number. You can also request IRP documents for the taxpayer's small business under the Employer Identification Number by calling the business PPS unit. Compare the IRP information against the return to be filed and correct any discrepancies before submitting the return.

Avoiding an Audit

Deductions and other things that tend to catch the eye of the IRS and bring audit notices:

- Gambling losses – Many Americans will win some type of lottery, slot machine bonus, or prize and then deduct everything they can as a gambling loss. The record keeping rules are very strict for gambling losses, the deduction is not that good, and your audit risk increases. Therefore, unless you have a detailed record of date, time, place, and amount of each gambling activity, don't even try this deduction.
- Using the wrong tax preparer – Some people get audited because their tax preparer got audited. The problem has become so bad that last year the IRS stepped in and attempted to set up licensing and continuing education requirements for tax preparers (however this was quashed by the judiciary). Avoid this problem by asking to see your preparer's license. Your preparer should be either a CPA, or an EA (IRS Enrolled Agent).
- Taking higher-than-average deductions. The Treasury Department publishes average tax deductions for each category, and exceeding the averages by more than 25% can trigger an audit.
- Taking large charitable deductions. If your charitable deductions are disproportionately large compared with your income, it raises a red flag.

- Schedule C filers who report a business loss. Losses from small businesses and unreported income can trigger an audit because they are often not truly businesses and can even represent an obvious tax cheating scheme.
- Failing to report all taxable income. Not reporting something on your tax return that was reported to the IRS by a third party. The IRS gets copies of all 1099s and W-2s you receive, so make sure you report all required income on your return. If you receive a 1099 showing income that isn't yours or listing incorrect income, get the issuer to file a corrected form with the IRS.
- Income other than wages, such as contract payments (1099-MISC).
- Home based businesses with home office expenses, especially if this in addition to salary income. The IRS is drawn to returns that claim home office write-offs due to the strict qualification requirements.
- Noncash charitable deductions. Particularly if you fail to file Form 8283 for donations over $500, the chances of audit increase.
- Deducting business meals, travel, and entertainment expenses, especially for self-employed persons. Large business meal and entertainment deductions are always ripe for audit, especially if the amount seems too high for the business.
- Claiming 100% business use of a vehicle (excessive business auto usage). The IRS knows that it's extremely rare for an individual to actually use a vehicle 100% of the time for business.
- Losses from an activity that could be viewed as a hobby rather than a business. If you have wage income and file a Schedule C with large losses and the loss-generating activity sounds like a hobby, it all but guarantees IRS scrutiny.
- Large casualty losses.
- Running a cash business like taxis, car washes, bars, hair salons, restaurants and the like are a tempting target for the IRS.
- Returns claiming the earned income tax credit.
- Failing to report a foreign bank account.
- Engaging in currency transactions. The IRS gets many reports of cash transactions in excess of $10,000 involving banks, casinos, car dealers, and other businesses, plus suspicious-activity reports from banks and disclosures of foreign accounts.
- Claiming rental losses. The IRS is scrutinizing rental real estate losses, especially those written off by taxpayers claiming to be real estate professionals. The IRS is hot on the audit trail of real estate professionals. They are required to maintain time records to show material participation in his/her rental activities. Without material participation, rental losses will be subject to the passive loss limitations ($25,000). Remember the *aggregation election* for real estate professionals. Without the election, he/she might be unable to show material participation in his/her rental activities.
- <u>And finally and probably the most important is making too much money</u>. Although the overall individual audit rate is about 1.11%, the odds increase dramatically for higher-income filers.

Data shows that Americans with more than $100,000 of income are nearly twice as likely to be audited as those with $50,000 - $100,000 of annual income. Once you hit $200,000 of income, your audit chances double again. If you somehow have $1,000,000 or more of income, your audit risk doubles yet again.

Criminal Investigations

The IRS can initiate a criminal investigation by either contacting the taxpayer first or the practitioner who prepared the tax return. If the taxpayer is contacted first and calls the tax preparer asking what to do, the tax preparer should resist the urge to investigate further and should immediately refer the taxpayer to an experienced criminal tax attorney. The AICPA Statement on Standards for Tax Services asserts that when the CPA has a reason to believe that a taxpayer may be charged with any type of fraud or criminal violation, the taxpayer should be advised to consult with a tax attorney before speaking to the CPA further in regard to the matter at hand. A CPA's communications surrounding the preparation of a taxpayer's original tax return that is under audit are never privileged (even where the original return was prepared by an attorney) given that a tax return is a public disclosure; therefore, no expectation of confidentially surrounds the communications at issue. A dilemma for CPAs instantly develops when a civil examination turns criminal and CPAs find themselves legally compelled to divulge the taxpayer's previously discussed secrets to the IRS under its subpoena power. Moreover, a conflict of interest inevitably arises where an actual or potential criminal tax issue arises surrounding a previous tax preparation engagement where CPAs have a vested interest in protecting their reputation with the investigating tax authority, which can place them at odds with the needs of the investigated taxpayer.

- CPAs should protect any materials or documents related to services rendered connected to an actual or potential criminal tax matter. Such documents will help an attorney identify potential issues and protect the CPA from any further exposure.
- When a CPA becomes aware that a taxpayer could be exposed to allegations of fraud or other criminal misconduct, the CPA should consider withdrawing from the performance of further tax or other services for the taxpayer. If the relationship continues, the CPA should work with the taxpayer's attorney to best protect the taxpayer's rights. <u>This means the CPA should avoid any unsupervised communication with the IRS</u>.
- Any and all information that is to be shared with the IRS should be approved by the taxpayer's attorney. This collaborative effort will provide the taxpayer's best chance of avoiding harsh penalties and possible jail time – and minimize the CPA's exposure.
- If the CPA is confronted first by the criminal investigators, the CPA should politely inform them that he recognizes he is a witness and will answer questions after first consulting with legal counsel. If a summons is part of the process, CPAs should comply. Generally a summons requires a future production of records, so there is time to confer with counsel. Also, the taxpayer will generally be notified of the existence of the summons and will be able to assert

any privilege claims to which he is entitled. Finally, if the investigators arrive to serve a search warrant and to seize records, CPAs must cooperate. It's common for the taxpayer to be served a warrant simultaneously.
- An alternative is for the CPA and attorney to team up in making a voluntary disclosure to the IRS on behalf of a taxpayer, i.e. the attorney approaches the IRS and concedes that a taxpayer has cheated in some way on his taxes and wants to remedy the situation. This can be achieved by amending the fraudulent return and making payment of taxes and penalties in exchange for the IRS passing on criminal prosecution. In practice, the IRS will generally refrain from prosecuting under such circumstances.

Dispute Over a Tax Liability

Interest continues to accrue during the period that the taxpayer and the IRS dispute a liability. To avoid the accrual of interest, taxpayer may deposit cash with the IRS that may subsequently be used to pay an underpayment. These payments may be withdrawn at any time if the taxpayer requests in writing (will be returned with interest). To make a deposit, remit a check or money order to the IRS Service Center or to the appropriate IRS Office from which you are under examination. Your check must be accompanied by a written statement that designates the remittance as a deposit for the particular item(s) under dispute – identifying the amount and the basis for the dispute.
- Payments made with an Extension (Form 4868) are <u>not</u> considered a deposit and cannot be credited against liabilities for later years.

Tax disagreements between taxpayers and the IRS can be settled either informally or through the formal appeals process (see below). Alternatives to the formal appeals process are:
- Fast Track Settlement Program – Allows the taxpayer to resolve an audit issue within less than 120 days by using the mediation skills of Appeals to shorten the audit period. It is jointly administered by the IRS Office of Appeals (OA) and the Large and Mid-size Business Division of IRS. Seeks to resolve issues through mediation between the IRS and taxpayer.
- Post-Appeals Mediation – Jointly administered by the IRS Office of Appeals (OA) and the Small Business/Self-Employed Compliance Division of the IRS. The mediator does not have settlement authority.
- Post-Appeals Arbitration – The Arbiter renders a decision on the facts being arbitrated. This decision is binding on both parties. Neither party can appeal or contest the Arbiter's decision in a judicial proceeding.

Most cases are disposed of by phone and mail (without a face-to-face meeting). If the Fast Track process doesn't work, taxpayer can file an appeal with the IRS Office of Appeals (OA).

IRS Office of Appeals (OA)

The last step in the administrative process before going to Court. Mission of OA: to settle tax disagreements between taxpayer and the IRS's Examination Division and/or Collection Division without having to go to court. Objective is to obtain a Closing Agreement. OA is available to help taxpayers who disagree with a tax decision made by the IRS. OA is supposed to be independent of any other IRS office, and provides a venue where disagreements <u>concerning the application of tax law</u> can be resolved on a fair and impartial basis by taking a "fresh look." A taxpayer is ready to request an appeals conference or hearing with the OA if he/she can explain why he/she disagrees with an IRS decision: (1) taxpayer believes IRS did not properly apply the law due to a misunderstanding of the facts (must be prepared to clarify and support position with records or other support); (2) taxpayer believes IRS is taking an inappropriate collection action against him; or (3) he does not agree with the Office of Collection's denial of his offer in compromise. OA looks at about 100,000 cases a year, of which ½ come from the Collection Division and resolves over 80% of these cases without going to Court. OA is the right choice if a taxpayer (call: <u>800-829-1040</u>):

- Receives correspondence from the IRS explaining that he/she has the right to come to OA to dispute an IRS decision.
- Does not agree with an IRS decision and is <u>not signing</u> an Agreement Form sent to taxpayer by the IRS.

OA is not the right choice if:

- A taxpayer's only concern is that he/she cannot afford to pay the amount owed.
- The correspondence the taxpayer received from the IRS was a bill and there was no mention of appeals (OA). A taxpayer can make an offer-in-compromise, which is an offer to settle an outstanding tax liability for less than is due, when (1) there is doubt that the total amount can be collected, or (2) there is doubt as to the liability, or to the collectability, and compromise would promote effective tax administration due to economic hardship of the taxpayer.

The following programs were created to permit taxpayers to be heard by the Office of Appeals (OA) before any levy and seizure is made on any property:

- <u>Collection Due Process Program (CDP)</u> - CDP is available if a taxpayer receives one of the following notices: Notice of Federal Tax Lien Filing and Your Right to a Hearing Under IRC 6320; Final Notice - Notice of Intent to Levy and Notice of Your Right to a Hearing; Notice of Jeopardy Levy and Right of Appeal; Notice of Levy on Your State tax Refund - Notice of Your Right to a Hearing; or Post Levy Collection Due Process (CDP) Notice.
- <u>Collection Appeals Program (CAP)</u> - CAP is available for taxpayers in the following situations: (1) before or after the IRS files a Notice of Federal Tax Lien or levies or seizes property; (2) if the IRS has terminated or proposed to terminate an installment agreement, rejected an installment agreement, or modified or proposed to modify an installment agreement.

The first step in a collection case is to take action immediately to freeze collection activities and allow the client and the representative a chance to collect their thoughts (and information) and consider how to work out a plan that works best for the taxpayer. If collection procedures are still in the earlier stages, liens may not have been filed in the local governmental office, and levies may not have been sent to employers, banks, customers, etc. An appeal of an IRS collection determination by OA in a CDP hearing or a CAP hearing may allow a taxpayer to avoid unwarranted collection action. CAP is available before or after IRS notices are filed and generally results in a quicker OA decision. A major advantage of a CDP hearing compared to a CAP hearing is that the determination in a CDP hearing may be appealed to the U.S. Tax Court, but the decision in a CAP hearing is binding on both the IRS and the taxpayer and cannot be appealed.

The timing for requesting consideration under the two methods is also different. A taxpayer must make a request for a CDP hearing within 30 days of receiving the first notice of a right to a hearing for a particular type of tax and period. If the taxpayer timely files the CDP hearing request, collection action ceases (and the statute of limitation under Sec. 6501 is suspended) until a final determination is made following the CDP hearing or a subsequent appeal to the U.S. Tax Court. If the 30-day window is missed, the taxpayer will be offered a chance for an "equivalent hearing," but that does not stop collection actions nor does it provide a chance to appeal the determination to Tax Court. The taxpayer makes a request for a CDP hearing by filing Form 12153, Request for a Collection Due Process or Equivalent Hearing at the address shown on the lien or levy notice. If the case has been assigned to a revenue officer, it is advisable to also send a copy of Form 12153 to him so he or she can suspend collection activities. A taxpayer can pursue an appeal through CAP before or after the filing of a lien or levy or the seizure of property. If the taxpayer disagrees with an IRS employee's decision and wants to appeal it, the taxpayer can ask the employee's manager to review the case. If the taxpayer and the manager are unable to resolve the disagreement (or in certain cases, where the taxpayer is not contacted by the manager within two days of making the request for a conference), the taxpayer can request a CAP hearing. The request in most cases is made by filing Form 9423, Collection Appeal Request. Normally in the case of liens, levies, and seizures, the IRS will not take any collection action until OA makes a decision, unless the IRS believes the collection of the tax is at risk.

When taxpayers cannot pay their tax liabilities, the IRS may proceed with the collection of taxes and penalties, and that, in turn, can result in the taxpayer's inability to borrow money to pay taxes or continue operating a business. By freezing collection activities, the CDP procedures and, to a lesser extent, the CAP procedures can provide tremendous benefits, resulting in a fair and equitable process for both the IRS and taxpayers.

Preparing a Request for Appeals

There are two types of ways to request an appeals hearing – A Small Case Request and a Formal written protest. When a taxpayer requests an appeals hearing, the request is typically forwarded by the Audit Agent to a local appeals office along with a copy of the Audit Agent's rebuttal to the taxpayer's protest. A "Small Case Request" should be prepared instead of a formal written request if the amount in dispute for any one tax period is $25,000 or less. A "Formal written protest" should be prepared when: (1) the total amount in dispute for any one tax period is greater than $25,000; (2) is a partnership or S-Corporation case without regard to the dollar amount at issue; or (3) is an employee plan and/or exempt organization case:

- Send a letter to OA requesting appeals consideration.
- Send Form 12203 indicating the proposed changes by the IRS that the taxpayer does not agree with, and the reason for the disagreement. If a Representative is signing the Form 12203, Form 2848 "Power of Attorney and Declaration of Representative" should be attached.
- A taxpayer can represent himself in the Appeals conference, and he/she may bring another person with him to support his position. If a taxpayer wants to be represented by someone, the person must be an Attorney, CPA, or an Enrolled Agent. If the taxpayer plans to have the Representative talk to the OA without him, the IRS needs a copy of a completed power of attorney (Form 2848). At the appeals conference, the taxpayer or his representative(s) will discuss the taxpayer's positions to the Appeals Officer. The focus for the appeals officer at an appeals hearing is to determine whether the IRS or the taxpayer has the most "Hazards of Litigation" if the case goes to court.

Closing Agreements

There are two types of closing agreements:

- Form 866 – Agreement as to final determination of tax liability (Deficiency Notice not required). If a case is agreed to or a settlement is reached, the taxpayer will receive closing documents to sign which set out the agreement/settlement that has been reached.
- Form 906 – Final agreement as to final determination covering specific matters (final only as to specific issues) – IRS can still issue a Deficiency Notice – 90 day letter.
- If the case remains un-agreed to, the IRS can issue a statutory Deficiency Notice, also known as a **90-Day Letter**. A 90-day letter is a formal legal notice, sent by certified or registered mail. Taxpayers have a 90-day window from the date of the notice to either agree to the adjustments or file a petition with the U.S. Tax Court. Failing to agree to the adjustments or timely file a petition with the Court will result in the assessment of the tax and actions to collect it. A 90-day letter is issued when one of three criteria are met: (1) the statute of limitation on assessment is imminent, and no extension can be obtained; (2) the taxpayer has not responded to or filed a valid protest to a 30-day letter (a preliminary notice of un-agreed deficiency that gives the taxpayer an opportunity to request an administrative review by the IRS's Office of

Appeals; or (3) the taxpayer asks for the notice to petition the case to the U.S. Tax Court. The 90-day letter contains detailed, plain-language instructions on how to contact the Tax Court (see below) for filing rules and forms, and the deadline for filing a petition with the Tax Court. Special rules govern small tax cases (disputed amounts up to $50,000 for any one year). The Court cannot consider untimely filed petitions so keeping track of the 90-day deadline is vital, and the 90 days include weekends and holidays (although the last day cannot fall on a weekend or holiday). Taxpayers may represent themselves in the Tax Court or be represented by CPAs, attorneys, or others admitted to practice before the Court.

Appeals Arbitration Program
Used when a binding arbitration is requested by taxpayer and OA on certain unresolved factual issues (used when all other issues are resolved except for specific factual issues). If Arbitration does not resolve a case:
- A Statutory Notice of Deficiency is issued to taxpayer, who will probably have to go to Court of Appeals.
- Taxpayer can appeal a determination to the U.S. Tax Court, District Court, or U.S. Court of Federal Claims.
- Form 12153 – taxpayer requests a Collection Due Process Hearing.

Taxpayers may recover fees and other costs incurred (including attorney's fees – maximum rate $170 in 2007) in any administrative proceeding before the IRS or court proceeding, including the Tax Court and Federal Claims Court, if he/she prevails.

Offers in Compromise (OIC)
An Offer in Compromise is an agreement between the taxpayer and government that settles a tax liability for payment of less than the full amount owed. This alternative should normally be used if a taxpayer's main concern is that he/she cannot afford to pay the amount owed. There are other alternatives to pursuing an Offer in Compromise in order to settle a tax assessment, including installment agreements, partial installment agreements, penalty and interest abatement requests, bankruptcy, etc. The ideal alternative depends on the individual circumstances of the taxpayer, including the amount of the tax liability as well as the ability of the taxpayer to pay it. If all of the other alternatives are not right for you, then Offer in Compromise may be the best course. However, you will waste valuable time processing the lengthy, detailed application required for an Offer in Compromise; incur thousands of dollars in costs in hiring professionals to assist you; and incur needless application fees and installment payments if other alternatives are available and preferable. **On May 22, 2012, the IRS announced that it is making the terms under which it will accept offers in comprise more flexible by expansion of its Fresh Start program, which is designed to help financially distressed taxpayers clear up tax problems more quickly.** In calculating whether a taxpayer is eligible for an offer in

compromise, the IRS will now look at only one year of future income for offers paid in five or fewer months (down from four years). It will look at two years of future income for offers paid in six to 24 months (down from five years). All offers must be fully paid within 24 months of the date the offer is accepted. Among other things, the new rules revise the calculation for the taxpayer's future income; allow taxpayers to repay their student loans and to pay state and local delinquent taxes; and expand the allowable living expense allowance category and amount.

The key in deciding whether an Offer in Compromise should be pursued is determining the amount of the offer that will be acceptable to the IRS. The IRS will generally accept an Offer in Compromise when it is unlikely that the tax liability can be collected in full and the amount offered reasonably reflects collection potential. Consequently, it is essential to do the math before deciding to pursue an Offer in Compromise. The offer should reflect what the IRS could potentially collect from you through liens on and seizure of your assets as well as garnishments on your wages. There is a mathematical algorithm consisting of variables and parameters that needs to be calculated to determine your offer. It is not simply a number picked out of the air or "pennies on the dollar." The process of determination is rigorous and driven by a mathematical procedure to minimize frivolous offers. You do not want to initiate a negotiation with the IRS with a ridiculous offer. **Not too long ago the Internal Revenue Service issued an alert to taxpayers to beware of promoters' claims on television and the Internet that tax debts can be settled for "pennies on the dollar" through their professional services, inappropriately advising indebted taxpayers to file an Offer in Compromise application with the IRS. The IRS characterized such advice as bad, only costing taxpayers additional money and time.**

- An OIC is generally not accepted if the IRS believes the liability can be paid in full as a lump sum or through a payment agreement. They look at the taxpayer's income and assets to make a determination of the taxpayer's reasonable collection potential. OICs are subject to acceptance on legal requirements. Other changes to the program include narrowed parameters and clarification of when a dissipated asset will be included in the calculation of reasonable collection potential. In addition, equity in income producing assets generally will not be included in the calculation of reasonable collection potential for on-going businesses.
- <u>Allowable living expenses</u> – The allowable Living Expenses standards are used in cases requiring financial analysis to determine a taxpayer's ability to pay. Under the Fresh Start initiative, taxpayers can now use the "miscellaneous allowance" for expenses such as credit card payments and bank fees and charges, payments for loans guaranteed by the federal government for post-high school education, payments for delinquent state and local taxes based on a percentage basis of tax owed to the state and IRS. Also, there is lien relief for taxpayers trying to refinance or sell a home.
- <u>Streamlined offers-in-compromise</u> – The IRS has raised the dollar limits for streamlined-offers-in-compromise agreements, allowing taxpayers with annual incomes of up to $100,000 and tax liability of less than $50,000 to participate, effectively doubling the dollar ceiling from its

previous $25,000 level. The IRS looks at the taxpayer's income and assets to make a determination regarding ability to pay.

If you are in a tax jam and want to apply for an OIC, you can use the IRS pre-qualifier tool (http://irs.treasury.gov/oic pre qualifier). This interactive questionnaire walks you through the eligibility standards. If the pre-qualifier tool indicates you may be eligible for an OIC, then you must submit Form 656, Offer Income Compromise, along with a $150 nonrefundable application fee. In addition, you must complete Form 433-A, Collection Information Statement, for individuals. You'll have to disclose your personal financial situation in detail.

Consider Alternative Reasons for Submitting an Offer in Compromise
When most practitioners think of an OIC, they think of a "doubt as to collectability" offer, where the taxpayer has insufficient income and assets to pay the full liability and the IRS allows a cash settlement on that liability. However, doubt as to collectability is just one of three possible reasons the IRS can accept an OIC. The other two reasons are "effective tax administration" and "doubt as to liability."

- Promoting effective tax administration (ETA) – when considering ETA, you should understand that the Internal Revenue Manual instructs IRS employees to consider ETA justifications as a last resort. However, the multiple elements under ETA make it an attractive alternative for many taxpayers. Under Treas. Reg. par 301.7122-1(b)(3), the IRS is allowed to compromise a tax liability based on ETA if (1) financial hardship exists; (2) public policy dictates it; or (3) sufficient equitable considerations exist. Financial hardship exists when a taxpayer is unable to pay reasonable basic living expenses. In most circumstances, the IRS will determine the existence of financial hardship by reducing a taxpayer's income (generally consisting of gross wages, interest and dividends, net self-employment and rental income) by the prescribed national and local expense standards (IRM 5.15.1). However, the IRM does allow deviations from those standards if taxpayers can show that they are inadequate to provide for the specific situation. Unlike the normal deviation provisions that require reasonable substantiation that an expense is necessary to provide for the taxpayer's and taxpayer's family's health and welfare and/or production of income, an ETA offer analysis can take into account more factors when departing from those standards. A practitioner should consider raising as a factor the taxpayer's age, employment status, dependents, education expenses, and any extraordinary circumstances when presenting the existence of a financial hardship. Raising these additional considerations is most successful if included both in a cover letter when filing the OIC and as an attachment to the financial disclosure forms, specifically, Form 433-A, Collection Information Statement for Wage Earners and Self-Employed Individuals. ETA offers are available only for individuals and not for corporations, partnerships, or other entities.

U.S. Tax Court

The U.S. Tax Court handles only tax litigation and judges are all tax experts. There are no juries. The Tax Court is the only court that will decide a case on a non-refund suit. Thus, the taxpayer does not have to pay the IRS monies owed on a disputed case in order to have standing to bring its case to the Tax Court. The taxpayer has a right to appeal a Tax Court decision to the U.S. Court of Appeals and U.S. Supreme Court. Statute of limitation for Tax Court is 90 days (see 90 letter above).

- Small Claims – Available for cases where the dispute amount is less than $50,000. Heard by the Small Case Division of the U.S. Tax Court, and are in informal settings (typically in conference rooms). Unlike regular Tax Court, the taxpayer will have no appeal rights, meaning that all decisions are final and binding.

Taxpayer Advocate Service (TAS)

The Taxpayer Advocate Service (TAS) is an independent organization within the IRS that helps taxpayers who are experiencing unresolved federal tax problems. Due to an unwieldy case load, the Taxpayer Advocate Service (TAS) is refocusing its workload in order to focus on taxpayers who need assistance the most. If the taxpayer is not currently facing an imminent threat of enforcement action or otherwise experiencing situations that meet the definition of an economic burden, TAS will probably refer the taxpayer to the appropriate IRS function specializing in return processing issues. In this respect, "economic burden" is defined according to four criteria: the taxpayer is experiencing economic harm or is about to suffer economic harm; the taxpayer is facing an immediate threat of adverse action; the taxpayer will incur significant costs if relief is not granted (including fees for professional representation); or the taxpayer will suffer irreparable injury or long-term adverse impact if relief is not granted. You can file **Form 911**, Request for Taxpayer Advocate Service Assistance, which can be faxed to a local office. There are local Taxpayer Advocates in each state.

- TAS assistance is free and tailored to meet your needs.
- You may be eligible for TAS help if you've tried to resolve your tax problem through normal IRS channels and have gotten nowhere, or if you are facing (or your business is facing) an immediate action from the IRS that will adversely affect you.
- TAS helps taxpayers whose tax problems are causing financial difficulty, which could include the cost of hiring professional representation such as a tax attorney.
- If you qualify for TAS help, you'll be assigned one advocate who will do everything possible to get your problem resolved.
- You can obtain the number of your local Taxpayer Advocate from the phone book, in Pub. 1546, and on the IRS website at IRS.gov/advocate. You can also call 1-877-777-4778.
- As a taxpayer, you have rights, which the toolkit website at www.TaxpayerAdvocate.irs.gov can help you understand.

- TAS also handles tax problems that may have an impact on more than just one taxpayer. You can report these "systemic" issues to TAS through the Systemic Advocacy Management System at IRS.gov/advocate.
- You can get updates on hot topics by visiting the TAS YouTube channel at www.youtube.com/TASNTA and the TAS Facebook page at www.facebook.com/YourVoiceAtIRS.

Tax Planning

The point of tax planning is to identify the best possible outcome. This is usually to lower tax liability and/or avoid underpayment penalties, based on the known components. Common variables include anticipating future changes in income, filing status, capital gains realizations, and fund distributions. Taking certain actions now will affect an individual's tax situation this year and in future years as compared to taking those actions in future years, or when possible, spreading income over multiple years. Tax planning isn't going to be perfectly accurate every time due to the likely changes in the tax code, particularly for longer-range, multi-year plans. Usually postponing income means postponing the payment of tax, but if you anticipate being in a higher tax bracket next year, you should explore shifting income into the current year ("income acceleration techniques") and pushing deductions into next year and beyond. However, the fundamentals of effective tax planning are **usually** to defer the recognition of income in that "time is money" (postponing income means postponing the payment of tax), and to accelerate deductible expenses and loses.

You should start tax planning early – **timing the receipt of income so that it is claimed in years when it will be taxed at the lowest tax rate, and claiming deductions in years when you are in the highest tax bracket. Many individuals find that they have more flexibility in accelerating or deferring expenses that generate tax deductions rather than trying to time income recognition**. You should maximize retirement savings account contributions (even upping your contribution by $1,000 cuts your taxes by $280 in the 28% tax bracket) and keep better track of your deductions – especially itemized deductions (consider "bunching" deductions) – "it's better to be able to take itemized deductions every other year than not take them at all". You can do this, for example, by paying two years' of real estate taxes in the same year, and by making charitable contributions twice as big this year and cutting back next year. Remember that if you want deductions to count in the current year, paying with a credit card counts even though you don't actually pay until the next year. Also, if you pay by check, the payment is considered made when the check is mailed. However, prepayment of an expense before it is incurred generally does not trigger the immediate right to a deduction in the year paid. Stock traded in the over-the-counter market or national exchange is considered sold on the trade date rather than the settlement date, unless it is a short sale. In the case of a short sale, gain is realized on the trade date (the stock price falls and a gain results), but a loss is not realized until the settlement date (the stock price rises and a loss results). Pledges to charitable organizations are not deductible until payment is made to the charity.

General Planning
There are a number of thresholds coming into play including the new Medicare 0.9% surtax and the 3.8% surtax on "net investment income" applicable to taxpayers with AGIs above $200,000 for single taxpayers and $250,000 for joint return filers, and the 3% phase-out of itemized deductions and the 2%

phase-out of exemptions in the area between $200,000 and $400,000. **Therefore, managing your AGI is probably the best planning technique available**. You should max out retirement contributions to IRAs, 401(k)s, and anything else that is tax deferred. If self-employed, set-up a self-employed retirement plan, and revisit decisions to contribute to traditional versus a Roth IRAs. Since distributions from Roth IRAs and 401(k)s are not subject to regular tax or the 3.8% surtax, they are a more attractive retirement vehicle for high-income individuals. On the contrary, if a taxpayer is hovering around the threshold for the surtax, maximizing contributions to deductible traditional IRAs could reduce taxable income below the threshold and, therefore, avoid the additional 3.8% surtax on net investment income. Another tool to use is an installment sales agreement, because it spreads out gains over future years, reducing taxable income in the current year. Tax-deferral mechanisms for significant tax gains should be considered, such as a Section 1031 exchange for real property sales or structuring the sale as an installment sale. Taxpayers should also consider realizing losses on existing stock holdings while maintaining their investment position by selling at a loss and repurchasing at least 31 days later, or swapping it out for a similar but not identical investment. Taxpayers might also consider reducing income by taking advantage of other tax-exempt investment vehicles, such as municipal bonds. If a loss from a flow-through (partnership or S-corporation) has been incurred, make sure that it's deductible (not a passive loss). Taxpayers can increase their basis in a partnership or S-corporation if doing so will enable them to deduct a loss from it this year. Also, if taxpayers have multiple passive activities, they should consider grouping the activities to reclassify them as non-passive. If a taxpayer has self-employment income, they should consider purchasing any capital expenditures that will be needed in the coming years, and taking favorable Section 179 expensing and bonus depreciation deductions that will go away after 2013. The maximum Section 179 deduction of $500,000 in 2013 is scheduled to drop to $25,000 in 2014 and future years. Also, the 50% bonus depreciation available in 2013 will expire at the end of 2013. Purchasing qualified property and placing it in service before year end will accelerate the depreciation deduction allowed on the assets in 2013 and reduce the earnings potentially subject to the 0.9% Medicare surtax. Where taxpayers are near the standard deduction amount, taxpayers should consider bunching expenditures for itemized deductions every other year, while claiming the standard deduction in the intervening years. Any tax-free benefits available through your employer should be maximized. If taxpayers are still eligible for the energy efficient housing tax credit, they should take advantage of it because it will expire at the end of 2013. Finally, consider donating appreciated securities, rather than cash, to a charity to receive a charitable deduction equal to the fair market value of the securities and avoid paying capital gains tax on them, and then consider purchasing new investments with the cash you would have donated, potentially lowering exposure to the 3.8% surtax in later years.

Planning for the Affordable Care Act (ACA)
Beginning in the 2013 tax year: (1) a surtax of 0.9% is added to the 1.45% Medicare hospital insurance payroll tax paid by high-income earners ($250,000 married filing jointly, and $200,000 singles); and (2)

there is also a 3.8% surtax on unearned income (investment income) of high-income earners ($250,000 married filing jointly, and $200,000 singles). Deferred compensation techniques and tax-free fringe benefits are among the standard tax planning strategies that may be used to reduce exposure to the additional 0.9% Medicare tax on high income earners beginning in 2013. High-income taxpayers should try to find ways of taking less wages in return for other benefits to avoid much of the increase in Medicare taxes. This includes ensuring that the maximum is contributed on a pre-tax basis to 401(k)s, IRAs, and other qualified retirement plans since these portions of wages are not subject to Medicare tax. The 3.8% surtax applies to whichever is less, "net investment income" or the amount by which modified adjusted gross income (MAGI) exceeds the stated income thresholds. Investment income includes taxable capital gains, dividends, interest income, annuities, royalties, and rents. The thresholds for both of these taxes will not be indexed for inflation, so they will snag an increasing number of taxpayers over time. Ensuring that the maximum is contributed to qualified retirement accounts will also reduce MAGI of high-income earners. A Roth IRA conversion is not itself subject to the 3.8% surtax, but the conversion is included in MAGI and may push a taxpayer's MAGI over the threshold amounts of $200,000/$250,000. Likewise, although lump-sum distributions from retirement plans; required minimum distributions (RMD); and all distributions from qualified plans, IRAs, and Roth IRAs are not subject to the surtax, they are included in MAGI and may push the taxpayer's MAGI over the threshold amounts. Also, gain over and above the $250,000/$500,000 exclusions from the sale of a principal residence may push a taxpayer's MAGI over the threshold amounts. Planning techniques to reduce exposure to the 3.8% surtax in 2013 and beyond might include making preparations to change the mix of investments by moving away from dividend-paying securities, investing in tax-free municipal bonds, investing in real estate (because depreciation offsets income from the property), and investing in tax-deferred non-qualified annuities. The higher cost of taxable investments might also tip the scales in favor of contributing more to a retirement plan from which eventual distributions are not subject to either the 0.9 % Medicare surtax or the 3.8% surtax. Contributing the maximum allowed to a qualified retirement plan in 2013 and future years may prove to be a good retirement strategy in two ways, first in reducing MAGI in the year of contribution and then in being exempt from the surtax when eventually distributed.

- Distributions from qualified plans, 401(k) plans, tax-sheltered annuities, IRAs, and eligible 457 plans are not subject to the 3.8% surtax. The exception for distributions from retirement plans suggests that taxpayers should shift wages and investments to retirement plans such as 401(k) plans, 403(b) annuities, and IRAs. This will reduce income and may help taxpayers stay below the thresholds.
- There is no exception for distributions from non-qualified deferred compensation plans subject to Code Sec. 409A. However, distributions from these plans (including amounts deemed as interest) are generally treated as compensation, not as investment income.

Employees who rely on employer-offered plans for their health insurance coverage should not automatically select the same coverage or plan they had in 2013, but instead should take time to compare plans since their 2013 choice may no longer be the most cost-effective. Many companies are using spousal surcharges to increase premiums. More commonly, they are creating different rates for different family situations (employee and spouse, employee plus children, etc.). If your spouse's employer also offers insurance coverage and the premiums plus the deductibles for each of you going with your own employer add up to less than the premiums and deductibles for both of you on any single plan, you should probably consider splitting up your coverage. Families with children should compare the cost of covering them on each spouse's plan, then with full coverage on each plan. You should consider setting-up a Health Savings Account (HSA) where in 2014 you can contribute up to $3,300 (single) and $6,550 (families); and those over 55 can contribute an additional $1,000. Amounts contributed to HSAs are deductible in computing adjusted gross income (AGI) on your tax return, which means these contributions are deductible even if you don't itemize deductions. Sometimes, your employer will offer a web based tool where you can compare plans and pick the best one for your particular situation. Be sure to check whether your doctors are in network and regular medications are covered by any new plan.

Planning to Avoid the Alternative Minimum Tax (AMT) Liability
The favorable tax benefits available under the regular income tax are curtailed for the AMT by a system of preferences and adjustments. The AMT is the excess of the Tentative Minimum Tax over regular income tax that is paid in addition to the regular income tax. Liability for the AMT is triggered when the taxpayer's tentative minimum tax exceeds regular tax liability for a particular year. For 2013, all nonrefundable personal and business tax credits are allowable for AMT. **The characteristics most likely to give rise to AMT liability for ordinary taxpayers are a large number of personal exemptions, high deductions for state and local taxes, a large amount of miscellaneous itemized deductions, and incentive stock options.** Perhaps the most important planning technique for taxpayers who are borderline candidates for the AMT is to do their best to maintain this situation. Bunching itemized deductions into one year causes the taxpayer to lose the value of these deductions in an AMT tax year. If deductions are not evenly distributed and the taxpayer has AMT and non-AMT years, the taxpayer should try to shift AMT preference items from AMT years to the regular tax years until the taxpayer arrives at the brink of AMT liability, therefore reducing regular tax to the point where it equals the tentative minimum tax. This technique provides the maximum benefit of AMT preference items. Thus, a taxpayer can recognize AMT preferences and adjustments up to the point in which the tentative minimum tax is equal to regular tax without incurring AMT liability – the AMT crossover point. For individual taxpayers, the AMT crossover point generally occurs when 26 percent of the first $175,000 of taxable excess (alternative minimum taxable income (AMTI) minus the applicable exemption amount, reduced by the AMT foreign tax credit) is greater than the taxpayer's regular taxable income.

- Timing Strategies – may be effective for non-preference adjustments. If the marginal tax rate for the regular tax is more than 26% or 28%, non-preference deductions should be shifted to the regular tax year. If the regular tax rate is 15%, this strategy should be reversed with non-preference deductions shifted to the AMT year. One way to take advantage of the rate differentials between an AMT year and a non-AMT year is to accelerate items of income into the AMT year and postpone deductions into the non-AMT year.
- Accelerating income – among other strategies, income can be accelerated by:
    - Making prepayments of salary and bonuses;
    - Redeeming Series EE savings bonds;
    - Recognizing short-term capital gains;
    - Converting tax-free bonds to higher yielding taxable bonds; and
    - Withdrawing money from IRAs and other retirement funds.
- Deferring deductions – deductions can be deferred by:
    - Depreciating rather than expensing business furniture and equipment; and
    - Delaying the payment of AMT preference items to a year when the AMT does not apply.
- Real estate and state income taxes – In a year in which the taxpayer is subject to AMT, prepaying real estate or state income taxes does not provide any benefit. If the taxpayer lives in a state where income taxes are high, then the taxpayer is more likely to be subject to the AMT. Instead of prepayment, payment should be delayed to another year, if possible.
- Mortgage interest – Because interest on mortgage borrowings used for purposes other than to buy, build, or improve the taxpayer's home is not deductible for AMT purposes, taxpayers subject to the AMT achieve no advantage from using a home equity line of credit to purchase a car or make some other expenditure. However, if the car is used in the taxpayer's business, a taxpayer may be able to deduct some of the auto loan interest or other costs as a business expense on Schedule C that is an allowable deduction for AMT purposes.

There is actually an **AMT Sweet Spot** where higher income persons can actually take advantage of the AMT and pay lower taxes on part of their income. The AMT Sweet Spot stretches from incomes of $447,800 to $680,400. At the bottom of the Sweet Spot the tax bill is $121,884 at a rate of 35%, but across this Sweet Spot $232,600 ($680,400 minus $447,800) of income is taxed at the maximum AMT rate of 28% which adds only $65,128 to the tax bill. So higher income persons would potentially pay $187,012 in taxes on $680,400 of income or 27.5%. At the top of the AMT Sweet Spot is where the regular tax kicks in again, so any income over $680,400 would be taxed at the 35% rate. Therefore, for planning purposes taxpayers in this category should accelerate income over the cross-over point, where the last dollar of income is taxed at 28%. At the cross-over point, all deductions reduce tax by 35%, and all income is taxed at 28%. This sounds impossible, but true.

Planning for Education Expenses

Among the most significant costs that higher-income families encounter are education expenses for children and grandchildren, and often at the same time, support for elderly parents. Taxpayers can reduce costs by prefunding expenses, for example, by transferring income-producing property to a person on whose behalf they would eventually have spent after-tax dollars. This transfer of property is called income shifting because, after the transfer, the income will be taxed to the new owner who may be in a lower tax bracket. Keep in mind that children are taxpayers in their own right for any money that they actually earn as well as for their investment income; but special rules, called the kiddie tax, apply to the investment income. Once the young people reach age 18 (24 for students who are dependents), their separate tax status permits investment income to be taxed at rates that may be significantly below their parents' rate, but not much benefit exists before that age, **unless they are not your dependents before those ages are reached**.

- By using some tax planning, a child's earned income can be inflated to an amount that is more than ½ of his/her support, even if it is not actually used for the child's support. This includes reasonable wages that self-employed parents can pay a student/child for services performed by the child. As a result, a contribution by the child to his/her own IRA using earned income could reduce taxable income and thereby reduce or completely eliminate the kiddie tax. Also, the child may be able to take an education tax credit which will offset the kiddie tax. But all of this can only be done when the parent cannot claim a student as a dependent. Students could also invest in tax-free investments, including Section 529 plans, which are not included in income.

- How to overcome the high cost of college if your income is too high to get financial aid: Like in the example above, attempt to make a child independent (income more than ½ of support). If a child is independent for tax purposes by meeting the ½ of support test, the child can claim the $3,900 personal exemption and the $6,100 standard deduction, and can benefit from the 10% tax rate on the 1st $8,925 of taxable income and the 15% tax rate on the next $36,250 of taxable income. In addition, the child will not have to pay the kiddie tax on the child's unearned income above $2,000. In order to accomplish this, the child can work during the summer, take advantage of internships and work study programs, and if his or her parent(s) own their own business, the parent can hire the child and shift some of his income to the child. The parent owning his own business can also set-up a tuition assistance program of up to $5,250 per year (which must be available to all employees). Also, a child who is tax independent might be able to take advantage of the "Education Tax Credits." For example, suppose a sophomore in college who earns $14,000 working for this father's business over the summer months also receives $1,700 in interest income from a UTMA account. Further suppose the child's grandparents make a $5,000 tuition payment on his behalf directly to the university, and his parents distribute $10,000 from the child's 529 plan (withdrawals from a 529 college savings plan are considered the child's income for purposes of establishing tax independence). Also, suppose he gets $5,250 from his father's company tuition program for a total of $35,950 toward his college expenses. $25,700 counts toward the child being independent for tax purposes ($14,000 + $1,700 + $10,000). The $5,000, $5,250, and the $10,000 are income tax free to the student and his family. Also, the child's father's business gets a deduction for the $5,250. The child's gross income is $15,700, and after applying the $3,900 personal exemption and the $6,100 standard deduction, the student's taxable income is $5,700.

Estate Tax Planning
Estate tax planning involves estate owners dealing with the building and preserving of their wealth, and eventually passing wealth to family members, charities, or other beneficiaries: (1) planning for succession of asset management; (2) consideration of income and estate tax consequences of a plan; and (3) building a team of advisors for the estate plan. "Zeroing out the taxable estate" can be accomplished through the following techniques: (1) Charitable giving, including living trusts; (2) life insurance proceeds to pay any estate tax due; and **by using family partnerships (FLP) and limited liability companies (LLC)** as "pass-through" entities for income tax treatment. An LLC is a better planning vehicle than a FLP; example: all family members can dump their real estate holdings into a LLC, and an appraiser can come up with a 60% discount at date of death. Make sure FLPs or LLCs have already been legally formed before transferring real estate or stock to it. Business valuation appraisers should have credentials with appraisal organizations, such as ASA (must always hire a good, independent appraiser). Due to the equivalent increase in the generation skipping transfer tax (GST) exemption to $5.25 million, even greater tax savings may be achieved by transfers to trusts in which all the beneficiaries are skip persons. If the GST exemption is sufficient to cover the entire trust, future distributions from the trust will "not be subject to transfer tax."

A properly implemented estate plan would have most, if not all, 1099s flowing into a trust. It may be a pass-through trust not requiring a separate tax return, but from an estate planning perspective, the trust is a far more efficient entity to hold and pass title upon death. Unless the estate falls under your state's probate limit, property passing from one individual to another due to death must go through probate. This can be expensive and time-consuming. Use of trusts can avoid this. Questions to ask: How current is your will and other estate documents? If they have children, who is named in the will as the guardian of minor children should both parents pass prematurely? If elderly parents are being claimed, ask about their asset structure, i.e. will they be able to pay for any long-term care issues they may encounter? What role are you intending to play in the settling of your parent estates? What is the succession plans for your company – do you have key man insurance? How will the transfer of ownership either to the next generation or partners be handled?

Avoiding an Audit
High levels of income can increase the risk of an IRS audit. Data shows that Americans with more than $100,000 of income are nearly twice as likely to be audited as those with $50,000 - $100,000 of annual

income. And once you hit $200,000 of income, your audit chances double again. And if you somehow have $1,000,000 or more of income, your audit risk doubles yet again. However, high levels of income can't be avoided. But other things such as the nature and amount of some deductions can catch the eye of the IRS and trigger an audit, as follows:

- Gambling losses – Many Americans will win some type of lottery, slot machine bonus or prize and then deduct everything they can as a gambling loss. The record keeping rules are very strict for gambling losses, the deduction is not that good, and your audit risk increases. Therefore, unless you have a detailed record of date, time, place and amount of each gambling activity, don't even try this deduction.
- Using the wrong tax preparer – Some people get audited because their tax preparer got audited. The problem has become so bad that last year the IRS stepped-in and tried (but failed) to set-up licensing and continuing education requirements for tax preparers. Avoid this problem by asking to see your preparer's license. Your preparer should be either a CPA or an EA (IRS Enrolled Agent).
- The Treasury Department publishes average tax deductions for each category, and exceeding the averages by more than 25% triggers an audit. Here are the averages:
  - AGI – under $15,000; Taxable income - $2,739: (1) interest expense - $8,838; (2) state taxes paid - $3,337; (3) charity - $1,496; (4) medical expenses - $8414; (5) total itemized deductions- $16,164.
  - AGI - $15,000 - $29,999; Taxable income - $9,279: (1) interest expense - $8434; (2) state taxes paid - $3,184; (3) charity - $2,048; (4) medical expenses - $7,783; total itemized deductions - $15,608.
  - AGI - $30,000 - $49,999; Taxable income - $24,428: (1) interest expense - $8,699; (2) state taxes paid - $3,943; (3) charity - $2,274; (4) medical expenses - $7,028; (5) total itemized deductions - $16,404.
  - AGI - $50,000 - $99,999; Taxable income - $46,401: (1) interest expense - $10,133; (2) state taxes paid - $6,247; (3) charity - $2,775; (4) medical expenses - $7,269; (5) total itemized deductions - $20,350.
  - AGI - $100,000 - $199,999; Taxable income - $97,042; (1) interest expense - $13,456; (2) state taxes paid - $11,069; (3) charity - $3,888; (4) medical expenses - $9,269; (5) total itemized deductions - $28,952.
  - AGI - $200,000 - $249,000; Taxable income - $171,938: (1) interest expense - $17,572; (2) state taxes paid - $18,524; (3) charity - $5,974; (4) medical expenses - $21,599; (5) total itemized deductions - $41,595.
  - AGI - $250,000 and above; Taxable income - $555,769: (1) interest expense - $25,527; (2) state taxes paid - $48,317; (3) charity - $18,488; (4) medical expenses - $38,149; (5) total itemized deductions - $89,432.

- Losses from small businesses and unreported income can trigger an audit because they are often not truly businesses and can even represent an obvious tax cheating scheme.
- The IRS is hot on the audit trail of real estate professionals. They are required to maintain time records to show material participation in his/her rental activities. Without material participation, rental losses will be subject to the passive loss limitations ($25,000). Remember the <u>aggregation election</u> for real estate professionals. Without the election, he/she might be unable to show material participation in his/her rental activities.